G. A. Chadwick

The Book of Exodus

G. A. Chadwick
The Book of Exodus
ISBN/EAN: 9783743329386
Manufactured in Europe, USA, Canada, Australia, Japa
Cover: Foto ©ninafisch / pixelio.de

Manufactured and distributed by brebook publishing software (www.brebook.com)

G. A. Chadwick

The Book of Exodus

THE EXPOSITOR'S BIBLE.

EDITED BY THE REV.
W. ROBERTSON NICOLL, M.A., LL.D.
Editor of "The Expositor."

THE BOOK OF EXODUS.

BY THE VERY REV.
G. A. CHADWICK, D.D.,
Dean of Armagh

London:
HODDER AND STOUGHTON,
27, PATERNOSTER ROW.

MDCCCXC.

THE EXPOSITOR'S BIBLE.

1889-90.

Crown 8vo. Cloth. Price 7s. 6d. each.

JUDGES AND RUTH. By the Rev. R. A. WATSON, M.A.

THE PROPHECIES OF JEREMIAH. By the Rev. C. J. BALL, M.A., Chaplain of Lincoln's Inn.

THE PROPHECIES OF ISAIAH. Vol. II. Completing the Work. By the Rev. GEORGE ADAM SMITH, M.A.

THE GOSPEL OF MATTHEW. By the Rev. J. MONRO GIBSON, D.D., London, Author of "The Mosaic Era," etc.

THE BOOK OF EXODUS. By the Very Rev. G. A. CHADWICK, D.D., Dean of Armagh.

THE BOOK OF THE ACTS OF THE APOSTLES. By the Rev. G. T. STOKES, D.D., Professor of Ecclesiastical History in the University of Dublin.

1888-89.

Crown 8vo. Cloth. Price 7s. 6d. each.

THE EPISTLE TO THE GALATIANS. By the Rev. Professor G. G. FINDLAY, B.A., Headingley College, Leeds.

THE BOOK OF ISAIAH. Chap. I. to XXXIX. By the Rev. GEORGE ADAM SMITH, M.A., Aberdeen.

THE PASTORAL EPISTLES. By the Rev. ALFRED PLUMMER, D.D., Master of University College, Durham.

THE FIRST EPISTLE TO THE CORINTHIANS. By the Rev. Professor MARCUS DODS, D.D. Second Edition.

THE REVELATION OF ST. JOHN. By the Rev. Professor W. MILLIGAN, D.D., of the University of Aberdeen.

THE EPISTLES OF ST. JOHN. By the Right Rev. W. ALEXANDER, D.D., D.C.L., Lord Bishop of Derry and Raphoe.

1887-88.

Crown 8vo. Cloth. Price 7s. 6d. each.

THE EPISTLE TO THE COLOSSIANS. By ALEXANDER MACLAREN, D.D., of Manchester. Fourth Edition.

THE GOSPEL ACCORDING TO ST. MARK. By the Rev. Prebendary G. A. CHADWICK, D.D., Dean of Armagh.

THE BOOK OF GENESIS. By the Rev. Professor MARCUS DODS, D.D. Fourth Edition.

THE FIRST BOOK OF SAMUEL. By the Rev. Professor W. G. BLAIKIE, D.D., LL.D.

THE SECOND BOOK OF SAMUEL. By the same Author.

THE EPISTLE TO THE HEBREWS. By the Rev. Principal T. C. EDWARDS, M.A.

THE BOOK OF EXODUS.

BY THE VERY REV.
G. A. CHADWICK, D.D.,
Dean of Armagh,
AUTHOR OF "CHRIST BEARING WITNESS TO HIMSELF," "AS HE THAT SERVETH," "THE GOSPEL OF ST. MARK," ETC.

London:
HODDER AND STOUGHTON,
27, PATERNOSTER ROW.

MDCCCXC.

Printed by Hazell, Watson, & Viney, Ld., London and Aylesbury.

PREFACE.

MUCH is now denied or doubted, within the Church itself, concerning the Book of Exodus, which was formerly accepted with confidence by all Christians.

But one thing can neither be doubted nor denied. Jesus Christ did certainly treat this book, taking it as He found it, as possessed of spiritual authority, a sacred scripture. He taught His disciples to regard it thus, and they did so.

Therefore, however widely His followers may differ about its date and origin, they must admit the right of a Christian teacher to treat this book, taking it as he finds it, as a sacred scripture and invested with spiritual authority. It is the legitimate subject of exposition in the Church.

Such work this volume strives, however imperfectly, to perform. Its object is to edify in the first place, and also, but in the second place, to inform. Nor has the author consciously shrunk from saying what seemed to him proper to be said because the utterance would be unwelcome, either to the latest critical theory, or to the last sensational gospel of an hour.

But since controversy has not been sought,

although exposition has not been suppressed when it carried weapons, by far the greater part of the volume appeals to all who accept their Bible as, in any true sense, a gift from God.

No task is more difficult than to exhibit the Old Testament in the light of the New, discovering the permanent in the evanescent, and the spiritual in the form and type which it inhabited and illuminated. This book is at least the result of a firm belief that such a connection between the two Testaments does exist, and of a patient endeavour to receive the edification offered by each Scripture, rather than to force into it, and then extort from it, what the expositor desires to find. Nor has it been supposed that by allowing the imagination to assume, in sacred things, that rank as a guide which reason holds in all other practical affairs, any honour would be done to Him Who is called the Spirit of knowledge and wisdom, but not of fancy and quaint conceits.

If such an attempt does, in any degree, prove successful and bear fruit, this fact will be of the nature of a scientific demonstration.

If this ancient Book of Exodus yields solid results to a sober devotional exposition in the nineteenth Christian century, if it is not an idle fancy that its teaching harmonises with the principles and theology of the New Testament, and even demands the New Testament as the true commentary upon the Old, what follows? How comes it that the oak is potentially in the acorn, and the living creature in the egg? No germ is a manufactured article: it is a part of the system of the universe.

ANALYSIS OF CONTENTS.

CHAPTER I.

THE PROLOGUE, i. 1—6.

Books linked by conjunction "And :" Scripture history a connected whole, 1.—So is secular history organic : " Philosophy of history." The Pentateuch being a still closer unity, Exodus rehearses the descent into Egypt, 2.—Heredity: the family of Jacob, 3.—Death of Joseph. Influence of Egypt on the shepherd race, 4.—A healthy stock : good breeding. Goethe's aphorism, 5.—Ourselves and our descendants, 6.

GOD IN HISTORY, i. 7.

In Exodus, national history replaces biography, 6.— Contrasted narratives of Jacob and Moses. Spiritual progress from Genesis to Exodus, 7.—St. Paul's view: Law prepares for Gospel, especially by our failures, 8.—This explains other phenomena : failures in various circumstances, of innocence in Eden ; of an elect family; now of a race, a nation, 9.—Israel, failing with all advantages, needs a Messiah. Faith justifies, in Old Testament as in New, 10.—Scripture history reveals God in this life, in all things, 11.—True spirituality owns God in the secular : this is a gospel for our days, 12-13.

THE OPPRESSION, i. 7—22.

Early prosperity: its dangers: political supports vain, 13.—Joseph forgotten. National responsibilities: despotism, 14.—Nations and their chiefs. Our subject races, 15.—The Church and her King : imputation. Pharaoh precipitates what he fears, 16.—Egypt and her aliens : modern parallels, 17.—Tyranny is tyrannous even when cultured, 18.—Our undue estrangement from the fallen : Jesus a brother. Toil crushes the spirit, 19.—Israel idolatrous. Religious dependence, 20.—Direct interposition required. Bitter oppression, 21.—

Pharaoh drops the mask. Defeated by the human heart. The midwives, 22.—Their falsehood. Morality is progressive, 23.—Culture and humanity, 24.—Religion and the child, 25.

CHAPTER II.

THE RESCUE OF MOSES, ii. 1—10.

Importance of the individual, 26.—A man *versus* "the Time-spirit," 27.—The parents of Moses, 28.—Their family: their goodly child, 29.—Emotion helps faith, 30.—The ark in the bulrushes, 31.—Pharaoh's daughter and Miriam, 32.—Guidance for good emotions: the Church for humanity, 33.

THE CHOICE OF MOSES, ii. 11—15.

God employs means, 34.—Value of endowment. Moses and his family. "The reproach of Christ," 35.—An impulsive act, 36.—Impulses not accidents. The hopes of Moses, 37.—Moses and his brethren. His flight, 38.

MOSES IN MIDIAN, ii. 16—22.

Energy in disaster, 39.—Disinterested bravery. Parallels with a variation, 40.—The Unseen a refuge. Duty of resisting small wrongs. His wife, 41.—A lonely heart, 42.

CHAPTER III.

THE BURNING BUSH, ii. 23—iii.

Death of Raamses. Misery continues, 43.—The cry of the oppressed, 44.—Discipline of Moses, 45.—How a crisis comes, 46.—God hitherto unmentioned. The Angel of the Lord, 47.—An unconsuming fire, 48.—Inquiry: reverence. God finds, not man, 49.—"Take off thy shoe." "The God of thy father," 50.—Immortality. "My people," not saints only, 51.—The good land. The commission, 52.—God with him. A strange token, 53.

A NEW NAME, iii. 14; vi. 2, 3.

Why Moses asked the name of God: idolatry: pantheism, 54.—A progressive revelation, 55.—Jehovah. The sound corrupted. Similar superstitions yet, 56.—What it told the Jews. Reality of being, 57.—Jews not saved by ideas. Streams of tendency. The Self-contained. We live in our past, 58.—And in our future, 59.—Yet Jehovah not the impassive God of Lucretius,

60.—The Immutable is Love. This is our help, 61.—Human will is not paralysed, 62.—The teaching of St. Paul. All this is practical, 63.—This gives stability to all other revelations. Our own needs, 64.

THE COMMISSION, iii. 10, 16—22.
    God comes where He sends, 65.—The Providential man. Prudence, 66.—Sincerity of demand for a brief respite, 67.—God has already visited them. By trouble He transplants, 68.—The " borrowing " o jewels, 69.

CHAPTER IV.

MOSES HESITATES, iv. 1—17.
    Scripture is impartial : Josephus, 70.—Hindrance from his own people. The rod, 71.—The serpent : the leprosy, 72. —" I am not eloquent," 73.—God with us. Aaron the Levite, 74.—Responsibility of *not* working. The errors of Moses, 75.—Power of fellowship. Vague fears, 76.—With his brother, Moses will go. The Church, 77.—This craving met by Christ, 78.—Family affection. Examples, 79.

MOSES OBEYS, iv. 18—31.
    Fidelity to his employer. Reticence, 80.—Resemblance to story of Jesus. He is the Antitype of all experiences, 81.—Counterpoint in history. "Israel is My son," 82.—A neglected duty Zipporah. Was she a helpmeet ? 83.—Domestic unhappiness. History *v.* myth, 84.—The failures of the good, 85.—Men of destiny are not irresponsible, 86.—His first followers : a joyful reception, 87.—Spiritual joy and reaction, 88.

CHAPTER V.

PHARAOH REFUSES, v. 1—23.
    Moses at court again. Formidable, 89.—Power of convictions but also of tyranny and pride. Menephtah : his story, 90.—Was the Pharaoh drowned ? The demand of Jehovah, 91.—The refusal, 92.—Is religion idleness? Hebrews were taskmasters, 93.—Demoralised by slavery. They are beaten, 94.—Murmurs against Moses. He returns to God. His remonstrance, 95.—His disappointment. Not really irreverent, 96. —Use of this abortive attempt, 97-8.

CHAPTER VI.

THE ENCOURAGEMENT OF MOSES, vi. 1—30.

> The word Jehovah known before: its consolations now, 99.—The new truth is often implicit in the old, 100.—Discernment more needed than revelation. "Judgments," 101.—My people: your God, 102.—The tie is of God's binding, 103.—Fatherhood and sonship, 104.—Faith becomes knowledge. The body hinders the soul, 105.—We are responsible for bodies. Israel weighs Moses down, 106.—We may hold back the saints, 107.—The pedigree, 107-8.—Indications of genuine history, 108-9.—"As a god to Pharaoh," 110.—We also, 111.

CHAPTER VII.

THE HARDENING OF PHARAOH'S HEART, vii. 3—13.

> The assertion offends many, 112.—Was he a free agent? When hardened. A.V. incorrect, 113.—He resists five plagues spontaneously. The last five are penal, 114.—Not "hardened" in wickedness, but in nerve. A.V. confuses three words: His heart is (*a*) "hardened," 115.—(*b*) it is made "strong" (*c*) "heavy," 116.—Other examples of these words, 117.—The warning implied, 117-19.—Moses returns with the signs, 119.—The functions of miracle, 120.

THE PLAGUES, vii. 14.

> Their vast range, 121.—Their relation to Pantheism, Idolatry, Philosophy, 122.—And to the gods of Egypt. Their retributive fitness, 123.—Their arrangement, 124.—Like our Lord's, not creative, 125.—God in common things, 126.—Some we inflict upon ourselves. Yet rationalistic analogies fail, 127.—Duration of the conflict, 128.

THE FIRST PLAGUE, vii. 14—25.

> The probable scene, 129.—Extent of the plague. The magicians. Its duration, 131.—Was Israel exempt? Contrast with first miracle of Jesus, 132.

CHAPTER VIII.

THE SECOND PLAGUE, viii. 1—15.

> Submission demanded. Severity of plague, 133.—Pharaoh humbles himself, 134.—"Glory over me." Pharaoh breaks faith, 135.

THE THIRD PLAGUE, viii. 16—19.

 Various theories. A surprise. Magicians baffled, 136—What they confess, 137.

THE FOURTH PLAGUE, viii. 20—32.

 "Rising up early," 137.—Bodily pain. Beetles or flies? "A mixture," 138—Goshen exempt. Pharaoh suffers. He surrenders, 139.—Respite and treachery. Would Moses have returned? 140.

CHAPTER IX.

THE FIFTH PLAGUE, ix. 1—7.

 First attack on life. Animals share our fortunes, 141. The new summons. Murrain, 142.—Pharaoh's curiosity, 143.

THE SIXTH PLAGUE, ix. 8—12.

 No warning, yet Author manifest. Ashes of the furnace, 144.—Suffering in the flesh. The magicians again. Pharaoh's heart "made strong," 145.—Dares not retaliate, 146.

THE SEVENTH PLAGUE, ix. 13—35.

 Expostulation not mockery, 146-7.—God is wronged by slavery, 147.—Civil liberty is indebted to religion. "Plagues upon thine heart," 148.—A mis-rendering: why he was not crushed, 149.—An opportunity of escape. The storm, 150.—Ruskin upon terrors of thunderstorm, 151.—Pharaoh confesses sin, 152.—Moses intercedes. The weather in history. Job's assertion, 153.

CHAPTER X.

THE EIGHTH PLAGUE, x. 1—20.

 Moses encouraged, 154.—Deliverances should be remembered. A sterner rebuke. Locusts in Egypt, 155.—Their effect. The court interferes. Yet "their hearts hardened" also, 156—Infatuation of Pharaoh. Parallel of Napoleon, 157.—Women and little ones did share in festivals, 158.—A gentle wind. Locusts. Another surrender, 159.—Relief. Our broken vows, 160.

THE NINTH PLAGUE, x. 21—29.

 Menephtah's sun-worship, 161.—Suddenness of the plague. Concentrated narrative, 162.—Darkness represents death, 163.—

The Book of Wisdom upon this plague, 164-5.—Isaiah's allusions. The Pharaoh's character, 165.—Altercation with Moses, 166.

CHAPTER XI.

THE LAST PLAGUE ANNOUNCED, xi. 1—10.

This chapter supplements the last. The blow is known to be impending. Uses of its delay, 167.—Israel shall claim wages. The menace, 168.—Parallel with St. John, 169-70.

CHAPTER XII.

THE PASSOVER, xii. 1—28.

Birthday of a nation. The calendar, 171.—"The congregation." The feast is social, 172.—The nation is based upon the family. No Egyptian house escapes, 173.—National interdependence. The Passover a sacrifice, 174.—What does the blood mean? Rationalistic theories. Harvest festivals, 175.—The unbelieving point of view: what theories of sacrifice were then current? "A sacrifice was a meal," 176.—Human sacrifices. The Passover "unhistorical." Kuenen rejects this view, 177.—Phenomena irreconcilable with it, 178-9. What is really expressed? Danger even to Jews, 179.—Salvation by grace. Not unbought, 180.—The lamb a ransom. All firstborn are forfeited. Tribe of Levi, 181.—Cash payment. Effect on Hebrew literature, 182.—Its prophetic import, 183.—The Jew must co-operate with God: must also become His guest, 184.—Sacred festivals. Lamb or kid. Four days reserved, 185.—Men are sheep. Heads of houses originally sacrifice. Transition to Levites in progress under Hezekiah, complete under Josiah, 186.—Unleavened bread. The lamb. Roast, not sodden, 187.—Complete consumption. Judgment upon gods of Egypt, 188.—The blood a token unto themselves. On their lintels, 189.—The word "pass-over," 190.—Domestic teaching, 191.—Many who ate the feast perished. Aliens might share, 192.

THE TENTH PLAGUE, xii. 29—36.

The blow falls. Pharaoh was not "firstborn": his son "sat upon his throne," 193.—The scene, 194.—The demands of Israel. St. Augustine's inference, 195.

THE EXODUS, xii. 37—42.

    The route, 195.—Their cattle, a suggested explanation, 196.—"Four hundred and thirty years," 197-8.

CHAPTER XIII.

THE LAW OF THE FIRSTBORN, xiii. 1.

    The consecration of the firstborn, 199.—The Levite. "They are Mine," 200.—Joy is hopeful. Tradition? 201.—Phylacteries. The ass, 202.—The Philistines. No spiritual miracle, 203.—Education, 204.

THE BONES OF JOSEPH, xiii. 19.

    Joseph influenced Moses, 204.—His faith, 205.—Circumstances overcome by soul. God in the cloud, 206.—Hebrew poetry and modern, 207.

CHAPTER XIV.

THE RED SEA, xiv. 1—31.

    Stopped on the march, 208.—Pharaoh presumes, 209. —The panic, 210.—Moses. Prayer and action. "Self-assertion"? 211.—The midnight march, 212.—The lost army, 213.

ON THE SHORE, xiv. 30, 31.

    Impressions deepened. "They believed in Jehovah." So the faith of the apostles grew, 214.

CHAPTER XV.

THE SONG OF MOSES, xv. 1—22.

    A song remembered in heaven. Its structure, 216-17.—The women join. Instruments. Dances, 218. God the Deliverer, not Moses. "My salvation," 219.—Gratitude. Anthropomorphism. "Ye are gods." "Jehovah is a Man—of war," 220-2. —The overthrow, 222.—First mention of Divine holiness, 223. —An inverted holiness, 224.—"Thou shalt bring them in," 225.

SHUR, xv. 22—27.

    Disillusion. Marah, 226.—A universal danger, 227.—Prayer, and the use of means, 228.—"A statute and an ordinance." Such compacts often repeated. The offered privilege, 229.—It is still enjoyed, 230.—"The Lord for the body." Elim, 231.

CHAPTER XVI.

MURMURING FOR FOOD, xvi. 1—14.

We too fear, although Divinely guarded, 232.—They would fain die satiated, 233.—Relief tries them as want does, 234.—The Sabbath. A rebuke, 235.—Moses is zealous. His "meekness," 236.—The glory appears, 237.—Quails and manna, 238.

MANNA, xvi. 15—36.

Their course of life is changed, 238.—A drug resembles manna, 239.—The supernatural follows nature, 240.—They must gather, prepare, be moderate, 241.—Nothing over and no lack. Socialistic perversion, 242.—Socialism. Christ in politics, 243-4.

SPIRITUAL MEAT, xvi. 15—36.

Manna is a type. When given, 244.—An unearthly sustenance, 245. What is spirituality? Christ the true Manna, 246. Universal, daily, abundant, 247.—The Sabbath. The pot of manna, 248.

CHAPTER XVII.

MERIBAH, xvii. 1—7.

A greater strain. What if Israel had stood it? 249.—They murmured against Moses. The position of Aaron. An exaggerated outcry, 250.—Witnesses to the miracle. The rock in Horeb, 251.—The rod. Privilege is not acceptance, 252.

AMALEK, xvii. 8—16.

A water-raid, 252.—God's sheep must become His warriors. War, 253-4.—Joshua. The rod of God, 255.—A silent prayer. Aaron and Hur must join in it, 256.—So now. But the army must fight, 257.—"The Lord my banner." Unlike a myth, 258.

CHAPTER XVIII.

JETHRO, xviii. 1—27.

Gentiles in new aspect. Church may learn from secular wisdom, 259.—Little is said of Zipporah: Jethro's pleasure, 260.—A Gentile priest recognised. Religious festivity, 261.—Jethro's advice: its importance, 262.—Divine help does not supersede human gift, 263.

THE TYPICAL BEARINGS OF THE HISTORY.

Narrative is also allegory. Danger of arbitrary fancies. Example from Bunyan. Scriptural teaching, 264.—Some resemblances are planned: others are reappearances of same principle, 265. So that these are evidential analogies, like Butler's, 266.—Others appear forced. "I called My Son out of Egypt" refers to Israel, 267.—But the condescending phrase promised more, and the subsequent coincidence is significant, 268. Truths cannot all be proved like Euclid's, 269.

CHAPTER XIX.

AT SINAI, xix. 1—25.

Sinai and Pentecost. The place. Ras Sufsâfeh. God speaks in nature, 270.—Moses is stopped; the people must pledge themselves. Dedication services, 271.—An appeal to gratitude, and a promise, 272.—"A peculiar treasure." "A kingdom and priests," 273.—The individual, and Church order. "On eagles' wings," 274.—Israel consents. The Lord in the cloud. Manifestations are transient, 275.—Precautions. The trumpet, 276. "The priests." A plébiscite. Contrast between Law and Gospel: Methodius, 277.—Theophanies, 278.—None like this, 279.

CHAPTER XX.

THE LAW, xx. 1—17.

What the law did. It could not justify. It reveals obligation, 280.—It convicts, not enables. It is an organic whole. And a challenge, 281.—The Spirit enables: love is fulfilment of law. Luther's paradox, 283.—Law and Gospel contrasted. Its spiritual beauty: two noble failures, 283.—The Jewish arrangement of the Commandments. St. Augustine's. The Anglican. An equal division, 284-6.

THE PROLOGUE, xx. 2.

Their experience of God, 286.—God and the first table. The true object of adoration: men must adore. Agnosticism, 287. God and the second table, 288.—Law appeals to noble motives, 289.

The First Commandment, xx. 3.

Monotheism and a real God, 289.—False creeds attractive. Spiritualism. Science indebted to Monotheism, 290.—Unity of nature a religious truth. Strength of our experimental argument, 291. Informal apostacy. Luther's position. Scripture. The Chaldeans, 292. Animal pleasure, 293.—The remedy: "Thou shalt have . . . Me," 294.

The Second Commandment, xx. 4—6.

Imagery not all idolatry. The subtler paganisms, 295. Spiritual worship, like a Gothic building, aspires: images lack expansiveness, 296.—God is jealous, 297.—The shadow of love, 298. Visiting sins on children, 299, 300.—Part of vast beneficent law, 300-2.—Gospel in law, 302.

The Third Commandment, xx. 7.

Meaning of "in vain," 302.—Jewish superstition. Where swearing is wholly forbidden, 303.—Fruitful and free use of God's name, 304-5.

The Fourth Commandment, xx. 8—11.

Law of Sabbath unique. Confession of Augsburg. Of Westminster, 305.—Anglican position. St. Paul, 306.—The first positive precept. Love not the abolition of the law, 307.—Property of our friends. The word "remember." The story of creation, 308.—The manna. Isaiah, Jeremiah, Ezekiel, 309.—Christ's freedom was that of a Jew. "Sabbath for man," 310.—Our help, not our fetter. "My Father worketh," 311.

The Fifth Commandment, xx. 12.

Bridge between duty to God and to neighbour, 312.—Father and child, 313.—"Whosoever hateth not." Christ and His mother. Its sanction, 314.

The Sixth Commandment, xx. 13.

Who is neighbour? Ethics and religion, 315-16.—Science and morals, 317.—A Divine creature. Capital punishment, 318.

The Seventh Commandment, xx. 14.

Justice forbids act: Christ forbids desire. Sacredness of body, 319.—Human body connects material and spiritual worlds. Modifies, while serves, 320.—Marriage a type, 321.

THE EIGHTH COMMANDMENT, xx. 15.
   Assailed by communism, by Rome. Various specious pleas, 322.
   —Laws of community binding, 323.—None may judge his own
   case. St. Paul enlarges the precept, 324.

THE NINTH COMMANDMENT, xx. 16.
   Importance of words. Various transgressions, 325. Slander
   against nations, against the race. Love, 326-7.

THE TENTH COMMANDMENT, xx. 17.
   The list of properties, 328.—The heart. The law searches, 329.

THE LESSER LAW, xx. 18-xxiii. 33.

A remarkable code. The circumstances, 331. Moses fears: yet
bids them fear not, 332-3.—Presumption v. awe. He receives
an expanded decalogue, an abridged code, 334. Laws should
educate a people; should not outrun their capabilities, 335-6.—
Five subdivisions, 337.

I. THE LAW OF WORSHIP, xx. 22—26.
   Images again forbidden, 337.—Splendour and simplicity. An
   objection, 338.—Modesty, 339.

CHAPTER XXI. THE LESSER LAW (*continued*).

II. RIGHTS OF THE PERSON, xxi. 1—32.
   The Hebrew slave. The seventh year. Year of jubilee. His
   family, 340.—The ear pierced. St. Paul's "marks of the Lord."
   Assaults, 341.—The Gentile slave, 342. The female slave,
   342-3.—Murder and blood-fiends, 343.—Parents. Kidnappers,
   344.—Eye for eye. Mitigations of *lex talionis*, 344-5.—Vicious
   cattle, 346.

III. RIGHTS OF PROPERTY, xxi. 33—xxii. 15.
   Negligence: indirect responsibility: various examples, 346-8.—
   Theft, 348.

CHAPTER XXII. THE LESSER LAW (*continued*).

IV. VARIOUS ENACTMENTS, xxii. 16—xxiii. 19.
   Disconnected precepts. No trace of systematic revision. Certain
   capital crimes, 348-9.

SORCERY, xxii. 18.

Abuses have recoiled against religion, 349.—Sorcerers are impostors, but they existed, and do still, 350.—Moses could not leave them to enlightened opinion. Propagated apostacy, 351. —Traitors in a theocracy, 352.—When shall witchcraft die? 353.

THE STRANGER, xxii. 21 ; xxiii. 9.

"Ye were strangers," 354.—A fruitful principle. Morality not expediency, 355.—Cruelty often ignorance: Moses educates, 356.—The widow. The borrower, 357.—Other precepts, 358.

CHAPTER XXIII. THE LESSER LAW (*continued*).

An enemy's cattle. A false report, 359.—Influence of multitude : the world and the Church, 360-1. Favour not the poor, 361-2. Other precepts. "A kid in his mother's milk," 362.

LESSER LAW, V. ITS SANCTIONS, xxiii. 20—33.

A bold transition : the Angel in Whom is "My Name," 363. — Not a mere messenger, 364.—Nor the substitute of chap. xxxiii. 2, 3, 365-6.—Parallel verses, 366-7.

CHAPTER XXIV.

THE COVENANT RATIFIED. THE VISION OF GOD, xxiv.

The code is accepted, written, ratified with blood, 368.—Exclusion and admittance. The elders see God : Moses goes farther. Theophanies of other creeds, 369.—How could they see God ? 370.—Moses feels not satisfaction, but desire, 371.—His progress is from vision to shadow and a Voice, 372.—We see not each other, 373.—St. Augustine, 373-4.—The vision suits the period : not post-Exilian, 374-5.—Contrast with revelation in Christ, 375.

CHAPTER XXV.

THE SHRINE AND ITS FURNITURE, xxv. 1—40.

The God of Sinai will inhabit a tent. His other tabernacles, 376-7.—The furniture is typical. Altar of incense postponed, 377.—The ark enshrines His law and its sanctions, 377-8.— The mercy-seat covers it, 378-81.—Man's homage. The table of shewbread, 382-3.—The golden candlestick (lamp-stand), 383-6.

THE PATTERN IN THE MOUNT, xxv. 9, 40.
    Use in Hebrews. Plato, 386.—Not a model, but an idea. Art, 387.—Provisional institutions, 387-8.—The ideal in creation, 388.—In life, 389.

CHAPTER XXVI.

THE TABERNACLE.
    "Temple" an ambiguous word, 390.—"Curtains of the Tabernacle," 391.—Other coverings, 392.—The boards and sockets, 392-3.—The bars. The tent, 393.—Position of veil, 394, and of the front, 395.

CHAPTER XXVII.

THE OUTER COURT.
    The altar, 396.—The quadrangle, 397.—General effect, 398-400.

CHAPTER XXVIII.

THE HOLY GARMENTS.
    Their import, 401.—The drawers. "Coat." Head-tires. Robe of the ephod. Ephod. Jewels, 402.—Breastplate. Urim and Thummim. Mitre. Symbolism, 403.

THE PRIESTHOOD.
    Universal desire and dread of God, 404.—Delegates, 405.—Scripture. First Moses, 406.—His family passed over. The double consciousness expressed, 407-9.—Messianic priesthood, 409.

CHAPTER XXIX.

CONSECRATION SERVICES.
    Why consecrate at all? 410.—Moses officiates. The offerings, 411.—Ablution, robing, anointing, 412-13.—The sin-offering, 413-14. "Without the camp," 414. The burnt-offering, 415.—The peace-offering ("ram of consecration"), 415.—The wave-offerings, 415-16.—The result, 416-17.

CHAPTER XXX.

INCENSE, xxx. 1—10.
    The impalpable in nature, 418.—"The golden altar," 419.—Represents prayer. Needs cleansing, 420.

A Census, xxx. 11—16.
>   A census not sinful. David's transgression. The half-shekel. Equality of man, 421.—Christ paid it, 422.—Its employment, 423.

The Laver, xxx. 17—21.
>   Behind the altar. Purity of priests, 423.—Made of the mirrors, 424.

Anointing Oil and Incense, xxx. 22—38.
>   Their ingredients. All the vessels anointed, 424.—Forbidden to secular uses, 425.—Modern analogies, 426-7.

CHAPTER XXXI.

Bezaleel and Aholiab, xxxi. 1—18.
>   Secular gifts are sacred, 428-30.—The Sabbath. The tables and "the finger of God," 431.

CHAPTER XXXII.

The Golden Calf.
>   Sin of the people; of Aaron. God rejects them, 432.—Intercession. The Christian antitype, 433-4.

CHAPTER XXXIII.

Prevailing Intercession.
>   The first concession. The angel, 435.—"The Tent of the Meeting," 436.

CHAPTER XXXIV.

The Vision of God.
>   To know is to desire to know. A fit season. The greater Name, 438.—The covenant renewed. The tables. The skin of his face shone, 439.—Lessons, 440.

CHAPTERS XXXV.—XL. CONCLUSION.

>   The people obey, 441.—The forming of the nation; review, 441-3.

CHAPTER I.

THE PROLOGUE.

EXODUS i. 1-6.

"And these are the names of the children of Israel which came into Egypt."

MANY books of the Old Testament begin with the conjunction And. This fact, it has been often pointed out, is a silent indication of truth, that each author was not recording certain isolated incidents, but parts of one great drama, events which joined hands with the past and future, looking before and after.

Thus the Book of the Kings took up the tale from Samuel, Samuel from Judges, and Judges from Joshua, and all carried the sacred movement forward towards a goal as yet unreached. Indeed, it was impossible, remembering the first promise that the seed of the woman should bruise the head of the serpent, and the later assurance that in the seed of Abraham should be the universal blessing, for a faithful Jew to forget that all the history of his race was the evolution of some grand hope, a pilgrimage towards some goal unseen. Bearing in mind that there is now revealed to us a world-wide tendency toward the supreme consummation, the bringing all things under the headship of Christ, it is not to be denied that this hope of the ancient Jew is given to all mankind. Each new stage in universal history may be said to open with this same conjunction. It links the history of England with that of Julius Cæsar and of the Red Indian; nor is the chain composed of accidents: it is forged by the hand of the God of providence. Thus, in the conjunction which binds these Old Testament narratives together, is found the germ of that instinctive and elevating phrase, the Philosophy of History. But there is nowhere in Scripture the notion which too often degrades and stiffens that Philosophy—the notion that history is urged forward by blind forces, amid which the individual man is too puny to assert himself. Without a Moses the Exodus is inconceivable, and God always achieves His purpose through the providential man.

The Books of the Pentateuch are held together in a yet stronger unity than the rest, being sections of one and the same narrative, and having been accredited with a common authorship from the earliest mention of them. Accordingly, the Book of Exodus not only begins with this conjunction (which assumes the previous narrative), but also rehearses the descent into Egypt. "And these are the names of the sons of Israel which came into Egypt,"—names blotted with many a crime, rarely suggesting any lovable or great association, yet the names of men with a marvellous heritage, as being "the sons of Israel," the Prince who prevailed with God. Moreover they are consecrated: their father's dying words had conveyed to every one of them some expectation, some mysterious import which the future should disclose. In the issue would be revealed the awful influence of the past upon the future, of the fathers upon the children even beyond the third and fourth generation—an influence which is nearer to destiny, in its stern, subtle and far-reaching strength, than any other recognised by religion. Destiny, however, it is not, or how should the name of Dan have faded out from the final list of "every tribe of the children of Israel" in the Apocalypse (Rev. vii. 5-8), where Manasseh is reckoned separately from Joseph to complete the twelve?

We read that with the twelve came their posterity, seventy souls in direct descent from Jacob; but in this number he is himself included, according to that well-known Orientalism which Milton strove to force upon our language in the phrase—

"The fairest of her daughters Eve."

Joseph is also reckoned, although he "was in Egypt already." Now, it must be observed that of these seventy, sixty-eight were males, and therefore the people of the Exodus must not be reckoned to have sprung in the interval from seventy, but (remembering polygamy) from more than twice that number, even if we refuse to make any account of the household which is mentioned as coming with every man. These households were probably smaller in each case than that of Abraham, and the famine in its early stages may have reduced the number of retainers; yet they account for much of what is pronounced incredible in the rapid expansion of the clan into a nation.* But when all

---

* Professor Curtiss quotes a volume of family memoirs which shows that 5,564 persons are known to be descended from Lieutenant John Hollister, who emigrated to America in the year 1642 (*Expositor*, Nov. 1887, p. 329). This is probably equal in ratio to the increase of Israel in Egypt.

allowance has been made, the increase continues to be, such as the narrator clearly regards it, abnormal, well-nigh preternatural, a fitting type of the expansion, amid fiercer persecutions, of the later Church of God, the true circumcision, who also sprang from the spiritual parentage of another Seventy and another Twelve.

"And Joseph died, and all his brethren, and all that generation." Thus the connection with Canaan became a mere tradition, and the powerful courtier who had nursed their interests disappeared. When they remembered him, in the bitter time which lay before them, it was only to reflect that all mortal help must perish. It is thus in the spiritual world also. Paul reminds the Philippians that they can obey in his absence and not in his presence only, working out their own salvation, as no apostle can work it out on their behalf. And the reason is that the one real support is ever present. Work out your own salvation, for it is God (not any teacher) Who worketh in you. The Hebrew race was to learn its need of Him, and in Him to recover its freedom. Moreover, the influences which mould all men's characters, their surroundings and mental atmosphere, were completely changed. These wanderers for pasture were now in the presence of a compact and impressive social system, vast cities, gorgeous temples, an imposing ritual. They were infected as well as educated there, and we find the men of the Exodus not only murmuring for Egyptian comforts, but demanding visible gods to go before them.

Yet, with all its drawbacks, the change was a necessary part of their development. They should return from Egypt relying upon no courtly patron, no mortal might or wisdom, aware of a name of God more profound than was spoken in the covenant of their fathers, with their narrow family interests and rivalries and their family traditions expanded into national hopes, national aspirations, a national religion.

Perhaps there is another reason why Scripture has reminded us of the vigorous and healthy stock whence came the race that multiplied exceedingly. For no book attaches more weight to the truth, so miserably perverted that it is discredited by multitudes, but amply vindicated by modern science, that good breeding, in the strictest sense of the word, is a powerful factor in the lives of men and nations. To be well born does not of necessity require aristocratic parentage, nor does such parentage involve it: but it implies a virtuous, temperate and pious stock. In extreme cases the doctrine of race is palpable; for who can doubt that the sins of dissolute parents are visited upon their puny and short-lived children, and that the posterity of the just inherit not only honour and a welcome in the world, "an open door," but also immunity from many a physical blemish and many a perilous craving? If the Hebrew race, after eighteen centuries of calamity, retains an unrivalled vigour and tenacity, be it remembered how its iron sinew has been twisted, from what a sire it sprang, through what ages of more than "natural selection" the dross was throughly purged out, and (as Isaiah loves to reiterate) a chosen remnant left. Already, in Egypt, in the vigorous multiplication of the race, was visible the germ of that amazing vitality which makes it, even in its overthrow, so powerful an element in the best modern thought and action.

It is a well-known saying of Goethe that the quality for which God chose Israel was probably toughness.

Perhaps the saying would better be inverted: it was among the most remarkable endowments, unto which Israel was called, and called by virtue of qualities in which Goethe himself was remarkably deficient.

Now, this principle is in full operation still, and ought to be solemnly pondered by the young. Self-indulgence, the sowing of wild oats, the seeing of life while one is young, the taking one's fling before one settles down, the having one's day (like "every dog," for it is to be observed that no person says, "every Christian"), these things seem natural enough. And their unsuspected issues in the next generation, dire and subtle and far-reaching, these also are more natural still, being the operation of the laws of God.

On the other hand, there is no youth living in obedience alike to the higher and humbler laws of our complex nature, in purity and gentleness and healthful occupation, who may not contribute to the stock of happiness in other lives beyond his own, to the future well-being of his native land, and to the day when the sadly polluted stream of human existence shall again flow clear and glad, a pure river of water of life.

GOD IN HISTORY.

i. 7.

With the seventh verse, the new narrative, the course of events treated in the main body of this book, begins.

And we are at once conscious of this vital difference between Exodus and Genesis,—that we have passed from the story of men and families to the history of a nation. In the first book the Canaanites and Egyptians concern us only as they affect Abraham or Joseph. In the second book, even Moses himself concerns us only for the sake of Israel. He is in some respects a more imposing and august character than any who preceded him; but what we are told is no longer the story of a soul, nor are we pointed so much to the development of his spiritual life as to the work he did, the tyrant overthrown, the nation moulded, the law and the ritual imposed on it.

For Jacob it was a discovery that God was in Bethel as well as in his father's house. But now the Hebrew nation was to learn that He could plague the gods of Egypt in their stronghold, that His way was in the sea, that Horeb in Arabia was the Mount of God, that He could lead them like a horse through the wilderness.

When Jacob in Peniel wrestles with God and prevails, he wins for himself a new name, expressive of the higher moral elevation which he has attained. But when Moses meets God in the bush, it is to receive a commission for the public benefit; and there is no new name for Moses, but a fresh revelation of God for the nation to learn. And in all their later history we feel that the national life which it unfolds was nourished and sustained by these glorious early experiences, the most unique as well as the most inspiring on record.

Here, then, a question of great moment is suggested. Beyond the fact that Abraham was the father of the Jewish race, can we discover any closer connection between the lives of the patriarchs and the history of Israel? Is there a truly spiritual coherence between them, or merely a genealogical sequence? For if the Bible can make good its claim to be vitalised throughout by the eternal Spirit of God, and leading forward steadily to His final revelation in Christ, then its parts will be symmetrical, proportionate and well designed.

If it be a universal book, there must be a better reason for the space devoted to preliminary and half secular stories, which is a greater bulk than the whole of the New Testament, than that these histories chance to belong to the nation whence Christ came. If no such reason can be found, the failure may not perhaps outweigh the great evidences of the faith, but it will score for something on the side of infidelity. But if upon examination it becomes plain that all has its part in one great movement, and that none can be omitted without marring the design, and if moreover this design has become visible only since the fulness of the time is come, the discovery will go far to establish the claim of Scripture to reveal throughout a purpose truly divine, dealing with man for ages, and consummated in the gift of Christ.

Now, it is to St. Paul that we turn for light upon the connection between the Old Testament and the New. And he distinctly lays down two great principles. The first is that the Old Testament is meant to educate men for the New; and especially that the sense of failure, impressed upon men's consciences by the stern demands of the Law, was necessary to make them accept the Gospel.

The law was our schoolmaster to bring us to Christ: it entered that sin might abound. And it is worth notice that this effect was actually wrought, not only upon the gross transgressor by the menace of its broken precepts, but even more perhaps upon the high-minded and pure, by the creation in their breasts of an ideal, inaccessible in its loftiness. He who says, All these things have I kept from my youth up, is the same who feels the torturing misgiving, What good thing must I do to attain life? . . . What lack I yet?

He who was blameless as touching the righteousness of the law, feels that such superficial innocence is worthless, that the law is spiritual and he is carnal, sold under sin.

Now, this principle need by no means be restricted to the Mosaic institutions. If this were the object of the law, it would probably explain much more. And when we return to the Old Testament with this clue, we find every condition in life examined, every social and political experiment exhausted, a series of demonstrations made with scientific precision, to refute the arch-heresy which underlies all others—that in favourable circumstances man might save himself, that for the evil of our lives our evil surroundings are more to be blamed than we.

Innocence in prosperous circumstances, unwarped by evil habit, untainted by corruption in the blood, uncompelled by harsh surroundings, simple innocence had its day in Paradise, a brief day with a shameful close. God made man upright, but he sought out many inventions, until the flood swept away the descendants of him who was made after the image of God.

Next we have a chosen family, called out from all the perilous associations of its home beyond the river, to begin a new career in a new land, in special covenant with the Most High, and with every endowment for the present and every hope for the future which could help to retain its loyalty. Yet the third generation reveals the thirst of Esau for his brother's blood, the treachery of Jacob, and the distraction and guilt of his fierce and sensual family. It is when individual and family life have thus proved ineffectual amid the happiest circumstances, that the tribe and the nation essay the task. Led up from the furnace of affliction, hardened and tempered in the stern free life of the desert, impressed by every variety of fortune, by slavery and escape, by the pursuit of an irresistible foe and by a rescue visibly divine, awed finally by the sublime revelations of Sinai, the nation is ready for the covenant (which is also a challenge)—The man that doeth these things shall live by them : if thou diligently hearken unto the voice of the Lord thy God . . . He shall set thee on high above all nations.

Such is the connection between this narrative and what went before. And the continuation of the same experiment, and the same failure, can be traced through all the subsequent history. Whether in so loose an organisation that every man does what is right in his own eyes, or under the sceptre of a hero or a sage,—whether so hard pressed that self-preservation ought to have driven them to their God, or so marvellously delivered that gratitude should have brought them to their knees,—whether engulfed a second time in a more hopeless captivity, or restored and ruled by a hierarchy whose authority is entirely spiritual,—in every variety of circumstances the same melancholy process repeats itself; and lawlessness, luxury, idolatry and self-righteousness combine to stop every mouth, to make every man guilty before God, to prove that a greater salvation is still needed, and thus to pave the way for the Messiah.

The second great principle of St. Paul is that faith in a divine help, in pardon, blessing and support, was the true spirit of the Old Testament as well as of the New. The challenge of the law was meant to produce self-despair, only that men might trust in God. Appeal was made especially to the cases of Abraham and David, the founder of the race and of the dynasty, clearly because the justification without works of the patriarch and of the king were precedents to decide the general question (Rom. iv. 1-8). Now, this is pre-eminently the distinction between Jewish history and all others, that in it God is everything and man is nothing. Every sceptical treatment of the story makes Moses to be the deliverer from Egypt, and shows us the Jewish nation gradually finding out God. But the nation itself believed nothing of the kind. It confessed itself to have been from the beginning vagrant and rebellious and unthankful: God had always found out Israel, never Israel God. The history is an expansion of the parable of the good shepherd. And this perfect harmony of a long record with itself and with abstract principles is both instructive and reassuring.

As the history of Israel opens before us, a third principle claims attention—one which the apostle quietly assumes, but which is forced on our consideration by the unhappy state of religious thought in these degenerate days.

"They are not to be heard," says the Seventh Article rightly, "which feign that the old fathers did look only for transitory promises." But certainly they also would be unworthy of a hearing who would feign that the early Scriptures do not give a vast, a preponderating weight, to the concerns of our life on earth. Only very slowly, and as the result of long training, does the future begin to reveal its supremacy over the present. It would startle many a devout reader out of his propriety to discover the small proportion of Old Testament scriptures in which eternity and its prospects are discussed, to reckon the passages, habitually applied to spiritual thraldom and emancipation, which were spoken at first of earthly tyranny and earthly deliverance, and to observe, even in the pious aspirations of the Psalms, how much of the gratitude and joy of the righteous comes from the sense that he is made wiser than the ancient, and need not fear though a host rose up against him, and can break a bow of steel, and has a table prepared for him, and an overflowing cup. Especially is this true of the historical books. God is here seen ruling states, judging in the earth, remembering Israel in bondage, and setting him free, providing supernatural food and water, guiding him by the fiery cloud. There is not a word about regeneration, conversion, hell, or heaven. And yet there is a profound sense of God. He is real, active, the most potent factor in the daily lives of men. Now, this may teach us a lesson, highly important to us all, and especially to those who must teach others. The difference between spirituality and secularity is not the difference between the future life and the present, but between a life that is aware of God and a godless one. Perhaps, when we find our gospel a matter of indifference and weariness to men who are absorbed in the bitter monotonous and dreary struggle for existence, we ourselves are most to blame. Perhaps, if Moses had approached the Hebrew drudges as we approach men equally weary and oppressed, they would not have bowed their heads and worshipped. And perhaps we should have better success, if we took care to speak of God in this world, making life a noble struggle, charging with new significance the dull and seemingly degraded lot of all who remember Him, such a God as Jesus revealed when He cleansed the leper, and gave sight to the blind, using one and the same word for the "healing" of diseases and the "saving" of souls, and connecting faith equally with both. Exodus will have little to teach us, unless we believe in that God who knoweth that we have need of food and clothing. And the higher spiritual truths which it expresses will only be found there in dubious and questionable allegory, unless we firmly grasp the great truth, that God is not the Saviour of souls, or of bodies, but of living men in their entirety, and treats their higher and lower wants upon much the same principle, because He is the same God, dealing with the same men, through both.

Moreover, He treats us as the men of other ages. Instead of dealing with Moses upon exceptional and strange lines, He made known His ways unto Moses, His characteristic and habitual ways. And it is on this account that whatsoever things were written aforetime are true admonition for us also, being not violent interruptions but impressive revelations of the steady silent methods of the judgment and the grace of God.

THE OPPRESSION.

i. 7-22.

At the beginning of the history of Israel we find a prosperous race. It was indeed their growing importance, and chiefly their vast numerical increase, which excited the jealousy of their rulers, at the very time when a change of dynasty removed the sense of obligation. It is a sound lesson in political as well as personal godliness that prosperity itself is dangerous, and needs special protection from on high.

Is it merely by chance again that we find in this first of histories examples of the folly of relying upon political connections? As the chief butler remembered not Joseph, nor did he succeed in escaping from prison by securing influence at court, so is the influence of

Joseph himself now become vain, although he was the father of Pharaoh and lord of all his house. His romantic history, his fidelity in temptation, and the services by which he had at once cemented the royal power and saved the people, could not keep his memory alive. The hollow wraith of dying fame died wholly. There arose a new king over Egypt who knew not Joseph.

Such is the value of the highest and purest earthly fame, and such the gratitude of the world to its benefactors. The nation which Joseph rescued from starvation is passive in Pharaoh's hands, and persecutes Israel at his bidding.

And when the actual deliverer arose, his rank and influence were only entanglements through which he had to break.

Meanwhile, except among a few women, obedient to the woman's heart, we find no trace of independent action, no revolt of conscience against the absolute behest of the sovereign, until selfishness replaces virtue, and despair wrings the cry from his servants, Knowest thou not yet that Egypt is destroyed?

Now, in Genesis we saw the fate of families, blessed in their father Abraham, or cursed for the offence of Ham. For a family is a real entity, and its members, like those of one body, rejoice and suffer together. But the same is true of nations, and here we have reached the national stage in the education of the world. Here is exhibited to us, therefore, a nation suffering with its monarch to the uttermost, until the cry of the maid-servant behind the mill is as wild and bitter as the cry of Pharaoh upon his throne. It is indeed the eternal curse of despotism that unlimited calamity may be drawn down upon millions by the caprice of one most unhappy man, himself blinded and half maddened by adulation, by the absence of restraint, by unlimited sensual indulgence if his tendencies be low and animal, and by the pride of power if he be high-spirited and aspiring.

If we assume, what seems pretty well established, that the Pharaoh from whom Moses fled was Rameses the Great, his spirit was of the nobler kind, and he exhibits a terrible example of the unfitness even of conquering genius for unbridled and irresponsible power. That lesson has had to be repeated, even down to the days of the Great Napoleon.

Now, if the justice of plaguing a nation for the offence of its head be questioned, let us ask first whether the nation accepts his despotism, honours him, and is content to regard him as its chief and captain. According to the principles of the Sermon on the Mount, whoever thinks a tyrant enviable, has already himself tyrannised with him in his heart. Do we ourselves, then, never sympathise with political audacity, bold and unscrupulous " resource," success that is bought at the price of strange compliances, and compromises, and wrongs to other men?

The great national lesson is now to be taught to Israel that the most splendid imperial force will be brought to an account for its treatment of the humblest —that there is a God Who judges in the earth. And they were bidden to apply in their own land this experience of their own, dealing kindly with the stranger in the midst of them, " for thou wast a stranger in the land of Egypt." That lesson we have partly learned, who have broken the chain of our slaves. But how much have we left undone! The subject races were never given into our hands to supplant them, as we have supplanted the Red Indian and the New Zealander, nor to debauch, as men say we are corrupting the African and the Hindoo, but to raise, instruct and Christianise. And if the subjects of a despotism are accountable for the actions of rulers whom they tolerate, how much more are we? What ought we to infer, from this old-world history, of the profound responsibilities of all free citizens?

We attain a principle which reaches far into the spiritual world, when we reflect that if evil deeds of a ruler can justly draw down vengeance upon his people, the converse also must hold good. Reverse the case before us. Let the kingdom be that of the noblest and purest virtue. Let no subject ever be coerced to enter it, nor to remain one hour longer than while his adoring loyalty consents. And shall not these subjects be the better for the virtues of the Monarch whom they love? Is it mere caprice to say that in choosing such a King they do, in a very real sense, appropriate the goodness they crown? If it be natural that Egypt be scourged for the sins of Pharaoh, is it palpably incredible that Christ is made of God unto His people wisdom and righteousness and sanctification and redemption? The doctrine of imputation can easily be so stated as to become absurd. But the imputation of which St. Paul speaks much can only be denied when we are prepared to assail the principle on which all bodies of men are treated, families and nations as well as the Church of God.

It was the jealous cruelty of Pharaoh which drew down upon his country the very perils he laboured to turn away. There was no ground for his fear of any league with foreigners against him. Prosperous and unambitious, the people would have remained well content beside the flesh-pots of Egypt, for which they sighed even when emancipated from heavy bondage and eating the bread of heaven. Or else, if they had gone forth in peace, from a land whose hospitality had not failed, to their inheritance in Canaan, they would have become an allied nation upon the side where the heaviest blows were afterwards struck by the Asiatic powers. Cruelty and cunning could not retain them, but it could decimate a population and lose an army in the attempt. And this law prevails in the modern world. England paid twenty millions to set her bondmen free. Because America would not follow her example, she ultimately paid the more terrible ransom of civil war. For the same God was in Jamaica and in Florida as in the field of Zoan. Nor was there ever yet a crooked policy which did not recoil either upon its author, or upon his successors when he had passed away. In this case it fulfilled the plans and the prophecies of God, and the wrath of man was made to praise Him.

There is independent reason for believing that at this period one-third at least of the population of Egypt was of alien blood (Brugsch, *History*, ii. 100). A politician might fairly be alarmed, especially if this were the time when the Hittites were threatening the eastern frontier, and had reduced Egypt to stand on the defensive, and erect barrier fortresses. And the circumstances of the country made it very easy to enslave the Hebrews. If any stain of Oriental indifference to the rights of the masses had mingled with the God-given insight of Joseph, when he made his benefactor the owner of all the soil, the Egyptian people were fully avenged upon him now. For this arrangement laid his pastoral race helpless at their oppressor's feet. Forced labour quickly degenerates into slavery, and men who find the story of their misery hard to credit should consider the state of France before the Revolution, and of the Russian serfs before their emancipation. Their wretchedness was probably as bitter as that of the Hebrews at any period but the last climax of their oppression. And they owed it to the same cause—the absolute ownership of the land by others, too remote from them to be sympathetic, to take due account of their feelings, to remember that they were their fellow-men. This was enough to slay compassion, even without the aggravation of dealing with an alien and suspected race.

Now, it is instructive to observe these reappearances of wholesale crime. They warn us that the utmost achievements of human wickedness are human still; not wild and grotesque importations by a fiend, originated in the abyss, foreign to the world we live in. Satan finds the material for his master-strokes in the estrangement of class from class, in the drying up of the fountains of reciprocal human feeling, in the failure of real, fresh, natural affection in our bosom for those who differ widely from us in rank or circumstances. All cruelties are possible when a man does not seem to us really a man, nor his woes really woeful. For when the man has sunk into an animal it is only a step to his vivisection.

Nor does anything tend to deepen such perilous estrangement, more than the very education, culture and refinement, in which men seek a substitute for religion and the sense of brotherhood in Christ. It is quite conceivable that the tyrant who drowned the Hebrew infants was an affectionate father, and pitied his nobles when their children died. But his sympathies could not reach beyond the barriers of a caste. Do *our* sympathies really overleap such barriers? Would God that even His Church believed aright in the reality of a human nature like our own, soiled, sorrowful, shamed, despairing, drugged into that apathetical insensibility which lies even below despair, yet aching still, in ten thousand bosoms, in every great city of Christendom, every day and every night! Would to God that she understood what Jesus meant, when He called one lost creature by the tender name which she had not yet forfeited, saying, "Woman, where are thine accusers?" and when He asked Simon, who scorned such another, "Seest thou this woman!" Would God that when she prays for the Holy Spirit of Jesus she would really seek a mind like His, not only in piety and prayerfulness, but also in tender and heart-felt brotherhood with all, even the vilest of the weary and heavy-laden!

Many great works of ancient architecture, the pyramids among the rest, were due to the desire of crushing, by abject toil, the spirit of a subject people. We cannot ascribe to Hebrew labour any of the more splendid piles of Egyptian masonry, but the store cities or arsenals which they built can be identified. They are composed of such crude brick as the narrative describes; and the absence of straw in the later portion of them can still be verified. Rameses was evidently named after their oppressor, and this strengthens the conviction that we are reading of events in the nineteenth dynasty, when the shepherd kings had recently been driven out, leaving the eastern frontier so weak as to demand additional fortresses, and so far depopulated as to give colour to the exaggerated assertion of Pharaoh, "the people are more and mightier than we." It is by such exaggerations and alarms that all the worst crimes of statesmen have been justified to consenting peoples. And we, when we carry what seems to us a rightful object, by inflaming the prejudice and misleading the judgment of other men, are moving on the same treacherous and slippery inclines. Probably no evil is committed without some amount of justification, which the passions exaggerate, while they ignore the prohibitions of the law.

How came it to pass that the fierce Hebrew blood, which was yet to boil in the veins of the Maccabees, and to give battle, not unworthily, to the Roman conquerors of the world, failed to resent the cruelties of Pharaoh?

Partly, of course, because the Jewish people was only now becoming aware of its national existence; but also because it had forsaken God. Its religion, if not supplanted, was at least adulterated by the influence of the mystic pantheism and the stately ritual which surrounded them.

Joshua bade his victorious followers to "put away the gods whom your fathers served beyond the River and in Egypt, and serve ye the Lord" (Josh. xxiv. 14). And in Ezekiel the Lord Himself complains, "They rebelled against Me and would not hearken unto Me; they did not cast away the abominations of their eyes, neither did they forsake the idols of Egypt" (Ezek. xx. 8).

Now, there is nothing which enfeebles the spirit and breaks the courage like religious dependence. A strong priesthood always means a feeble people, most of all when they are of different blood. And Israel was now dependent on Egypt alike for the highest and lowest needs—grass for the cattle and religion for the soul. And when they had sunk so low, it is evident that their emancipation had to be wrought for them entirely without their help. From first to last they were passive, not only for want of spirit to help themselves, but because the glory of any exploit of theirs might have illuminated some false deity whom they adored.

Standing still, they saw the salvation of God, and it was not possible to give His glory to another.

For this cause also, judgment had, first of all, to be wrought upon the gods of Egypt.

In the meantime, without spirit enough to resist, they saw complete destruction drawing nearer to them by successive strides. At first Pharaoh "dealt wisely with them," and they found themselves entrapped into a hard bondage almost unawares. But a strange power upheld them, and the more they were afflicted the more they multiplied and spread abroad. In this they ought to have discerned a divine support, and remembered the promise to Abraham that God would multiply his seed as the stars of heaven. It may have helped them presently to "cry unto the Lord." And the Egyptians were not merely "grieved" because of them: they felt as the Israelites afterwards felt towards that monotonous diet of which they used the same word, and said, "our soul loatheth this light bread." Here it expresses that fierce and contemptuous attitude which the Californian and Australian are now assuming toward the swarms of Chinamen whose labour is so indispensable, yet the infusion of whose blood into the population is so hateful. Then the Egyptians make their service rigorous, and their lives bitter.

And at last that happens which is a part of every downward course: the veil is dropped; what men have done by stealth, and as if they would deceive themselves, they soon do consciously, avowing to their conscience what at first they could not face. Thus Pharaoh began by striving to check a dangerous population; and ended by committing wholesale murder. Thus men become drunkards through conviviality, thieves through borrowing what they mean to restore, and hypocrites through slightly overstating what they really feel. And, since there are nice gradations in evil, down to the very last, Pharaoh will not yet avow publicly the atrocity which he commands a few humble women to perpetrate; decency is with him, as it is often, the last substitute for a conscience.

Among the agents of God for the shipwreck of all full-grown wrongs, the chief is the revolt of human nature, since, fallen though we know ourselves to be, the image of God is not yet effaced in us. The better instincts of humanity are irrepressible—most so perhaps among the poor. It is by refusing to trust its intuitions that men grow vile; and to the very last that refusal is never absolute, so that no villainy can reckon upon its agents, and its agents cannot always reckon upon themselves. Above all, the heart of every woman is in a plot against the wrong; and as Pharaoh was afterwards defeated by the ingenuity of a mother and the sympathy of his own daughter, so his first scheme was spoiled by the disobedience of the midwives, themselves Hebrews, upon whom he reckoned.

Let us not fear to avow that these women, whom God rewarded, lied to the king when he reproached them, since their answer, even if it were not unfounded, was palpably a misrepresentation of the facts. The reward was not for their falsehood, but for their humanity. They lived when the notion of martyrdom for an avowal so easy to evade was utterly unknown.

Abraham lied to Abimelech. Both Samuel and David equivocated with Saul. We have learned better things from the King of truth, Who was born and came into the world to bear witness to the truth. We know that the martyr's bold protest against unrighteousness is the highest vocation of the Church, and is rewarded in the better country. But they knew nothing of this, and their service was acceptable according as they had, not according as they had not. As well might we blame the patriarchs for having been slave-owners, and David for having invoked mischief upon his enemies, as these women for having fallen short of the Christian ideal of veracity. Let us beware lest we come short of it ourselves. And let us remember that the way of the Church through time is the path of the just, beset with mist and vapour at the dawn, but shining more and more unto the perfect day.

In the meantime, God acknowledges, and Holy Scripture celebrates, the service of these obscure and lowly heroines. Nothing done for Him goes unrewarded. To slaves it was written that "From the Lord ye shall receive the reward of the inheritance: ye serve the Lord Christ" (Col. iii. 24). And what these women saved for others was what was recompensed to themselves, domestic happiness, family life and its joys. God made them houses.

The king is now driven to avow himself in a public command to drown all the male infants of the Hebrews; and the people become his accomplices by obeying him. For this they were yet to experience a terrible retribution, when there was not a house in Egypt that had not one dead.

The features of the king to whom these atrocities are pretty certainly brought home are still to be seen in the museum at Boulak. Seti I. is the most beautiful of all the Egyptian monarchs whose faces lie bare to the eyes of modern sightseers; and his refined features, intelligent, high-bred and cheerful, resemble wonderfully, yet surpass, those of Rameses II., his successor, from whom Moses fled. This is the builder of the vast and exquisite temple of Amon at Thebes, the grandeur of which is amazing even in its ruins; and his culture and artistic gifts are visible, after all these centuries, upon his face. It is a strange comment upon the modern doctrine that culture is to become a sufficient substitute for religion. And his own record of his exploits is enough to show that the sense of beauty is not that of pity: he is the jackal leaping through the land of his enemies, the grim lion, the powerful bull with sharpened horns, who has annihilated the peoples.

There is no greater mistake than to suppose that artistic refinement can either inspire morality or replace it. Have we quite forgotten Nero, and Lucretia Borgia, and Catherine de Medici?

Many civilisations have thought little of infant life. Ancient Rome would have regarded this atrocity as lightly as modern China, as we may see by the absolute silence of its literature concerning the murder of the innocents—an event strangely parallel with this in its nature and political motives, and in the escape of one mighty Infant.

Is it conceivable that the same indifference should return, if the sanctions of religion lose their power? Every one remembers the callousness of Rousseau. Strange things are being written by pessimistic unbelief about the bringing of more sufferers into the world. And a living writer in France has advocated the legalising of infanticide, and denounced St. Vincent de Paul because, "thanks to his odious precautions, this man deferred for years the death of creatures without intelligence," etc.*

It is to the faith of Jesus, not only revealing by the light of eternity the value of every soul, but also replenishing the fountains of human tenderness that had well-nigh become exhausted, that we owe our modern love of children. In the very helplessness which the ancient masters of the world exposed to destruction without a pang, we see the type of what we must ourselves become, if we would enter heaven. But we cannot afford to forget either the source or the sanctions of the lesson.

* J. K. Huysmans—quoted in *Nineteenth Century*, May 1888, p. 673.

CHAPTER II.

THE RESCUE OF MOSES.

ii. 1-10.

WE have said that the Old Testament history teems with political wisdom, lessons of permanent instruction for mankind, on the level of this life, yet godly, as all true lessons must be, in a world of which Christ is King. These our religion must learn to recognise and proclaim, if it is ever to win the respect of men of affairs, and "leaven the whole lump" of human life with sacred influence.

Such a lesson is the importance of the individual in the history of nations. History, as read in Scripture, is indeed a long relation of heroic resistance or of base compliance in the presence of influences which are at work to debase modern peoples as well as those of old. The holiness of Samuel, the gallant faith of David, the splendour and wisdom of Solomon, the fervid zeal of Elijah, the self-respecting righteousness of Nehemiah, —ignore these, and the whole course of affairs becomes vague and unintelligible. Most of all this is true of Moses, whose appearance is now related.

In profane history it is the same. Alexander, Mahomet, Luther, William the Silent, Napoleon,—will any one pretend that Europe uninfluenced by these personalities would have become the Europe that we know?

And this truth is not at all a speculative, unpractical theory: it is vital. For now there is a fashion of speaking about the tendency of the age, the time-spirit, as an irresistible force which moulds men like potters' clay, crowning those who discern and help it, but grinding to powder all who resist its course. In reality there are always a hundred time-spirits and tendencies competing for the mastery—some of them violent, selfish, atheistic, or luxurious (as we see with our own eyes to-day)—and the shrewdest judges are continually at fault as to which of them is to be victorious, and recognised hereafter as the spirit of the age.

This modern pretence that men are nothing, and streams of tendency are all, is plainly a gospel of capitulations, of falsehood to one's private convictions, and of servile obedience to the majority and the popular cry. For, if individual men are nothing, what am I? If we are all bubbles floating down a stream, it is folly to strive to breast the current. Much practical baseness and servility is due to this base and servile creed. And the cure for it is belief in another spirit than that of the present age, trust in an inspiring God, who rescued a herd of slaves and their fading convictions from the greatest nation upon earth by matching one man, shrinking and reluctant yet obedient to his mission, against Pharaoh and all the tendencies of the age.

And it is always so. God turns the scale of events by the vast weight of a man, faithful and true, and sufficiently aware of Him to refuse, to universal clamour, the surrender of his liberty or his religion. In small matters, as in great, there is no man, faithful to a lonely duty or conviction, understanding that to have discerned it is a gift and a vocation, but makes the world better and stronger, and works out part of the answer to that great prayer "Thy will be done."

We have seen already that the religion of the Hebrews in Egypt was corrupted and in danger of being lost. To this process, however, there must have been bright exceptions; and the mother of Moses bore witness, by her very name, to her fathers' God. The first syllable of Jochebed is proof that the name of God, which became the keynote of the new revelation, was not entirely new.

As yet the parents of Moses are not named; nor is there any allusion to the close relationship which would have forbidden their union at a later period (chap. vi. 20). And throughout all the story of his youth and early manhood there is no mention whatever of God or of religion. Elsewhere it is not so. The Epistle to the Hebrews declares that through faith the babe was hidden, and through faith the man refused Egyptian rank. Stephen tells us that he expected his brethren to know that God by his hand was giving them deliverance. But the narrative in Exodus is wholly untheological. If Moses were the author, we can see why he avoided reflections which directly tended to glorify himself. But if the story were a subsequent invention, why is the tone so cold, the light so colourless?

Now, it is well that we are invited to look at all these things from their human side, observing the play of human affection, innocent subtlety, and pity. God commonly works through the heart and brain which He has given us, and we do not glorify Him at all by ignoring these. If in this case there were visible a desire to suppress the human agents, in favour of the Divine Preserver, we might suppose that a different historian would have given a less wonderful account of the plagues, the crossing of the Sea, and the revelation from Sinai. But since full weight is allowed to second causes in the early life of Moses, the story is entitled to the greater credit when it tells of the burning bush and the flaming mountain.

Let us, however, put together the various narratives and their lessons. At the outset we read of a marriage celebrated between kinsfolk, when the storm of persecution was rising. And hence we infer that courage or strong affection made the parents worthy of him through whom God should show mercy unto thousands. The first child was a girl, and therefore safe; but we may suppose, although silence in Scripture proves little, that Aaron, three years before the birth of Moses, had not come into equal peril with him. Moses was therefore born just when the last atrocity was devised, when trouble was at its height.

"At this time Moses was born," said Stephen. Edifying inferences have been drawn from the statement in Exodus that "the woman . . . hid him." Perhaps the stronger man quailed, but the maternal instinct was not at fault, and it was rewarded abundantly. From which we only learn, in reality, not to overstrain the words of Scripture; since the Epistle to the Hebrews distinctly says that he "was hid three months by his parents"—both of them, while naturally the mother is the active agent.

All the accounts agree that he was thus hidden, "because they saw that he was a goodly child" (Heb. xi. 23). It is a pathetic phrase. We see them, before the crisis, vaguely submitting in theory to an unrealised atrocity, ignorant how imperiously their nature would forbid the crime, not planning disobedience in advance, nor led to it by any reasoning process. All is changed when the little one gazes at them with that marvellous appeal in its unconscious eyes, which is known to every parent, and helps him to be a better man. There is a great difference between one's thought about an infant, and one's feeling towards the actual baby. He was their child, their beautiful child; and this it was that turned the scale. For him they would now dare anything, "because they saw he was a goodly child, and they were not afraid of the king's commandment." Now, impulse is often a great power for evil, as when appetite or fear, suddenly taking visible shape, overwhelms the judgment and plunges men into guilt. But good impulses may be the very voice of God, stirring whatever is noble and generous within us. Nor are they accidental: loving and brave emotions belong to warm and courageous hearts; they come of themselves, like song birds, but they come surely where sunshine and still groves invite them, not into clamour and foul air. Thus arose in their bosoms the sublime thought of God as an active power to be reckoned upon. For as certainly as every bad passion that we harbour preaches atheism, so does all goodness tend to sustain itself by the consciousness of a supreme Goodness in reserve. God had sent them their beautiful child, and who was Pharaoh to forbid the gift? And so religion and natural pity joined hands, their supreme convictions and their yearning for their infant. "By faith Moses was hid ... because they saw he was a goodly child, and they were not afraid of the king's commandment."

Such, if we desire a real and actual salvation, is always the faith which saves. Postpone salvation to an indefinite future; make it no more than the escape from vaguely realised penalties for sins which do not seem very hateful; and you may suppose that faith in theories can obtain this indulgence; an opinion may weigh against a misgiving. But feel that sin is not only likely to entail damnation, but is really and in itself damnable meanwhile, and then there will be no deliverance possible, but from the hand of a divine Friend, strong to sustain and willing to guide the life. We read that Amram lived a hundred and thirty and seven years, and of all that period we only know that he helped to save the deliverer of his race, by practical faith which made him not afraid, and did not paralyse but stimulate his energies.

When the mother could no longer hide the child, she devised the plan which has made her for ever famous. She placed him in a covered ark, or casket,[*] plaited (after what we know to have been the Egyptian fashion) of the papyrus reed, and rendered watertight with bitumen, and this she laid among the rushes—a lower vegetation, which would not, like the tall papyrus, hide her treasure—in the well-known and secluded place where the daughter of Pharaoh used to bathe. Something in the known character of the princess may have inspired this ingenious device to move her pity; but it is more likely that the woman's heart, in her extremity, prompted a simple appeal to the woman who could help her if she would. For an Egyptian princess was an important personage, with an establishment of her own, and often possessed of much political influence. The most sanguinary agent of a tyrant would be likely to respect the client of such a patron.

---

[*] The same word is used for Noah's ark, but not elsewhere; not, for example, of the ark in the Temple, the name of which occurs elsewhere in Scripture only of the "coffin" of Joseph, and the "chest" for the Temple revenues (Gen. l. 26; 2 Chron. xxiv. 8, 10, 11).

The heart of every woman was in a plot against the cruelty of Pharaoh. Once already the midwives had defeated him; and now, when his own daughter* unexpectedly found, in the water at her very feet, a beautiful child sobbing silently (for she knew not what was there until the ark was opened), her indignation is audible enough in the words, "This is one of the Hebrews' children." She means to say "This is only one specimen of the outrages that are going on."

This was the chance for his sister, who had been set in ambush, not prepared with the exquisite device which follows, but simply "to know what would be done to him." Clearly the mother had reckoned upon his being found, and neglected nothing, although unable herself to endure the agony of watching, or less easily hidden in that guarded spot. And her prudence had a rich reward. Hitherto Miriam's duty had been to remain passive—that hard task so often imposed upon the affection, especially of women, by sickbeds, and also in many a more stirring hazard, and many a spiritual crisis, where none can fight his brother's battle. It is a trying time, when love can only hold its breath, and pray. But let not love suppose that to watch is to do nothing. Often there comes a moment when its word, made wise by the teaching of the heart, is the all-important consideration in deciding mighty issues.

This girl sees the princess at once pitiful and embarrassed, for how can she dispose of her strange charge? Let the moment pass, and the movement of her heart subside, and all may be lost; but Miriam is prompt and bold, and asks "Shall I go and call to thee a nurse of the Hebrew women, that she may nurse the child for thee?" It is a daring stroke, for the

---

* Or his sister, the daughter of a former Pharoah.

princess must have understood the position thoroughly, the moment the eager Hebrew girl stepped forward. The disguise was very thin. And at least the heart which pitied the infant must have known the mother when she saw her face, pale with longing. It is therefore only as a form, exacted by circumstances, but well enough though tacitly understood upon both sides, that she bids her nurse the child for her, and promises wages. What reward could equal that of clasping her child to her own agitated bosom in safety, while the destroyers were around?

This incident teaches us that good is never to be despaired of, since this kindly woman grew up in the family of the persecutor.

And the promptitude and success of Miriam suggest a reflection. Men do pity, when it is brought home to them, the privation, suffering, and wrong, which lie around. Magnificent sums are contributed yearly for their relief by the generous instincts of the world. The misfortune is that sentiment is evoked only by visible and pathetic griefs, and that it will not labour as readily as it will subscribe. It is a harder task to investigate, to devise appeals, to invent and work the machinery by which misery may be relieved. Mere compassion will accomplish little, unless painstaking affection supplement it. Who supplies that? Who enables common humanity to relieve itself by simply paying "wages," and confiding the wretched to a painstaking, laborious, loving guardian? The streets would never have known Hospital Saturday, but for Hospital Sunday in the churches. The orphanage is wholly a Christian institution. And so is the lady nurse. The old-fashioned phrase has almost sunk into a party cry, but in a large and noble sense it will continue to be true to nature as long as bereavement, pain or penitence requires a tender bosom and soothing touch, which speaks of Mother Church.

Thus did God fulfil His mysterious plans. And according to a sad but noble law, which operates widely, what was best in Egypt worked with Him for the punishment of its own evil race. The daughter of Pharaoh adopted the perilous foundling, and educated him in the wisdom of Egypt.

THE CHOICE OF MOSES.
ii. 11-15.

God works even His miracles by means. As He fed the multitude with barley-loaves, so He would emancipate Israel by human agency. It was therefore necessary to educate one of the trampled race "in all the learning of Egypt," and Moses was planted in the court of Pharaoh, like the German Arminius in Rome. Wonderful legends may be read in Josephus of his heroism, his wisdom, and his victories; and these have some foundation in reality, for Stephen tells us that he was mighty in his words and works. Might in words need not mean the fluent utterance which he so earnestly disclaimed (iv. 10), even if forty years' disuse of the language were not enough to explain his later diffidence. It may have meant such power of composition as appears in the hymn by the Red Sea, and in the magnificent valediction to his people.

The point is that among a nation originally pastoral, and now sinking fast into the degraded animalism of slaves, which afterwards betrayed itself in their complaining greed, their sighs for the generous Egyptian dietary, and their impure carouse under the mountain, one man should possess the culture and mental grasp needed by a leader and lawgiver. "Could not the grace of God have supplied the place of endowment and attainment?" Yes, truly; and it was quite as likely to do this for one who came down from His immediate presence with his face intolerably bright, as for the last impudent enthusiast who declaims against the need of education in sentences which at least prove that for him the want has by no substitute been completely met. But the grace of God chose to give the qualification, rather than replace it, alike to Moses and St. Paul. Nor is there any conspicuous example among the saints of a man being thrust into a rank for which he was not previously made fit.

The painful contrast between his own refined tastes and habits, and the coarser manners of his nation, was no doubt one difficulty of the choice of Moses, and a lifelong trial to him afterwards. He is an example not only to those whom wealth and power would entangle, but to any who are too fastidious and sensitive for the humble company of the people of God.

While the intellect of Moses was developing, it is plain that his connection with his family was not entirely broken. Such a tie as often binds a foster-child to its nurse may have been permitted to associate him with his real parents. Some means were evidently found to instruct him in the history and messianic hopes of Israel, for he knew that their reproach was that of "the Christ," greater riches than all the treasure of Egypt, and fraught with a reward for which he looked in faith (Heb. xi. 26). But what is meant by naming as part of his burden their "reproach," as distinguished from their sufferings?

We shall understand, if we reflect, that his open rupture with Egypt was unlikely to be the work of a moment. Like all the best workers, he was led forward gradually, at first unconscious of his vocation. Many a protest he must have made against the cruel and unjust policy that steeped the land in innocent blood. Many a jealous councillor must have known how to weaken his dangerous influence by some cautious taunt, some insinuated "reproach" of his own Hebrew origin. The warnings put by Josephus into the lips of the priests in his childhood, were likely enough to have been spoken by some one before he was forty years old. At last, when driven to make his choice, he "refused to be called the son of Pharaoh's daughter," a phrase, especially in its reference to the rejected title as distinguished from "the pleasures of sin," which seems to imply a more formal rupture than Exodus records.

We saw that the piety of his parents was not unhelped by their emotions: they hid him by faith when they saw that he was a goodly child. Such was also the faith by which Moses broke with rank and fortune. He went out unto his brethren, and looked on their burdens, and he saw an Egyptian smiting an Hebrew, one of his brethren. Twice the word of kinship is repeated; and Stephen tells us that Moses himself used it in rebuking the dissensions of his fellow-countrymen. Filled with yearning and pity for his trampled brethren, and with the shame of generous natures who are at ease while others suffer, he saw an Egyptian smiting an Hebrew. With that blended caution and vehemence which belong to his nation still, he looked and saw that there was no man, and slew the Egyptian. Like most acts of passion, this was at once an impulse of the moment, and an outcome of long gathering forces— just as the lightning flash, sudden though it seem, has been prepared by the accumulated electricity of weeks.

And this is the reason why God allows the issues of a lifetime, perhaps of an eternity, to be decided by a sudden word, a hasty blow. Men plead that if time had been given, they would have stifled the impulse which ruined them. But what gave the impulse such violent and dreadful force that it overwhelmed them before they could reflect? The explosion in the coal-mine is not caused by the sudden spark, without the accumulation of dangerous gases, and the absence of such wholesome ventilation as would carry them away. It is so in the breast where evil desires or tempers are harboured, unsubdued by grace, until any accident puts them beyond control. Thank God that such sudden movements do not belong to evil only! A high soul is surprised into heroism, as often perhaps as a mean one into theft or falsehood. In the case of Moses there was nothing unworthy, but much that was unwarranted and presumptuous. The decision it involved was on the right side, but the act was self-willed and unwarranted, and it carried heavy penalties. "The trespass originated not in inveterate cruelty," says St. Augustine, "but in a hasty zeal which admitted of correction . . . resentment against injury was accompanied by love for a brother. . . . Here was evil to be rooted out, but the heart with such capabilities, like good soil, needed only cultivation to make it fruitful in virtue."

Stephen tells us, what is very natural, that Moses expected the people to accept him as their heaven-born deliverer. From which it appears that he cherished high expectations for himself, from Israel if not from Egypt. When he interfered next day between two Hebrews, his question as given in Exodus is somewhat magisterial: "Wherefore smitest thou thy fellow?" In

Stephen's version it dictates less, but it lectures a good deal: "Sirs, ye are brethren, why do ye wrong one to another?" And it was natural enough that they should dispute his pretensions, for God had not yet given him the rank he claimed. He still needed a discipline almost as sharp as that of Joseph, who, by talking too boastfully of his dreams, postponed their fulfilment until he was chastened by slavery and a dungeon. Even Saul of Tarsus, when converted, needed three years of close seclusion for the transformation of his fiery ardour into divine zeal, as iron to be tempered must be chilled as well as heated. The precipitate and violent zeal of Moses entailed upon him forty years of exile.

And yet his was a noble patriotism. There is a false love of country, born of pride, which blinds one to her faults; and there is a loftier passion which will brave estrangement and denunciation to correct them. Such was the patriotism of Moses, and of all whom God has ever truly called to lead their fellows. Nevertheless he had to suffer for his error.

His first act had been a kind of manifesto, a claim to lead, which he supposed that they would have understood; and yet, when he found his deed was known, he feared and fled. His false step told against him. One cannot but infer also that he was conscious of having already forfeited court favour—that he had before this not only made his choice, but announced it, and knew that the blow was ready to fall on him at any provocation. We read that he dwelt in the land of Midian, a name which was applied to various tracts according to the nomadic wanderings of the tribe, but which plainly included, at this time, some part of the peninsula formed by the tongues of the Red Sea. For, as he fed his flocks, he came to the Mount of God.

MOSES IN MIDIAN.

ii. 16-22.

The interference of Moses on behalf of the daughters of the priest of Midian is a pleasant trait, courteous, and expressive of a refined nature. With this remark, and reflecting that, like many courtesies, it brought its reward, we are often content to pass it by. And yet it deserves a closer examination.

1. For it expresses great energy of character. He might well have been in a state of collapse. He had smitten the Egyptian for Israel's sake: he had appealed to his own people to make common cause, like brethren, against the common foe; and he had offered himself to them as their destined leader in the struggle. But they had refused him the command, and he was rudely awakened to the consciousness that his life was in danger through the garrulous ingratitude of the man he rescued. Now he was a ruined man and an exile, marked for destruction by the greatest of earthly monarchs, with the habits and tastes of a great noble, but homeless among wild races.

It was no common nature which was alert and energetic at such a time. The greatest men have known a period of prostration in calamity: it was enough for honour that they should rally and re-collect their forces. Thinking of Frederick, after Kunersdorf, resigning the command ("I have no resources more, and will not survive the destruction of my country"), and of his subsequent despatch, "I am now recovered from my illness"; and of Napoleon, trembling and weeping on the road to Elba, one turns with fresh admiration to the fallen prince, the baffled liberator, sitting exhausted by the well, but as keen on behalf of liberty as when Pharaoh trampled Israel, though now the oppressors are a group of rude herdsmen, and the oppressed are Midianite women, driven from the troughs which they have toiled to fill. One remembers Another, sitting also exhausted by the well, defying social usage on behalf of a despised woman, and thereby inspired and invigorated as with meat to eat which His followers knew not of.

2. Moreover there is disinterested bravery in the act, since he hazards the opposition of the men of the land, among whom he seeks refuge, on behalf of a group from which he can have expected nothing. And here it is worth while to notice the characteristic variations in three stories which have certain points of contact. The servant of Abraham, servant-like, was well content that Rebekah should draw for all his camels, while he stood still. The prudent Jacob, anxious to introduce himself to his cousin, rolled away the stone and watered her camels. Moses sat by the well, but did not interfere while the troughs were being filled: it was only the overt wrong which kindled him. But as in great things, so it is in small: our actions never stand alone; having once befriended them, he will do it thoroughly, "and moreover he drew water for us, and watered the flock." Such details could hardly have been thought out by a fabricator; a legend would not have allowed Moses to be slower in courtesy than Jacob;* but the story fits the case exactly: his eyes were with his heart, and that was far away, until the injustice of the shepherds roused him.

---

* Nor would it have made the women call their deliverer "an Egyptian," for the Hebrew cast of features is very dissimilar. But Moses wore Egyptian dress, and the Egyptians worked mines in the peninsula, so that he was naturally taken for one of them.

And why was Moses thus energetic, fearless, and chivalrous? Because he was sustained by the presence of the Unseen: he endured as seeing Him who is invisible; and having, despite of panic, by faith forsaken Egypt, he was free from the absorbing anxieties which prevent men from caring for their fellows, free also from the cynical misgivings which suspect that violence is more than justice, that to be righteous overmuch is to destroy oneself, and that perhaps, after all, one may see a good deal of wrong without being called upon to interfere. It would be a different world to-day, if all who claim to be "the salt of the earth" were as eager to repress injustice in its smaller and meaner forms as to make money or influential friends. If all petty and cowardly oppression were sternly trodden down, we should soon have a state of public opinion in which gross and large tyranny would be almost impossible. And it is very doubtful whether the flagrant wrongs, which must be comparatively rare, cause as much real mental suffering as the frequent small ones. Does mankind suffer more from wild beasts than from insects? But how few that aspire to emancipate oppressed nations would be content, in the hour of their overthrow, to assert the rights of a handful of women against a trifling fraud, to which indeed they were so well accustomed that its omission surprised their father!

Is it only because we are reading a history, and not a biography, that we find no touch of tenderness, like the love of Jacob for Rachel, in the domestic relations of Moses?

Joseph also married in a strange land, yet he called the name of his first son Manasseh, because God had made him to forget his sorrows: but Moses remembered his. Neither wife nor child could charm away his home sickness; he called his firstborn Gershom, because he was a sojourner in a strange land. In truth, his whole life seems to have been a lonely one. Miriam is called "the sister of Aaron" even when joining in the song of Moses (xv. 20), and with Aaron she made common cause against their greater brother (Num. xii. 1-2). Zipporah endangered his life rather than obey the covenant of circumcision; she complied at last with a taunt (iv. 24-6), and did not again join him until his victory over Amalek raised his position to the utmost height (xviii. 2).

His children are of no account, and his grandson is the founder of a dangerous and enduring schism (Judges xviii. 30, R.V.).

There is much reason to see here the earliest example of the sad rule that a prophet is not without honour save in his own house; that the law of compensations reaches farther into life than men suppose; and high position and great powers are too often counterbalanced by the isolation of the heart.

CHAPTER III.

THE BURNING BUSH.

ii. 23 -iii.

"IN process of time the king of Egypt died," probably the great Raamses, no other of whose dynasty had a reign which extended over the indicated period of time. If so, he had while living every reason to expect an immortal fame, as the greatest among Egyptian kings, a hero, a conqueror on three continents, a builder of magnificent works. But he has only won an immortal notoriety. "Every stone in his buildings was cemented in human blood." The cause he persecuted has made deathless the banished refugee, and has gibbeted the great monarch as a tyrant, whose misplanned severities wrought the ruin of his successor and his army. Such are the reversals of popular judgment: and such the vanity of fame. For all the contemporary fame was his.

"The children of Israel sighed by reason of the bondage, and they cried." Another monarch had come at last, a change after sixty-seven years, and yet no change for them! It filled up the measure of their patience, and also of the iniquity of Egypt. We are not told that their cry was addressed to the Lord; what we read is that it reached Him, Who still overhears and pities many a sob, many a lament, which ought to have been addressed to Him, and is not. Indeed, if His compassion were not to reach men until they had remembered and prayed to Him, who among us would ever have learned to pray to Him at all? Moreover He remembered His covenant with their forefathers, for the fulfilment of which the time had now arrived. "And God saw the children of Israel, and God took knowledge of them."

These were not the cries of religious individuals, but of oppressed masses. It is therefore a solemn question to ask How many such appeals ascend from Christian England? Behold, the hire of labourers . . . held back by fraud crieth out. The half-paid slaves of our haste to be rich, and the victims of our drinking institutions, and of hideous vices which entangle and destroy the innocent and unconscious, what cries to heaven are theirs! As surely as those which St. James records, these have entered into the ears of the Lord of Sabaoth. Of these sufferers every one is His own by purchase, most of them by a covenant and sacrament more solemn than bound Him to His ancient Israel. Surely He hears their groaning. And all whose hearts are touched with compassion, yet who hesitate whether to bestir themselves or to remain inert while evil is masterful and cruel, should remember the anger of God when Moses said, " Send, I pray Thee, by whom Thou wilt send." The Lord is not indifferent. Much less than other sufferers should those who know God be terrified by their afflictions. Cyprian encouraged the Church of his time to endure even unto martyrdom, by the words recorded of ancient Israel, that the more they afflicted them, so much the more they became greater and waxed stronger. And he was right. For all these things happened to them for ensamples, and were written for our admonition.

It is further to be observed that the people were quite unconscious, until Moses announced it afterwards, that they were heard by God. Yet their deliverer had now been prepared by a long process for his work. We are not to despair because relief does not immediately appear: though He tarry, we are to wait for Him.

While this anguish was being endured in Egypt, Moses was maturing for his destiny. Self-reliance, pride of place, hot and impulsive aggressiveness, were dying in his bosom. To the education of the courtier and scholar was now added that of the shepherd in the wilds, amid the most solemn and awful scenes of nature, in solitude, humiliation, disappointment, and, as we learn from the Epistle to the Hebrews, in enduring faith. Wordsworth has a remarkable description of the effect of a similar discipline upon the good Lord Clifford. He tells—

> "How he, long forced in humble paths to go,
> Was softened into feeling, soothed and tamed.
>
> "Love had he found in huts where poor men lie,
> His daily teachers had been woods and rills,
> The silence that is in the starry sky,
> The sleep that is among the lonely hills.
>
> "In him the savage virtues of the race,
> Revenge, and all ferocious thoughts, were dead;
> Nor did he change, but kept in lofty place
> The wisdom which adversity had bred."

There was also the education of advancing age, which teaches many lessons, and among them two which are essential to leadership,—the folly of a hasty blow, and of impulsive reliance upon the support of mobs.

Moses the man-slayer became exceeding meek; and he ceased to rely upon the perception of his people that God by him would deliver them. His distrust, indeed, became as excessive as his temerity had been, but it was an error upon the safer side. "Behold, they will not believe me," he says, "nor hearken unto my voice."

It is an important truth that in very few lives the decisive moment comes just when it is expected. Men allow themselves to be self-indulgent, extravagant and even wicked, often upon the calculation that their present attitude matters little, and they will do very differently when the crisis arrives, the turning-point in their career to nerve them. And they waken up with a start to find their career already decided, their character moulded. As a snare shall the day of the Lord come upon all flesh; and as a snare come all His great visitations meanwhile. When Herod was drinking among bad companions, admiring a shameless dancer, and boasting loudly of his generosity, he was sobered and saddened to discover that he had laughed away the life of his only honest adviser. Moses, like David, was "following the ewes great with young," when summoned by God to rule His people Israel. Neither did the call arrive when he was plunged in moody reverie and abstraction, sighing over his lost fortunes and his defeated aspirations, rebelling against his lowly duties. The humblest labour is a preparation for the brightest revelations, whereas discontent, however lofty, is a preparation for nothing. Thus, too, the birth of Jesus was first announced to shepherds keeping watch over their flock. Yet hundreds of third-rate young persons in every city in this land to-day neglect their work, and unfit themselves for any insight, or any leadership whatever, by chafing against the obscurity of their vocation.

Who does not perceive that the career of Moses hitherto was divinely directed? The fact that we feel this, although, until now, God has not once been mentioned in his personal story, is surely a fine lesson for those who have only one notion of what edifies—the dragging of the most sacred names and phrases into even the most unsuitable connections. In truth, such a phraseology is much less attractive than a certain tone, a recognition of the unseen, which may at times be more consistent with reverential silence than with obtrusive utterance. It is enough to be ready and fearless when the fitting time comes, which is sure to arrive, for the religious heart as for this narrative—the time for the natural utterance of the great word, God.

We read that the angel of the Lord appeared to him—a remarkable phrase, which was already used in connection with the sacrifice of Isaac (Gen. xxii. 11). How much it implies will better be discussed in the twenty-third chapter, where a fuller statement is made. For the present it is enough to note, that this is one pre-eminent angel, indicated by the definite article; that he is clearly the medium of a true divine appearance, because neither the voice nor form of any lesser being is supposed to be employed, the appearance being that of fire, and the words being said to be the direct utterance of the Lord, not of any one who says, Thus saith the Lord. We shall see hereafter that the story of the Exodus is unique in this respect, that in training a people tainted with Egyptian superstitions, no 'similitude' is seen, as when there wrestled a man with Jacob, or when Ezekiel saw a human form upon the sapphire pavement.

Man is the true image of God, and His perfect revelation was in flesh. But now that expression of Himself was perilous, and perhaps unsuitable besides; for He was to be known as the Avenger, and presently as the Giver of Law, with its inflexible conditions and its menaces. Therefore He appeared as fire, which is intense and terrible, even when "the flame of the grace of God does not consume, but illuminates."

There is a notion that religion is languid, repressive, and unmanly. But such is not the scriptural idea. In His presence is the fulness of joy. Christ has come that we might have life, and might have it more abundantly. They who are shut out from His blessedness are said to be asleep and dead. And so Origen quotes this passage among others, with the comment that "As God is a fire, and His angels a flame of fire, and all the saints fervent in spirit, so they who have fallen away from God are said to have cooled, or to have become cold" (*De Princip.*, ii. 8). A revelation by fire involves intensity.

There is indeed another explanation of the burning bush, which makes the flame express only the afflictions that did not consume the people. But this would be a strange adjunct to a divine appearance for their deliverance, speaking rather of the continuance of suffering than of its termination, for which the extinction of such fire would be a more appropriate symbol.

Yet there is an element of truth even in this view, since fire is connected with affliction. In His holiness God is light (with which, in the Hebrew, the very word for holiness seems to be connected); in His judgments He is fire. "The Light of Israel shall be for a fire, and his Holy One for a flame, and it shall burn and devour his thorns and his briers in one day" (Isa. x. 17).

But God reveals Himself in this thorn bush as a fire which does not consume; and such a revelation tells at once Who has brought the people into affliction, and also that they are not abandoned to it.

To Moses at first there was visible only an extraordinary phenomenon; He turned to see a great sight. It is therefore out of the question to find here the truth, so easy to discover elsewhere, that God rewards the religious inquirer—that they who seek after Him shall find Him. Rather we learn the folly of deeming that the intellect and its inquiries are at war with religion and its mysteries, that revelation is at strife with mental insight, that he who most stupidly refuses to "see the great sights" of nature is best entitled to interpret the voice of God. When the man of science gives ear to voices not of earth, and the man of God has eyes and interest for the divine wonders which surround us, many a discord will be harmonised. With the revival of classical learning came the Reformation.

But it often happens that the curiosity of the intellect is in danger of becoming irreverent, and obtrusive into mysteries not of the brain, and thus the voice of God must speak in solemn warning: "Moses, Moses, . . . Draw not nigh hither: put off thy shoes from off thy feet, for the place whereon thou standest is holy ground."

After as prolonged a silence as from the time of Malachi to the Baptist, it is God Who reveals Himself once more—not Moses who by searching finds Him out. And this is the established rule. Tidings of the Incarnation came from heaven, or man would not have discovered the Divine Babe. Jesus asked His two first disciples "What seek ye?" and told Simon "Thou shalt be called Cephas," and pronounced the listening

Nathaniel "an Israelite indeed," and bade Zaccheus "make haste and come down," in each case before He was addressed by them.

The first words of Jehovah teach something more than ceremonial reverence. If the dust of common earth on the shoe of Moses may not mingle with that sacred soil, how dare we carry into the presence of our God mean passions and selfish cravings? Observe, too, that while Jacob, when he awoke from his vision, said, "How dreadful is this place!" (Gen. xxviii. 17), God Himself taught Moses to think rather of the holiness than the dread of His abode. Nevertheless Moses also was afraid to look upon God, and hid the face which was thereafter to be veiled, for a nobler reason, when it was itself illumined with the divine glory. Humility before God is thus the path to the highest honour, and reverence, to the closest intercourse.

Meantime the Divine Person has announced Himself: "I am the God of thy father" (father is apparently singular with a collective force), "the God of Abraham, the God of Isaac, and the God of Jacob." It is a blessing which every Christian parent should bequeath to his child, to be strengthened and invigorated by thinking of God as his father's God.

It was with this memorable announcement that Jesus refuted the Sadducees and established His doctrine of the resurrection. So, then, the bygone ages are not forgotten: Moses may be sure that a kindly relation exists between God and himself, because the kindly relation still exists in all its vital force which once bound Him to those who long since appeared to die. It was impossible, therefore, our Lord inferred, that they had really died at all. The argument is a forerunner of that by which St. Paul concludes, from the resurrection of Christ, that none who are "in Christ" have perished. Nay, since our Lord was not disputing about immortality only, but the resurrection of the body, His argument implied that a vital relationship with God involved the imperishability of the whole man, since all was His, and in truth the very seal of the covenant was imprinted upon the flesh. How much stronger is the assurance for us, who know that our very bodies are His temple! Now, if any suspicion should arise that the argument, which is really subtle, is over-refined and untrustworthy, let it be observed that no sooner was this announcement made, than God added the proclamation of His own immutability, so that it cannot be said He was, but from age to age His title is I AM. The inference from the divine permanence to the living and permanent vitality of all His relationships is not a verbal quibble, it is drawn from the very central truth of this great scripture.

And now for the first time God calls Israel My people, adopting a phrase already twice employed by earthly rulers (Gen. xxiii. 11, xli. 40), and thus making Himself their king and the champion of their cause. Often afterwards it was used in pathetic appeal :— " Thou hast showed Thy people hard things,"—" Thou sellest Thy people for nought,"—" Behold, look, we beseech Thee; we are all Thy people" (Ps. lx. 3, xliv. 12; Isa. lxiv. 9). And often it expressed the returning favour of their king: "Hear, O My people, and I will speak"; "Comfort ye, comfort ye My people" (Ps. l. 7; Isa. xl. 1).

It is used of the nation at large, all of whom were brought into the covenant, although with many of them God was not well pleased. And since it does not belong only to saints, but speaks of a grace which might be received in vain, it is a strong appeal to all Christian people, all who are within the New Covenant. Them also the Lord claims and pities, and would gladly emancipate: their sorrows also He knows. "I have surely seen the affliction of My people which are in Egypt, and have heard their cry by reason of their taskmasters; for I know their sorrows; and I am come down to deliver them out of the hand of the Egyptians, and to bring them up out of that land unto a good land and a large, unto a land flowing with milk and honey." Thus the ways of God exceed the desires of men. Their subsequent complaints are evidence that Egypt had become their country: gladly would they have shaken off the iron yoke, but a successful rebellion is a revolution, not an Exodus. Their destined home was very different: with the widest variety of climate, scenery, and soil, a land which demanded much more regular husbandry, but rewarded labour with exuberant fertility. Secluded from heathenism by deserts on the south and east, by a sublime range of mountains on the north, and by a sea with few havens on the west, yet planted in the very bosom of all the ancient civilisation which at the last it was to leaven, it was a land where a faithful people could have dwelt alone and not been reckoned among the nations, yet where the scourge for disobedience was never far away.

Next after the promise of this good land, the commission of Moses is announced. He is to act, because God is already active: "*I* am come down to deliver them . . . come now, therefore, and I will send *thee* unto Pharaoh, that thou mayest bring forth My people.' And let this truth encourage all who are truly sent of God, to the end of time, that He does not send us to deliver man, until He is Himself prepared to do so, that when our fears ask, like Moses, Who am I, that I should go? He does not answer, Thou art capable, but Certainly I will go with thee. So, wherever the ministry of the word is sent, there is a true purpose of grace. There is also the presence of One who claims the right to bestow upon us the same encouragement which was given to Moses by Jehovah, saying, "Lo, I am with you alway." In so saying, Jesus made Himself equal with God.

And as this ancient revelation of God was to give rest to a weary and heavy-laden people, so Christ bound together the assertion of a more perfect revelation, made in Him, with the promise of a grander emancipation. No man knoweth the Father save by revelation of the Son is the doctrine which introduces the great offer "Come unto Me, all ye that labour and are heavy-laden, and I will give you rest" (Matt. xi. 27, 28). The claims of Christ in the New Testament will never be fully recognised until a careful study is made of His treatment of the functions which in the Old Testament are regarded as Divine. A curious expression follows: "This shall be a token unto thee that I have sent thee: When thou hast brought forth the people out of Egypt, ye shall serve God upon this mountain." It seems but vague encouragement, to offer Moses, hesitating at the moment, a token which could take effect only when his task was wrought. And yet we know how much easier it is to believe what is thrown into distinct shape and particularised. Our trust in good intentions is helped when their expression is detailed and circumstantial, as a candidate for office will reckon all general assurances of support much cheaper than a pledge to canvass certain electors within a certain time. Such is the constitution of human nature; and its Maker has often deigned to sustain its weakness by going thus into particulars. He does the same for us, condescending to embody the most profound of all mysteries in sacramental emblems, clothing his promises of our future blessedness in much detail, and in concrete figures which at least symbolise, if they do not literally describe, the glories of the Jerusalem which is above.

A NEW NAME.

iii. 14. vi. 2, 3.

"God said unto Moses, I AM THAT I AM: and He said, Thus shalt thou say unto the children of Israel, I AM hath sent me unto you."

We cannot certainly tell why Moses asked for a new name by which to announce to his brethren the appearance of God. He may have felt that the memory of their fathers, and of the dealings of God with them, had faded so far out of mind that merely to indicate their ancestral God would not sufficiently distinguish Him from the idols of Egypt, whose worship had infected them.

If so, he was fully answered by a name which made this God the one reality, in a world where all is a phantasm except what derives stability from Him.

He may have desired to know, for himself, whether there was any truth in the dreamy and fascinating pantheism which inspired so much of the Egyptian superstition.

In that case, the answer met his question by declaring that God existed, not as the sum of things or soul of the universe, but in Himself, the only independent Being.

Or he may simply have desired some name to

express more of the mystery of deity, remembering how a change of name had accompanied new discoveries of human character and achievement, as of Abraham and Israel; and expecting a new name likewise when God would make to His people new revelations of Himself.

So natural an expectation was fulfilled not only then, but afterwards. When Moses prayed "Show me, I pray Thee, Thy glory," the answer was "I will make all My goodness pass before thee, and I will proclaim the name of the Lord." The proclamation was again Jehovah, but not this alone. It was "The Lord, the Lord, a God full of compassion and gracious, slow to anger, and plenteous in mercy and truth" (xxxiii. 18, 19, xxxiv. 6, R.V.) Thus the life of Moses, like the agelong progress of the Church, advanced towards an ever-deepening knowledge that God is not only the Independent but the Good. All sets toward the final knowledge that His highest name is Love.

Meanwhile, in the development of events, the exact period was come for epithets, which were shared with gods many and lords many, to be supplemented by the formal announcement and authoritative adoption of His proper name Jehovah. The infant nation was to learn to think of Him, not only as endowed with attributes of terror and power, by which enemies would be crushed, but as possessing a certain well-defined personality, upon which the trust of man could repose. Soon their experience would enable them to receive the formal announcement that He was merciful and gracious. But first they were required to trust His promise amid all discouragements; and to this end, stability was the attribute first to be insisted upon.

It is true that the derivation of the word Jehovah is

still a problem for critical acumen. It has been sought in more than one language, and various shades of meaning have been assigned to it, some untenable in the abstract, others hardly, or not at all, to be reconciled with the Scriptural narrative.

Nay, the corruption of the very sound is so notorious, that it is only worth mention as illustrating a phase of superstition.

We smile at the Jews, removing the correct vowels lest so holy a word should be irreverently spoken, placing the sanctity in the cadence, hoping that light and flippant allusions may offend God less, so long as they spare at least the vowels of His name, and thus preserve some vestige undesecrated, while profaning at once the conception of His majesty and the consonants of the mystic word.

A more abject superstition could scarcely have made void the spirit, while grovelling before the letter of the commandment.

But this very superstition is alive in other forms to-day. Whenever one recoils from the sin of coarse blasphemy, yet allows himself the enjoyment of a polished literature which profanes holy conceptions,—whenever men feel bound to behave with external propriety in the house of God, yet bring thither wandering thoughts, vile appetites, sensuous imaginations, and all the chamber of imagery which is within the unregenerate heart,—there is the same despicable superstition which strove to escape at least the extreme of blasphemy by prudently veiling the Holy Name before profaning it.

But our present concern is with the practical message conveyed to Israel when Moses declared that Jehovah, I AM, the God of their fathers, had appeared unto him.

And if we find in it a message suited for the time, and which is the basis, not the superstructure, both of later messages and also of the national character, then we shall not fail to observe the bearing of such facts upon an urgent controversy of this time.

Some significance must have been in that Name, not too abstract for a servile and degenerate race to apprehend. Nor was it soon to pass away and be replaced; it was His memorial throughout all generations; and therefore it has a message for us to-day, to admonish and humble, to invigorate and uphold.

That God would be the same to them as to their fathers was much. But that it was of the essence of His character to be evermore the same, immutable in heart and mind and reality of being, however their conduct might modify His bearing towards them, this indeed would be a steadying and reclaiming consciousness.

Accordingly Moses receives the answer for himself, "I AM THAT I AM"; and he is bidden to tell his people " I AM hath sent me unto you," and yet again " JEHOVAH the God of your fathers hath sent me unto you." The spirit and tenor of these three names may be said to be virtually comprehended in the first; and they all speak of the essential and self-existent Being, unchanging and unchangeable.

I AM expresses an intense reality of being. No image in the dark recesses of Egyptian or Syrian temples, grotesque and motionless, can win the adoration of him who has had communion with such a veritable existence, or has heard His authentic message. No dreamful pantheism, on its knees to the beneficent principle expressed in one deity, to the destructive in another, or to the reproductive in a third, but all of them dependent upon nature, as the rainbow upon the cataract which it spans, can ever again satisfy the soul which is athirst for the living God, the Lord, Who is not personified, but IS.

This profound sense of a living Person within reach, to be offended, to pardon, and to bless, was the one force which kept the Hebrew nation itself alive, with a vitality unprecedented since the world began. They could crave His pardon, whatever natural retributions they had brought down upon themselves, whatever tendencies of nature they had provoked, because He was not a dead law without ears or a heart, but their merciful and gracious God.

Not the most exquisite subtleties of innuendo and irony could make good for a day the monstrous paradox that the Hebrew religion, the worship of I AM, was really nothing but the adoration of that stream of tendencies which makes for righteousness.

Israel did not challenge Pharaoh through having suddenly discovered that goodness ultimately prevails over evil, nor is it any cold calculation of the sort which ever inspires a nation or a man with heroic fortitude. But they were nerved by the announcement that they had been remembered by a God Who is neither an ideal nor a fancy, but the Reality of realities, beside Whom Pharaoh and his host were but as phantoms.

I AM THAT I AM is the style not only of permanence, but of permanence self-contained, and being a distinctive title, it denies such self-contained permanence to others.

Man is as the past has moulded him, a compound of attainments and failures, discoveries and disillusions, his eyes dim with forgotten tears, his hair grey with surmounted anxieties, his brow furrowed with bygone studies, his conscience troubled with old sin. Modern unbelief is ignobly frank respecting him. He is the sum of his parents and his wet-nurse. He is what he eats. If he drinks beer, he thinks beer. And it is the element of truth in these hideous paradoxes which makes them rankle, like an unkind construction put upon a questionable action. As the foam is what wind and tide have made of it, so are we the product of our circumstances, the resultant of a thousand forces, far indeed from being self-poised or self-contained, too often false to our best self, insomuch that probably no man is actually what in the depth of self-consciousness he feels himself to be, what moreover he should prove to be, if only the leaden weight of constraining circumstance were lifted off the spring which it flattens down to earth. Moses himself was at heart a very different person from the keeper of the sheep of Jethro. Therefore man says, Pity and make allowance for me : this is not my true self, but only what by compression, by starvation and stripes and bribery and error, I have become. Only God says, I AM THAT I AM.

Yet in another sense, and quite as deep a one, man is not the coarse tissue which past circumstances have woven : he is the seed of the future, as truly as the fruit of the past. Strange compound that he is of memory and hope, while half of the present depends on what is over, the other half is projected into the future ; and like a bridge, sustained on these two banks, life throws its quivering shadow on each moment that fleets by. It is not attainment, but degradation to live upon the level of one's mere attainment, no longer uplifted by any aspiration, fired by any emulation, goaded by any but carnal fears. If we have been shaped by circumstances, yet we are saved by hope.

Do not judge me, we are all entitled to plead, by anything that I am doing or have done: He only can appraise a soul a right Who knows what it yearns to become, what within itself it hates and prays to be delivered from, what is the earnestness of its self-loathing, what the passion of its appeal to heaven. As the bloom of next April is the true comment upon the dry bulb of September, as you do not value the fountain by the pint of water in its basin, but by its inexhaustible capabilities of replenishment, so the present and its joyless facts are not the true man; his possibilities, the fears and hopes that control his destiny and shall unfold it, these are his real self.

I am not merely what I am: I am very truly that which I long to be. And thus, man may plead, I am what I move towards and strive after, my aspiration is myself. But God says, I AM WHAT I AM. The stream hurries forward: the rock abides. And this is the Rock of Ages.

Now, such a conception is at first sight not far removed from that apathetic and impassive kind of deity which the practical atheism of ancient materialists could well afford to grant;—" ever in itself enjoying immortality together with supreme repose, far removed and withdrawn from our concerns, since it, exempt from every pain, exempt from all danger, strong in its own resources and wanting nought from us, is neither gained by favour nor moved by wrath."

Thus Lucretius conceived of the absolute Being as by the necessity of its nature entirely outside our system.

But Moses was taught to trust in Jehovah as intervening, pitying sorrow and wrong, coming down to assist His creatures in distress.

How could this be possible? Clearly the movement

towards them must be wholly disinterested, and wholly from within ; unbought, since no external influence can modify His condition, no puny sacrifice can propitiate Him Who sitteth upon the circle of the earth and the inhabitants thereof are as grasshoppers : a movement prompted by no irregular emotional impulse, but an abiding law of His nature, incapable of change, the movement of a nature, personal indeed, yet as steady, as surely to be reckoned upon in like circumstances, as the operations of gravitation are.

There is no such motive, working in such magnificent regularity for good, save one. The ultimate doctrine of the New Testament, that God is Love, is already involved in this early assertion, that being wholly independent of us and our concerns, He is yet not indifferent to them, so that Moses could say unto the children of Israel " I AM hath sent me unto you."

It is this unchangeable consistency of Divine action which gives the narrative its intense interest to us. To Moses, and therefore to all who receive any commission from the skies, this title said, Frail creature, sport of circumstances and of tyrants, He who commissions thee sits above the waterfloods, and their rage can as little modify or change His purpose, now committed to thy charge, as the spray can quench the stars. Perplexed creature, whose best self lives only in aspiration and desire, now thou art an instrument in the hand of Him with Whom desire and attainment, will and fruition, are eternally the same. None truly fails in fighting for Jehovah, for who hath resisted His will ?

To Israel, and to all the oppressed whose minds are open to receive the tidings and their faith strong to embrace it, He said, Your life is blighted, and your future is in the hand of taskmasters, yet be of good cheer, for now your deliverance is undertaken by Him Whose being and purpose are one, Who *is* in perfection of enjoyment all that He *is* in contemplation and in will. The rescue of Israel by an immutable and perfect God is the earnest of the breaking of every yoke.

And to the proud and godless world which knows Him not, He says, Resistance to My will can only show forth all its power, which is not at the mercy of opinion or interest or change: I sit upon the throne, not only supreme but independent, not only victorious but unassailable; self-contained, self-poised and self-sufficing, I AM THAT I AM.

Have we now escaped the inert and self-absorbed deity of Lucretius, only to fall into the palsying grasp of the tyrannous deity of Calvin? Does our own human will shrivel up and become powerless under the compulsion of that immutability with which we are strangely brought into contact?

Evidently this is not the teaching of the Book of Exodus. For it is here, in this revelation of the Supreme, that we first hear of a nation as being His: "I have seen the affliction of My people which is in Egypt . . . and I have come down to bring them into a good land." They were all baptized into Moses in the cloud and in the sea. Yet their carcases fell in the wilderness. And these things were written for our learning. The immutability, which suffers no shock when we enter *into* the covenant, remains unshaken also if we depart from the living God. The sun shines alike when we raise the curtain and when we drop it, when our chamber is illumined and when it is dark. The immutability of God is not in His operations, for sometimes He gave His people into the hand of their enemies, and again He turned and helped them. It is in His nature, His mind, in the principles which guide His actions. If He had not chastened David for his sin, then, by acting as before, He would have been other at heart than when He rejected Saul for disobedience and chose the son of Jesse to fulfil all His word. The wind has veered, if it continues to propel the vessel in the same direction, although helm and sails are shifted.

Such is the Pauline doctrine of His immutability. "If we endure we shall also reign with Him: if we shall deny Him, He also will deny us,"—and such is the necessity of His being, for we cannot sway Him with our changes: "if we are faithless, He abideth faithful, for He cannot deny Himself." And therefore it is presently added that "the firm foundation of the Lord standeth sure, having" not only "this seal, that the Lord knoweth those that are His,"—but also this, "Let every one that nameth the name of the Lord depart from unrighteousness" (2 Tim. ii. 12, 13, 19, R.V.).

The Lord knew that Israel was His, yet for their unrighteousness He sware in His wrath that they should not enter into His rest.

It follows from all this that the new name of God was no academic subtlety, no metaphysical refinement of the schools, unfitly revealed to slaves, but a most practical and inspiring truth, a conviction to warm their blood, to rouse their courage, to convert their despair into confidence and their alarms into defiance.

They had the support of a God worthy of trust. And thenceforth every answer in righteousness, every new disclosure of fidelity, tenderness, love, was not an abnormal phenomenon, the uncertain grace of a capricious despot; no, its import was permanent as an observation of the stars by an astronomer, ever more to be remembered in calculating the movements of the universe.

In future troubles they could appeal to Him to awake as in the ancient days, as being He who "cut Rahab and wounded the Dragon." "I am the Lord, I change not, therefore ye sons of Jacob are not consumed."

And as the sublime and beautiful conception of a loving spiritual God was built up slowly, age by age, tier upon tier, this was the foundation which insured the the stability of all, until the Head Stone of the Corner gave completeness to the vast design, until men saw and could believe in the very Incarnation of all Love, unshaken amid anguish and distress and seeming failure, immovable, victorious, while they heard from human lips the awful words, "Before Abraham was, I AM." Then they learned to identify all this ancient lesson of trustworthiness with new and more pathetic revelations of affection: and the martyr at the stake grew strong as he emembered that the Man of Sorrows was the same yesterday and to-day and for ever; and the great apostle, prostrate before the glory of his Master, was restored by the touch of a human hand, and by the voice of Him upon Whose bosom he had leaned, saying, Fear not, I am the First and the Last and the Living One.

And if men are once more fain to rend from humanity that great assurance, which for ages, amid all shocks, has made the frail creature of the dust to grow strong and firm and fearless, partaker of the Divine Nature, what will they give us in its stead? Or do they think us too strong of will, too firm of purpose? Looking around us, we see nations heaving with internal agitations, armed to the teeth against each other, and all things like a ship at sea reeling to and fro, and staggering like a drunken man. There is no stability for us in constitutions or old formulæ—none anywhere, if it be not in the soul of man. Well for us, then, that the anchor of the soul is sure and steadfast! well that unnumbered millions take courage from their Saviour's word, that the world's worst anguish is the beginning, not of dissolution, but of the birth-pangs of a new heaven and earth,—that when the clouds are blackest because the light of sun and moon is quenched, then, then we shall behold the Immutable unveiled, the Son of Man, who is brought nigh unto the Ancient of Days, now sitting in the clouds of heaven, and coming in the glory of His Father!

THE COMMISSION.

iii. 10, 16-22.

We have already learned from the seventh verse that God commissioned Moses, only when He had Himself descended to deliver Israel. He sends none, except with the implied or explicit promise that certainly He will be with them. But the converse is also true. If God sends no man but when He comes Himself, He never comes without demanding the agency of man. The overruled reluctance of Moses, and the inflexible urgency of his commission, may teach us the honour set by God upon humanity. He has knit men together in the mutual dependence of nations and of families, that each may be His minister to all; and in every great crisis of history He has respected His own principle, and has visited the race by means of the providential man. The gospel was not preached by angels. Its first agents found themselves like sheep among wolves:

they were an exhibition to the world and to angels and men, yet necessity was laid upon them, and a woe if they preached it not.

All the best gifts of heaven come to us by the agency of inventor and sage, hero and explorer, organiser and philanthropist, patriot, reformer and saint. And the hope which inspires their grandest effort is never that of selfish gain, nor even of fame, though fame is a keen spur, which perhaps God set before Moses in the noble hope that "thou shalt bring forth the people" (ver. 12). But the truly impelling force is always the great deed itself, the haunting thought, the importunate inspiration, the inward fire; and so God promises Moses neither a sceptre, nor share in the good land: He simply proposes to him the work, the rescue of the people; and Moses, for his part, simply objects that he is unable, not that he is solicitous about his reward. Whatever is done for payment can be valued by its cost: all the priceless services done for us by our greatest were, in very deed, unpriced.

Moses, with the new name of God to reveal, and with the assurance that He is about to rescue Israel, is bidden to go to work advisedly and wisely. He is not to appeal to the mob, nor yet to confront Pharaoh without authority from his people to speak for them, nor is he to make the great demand for emancipation abruptly and at once. The mistake of forty years ago must not be repeated now. He is to appeal to the elders of Israel; and with them, and therefore clearly representing the nation, he is respectfully to crave permission for a three days' journey, to sacrifice to Jehovah in the wilderness. The blustering assurance with which certain fanatics of our own time first assume that they possess a direct commission from the skies, and thereupon that they are freed from all order, from all recognition of any human authority, and then that no considerations of prudence or of decency should restrain the violence and bad taste which they mistake for zeal, is curiously unlike anything in the Old Testament or the New. Was ever a commission more direct than those of Moses and of St. Paul? Yet Moses was to obtain the recognition of the elders of his people; and St. Paul received formal ordination by the explicit command of God (Acts xiii. 3).

Strangely enough, it is often assumed that this demand for a furlough of three days was insincere. But it would only have been so, if consent were expected, and if the intention were thereupon to abuse the respite and refuse to return. There is not the slightest hint of any duplicity of the kind. The real motives for the demand are very plain. The excursion which they proposed would have taught the people to move and act together, reviving their national spirit, and filling them with a desire for the liberty which they tasted. In the very words which they should speak, "The Lord, the God of the Hebrews, hath met with us," there is a distinct proclamation of nationality, and of its surest and strongest bulwark, a national religion. From such an excursion, therefore, the people would have returned, already well-nigh emancipated, and with recognised leaders. Certainly Pharaoh could not listen to any such proposal, unless he were prepared to reverse the whole policy of his dynasty toward Israel.

But the refusal answered two good ends. In the first place it joined issue on the best conceivable ground, for Israel was exhibited making the least possible demand with the greatest possible courtesy—" Let us go, we pray thee, three days' journey into the wilderness." Not even so much would be granted. The tyrant was palpably in the wrong, and thenceforth it was perfectly reasonable to increase the severity of the terms after each of his defeats, which proceeding in its turn made concession more and more galling to his pride. In the second place, the quarrel was from the first avowedly and undeniably religious: the gods of Egypt were matched against Jehovah; and in the successive plagues which desolated his land Pharaoh gradually learnt Who Jehovah was.

In the message which Moses should convey to the elders there are two significant phrases. He was to announce in the name of God, "I have surely visited you, and seen that which is done unto you in Egypt." The silent observation of God before He interposes is very solemn and instructive. So in the Revelation, He walks among the golden candlesticks, and knows the work, the patience, or the unfaithfulness of each. So He is not far from any one of us. When a heavy blow falls we speak of it as "a Visitation of Providence," but in reality the visitation has been long before. Neither Israel nor Egypt was conscious of the solemn presence. Who knows what soul of man, or what nation, is thus visited to-day, for future deliverance or rebuke?

Again it is said, "I will bring you up out of the affliction of Egypt into . . . a land flowing with milk and honey." Their affliction was the divine method of uprooting them. And so is our affliction the method by which our hearts are released from love of earth and life, that in due time He may "surely bring us in" to a better and an enduring country. Now, we wonder that the Israelites clung so fondly to the place of their captivity. But what of our own hearts? Have they a desire to depart? or do they groan in bondage, and yet recoil from their emancipation?

The hesitating nation is not plainly told that their affliction will be intensified and their lives made burdensome with labour. That is perhaps implied in the certainty that Pharaoh "will not let you go, no, not by a mighty hand." But it is with Israel as with us: a general knowledge that in the world we shall have tribulation is enough; the catalogue of our trials is not spread out before us in advance. They were assured for their encouragement that all their long captivity should at last receive its wages, for they should not borrow* but ask of the Egyptians jewels of silver, and gold, and raiment, and they should spoil the Egyptians. So are we taught to have "respect unto the recompense of the reward."

---

* So much ignorant capital has been made by sceptics out of this unfortunate mistranslation, that it is worth while to inquire whether the word "borrow" would suit the context in other passages. "He *borrowed* water and she gave him milk" (Judges v. 25). "The Lord said unto Solomon, Because thou hast *borrowed* this thing, and hast not *borrowed* long life for thyself, neither hast *borrowed* riches for thyself, nor hast *borrowed* the life of thine enemies" (1 Kings iii. 11). "And Elijah said unto Elisha, Thou hast *borrowed* a hard thing" (2 Kings ii. 10). The absurdity of the cavil is self-evident.

CHAPTER IV.

MOSES HESITATES.

iv. 1-17.

HOLY Scripture is impartial, even towards its heroes. The sin of David is recorded, and the failure of Peter. And so is the reluctance of Moses to accept his commission, even after a miracle had been vouchsafed to him for encouragement. The absolute sinlessness of Jesus is the more significant because it is found in the records of a creed which knows of no idealised humanity.

In Josephus, the refusal of Moses is softened down. Even the modest words, "Lord, I am still in doubt how I, a private man and of no abilities, should persuade my countrymen or Pharaoh," are not spoken after the sign is given. Nor is there any mention of the transfer to Aaron of a part of his commission, nor of their joint offence at Meribah, nor of its penalty, which in Scripture is bewailed so often. And Josephus is equally tender about the misdeeds of the nation. We hear nothing of their murmurs against Moses and Aaron when their burdens are increased, or of their making the golden calf. Whereas it is remarkable and natural that the fear of Moses is less anxious about his reception by the tyrant than by his own people: "Behold, they will not believe me, nor hearken unto my voice; for they will say, The Lord hath not appeared unto thee." This is very unlike the invention of a later period, glorifying the beginnings of the nation; but it is absolutely true to life. Great men do not fear the wrath of enemies if they can be secured against the indifference and contempt of friends; and Moses in particular was at last persuaded to undertake his mission by the promise of the support of Aaron. His hesitation is therefore the earliest example of what has been so often since observed—the discouragement of heroes, reformers and messengers from God, less by fear of the attacks of the world than of the contemptuous scepticism of the people of God. We often sigh for the appearing, in our degenerate days, of

> "A man with heart, head, hand,
> Like some of the simple great ones gone."

Yet who shall say that the want of them is not our own fault? The critical apathy and incredulity, not of the world but of the Church, is what freezes the fountains of Christian daring and the warmth of Christian zeal.

For the help of the faith of his people, Moses is commissioned to work two miracles; and he is caused to rehearse them, for his own.

Strange tales were told among the later Jews about his wonder-working rod. It was cut by Adam before leaving Paradise, was brought by Noah into the ark, passed into Egypt with Joseph, and was recovered by Moses while he enjoyed the favour of the court. These legends arose from downright moral inability to receive the true lesson of the incident, which is the confronting of the sceptre of Egypt with the simple staff of the shepherd, the choosing of the weak things of earth to confound the strong, the power of God to work His miracles by the most puny and inadequate means.

Anything was more credible than that He who led His people like sheep did indeed guide them with a common shepherd's crook. And yet this was precisely the lesson meant for us to learn—the glorification of poor resources in the grasp of faith.

Both miracles were of a menacing kind. First the rod became a serpent, to declare that at God's bidding enemies would rise up against the oppressor, even where all seemed innocuous, as in truth the waters of the river and the dust of the furnace and the winds of heaven conspired against him. Then, in the grasp of Moses, the serpent from which he fled became a rod again, to intimate that these avenging forces were subject to the servant of Jehovah.

Again, his hand became leprous in his bosom, and was presently restored to health again—a declaration that he carried with him the power of death, in its most dreadful form; and perhaps a still more solemn admonition to those who remember what leprosy betokens, and how every approach of God to man brings first the knowledge of sin, to be followed by the assurance that He has cleansed it.*

If the people would not hearken to the voice of the first sign, they should believe the second; but at the

---

* Tertullian appealed to the second of these miracles to illustrate the possibility of the resurrection. "The hand of Moses is changed and becomes like that of the dead, bloodless, colourless, and stiff with cold. But on the recovery of heat and restoration of its natural colour, it is the same flesh and blood. . . So will changes, conversions and reformation be needed to bring about the resurrection, yet the substance will be preserved safe." (*De Res.*, lv.) It is far wiser to be content with the declaration of St. Paul that the identity of the body does not depend on that of its corporeal atoms. "Thou sowest not that body that shall be, but a naked grain. . . . But God giveth . . . to every seed his own body" (1 Cor. xv. 37-8).

worst, and if they were still unconvinced, they would believe when they saw the water of the Nile, the pride and glory of their oppressors, turned into blood before their eyes. That was an omen which needs no interpretation. What follows is curious. Moses objects that he has not hitherto been eloquent, nor does he experience any improvement "since Thou hast spoken unto Thy servant" (a graphic touch!), and he seems to suppose that the popular choice between liberty and slavery would depend less upon the evidence of a Divine power than upon sleight of tongue, as if he were in modern England.

But let it be observed that the self-consciousness which wears the mask of humility while refusing to submit its judgment to that of God, is a form of selfishness—self-absorption blinding one to other considerations beyond himself—as real, though not as hateful, as greed and avarice and lust.

How can Moses call himself slow of speech and of a slow tongue, when Stephen distinctly declares that he was mighty in word as well as deed? (Acts vii. 22). Perhaps it is enough to answer that many years of solitude in a strange land had robbed him of his fluency. Perhaps Stephen had in mind the words of the Book of Wisdom, that "Wisdom entered into the soul of the servant of the Lord, and withstood dreadful kings in wonders and signs. . . . For Wisdom opened the mouth of the dumb, and made the tongues of them that cannot speak eloquent" (Wisdom x. 16, 21).

To his scruple the answer was returned, "Who hath made man's mouth? . . . Have not I the Lord? Now therefore go, and I will be with thy mouth, and teach thee what thou shalt say." The same encouragement belongs to every one who truly executes a mandate from above: "Lo, I am with you alway." For surely this encouragement *is* the same. Surely Jesus did not mean to offer His own presence as a substitute for that of God, but as being in very truth Divine, when He bade His disciples, in reliance upon Him, to go forth and convert the world.

And this is the true test which divides faith from presumption, and unbelief from prudence: do we go because God is with us in Christ, or because we ourselves are strong and wise? Do we hold back because we are not sure of *His* commission, or only because we distrust ourselves? "Humility without faith is too timorous; faith without humility is too hasty." The phrase explains the conduct of Moses both now and forty years before.

Moses, however, still entreats that any one may be chosen rather than himself: "Send, I pray Thee, by the hand of him whom Thou wilt send."

And thereupon the anger of the Lord was kindled against him, although at the moment his only visible punishment was the partial granting of his prayer— the association with him in his commission of Aaron, who could speak well, the forfeiting of a certain part of his vocation, and with it of a certain part of its reward. The words, "Is not Aaron thy brother the Levite?" have been used to insinuate that the tribal arrangement was not perfected when they were written, and so to discredit the narrative. But when so interpreted they yield no adequate sense, they do not reinforce the argument; while they are perfectly intelligible as implying that Aaron is already the leader of his tribe, and therefore sure to obtain the hearing of which Moses despaired. But the arrangement involved grave consequences sure to be developed in due time : among others, the reliance of Israel upon a feebler will, which could be forced by their clamour to make them a calf of gold. Moses was yet to learn that lesson which our century knows nothing of,—that a speaker and a leader of nations are not the same. When he cried to Aaron, in the bitterness of his soul, "What did this people to thee, that thou hast brought so great a sin upon them?" did he remember by whose unfaithfulness Aaron had been thrust into the office, the responsibilities of which he had betrayed?

Now, it is the duty of every man, to whom a special vocation presents itself, to set opposite each other two considerations. Dare I undertake this task? is a solemn question, but so is this: Dare I let this task go past me? Am I prepared for the responsibility of allowing it to drift into weaker hands? These are days when the Church of Christ is calling for the help of every one capable of aiding her, and we ought to hear it said more often that one is afraid *not* to teach in Sunday School, and another dares not refuse a proffered district, and a third fears to leave charitable tasks undone. To him that knoweth to do good, and doeth it not, to him it is sin; and we hear too much about the terrible responsibility of working for God, but too little about the still graver responsibility of refusing to work for Him when called.

Moses indeed attained so much that we are scarcely conscious that he might have been greater still. He had once presumed to go unsent, and brought upon himself the exile of half a lifetime. Again he presumed almost to say, I go not, and well-nigh to incur the guilt of Jonah when sent to Nineveh, and in so doing he forfeited the fulness of his vocation. But who reaches the level of his possibilities? Who is not haunted by faces, "each one a murdered self," a nobler self, that might have been, and is now impossible for ever? Only Jesus could say "I have finished the work which Thou gavest Me to do." And it is notable that while Jesus deals, in the parable of the labourers, with the problem of equal faithfulness during longer and shorter periods of employment; and in the parable of the pounds with that of equal endowment variously improved; and yet again, in the parable of the talents, with the problem of various endowments all doubled alike, He always draws a veil over the treatment of five talents which earn but two or three besides.

A more cheerful reflection suggested by this narrative is the strange power of human fellowship. Moses knew and was persuaded that God, Whose presence was even then miraculously apparent in the bush, and Who had invested him with superhuman powers, would go with him. There is no trace of incredulity in his behaviour, but only of failure to rely, to cast his shrinking and reluctant will upon the truth he recognised and the God Whose presence he confessed. He held back, as many a one does, who is honest when he repeats the Creed in church, yet fails to submit his life to the easy yoke of Jesus. Nor is it from physical peril that he recoils: at the bidding of God he has just grasped the serpent from which he fled; and in confronting a tyrant with armies at his back, he could hope for small assistance from his brother. But highly strung spirits, in every great crisis, are aware of vague indefinite apprehensions that are not cowardly but imaginative. Thus Cæsar, when defying the hosts of Pompey, is said to have been disturbed by an apparition. It is vain to put these apprehensions into logical form, and argue them down: the slowness of speech of

Moses was surely refuted by the presence of God, Who makes the mouth and inspires the utterance; but such fears lie deeper than the reasons they assign, and when argument fails, will yet stubbornly repeat their cry: "Send, I pray Thee, by the hand of him whom Thou wilt send." Now this shrinking, which is not craven, is dispelled by nothing so effectually as by the touch of a human hand. It is like the voice of a friend to one beset by ghostly terrors: he does not expect his comrade to exorcise a spirit, and yet his apprehensions are dispelled. Thus Moses cannot summon up courage from the protection of God, but when assured of the companionship of his brother he will not only venture to return to Egypt, but will bring with him his wife and children. Thus, also, He Who knew what was in men's hearts sent forth His missionaries, both the Twelve and the Seventy (as we have yet to learn the true economy of sending ours), "by two and two" (Mark vi. 7; Luke x. 1).

This is the principle which underlies the institution of the Church of Christ, and the conception that Christians are brothers, among whom the strong must help the weak. Such help from their fellow-mortals would perhaps decide the choice of many hesitating souls, upon the verge of the divine life, recoiling from its unknown and dread experiences, but longing for a sympathising comrade. Alas for the unkindly and unsympathetic religion of men whose faith has never warmed a human heart, and of congregations in which emotion is a misdemeanour!

There is no stronger force, among all that make for the abuses of priestcraft, than this same yearning for human help becomes when robbed of its proper nourishment, which is the communion of saints, and the pastoral care of souls. Has it no further nourishment than these? This instinctive craving for a Brother to help as well as a Father to direct and govern,—this social instinct, which banished the fears of Moses and made him set out for Egypt long before Aaron came in sight, content when assured of Aaron's co-operation,— is there nothing in God Himself to respond to it? He Who is not ashamed to call us brethren has profoundly modified the Church's conception of Jehovah, the Eternal, Absolute and Unconditioned. It is because He can be touched with the feeling of our infirmities, that we are bidden to draw near with boldness unto the Throne of Grace. There is no heart so lonely that it cannot commune with the lofty and kind humanity of Jesus.

There is a homelier lesson to be learned. Moses was not only solaced by human fellowship, but nerved and animated by the thought of his brother, and the mention of his tribe. "Is not Aaron thy brother the Levite?" They had not met for forty years. Vague rumours of deadly persecution were doubtless all that had reached the fugitive, whose heart had burned, in solitary communion with Nature in her sternest forms, as he brooded over the wrongs of his family, of Aaron, and perhaps of Miriam.

And now his brother lived. The call which Moses would have put from him was for the emancipation of his own flesh and blood, and for their greatness. In that great hour, domestic affection did much to turn the scale wherein the destinies of humanity were trembling. And his was affection well returned. It might easily have been otherwise, for Aaron had seen his younger brother called to a dazzling elevation, living in enviable magnificence, and earning fame by "word and deed"; and then, after a momentary fusion of sympathy and of condition, forty years had poured between them a torrent of cares and joys estranging because unshared. But it was promised that Aaron, when he saw him, should be glad at heart; and the words throw a beam of exquisite light into the depths of the mighty soul which God inspired to emancipate Israel and to found His Church, by thoughts of his brother's joy on meeting him.

Let no man dream of attaining real greatness by stifling his affections. The heart is more important than the intellect; and the brief story of the Exodus has room for the yearning of Jochebed over her infant "when she saw him that he was a goodly child," for the bold inspiration of the young poetess, who "stood afar off to know what should be done to him," and now for the love of Aaron. So the Virgin, in the dread hour of her reproach, went in haste to her cousin Elizabeth. So Andrew "findeth first his own brother Simon." And so the Divine Sufferer, forsaken of God, did not forsake His mother.

The Bible is full of domestic life. It is the theme of the greater part of Genesis, which makes the family the seed-plot of the Church. It is wisely recognised again at the moment when the larger pulse of the nation begins to beat. For the life-blood in the heart of a nation must be the blood in the hearts of men.

MOSES OBEYS.

iv. 18-31.

Moses is now commissioned: he is to go to Egypt, and Aaron is coming thence to meet him. Yet he first returns to Midian, to Jethro, who is both his employer and the head of the family, and prays him to sanction his visit to his own people.

There are duties which no family resistance can possibly cancel, and the direct command of God made it plain that this was one of them. But there are two ways of performing even the most imperative obligation, and religious people have done irreparable mischief before now, by rudeness, disregard to natural feeling and the rights of their fellow-men, under the impression that they showed their allegiance to God by outraging other ties. It is a theory for which no sanction can be found either in Holy Scripture or in common sense.

When he asks permission to visit "his brethren" we cannot say whether he ever had brothers besides Aaron, or uses the word in the same larger national sense as when we read that, forty years before, he went out unto his brethren and saw their burdens. What is to be observed is that he is reticent with respect to his vast expectations and designs.

He does not argue that, because a Divine promise must needs be fulfilled, he need not be discreet, wary and taciturn, any more than St. Paul supposed, because the lives of his shipmates were promised to him, that it mattered nothing whether the sailors remained on board.

The decrees of God have sometimes been used to justify the recklessness of man, but never by His chosen followers. They have worked out their own salvation the more earnestly because God worked in them. And every good cause calls aloud for human energy and wisdom, all the more because its consummation is the will of God, and sooner or later is assured. Moses has unlearned his rashness.

When the Lord said unto Moses in Midian, "Go, return unto Egypt, for all the men are dead which sought thy life," there is an almost verbal resemblance to the words in which the infant Jesus is recalled from exile. We shall have to consider the typical aspect of the whole narrative, when a convenient stage is reached for pausing to survey it in its completeness. But resemblances like this have been treated with so much scorn, they have been so freely perverted into evidence of the mythical nature of the later story, that some passing allusion appears desirable. We must beware equally of both extremes. The Old Testament is tortured, and genuine prophecies are made no better than coincidences, when coincidences are exalted to all the dignity of express predictions. One can scarcely venture to speak of the death of Herod when Jesus was to return from Egypt, as being deliberately typified in the death of those who sought the life of Moses. But it is quite clear that the words in St. Matthew do intentionally point the reader back to this narrative. For, indeed, under both, there are to be recognised the same principles: that God does not thrust His servants into needless or excessive peril; and that when the life of a tyrant has really become not only a trial but a barrier, it will be removed by the King of kings. God is prudent for His heroes.

Moreover, we must recognise the lofty fitness of what is very visible in the Gospels—the coming to a head in Christ of the various experiences of the people of God; and at the recurrence, in His story, of events already known elsewhere, we need not be disquieted, as if the suspicion of a myth were now become difficult to refute; rather should we recognise the fulness of the supreme life, and its points of contact with all lives, which are but portions of its vast completeness. Who does not feel that in the world's greatest events a certain harmony and correspondence are as charming as they are in music? There is a sort of counterpoint in history. And to this answering of deep unto deep, this responsiveness of the story of Jesus to all history, our attention is silently beckoned by St. Matthew, when, without asserting any closer link between the incidents, he borrows this phrase so aptly.

A much deeper meaning underlies the profound expression which God now commands Moses to employ; and although it must await consideration at a future time, the progressive education of Moses himself is meantime to be observed. At first he is taught that the Lord is the God of their fathers, in whose descendants He is therefore interested. Then the present Israel is His people, and valued for its own sake. Now he hears, and is bidden to repeat to Pharaoh, the amazing phrase, "Israel is My son, even My firstborn: let My son go that he may serve Me; and if thou refuse to let him go, behold I will slay thy son, even thy firstborn." Thus it is that infant faith is led from height to height. And assuredly there never was an utterance better fitted than this to prepare human minds, in the fulness of time, for a still clearer revelation of the nearness of God to man, and for the possibility of an absolute union between the Creator and His creature.

It was on his way into Egypt, with his wife and children, that a mysterious interposition forced Zipporah reluctantly and tardily to circumcise her son.

The meaning of this strange episode lies perhaps below the surface, but very near it. Danger in some form, probably that of sickness, pressed Moses hard, and he recognised in it the displeasure of his God. The form of the narrative leads us to suppose that he had no previous consciousness of guilt, and had now to infer the nature of his offence without any explicit announcement, just as we infer it from what follows.

If so, he discerned his transgression when trouble awoke his conscience; and so did his wife Zipporah. Yet her resistance to the circumcision of their younger son was so tenacious, with such difficulty was it overcome by her husband's peril or by his command, that her tardy performance of the rite was accompanied by an insulting action and a bitter taunt. As she submitted, the Lord "let him go"; but we may perhaps conclude that the grievance continued to rankle, from the repetition of her gibe, "So she said, A bridegroom of blood art thou because of the circumcision." The words mean, "We are betrothed again in blood," and might of themselves admit a gentler, and even a tender significance; as if, in the sacrifice of a strong prejudice for her husband's sake, she felt a revival of "the kindness of her youth, the love of her espousals." For nothing removes the film from the surface of a true affection, and makes the heart aware how bright it is, so well as a great sacrifice, frankly offered for the sake of love.

But such a rendering is excluded by the action which went with her words, and they must be explained as meaning, This is the kind of husband I have wedded: these are our espousals. With such an utterance she fades almost entirely out of the story: it does not even tell how she drew back to her father; and thenceforth all we know of her is that she rejoined Moses only when the fame of his victory over Amalek had gone abroad.

Their union seems to have been an ill-assorted or at

least an unprosperous one. In the tender hour when their firstborn was to be named, the bitter sense of loneliness had continued to be nearer to the heart of Moses than the glad new consciousness of paternity, and he said, "I am a stranger in a strange land." Different indeed had been the experience of Joseph, who called his "firstborn Manasseh, for God, said he, hath made me forget all my toil, and all my father's house" (Gen. xli. 51). The home-life of Moses had not made him forget that he was an exile. Even the removal of imminent death from her husband could not hush these selfish complaints of Zipporah, not because he was a father of blood to her little one, but because he was a bridegroom of blood to her own shrinking sensibilities. It is Miriam the sister, not Zipporah the wife, who gives lyrical and passionate voice to his triumph, and is mourned by the nation when she dies. Both what we read of her and what we do not read goes far to explain the insignificance of their children in history, and the more startling fact that the grandson of Moses became the venal instrument of the Danites in their schismatic worship (Judges xviii. 30, R.V.).

Domestic unhappiness is a palliation, but not a justification, for an unserviceable life. It is a great advantage to come into action with the dew and freshness of affection upon the soul. Yet it is not once nor twice that men have carried the message of God back from the barren desert and the lonely ways of their unhappiness to the not too happy race of man.

Now, who can fail to discern real history in all this? Is it in such a way that myth or legend would have dealt with the wife of the great deliverer? Still less conceivable is it that these should have treated Moses himself as the narrative hitherto has consistently done.

At every step he is made to stumble. His first attempt was homicidal, and brought upon him forty years of exile. When the Divine commission came he drew back wilfully, as he had formerly pressed forward unsent. There is not even any suggestion offered us of Stephen's apology for his violent deed—namely, that he supposed his brethren understood how that God by his hand was giving them deliverance (Acts vii. 25). There is nothing that resembles the eulogium of the Epistle to the Hebrews upon the faith which glorified his precipitancy, like the rainbow in a torrent, because that rash blow committed him to share the affliction of the people of God, and renounced the rank of a grand son of the Pharaoh (Heb. xi. 24-5). All this is very natural, if Moses himself be in any degree responsible for the narrative. It is incredible, if the narrative were put together after the Captivity, to claim the sanction of so great a name for a newly forged hierarchical system. Such a theory could scarcely be refuted more completely, if the narrative before us were invented with the deliberate aim to overthrow it.

But in truth the failures of the good and great are written for our admonition, teaching us how inconsistent are even the best of mortals, and how weak the most resolute. Rather than forfeit his own place among the chosen people, Moses had forsaken a palace and become a proscribed fugitive; yet he had neglected to claim for his child its rightful share in the covenant, its recognition among the sons of Abraham. Perhaps procrastination, perhaps domestic opposition, more potent than a king's wrath to shake his purpose, perhaps the insidious notion that one who had sacrificed so much might be at ease about slight negligences,— some such influence had left the commandment unobserved. And now, when the dream of his life was being realised at last, and he found himself the chosen instrument of God for the rebuke of one nation and the making of another, how pardonable it must have seemed to leave an unpleasant small domestic duty over until a more convenient season! How natural it still seems to merge the petty task in the high vocation, to excuse small lapses in pursuit of lofty aims! But this was the very time when God, hitherto forbearing, took him sternly to task for his neglect, because men who are especially honoured should be more obedient and reverential than their fellows. Let young men who dream of a vast career, and meanwhile indulge themselves in small obliquities, let all who cast out demons in the name of Christ, and yet work iniquity, reflect upon this chosen and long-trained, self-sacrificing and ardent servant of the Lord, whom Jehovah seeks to kill because he wilfully disobeys even a purely ceremonial precept.

Moses was not only religious, but "a man of destiny," one upon whom vast interests depended. Now, such men have often reckoned themselves exempt from the ordinary laws of conduct.*

It is not a light thing, therefore, to find God's indignant protest against the faintest shadow of a doctrine so insidious and so deadly, set in the forefront of sacred history, at the very point where national concerns and those of religion begin to touch. If our politics are to be kept pure and clean, we must learn to exact a higher fidelity, and not a relaxed morality, from those who propose to sway the destinies of nations.

---

* "I am not an ordinary man," Napoleon used to say, "and the laws of morals and of custom were never made for me."—*Memoirs of Madame de Rémusat*, i. 91.

And now the brothers meet, embrace, and exchange confidences. As Andrew, the first disciple who brought another to Jesus, found first his own brother Simon, so was Aaron the earliest convert to the mission of Moses. And that happened which so often puts our faithlessness to shame. It had seemed very hard to break his strange tidings to the people : it was in fact very easy to address one whose love had not grown cold during their severance, who probably retained faith in the Divine purpose for which the beautiful child of the family had been so strangely preserved, and who had passed through trial and discipline unknown to us in the stern intervening years.

And when they told their marvellous story to the elders of the people, and displayed the signs, they believed; and when they heard that God had visited them in their affliction, then they bowed their heads and worshipped.

This was their preparation for the wonders that should follow: it resembled Christ's appeal, "Believest thou that I am able to do this?" or Peter's word to the impotent man, "Look on us."

For the moment the announcement had the desired effect, although too soon the early promise was succeeded by faithlessness and discontent. In this, again, the teaching of the earliest political movement on record is as fresh as if it were a tale of yesterday. The offer of emancipation stirs all hearts ; the romance of liberty is beautiful beside the Nile as in the streets of Paris ; but the cost has to be gradually learned ; the losses displace the gains in the popular attention ; the labour, the self-denial and the self-control grow wearisome, and Israel murmurs for the flesh-pots of Egypt, much as the modern revolution reverts to a despotism. It is one thing to admire abstract freedom, but a very different thing to accept the austere conditions of the life of genuine freemen. And surely the same is true of the soul. The gospel gladdens the young convert: he bows his head and worships; but he little dreams of his long discipline, as in the forty desert years, of the solitary places through which his soul must wander, the drought, the Amalekite, the absent leader, and the temptations of the flesh. In mercy, the long future is concealed; it is enough that, like the apostles, we should consent to follow; gradually we shall obtain the courage to which the task may be revealed.

CHAPTER V.

PHARAOH REFUSES.

v. 1-23.

AFTER forty years of obscurity and silence, Moses re-enters the magnificent halls where he had formerly turned his back upon so great a place. The rod of a shepherd is in his hand, and a lowly Hebrew by his side. Men who recognise him shake their heads, and pity or despise the fanatic who had thrown away the most dazzling prospects for a dream. But he has long since made his choice, and whatever misgivings now beset him have regard to his success with Pharaoh or with his brethren, not to the wisdom of his decision.

Nor had he reason to repent of it. The pomp of an obsequious court was a poor thing in the eyes of an ambassador of God, who entered the palace to speak such lofty words as never passed the lips of any son of Pharaoh's daughter. He was presently to become a god unto Pharaoh, with Aaron for his prophet.

In itself, his presence there was formidable. The Hebrews had been feared when he was an infant. Now their cause was espoused by a man of culture, who had allied himself with their natural leaders, and was returned, with the deep and steady fire of a zeal which forty years of silence could not quench, to assert the rights of Israel as an independent people.

There is a terrible power in strong convictions, especially when supported by the sanctions of religion. Luther on one side, Loyola on the other, were mightier than kings when armed with this tremendous weapon. Yet there are forces upon which patriotism and fanaticism together break in vain. Tyranny and pride of race have also strong impelling ardours, and carry men far. Pharaoh is in earnest as well as Moses, and can act with perilous energy. And this great narrative begins the story of a nation's emancipation with a human demand, boldly made, but defeated by the pride and vigour of a startled tyrant and the tameness of a downtrodden people. The limitations of human energy are clearly exhibited before the direct interference of God begins. All that a brave man can do, when nerved by lifelong aspiration and by a sudden conviction that the hour of destiny has struck, all therefore upon which rationalism can draw, to explain the uprising of Israel, is exhibited in this preliminary attempt, this first demand of Moses.

Menephtah was no doubt the new Pharaoh whom the brothers accosted so boldly. What we glean of him elsewhere is highly suggestive of some grave event left unrecorded, exhibiting to us a man of uncontrollable temper yet of broken courage, a ruthless, godless, daunted man. There is a legend that he once hurled his spear at the Nile when its floods rose too high, and was punished with ten years of blindness. In the Libyan war, after fixing a time when he should join his vanguard, with the main army, a celestial vision forbade him to keep his word in person, and the victory was gained by his lieutenants. In another war, he boasts of having slaughtered the people and set fire to them, and netted the entire country as men net birds. Forty years then elapse without war and without any great buildings; there are seditions and internal troubles, and the dynasty closes with his son.* All this is exactly what we should expect, if a series of tremendous blows had depopulated a country, abolished an army, and removed two millions of the working classes in one mass.

But it will be understood that this identification, concerning which there is now a very general consent of competent authorities, implies that the Pharaoh was not himself engulfed with his army. Nothing is on the other side except a poetic assertion in Psalm cxxxvi. 15, which is not that God destroyed, but that He "shook off" Pharaoh and his host in the Red Sea, because His mercy endureth for ever.

To this king, then, whose audacious family had usurped the symbols of deity for its head-dress, and whose father boasted that in battle "he became like the god Mentu" and "was as Baal," the brothers came as yet without miracle, with no credentials except from slaves, and said, "Thus saith Jehovah, the God of Israel, Let My people go, that they may hold a feast unto Me in the wilderness." The issue was distinctly raised: did Israel belong to Jehovah or to the king? And Pharaoh answered, with equal decision, "Who is Jehovah, that I should hearken unto His voice? I know not Jehovah, and what is more, I will not let Israel go."

Now, the ignorance of the king concerning Jehovah was almost or quite blameless: the fault was in his practical refusal to inquire. Jehovah was no concern of his: without waiting for information, he at once decided

---

* Robinson, "The Pharaohs of the Bondage."

that his grasp on his captives should not relax. And his second fault, which led to this, was the same grinding oppression of the helpless which for eighty years already had brought upon his nation the guilt of blood. Crowned and national cupidity, the resolution to wring from their slaves the last effort consistent with existence, such greed as took offence at even the momentary pause of hope while Moses pleaded, because "the people of the land are many, and ye make them rest from their burdens,"—these shut their hearts against reason and religion, and therefore God presently hardened those same hearts against natural misgiving and dread and awe-stricken submission to His judgments.

For it was against religion also that he was unyielding. In his ample Pantheon there was room at least for the possibility of the entrance of the Hebrew God, and in refusing to the subject people, without investigation, leisure for any worship, the king outraged not only humanity, but Heaven.

The brothers proceed to declare that they have themselves met with the deity, and there must have been many in the court who could attest at least the sincerity of Moses; they ask for liberty to spend a day in journeying outward and another in returning, with a day between for their worship, and warn the king of the much greater loss to himself which may be involved in vengeance upon refusal, either by war or pestilence. But the contemptuous answer utterly ignores religion: "Wherefore do ye, Moses and Aaron, loose the people from their work? Get ye unto your burdens."

And his counter-measures are taken without loss of time: "that same day" the order goes out to exact the regular quantity of brick, but supply no straw for binding it together. It is a pitiless mandate, and illustrates the fact, very natural though often forgotten, that men as a rule cannot lose sight of the religious value of their fellow-men, and continue to respect or pity them as before. We do not deny that men who professed religion have perpetrated nameless cruelties, nor that unbelievers have been humane, sometimes with a pathetic energy, a tenacious grasp on the virtue still possible to those who have no Heaven to serve. But it is plain that the average man will despise his brother, and his brother's rights, just in proportion as the Divine sanctions of those rights fade away, and nothing remains to be respected but the culture, power and affluence which the victim lacks. "I know not Israel's God" is a sure prelude to the refusal to let Israel go, and even to the cruelty which beats the slave who fails to render impossible obedience.

"They be idle, therefore they cry, saying, Let us go and sacrifice to our God." And still there are men who hold the same opinion, that time spent in devotion is wasted, as regards the duties of real life. In truth, religion means freshness, elasticity and hope: a man will be not slothful in business, but fervent in spirit, if he serves the Lord. But perhaps immortal hope, and the knowledge that there is One Who shall break all prison bars and let the oppressed go free, are not the best narcotics to drug down the soul of a man into the monotonous tameness of a slave.

In the tenth verse we read that the Egyptian taskmasters and the officers combined to urge the people to their aggravated labours. And by the fourteenth verse we find that the latter officials were Hebrew officers whom Pharaoh's taskmasters had set over them.

So that we have here one of the surest and worst

effects of slavery—namely, the demoralisation of the oppressed, the readiness of average men, who can obtain for themselves a little relief, to do so at their brethren's cost. These officials were scribes, "writers": their business was to register the amount of labour due, and actually rendered. These were doubtless the more comfortable class, of whom we read afterwards that they possessed property, for their cattle escaped the murrain and their trees the hail. And they had the means of acquiring quite sufficient skill to justify whatever is recorded of the works done in the construction of the tabernacle. The time is long past when scepticism found support for its incredulity in these details.

One advantage of the last sharp agony of persecution was that it finally detached this official class from the Egyptian interest, and welded Israel into a homogeneous people, with officers already provided. For, when the supply of bricks came short, these officials were beaten, and, as if no cause of the failure were palpable, they were asked, with a malicious chuckle, "Wherefore have ye not fulfilled your task both yesterday and to-day, as heretofore?" And when they explain to Pharaoh, in words already expressive of their alienation, that the fault is with "thine own people," they are repulsed with insult, and made to feel themselves in evil case. For indeed they needed to be chastised for their forgetfulness of God. How soon would their hearts have turned back, how much more bitter yet would have been their complaints in the desert, if it were not for this last experience! But if judgment began with them, what should presently be the fate of their oppressors?

Their broken spirit shows itself by murmuring, not

against Pharaoh, but against Moses and Aaron, who at least had striven to help them. Here, as in the whole story, there is not a trace of either the lofty spirit which could have evolved the Mosaic law, or the hero-worship of a later age.

It is written that Moses, hearing their reproaches, "returned unto the Lord," although no visible shrine, no consecrated place of worship, can be thought of.

What is involved is the consecration which the heart bestows upon any place of privacy and prayer, where, in shutting out the world, the soul is aware of the special nearness of its King. In one sense we never leave Him, never return to Him. In another sense, by direct address of the attention and the will, we enter into His presence; we find Him in the midst of us, Who is everywhere. And all ceremonial consecrations do their office by helping us to realise and act upon the presence of Him in Whom, even when He is forgotten, we live and move and have our being. Therefore in the deepest sense each man consecrates or desecrates for himself his own place of prayer. There is a city where the Divine presence saturates every consciousness with rapture. And the seer beheld no temple therein, for the Lord God the Almighty, and the Lamb, are the temple of it.

Startling to our notions of reverence are the words in which Moses addresses God. "Lord, why hast Thou evil entreated this people? Why is it that Thou hast sent me? for since I came to Pharaoh to speak in Thy name, he hath evil entreated this people; neither hast Thou delivered Thy people at all." It is almost as if his faith had utterly given way, like that of the Psalmist when he saw the wicked in great prosperity, while waters of a full cup were wrung out by the people of God (Ps. lxxiii. 3, 10). And there is always a dangerous moment when the first glow of enthusiasm burns down, and we realise how long the process, how bitter the disappointments, by which even a scanty measure of success must be obtained. Yet God had expressly warned Moses that Pharaoh would not release them until Egypt had been smitten with all His plagues. But the warning passed unapprehended, as we let many a truth pass intellectually accepted it is true, but only as a theorem, a vague and abstract formula. As we know that we must die, that worldly pleasures are brief and unreal, and that sin draws evil in its train, yet wonder when these phrases become solid and practical in our experience, so, in the first flush and wonder of the promised emancipation, Moses had forgotten the predicted interval of trial.

His words would have been profane and irreverent indeed but for one redeeming quality. They were addressed to God Himself. Whenever the people murmured, Moses turned for help to Him Who reckons the most unconventional and daring appeal to Him far better than the most ceremonious phrases in which men cover their unbelief: "Lord, wherefore hast Thou evil entreated this people?" is in reality a much more pious utterance than "I will not ask, neither will I tempt the Lord." Wherefore Moses receives large encouragement, although no formal answer is vouchsafed to his daring question.

Even so, in our dangers, our torturing illnesses, and many a crisis which breaks through all the crust of forms and conventionalities, God may perhaps recognise a true appeal to Him, in words which only scandalise the orthodoxy of the formal and precise. In the bold rejoinder of the Syro-Phœnician woman He recognised great faith. His disciples would simply have sent her away as clamorous.

Moses had again failed, even though Divinely commissioned, in the work of emancipating Israel, and thereupon he had cried to the Lord Himself to undertake the work. This abortive attempt, however, was far from useless: it taught humility and patience to the leader, and it pressed the nation together, as in a vice, by the weight of a common burden, now become intolerable. At the same moment, the iniquity of the tyrant was filled up.

But the Lord did not explain this, in answer to the remonstrance of Moses. Many things happen, for which no distinct verbal explanation is possible, many things of which the deep spiritual fitness cannot be expressed in words. Experience is the true commentator upon Providence, if only because the slow building of character is more to God than either the hasting forward of deliverance or the clearing away of intellectual mists. And it is only as we take His yoke upon us that we truly learn of Him. Yet much is implied, if not spoken out, in the words, "Now (because the time is ripe) shalt thou see what I will do to Pharaoh (I, because others have failed); for by a strong hand shall he let them go, and by a strong hand shall he drive them out of the land." It is under the weight of the "strong hand" of God Himself that the tyrant must either bend or break.

Similar to this is the explanation of many delays in answering our prayer, of the strange raising up of tyrants and demagogues, and of much else that perplexes Christians in history and in their own experience. These events develop human character, for good or evil. And they give scope for the revealing of the fulness of the power which rescues. We have no means of measuring the supernatural force which overcomes but by the amount of the resistance offered. And if all good things came to us easily and at once, we should not become aware of the horrible pit, our rescue from which demands gratitude. The Israelites would not have sung a hymn of such fervent gratitude when the sea was crossed, if they had not known the weight of slavery and the anguish of suspense. And in heaven the redeemed who have come out of great tribulation sing the song of Moses and of the Lamb.

Fresh air, a balmy wind, a bright blue sky—which of us feels a thrill of conscious exultation for these cheap delights? The released prisoner, the restored invalid, feels it:

> "The common earth, the air, the skies,
> To him are opening paradise."

Even so should Israel be taught to value deliverance. And now the process could begin.

CHAPTER VI.

THE ENCOURAGEMENT OF MOSES.

vi. 1-30.

WE have seen that the name Jehovah expresses not a philosophic meditation, but the most bracing and reassuring truth—viz., that an immutable and independent Being sustains His people; and this great title is therefore reaffirmed with emphasis in the hour of mortal discouragement. It is added that their fathers knew God by the name of God Almighty, but by His name Jehovah was He not known, or made known, unto them. Now, it is quite clear that they were not utterly ignorant of this title, for no such theory as that it was hitherto mentioned by anticipation only, can explain the first syllable in the name of the mother of Moses himself, nor the assertion that in the time of Seth men began to call upon the name of Jehovah (Gen. iv. 26); nor the name of the hill of Abraham's sacrifice, Jehovah-jireh (Gen. xxii. 14). Yet the statement cannot be made available for the purposes of any reasonable and moderate scepticism, since the sceptical theory demands a belief in successive redactions of the work in which an error so gross could not have escaped detection.

And the true explanation is that this Name was now, for the first time, to be realised as a sustaining power. The patriarchs had known the name; how its fitness should be realised: God should be known by it. They had drawn support and comfort from that simpler view of the Divine protection which said, "I am the Almighty God: walk before Me and be thou perfect" (Gen. xvii. 1). But thenceforth all the experience of the past was to reinforce the energies of the present, and men were to remember that their promises came from One who cannot change. Others, like Abraham, had been stronger in faith than Moses. But faith is not the same as insight, and Moses was the greatest of the prophets (Deut. xxxiv. 10). To him, therefore, it was given to confirm the courage of his nation by this exalting thought of God. And the Lord proceeds to state what His promises to the patriarchs were, and joins together (as we should do) the assurance of His compassionate heart and of His inviolable pledges: "I have heard the groaning of the children of Israel, . . . and I have remembered My covenant."

It has been the same, in turn, with every new revelation of the Divine. The new was implicit in the old, but when enforced, unfolded, reapplied, men found it charged with unsuspected meaning and power, and as full of vitality and development as a handful of dry seeds when thrown into congenial soil. So it was pre-eminently with the doctrine of the Messiah. It will be the same hereafter with the doctrine of the kingdom of peace and the reign of the saints on earth. Some day men will smile at our crude theories and ignorant controversies about the Millennium. We, meantime, possess the saving knowledge of Christ amid many perplexities and obscurities. And so the patriarchs, who knew God Almighty, but not by His name Jehovah, were not lost for want of the knowledge of His name, but saved by faith in Him, in the living Being to

Whom all these names belong, and Who shall yet write upon the brows of His people some new name, hitherto undreamed by the ripest of the saints and the purest of the Churches. Meantime, let us learn the lessons of tolerance for other men's ignorance, remembering the ignorance of the father of the faithful, tolerance for difference of views, remembering how the unusual and rare name of God was really the precursor of a brighter revelation, and yet again, when our hearts are faint with longing for new light, and weary to death of the babbling of old words, let us learn a sober and cautious reconsideration, lest perhaps the very truth needed for altered circumstance and changing problem may lie, unheeded and dormant, among the dusty old phrases from which we turn away despairingly. Moreover, since the fathers knew the name Jehovah, yet gained from it no special knowledge of God, such as they had from His Almightiness, we are taught that discernment is often more at fault than revelation. To the quick perception and plastic imagination of the artist, our world reveals what the boor will never see. And the saint finds, in the homely and familiar words of Scripture, revelations for His soul that are unknown to common men. Receptivity is what we need far more than revelation.

Again is Moses bidden to appeal to the faith of his countrymen, by a solemn repetition of the Divine promise. If the tyranny is great, they shall be redeemed with a stretched out arm, that is to say, with a palpable interposition of the power of God, "and with great judgments." It is the first appearance in Scripture of this phrase, afterwards so common. Not mere vengeance upon enemies or vindication of subjects is in question: the thought is that of a deliberate weighing of merits, and rendering out of measured penalties. Now, the Egyptian mythology had a very clear and solemn view of judgment after death. If king and people had grown cruel, it was because they failed to realise remote punishments, and did not believe in present judgments, here, in this life. But there is a God that judgeth in the earth. Not always, for mercy rejoiceth over judgment. We may still pray, "Enter not into judgment with Thy servants, O Lord, for in Thy sight shall no man living be justified." But when men resist warnings, then retribution begins even here. Sometimes it comes in plague and overthrow, sometimes in the worse form of a heart made fat, the decay of sensibilities abused, the dying out of spiritual faculty. Pharaoh was to experience both, the hardening of his heart and the ruin of his fortunes.

It is added, "I will take you to Me for a people, and I will be to you for a God." This is the language, not of a mere purpose, a will that has resolved to vindicate the right, but of affection. God is about to adopt Israel to Himself, and the same favour which belonged to rare individuals in the old time is now offered to a whole nation. Just as the heart of each man is gradually educated, learning first to love a parent and a family, and so led on to national patriotism, and at last to a world-wide philanthropy, so was the religious conscience of mankind awakened to believe that Abraham might be the friend of God, and then that His oath might be confirmed unto the children, and then that He could take Israel to Himself for a people, and at last that God loved the world.

It is not religion to think that God condescends merely to save us. He cares for us. He takes us to Himself. He gives Himself away to us, in return, to be our God.

Such a revelation ought to have been more to Israel than any pledge of certain specified advantages. It was meant to be a silken tie, a golden clasp, to draw together the almighty Heart and the hearts of these downtrodden slaves. Something within Him desires their little human love; they shall be to Him for a people. So He said again, "My son, give Me thine heart." And so, when He carried to the uttermost these unsought, unhoped for, and, alas! unwelcomed overtures of condescension, and came among us, He would have gathered, as a hen gathers her chickens under her wings, those who would not. It is not man who conceives, from definite services received, the wild hope of some spark of real affection in the bosom of the Eternal and Mysterious One. It is not man, amid the lavish joys and splendours of creation, who conceives the notion of a supreme Heart, as the explanation of the universe. It is God Himself Who says, "I will take you to Me for a people, and I will be to you a God."

Nor is it human conversion that begins the process, but a Divine covenant and pledge, by which God would fain convert us to Himself; even as the first disciples did not accost Jesus, but He turned and spoke to them the first question and the first invitation: "What seek ye? . . . Come, and ye shall see."

To-day, the choice of the civilised world has to be made between a mechanical universe and a revealed love, for no third possibility survives.

This promise establishes a relationship, which God never afterwards cancelled. Human unbelief rejected its benefits, and chilled the mutual sympathies which it involved; but the fact always remained, and in their darkest hour they could appeal to God to remember His covenant and the oath which He sware.

And this same assurance belongs to us. We are not to become good, or desirous of goodness, in order that God may requite with affection our virtues or our wistfulness. Rather we are to arise and come to our Father, and to call Him Father, although we are not worthy to be called His sons. We are to remember how Jesus said, "If ye being evil know how to give good gifts unto your children, how much more shall your heavenly Father give His Holy Spirit to them that ask Him!" and to learn that He is the Father of those who are evil, and even of those who are still unpardoned, as He said again, "If ye forgive not . . . neither will your heavenly Father forgive you."

Much controversy about the universal Fatherhood of God would be assuaged if men reflected upon the significant distinction which our Saviour drew between His Fatherhood and our sonship, the one always a reality of the Divine affection, the other only a possibility, for human enjoyment or rejection: "Love your enemies, and pray for them that persecute you, that ye may be sons of your Father Which is in heaven" (Matt. v. 45). There is no encouragement to presumption in the assertion of the Divine Fatherhood upon such terms. For it speaks of a love which is real and deep without being feeble and indiscriminate. It appeals to faith because there is an absolute fact to lean upon, and to energy because privilege is conditional. It reminds us that our relationship is like that of the ancient Israel,—that we are in a covenant, as they were, but that the carcases of many of them fell in the wilderness; although God had taken them for a people, and was to them a God, and said, "Israel is My son, even My firstborn."

It is added that faith shall develop into knowledge. Moses is to assure them now that they "shall know" hereafter that the Lord is Jehovah their God. And this, too, is a universal law, that we shall know if we follow on to know: that the trial of our faith worketh patience, and patience experience, and we have so dim and vague an apprehension of Divine realities, chiefly because we have made but little trial, and have not tasted and seen that the Lord is gracious.

In this respect, as in so many more, religion is analogous with nature. The squalor of the savage could be civilised, and the distorted and absurd conceptions of mediæval science could be corrected, only by experiment, persistently and wisely carried out.

And it is so in religion: its true evidence is unknown to those who never bore its yoke; it is open to just such raillery and rejection as they who will not love can pour upon domestic affection and the sacred ties of family life; but, like these, it vindicates itself, in the rest of their souls, to those who will take the yoke and learn. And its best wisdom is not of the cunning brain but of the open heart, that wisdom from above, which is first pure, then peaceable, gentle, and easy to be entreated.

And thus, while God leads Israel, they shall know that He is Jehovah, and true to His highest revelations of Himself.

All this they heard, and also, to define their hope and brighten it, the promise of Palestine was repeated; but they hearkened not unto Moses for anguish of spirit and for cruel bondage. Thus the body often holds the spirit down, and kindly allowance is made by Him Who knoweth our frame and remembereth that we are dust, and Who, in the hour of His own agony, found the excuse for His unsympathising followers that the spirit was willing although the flesh was weak. So when Elijah made request for himself that he might die, in the utter reaction which followed his triumph on Carmel and his wild race to Jezreel, the good Physician did not dazzle him with new splendours of revelation until after he had slept, and eaten miraculous food, and a second time slept and eaten.

But if the anguish of the body excuses much weakness of the spirit, it follows, on the other hand, that men are responsible to God for that heavy weight which is laid upon the spirit by pampered and luxurious bodies, incapable of self-sacrifice, rebellious against the lightest of His demands. It is suggestive, that Moses, when sent again to Pharaoh, objected, as at first: "Behold, the children of Israel have not hearkened unto me; how then shall Pharaoh hear me, who am of uncircumcised lips?"

Every new hope, every great inspiration which calls the heroes of God to a fresh attack upon the powers of Satan, is checked and hindered more by the coldness of the Church than by the hostility of the world. That hostility is expected, and can be defied. But the infidelity of the faithful is appalling indeed.

We read with wonder the great things which Christ has promised to believing prayer, and, at the same time, although we know painfully that we have never claimed and dare not claim these promises, we wonder equally at the foreboding question, "When the Son of Man cometh, shall He find the faith (faith in its fulness) on the earth?" (Luke xviii. 8). But we ought to remember that our own low standard helps to form the standard of attainment for the Church at large —that when one member suffers, all the members suffer with it—that many a large sacrifice would be readily made for Christ, at this hour, if only ease and pleasure were at stake, which is refused because it is too hard to be called well-meaning enthusiasts by those who ought to glorify God in such attainment, as the first brethren did in the zeal and the gifts of Paul.

The vast mountains raise their heads above mountain ranges which encompass them; and it is not when the level of the whole Church is low, that giants of faith and of attainment may be hoped for. Nay, Christ stipulates for the agreement of two or three, to kindle and make effectual the prayers which shall avail.

For the purification of our cities, for the shaming of our legislation until it fears God as much as a vested interest, for the reunion of those who worship the same Lord, for the conversion of the world, and first of all for the conversion of the Church, heroic forces are demanded. But all the tendency of our half-hearted, abject, semi-Christianity is to repress everything that is unconventional, abnormal, likely to embroil us with our natural enemy, the world; and who can doubt that, when the secrets of all hearts shall be revealed, we shall know of many an aspiring soul, in which the sacred fire had begun to burn, which sank back into lethargy and the commonplace, murmuring in its despair, "Behold, the children of Israel have not hearkened unto me; how then shall Pharaoh hear me?"

It was the last fear which ever shook the great heart of the emancipator Moses.

At the beginning of the grand historical work, of which all this has been the prelude, there is set the pedigree of Moses and Aaron, according to "the heads of their fathers' houses,"—an epithet which indicates a subdivision of the "family," as the family is a subdivision of the tribe. Of the sons of Jacob, Reuben and Simeon are mentioned, to put Levi in his natural third place. And from Levi to Moses only four generations are mentioned, favouring somewhat the briefer scheme of chronology which makes four centuries cover all the time from Abraham, and not the captivity alone. But it is certain that this is a mere recapitulation of the more important links in the genealogy. In Num. xxvi. 58, 59, six generations are reckoned instead of four; in 1 Chron. ii. 3 there are seven generations; and elsewhere in the same book (vi. 22) there are ten. It is well known that similar omissions of obscure or unworthy links occur in St. Matthew's pedigree of our Lord, although some stress is there laid upon the recurrent division into fourteens. And it is absurd to found any argument against the trustworthiness of the narrative upon a phenomenon so frequent, and so sure to be avoided by a forger, or to be corrected by an unscrupulous editor. In point of fact, nothing is less likely to have occurred, if the narrative were a late invention.

Neither, in that case, would the birth of the great emancipator be ascribed to the union of Amram with his father's sister, for such marriages were distinctly forbidden by the law (Lev. xviii. 14).

Nor would the names of the children of the founder of the nation be omitted, while those of Aaron are recorded, unless we were dealing with genuine history, which knows that the sons of Aaron inherited the lawful priesthood, while the descendants of Moses were the jealous founders of a mischievous schism (Judges xviii. 30, R.V.).

Nor again, if this were a religious romance, designed to animate the nation in its later struggles, should we read of the hesitation and the fears of a leader "of uncircumcised lips," instead of the trumpet-like calls to action of a noble champion.

Nor does the broken-spirited meanness of Israel at all resemble the conception, popular in every nation, of a virtuous and heroic antiquity, a golden age. It is indeed impossible to reconcile the motives and the date to which this narrative is ascribed by some, with the plain phenomena, with the narrative itself.

Nor is it easy to understand why the Lord, Who speaks of bringing out "My hosts, My people, the children of Israel" (vii. 4, etc.), should never in the Pentateuch be called the Lord of Hosts, if that title were in common use when it was written; for no epithet would better suit the song of Miriam or the poetry of the Fifth Book.

When Moses complained that he was of uncircumcised lips, the Lord announced that He had already made His servant as a god unto Pharaoh, having armed him, even then, with the terrors which are soon to shake the tyrant's soul.

It is suggestive and natural that his very education in a court should render him fastidious, less willing than a rougher man might have been to appear before the king after forty years of retirement, and feeling almost physically incapable of speaking what he felt so deeply, in words that would satisfy his own judgment. Yet God had endowed him, even then, with a supernatural power far greater than any facility of expression. In his weakness he would thus be made strong; and the less fit he was to assert for himself any ascendency over Pharaoh, the more signal would be the victory of his Lord, when he became "very great in the land of Egypt, in the sight of Pharaoh's servants, and in the sight of the people" (xi. 3).

As a proof of this mastery he was from the first to speak to the haughty king through his brother, as a god through some prophet, being too great to reveal himself directly. It is a memorable phrase; and so lofty an assertion could never, in the myth of a later period, have been ascribed to an origin so lowly as the reluctance of Moses to expose his deficiency in elocution.

Therefore he should henceforth be emboldened by the assurance of qualification bestowed already: not only by the hope of help and achievement yet to come, but by the certainty of present endowment. And so should each of us, in his degree, be bold, who have gifts differing according to the grace given unto us.

It is certain that every living soul has at least one talent, and is bound to improve it. But how many of us remember that this loan implies a commission from God, as real as that of prophet and deliverer, and that nothing but our own default can prevent it from being, at the last, received again with usury?

The same bravery, the same confidence when standing where his Captain has planted him, should inspire the prophet, and him that giveth alms, and him that showeth mercy; for all are members in one body, and therefore animated by one invincible Spirit from above (Rom. xii. 4-9).

The endowment thus given to Moses made him "as a god" to Pharaoh.

We must not take this to mean only that he had a prophet or spokesman, or that he was made formidable, but that the peculiar nature of his prowess would be felt. It was not his own strength. The supernatural would become visible in him. He who boasted "I know not Jehovah" would come to crouch before Him in His agent, and humble himself to the man whom once he contemptuously ordered back to his burdens, with the abject prayer, "Forgive, I pray thee, my sin only this once, and entreat Jehovah your God that He may take away from me this death only."

Now, every consecrated power may bear witness to the Lord: it is possible to do all to the glory of God. Not that every separate action will be ascribed to a preternatural source, but the sum total of the effect produced by a holy life will be sacred. He who said, "I have made thee a god unto Pharaoh," says of all believers, "I in them, and Thou, Father, in Me, that the world may know that Thou hast sent Me."

CHAPTER VII.

THE HARDENING OF PHARAOH'S HEART.

vii. 3-13.

WHEN Moses received his commission, at the bush, words were spoken which are now repeated with more emphasis, and which have to be considered carefully. For probably no statement of Scripture has excited fiercer criticism, more exultation of enemies and perplexity of friends, than that the Lord said, "I will harden Pharaoh's heart, and he shall not let the people go," and that in consequence of this Divine act Pharaoh sinned and suffered. Just because the words are startling, it is unjust to quote them without careful examination of the context, both in the prediction and the fulfilment. When all is weighed, compared, and harmonised, it will at last be possible to draw a just conclusion. And although it may happen long before then, that the objector will charge us with special pleading, yet he will be the special pleader himself, if he seeks to hurry us, by prejudice or passion, to give a verdict which is based upon less than all the evidence, patiently weighed.

Let us in the first place find out how soon this dreadful process began; when was it that God fulfilled His threat, and hardened, in any sense whatever, the heart of Pharaoh? Did He step in at the beginning, and render the unhappy king incapable of weighing the remonstrances which He then performed the cruel mockery of addressing to him? Were these as insincere and futile as if one bade the avalanche to pause which his own act had started down the icy slopes? Was Pharaoh as little responsible for his pursuit of Israel as his horses were—being, like them, the blind agents of a superior force? We do not find it so. In the fifth chapter, when a demand is made, without any sustaining miracle, simply appealing to the conscience of the ruler, there is no mention of any such process, despite the insults with which Pharaoh then assails both the messengers and Jehovah Himself, Whom he knows not. In the seventh chapter there is clear evidence that the process is yet unaccomplished; for, speaking of an act still future, it declares, "I will harden Pharaoh's heart, and multiply My signs and My wonders in the land of Egypt" (vii. 3). And this terrible act is not connected with the remonstrances and warnings of God, but entirely with the increasing pressure of the miracles.

The exact period is marked when the hand of doom closed upon the tyrant. It is not where the Authorised Version places it. When the magicians imitated the earlier signs of Moses, "his heart was strong," but the original does not bear out the assertion that at this time the Lord made it so by any judicial act of His (vii. 13). That only comes with the sixth plague; and the course of events may be traced, fairly well, by the help of the margin of the Revised Version.

After the plague of blood "Pharaoh's heart was strong" ("hardened"), and this is distinctly ascribed to his own action, because "he set his heart even to this" (vii. 22, 23).

After the second plague, it was still he himself who "made his heart heavy" (viii. 15).

After the third plague the magicians warned him that the very finger of some god was upon him indeed: their rivalry, which hitherto might have been somewhat of a palliation for his obstinacy, was now ended; but yet "his heart was strong" (viii. 19).

Again, after the fourth plague he "made his heart heavy"; and it "was heavy" after the fifth plague, (viii. 32, ix. 7).

Only thenceforward comes the judicial infatuation upon him who has resolutely infatuated himself hitherto.

But when five warnings and penalties have spent their force in vain, when personal agony is inflicted in the plague of boils, and the magicians in particular cannot stand before him through their pain, would it have been proof of virtuous contrition if he had yielded then? If he had needed evidence, it was given to him long before. Submission now would have meant prudence, not penitence; and it was against prudence, not penitence, that he was hardened. Because he had resisted evidence, experience, and even the testimony of his own magicians, he was therefore stiffened against the grudging and unworthy concessions which must otherwise have been wrested from him, as a wild beast will turn and fly from fire. He was henceforth himself to become an evidence and a portent; and so "The Lord made strong the heart of Pharaoh, and he hearkened not unto them" (ix. 12). It was an awful doom, but it is not open to the attacks so often made upon it. It only means that for him the last five plagues were not disciplinary, but wholly penal.

Nay, it stops short of asserting even this: they might still have appealed to his reason; they were only not allowed to crush him by the agency of terror. Not once is it asserted that God hardened his heart against any nobler impulse than alarm, and desire to evade danger and death. We see clearly this meaning in the phrase, when it is applied to his army entering the Red Sea: "I will make strong the hearts of the Egyptians, and they shall go in" (xiv. 17). It needed no greater moral turpitude to pursue the Hebrews over the sands than on the shore, but it certainly required more hardihood. But the unpursued departure which the good-will of Egypt refused, their common sense was not allowed to grant. Callousness was followed by infatuation, as even the pagans felt that whom God wills to ruin He first drives mad.

This explanation implies that to harden Pharaoh's heart was to inspire him, not with wickedness, but with nerve.

And as far as the original language helps us at all, it decidedly supports this view. Three different expressions have been unhappily rendered by the same English word, to harden; but they may be discriminated throughout the narrative in Exodus, by the margin of the Revised Version.

One word, which commonly appears without any marginal explanation, is the same which is employed elsewhere about "the cause which is too *hard* for" minor judges (Deut. i. 17, cf. xv. 18, etc.). Now, this word is found (vii. 13) in the second threat that "I will harden Pharaoh's heart," and in the account which was to be given to posterity of how "Pharaoh hardened himself to let us go" (xiii. 15). And it is said likewise of Sihon, king of Heshbon, that he "would not let us pass by him, for the Lord thy God hardened his spirit and made his heart strong" (Deut. ii. 30). But since it does not occur anywhere in all the narrative of what God actually did with Pharaoh, it is only just to interpret this phrase in the prediction by what we read elsewhere of the manner of its fulfilment.

The second word is explained in the margin as meaning *to make strong*. Already God had employed it when He said "I will *make strong* his heart" (iv. 21), and this is the term used of the first fulfilment of the menace, after the sixth plague (ix. 12). God is not said to interfere again after the seventh, which had few special terrors for Pharaoh himself; but from henceforth the expression "to make *strong*" alternates with the phrase "to make *heavy*." "Go in unto Pharaoh, for I have made heavy his heart and the heart of his servants, that I might show these My signs in the midst of them" (x. 1).

It may be safely assumed that these two expressions cover between them all that is asserted of the judicial action of God in preventing a recoil of Pharaoh from his calamities. Now, the strengthening of a heart, however punitive and disastrous when a man's will is evil (just as the strengthening of his arm is disastrous then), has in itself no immorality inherent. It is a thing as often good as bad,—as when Israel and Joshua are exhorted to "Be *strong* and of a good courage" (Deut. xxxi. 6, 7, 23), and when the angel laid his hand upon Daniel and said, "Be strong, yea, be strong" (Dan. x. 19). In these passages the phrase is identical with that which describes the process by which Pharaoh was prevented from cowering under the tremendous blows he had provoked.

The other expression is to make heavy or dull. Thus "the eyes of Israel were *heavy* with age" (Gen. xlviii. 10), and as we speak of a *weight* of honour, equally with the heaviness of a dull man, so we are twice commanded, "Make heavy (honour) thy father and thy mother"; and the Lord declares, "I will make Myself heavy (get Me honour) upon Pharaoh" (Deut. v. 16, Exod. xx. 12, xiv. 4, 17, 18). In these latter references it will be observed that the making "strong" the heart of Pharaoh, and the making "Myself heavy" are so connected as almost to show a design of indicating how far is either expression from conveying the notion of immorality, infused into a human heart by God. For one of the two phrases which have been thus interpreted is still applied to Pharaoh; but the other (and the more sinister, as we should think, when thus applied) is appropriated by God to Himself: He makes Himself heavy.

It is also a curious and significant coincidence that the same word was used of the burdens that were made *heavy* when first they claimed their freedom, which is now used of the treatment of the heart of their oppressor (v. 9).

It appears, then, that the Lord is never said to debauch Pharaoh's heart, but only to strengthen it against prudence and to make it dull; that the words used do not express the infusion of evil passion, but the animation of a resolute courage, and the overclouding of a natural discernment; and, above all, that every one of the three words, to make hard, to make strong, and to make heavy, is employed to express Pharaoh's own treatment of himself, before it is applied to any work of God, as actually taking place already.

Nevertheless, there is a solemn warning for all time, in the assertion that what he at first chose, the vengeance of God afterward chose for him. For indeed the same process, working more slowly but on identical lines, is constantly seen in the hardening effect of vicious habit. The gambler did not mean to stake all his fortune upon one chance, when first he timidly laid down a paltry stake; nor has he changed his mind since then as to the imprudence of such a hazard. The drunkard, the murderer himself, is a man who at first did evil as far as he dared, and afterwards dared to do evil which he would once have shuddered at.

Let no man assume that prudence will always save him from ruinous excess, if respect for righteousness cannot withhold him from those first compliances which sap the will, destroy the restraint of self-respect, wear away the horror of great wickedness by familiarity with the same guilt in its lesser phases, and, above all, forfeit the enlightenment and calmness of judgment which come from the Holy Spirit of God, Who is the Spirit of wisdom and of counsel, and makes men to be of quick understanding in the fear of the Lord.

Let no man think that the fear of damnation will bring him to the mercy-seat at last, if the burden and gloom of being "condemned already" cannot now bend his will. "Even as they refused to have God in their knowledge, God gave them up unto a reprobate mind" (Rom. i. 28). "I gave them My statutes and showed them My judgments, which if a man do, he shall even live in them. . . . I gave them statutes that were not good, and judgments wherein they should not live" (Ezek. xx. 11, 25).

This is the inevitable law, the law of a confused and darkened judgment, a heart made heavy and ears shut, a conscience seared, an infatuated will kicking against the pricks, and heaping to itself wrath against the day of wrath. Wilful sin is always a challenge to God, and it is avenged by the obscuring of the lamp of God in the soul. Now, a part of His guiding light is prudence; and it is possible that men who will not be warned by the fear of injury to their conscience, such as they suppose that Pharaoh suffered, may be sobered by the danger of such derangement of their intellectual efficiency as really befel him.

In this sense men are, at last, impelled blindly to their fate (and this is a judicial act of God, although it comes in the course of nature), but first they launch themselves upon the slope which grows steeper at every downward step, until arrest is impossible.

On the other hand, every act of obedience helps to release the will from its entanglement, and to clear the judgment which has grown dull, anointing the eyes with eye-salve that they may see. Not in vain is the assertion of the bondage of the sinner and the glorious liberty of the children of God.

A second time, then, Moses presented himself before Pharaoh with his demands; and, as he had been forewarned, he was now challenged to give a sign in proof of his commission from a god.

And the demand was treated as reasonable; a sign was given, and a menacing one. The peaceable rod of the shepherd, a fit symbol of the meek man who bore it, became a serpent* before the king, as Moses was to become destructive to his realm. But when the wise men of Egypt and the enchanters were called, they did likewise; and although a marvel was added

---

* It is true that the word means any large reptile, as when "God created great *whales*"; but doubtless our English version is correct. It was certainly a serpent which he had recently fled from, and then taken by the tail (iv. 4). And unless we suppose the magicians to have wrought a genuine miracle, no other creature can be suggested, equally convenient for their sleight of hand.

which incontestably declared the superior power of the Deity Whom Aaron represented, yet their rivalry sufficed to make strong the heart of Pharaoh, and he would not let the people go. The issue was now knit: the result would be more signal than if the quarrel were decided at one blow, and upon all the gods of Egypt the Lord would exercise vengeance.

What are we to think of the authentification of a religion by a sign? Beyond doubt, Jesus recognised this aspect of His own miracles, when He said, "If I had not done among them the works that none other man did, they had not had sin" (John xv. 24). And yet there is reason in the objection that no amount of marvel ought to deflect by one hair's breadth our judgment of right and wrong, and the true appeal of a religion must be to our moral sense.

No miracle can prove that immoral teaching is sacred. But it can prove that it is supernatural. And this is precisely what Scripture always proclaims. In the New Testament, we are bidden to take heed, because a day will come, when false prophets shall work great signs and wonders, to deceive, if possible, even the elect (Mark xiii. 22). In the Old Testament, a prophet may seduce the people to worship other gods, by giving them a sign or a wonder which shall come to pass, but they must surely stone him: they must believe that his sign is only a temptation; and above whatever power enabled him to work it, they must recognise Jehovah proving them, and know that the supernatural has come to them in judgment, not in revelation (Deut. xiii. 1-5).

Now, this is the true function of the miraculous. At the most, it cannot coerce the conscience, but only challenge it to consider and to judge.

A teacher of the purest morality may be only a human teacher still; nor is the Christian bound to follow into the desert every clamorous innovator, or to seek in the secret chamber every one who whispers a private doctrine to a few. We are entitled to expect that one who is commissioned directly from above will bear special credentials with him; but when these are exhibited, we must still judge whether the document they attest is forged. And this may explain to us why the magicians were allowed for awhile to perplex the judgment of Pharaoh whether by fraud, as we may well suppose, or by infernal help. It was enough that Moses should set his claims upon a level with those which Pharaoh reverenced: the king was then bound to weigh their relative merits in other and wholly different scales.

THE PLAGUES.

vii. 14

There are many aspects in which the plagues of Egypt may be contemplated.

We may think of them as ranging through all nature, and asserting the mastery of the Lord alike over the river on which depended the prosperity of the realm, over the minute pests which can make life more wretched than larger and more conspicuous ills (the frogs of the water, the reptiles that disgrace humanity, and the insects that infest the air), over the bodies of animals stricken with murrain, and those of man tortured with boils, over hail in the cloud and blight in the crop, over the breeze that bears the locust and the sun that grows dark at noon, and at last over the secret springs of human life itself.

No pantheistic creed (and the Egyptian religion struck its roots deep into pantheistic speculation) could thus completely exalt God above nature, as a superior and controlling Power, not one with the mighty wheels of the universe, of which the height is terrible, but, as Ezekiel saw Him, enthroned above them in the likeness of fire, and yet in the likeness of humanity.

No idolatrous creed, however powerful be its conception of one god of the hills and another of the valleys, could thus represent a single deity as wielding all the arrows of adverse fortune, able to assail us from earth and sky and water, formidable alike in the least things and in the greatest. And presently the demonstration is completed, when at His bidding the tempest heaps up the sea, and at His frown the waters return to their strength again.

And no philosophic theory condescends to bring the Ideal, the Absolute, and the Unconditioned, into such close and intimate connection with the frog-spawn of the ditch and the blain upon the tortured skin.

We may, with ample warrant from Scripture, make the controversial application still more simple and direct, and think of the plagues as wreaking vengeance, for the worship they had usurped and the cruelties they had sanctioned, upon all the gods of Egypt, which are conceived of for the moment as realities, and as humbled, if not in fact, yet in the sympathies of priest and worshipper (xii. 12).

Then we shall see the domain of each impostor invaded, and every vaunted power to inflict evil or to remove it triumphantly wielded by Him Who proves His equal mastery over all, and thus we shall find here the justification of that still bolder personification which says, " Worship Him, all ye gods " (Psalm xcvii. 7).

The Nile had a sacred name, and was adored as "Hapee, or Hapee Mu, the Abyss, or the Abyss of Waters, or the Hidden," and the king was frequently portrayed standing between two images of this god, his throne wreathed with water-lilies. The second plague struck at the goddess HEKT, whose head was that of a frog. The uncleanness of the third plague deranged the whole system of Egyptian worship, with its punctilious and elaborate purifications. In every one there is either a presiding divinity attacked, or a blow dealt upon the priesthood or the sacrifice, or a sphere invaded which some deity should have protected, until the sun himself is darkened, the great god RA, to whom their sacred city was dedicated, and whose name is incorporated in the title of his earthly representative, the Pharaoh or PH-RA. Then at last, after all these premonitions, the deadly blow struck home.

Or we may think of the plagues as retributive, and then we shall discover a wonderful suitability in them all. It was a direful omen that the first should afflict the nation through the river, into which, eighty years before, the Hebrew babes had been cast to die, which now rolled bloody, and seemed to disclose its dead. It was fit that the luxurious homes of the oppressors should become squalid as the huts of the slaves they trampled; that their flesh should suffer torture worse than that of the whips they used so unmercifully; that the loss of crops and cattle should bring home to them the hardships of the poor who toiled for their magnificence; that physical darkness should appal them with vague terrors and undefined apprehensions, such as ever haunt the bosom of the oppressed, whose life is the sport of a caprice; and at last that the aged should learn by the deathbed of the prop and pride of their declining feebleness, and the younger feel beside the cradle of the first blossom and fruit of love, all the agony of such bereavement as they had wantonly inflicted on the innocent.

And since the fear of disadvantage in war had prompted the murder of the Hebrew children, it was right that the retributive blow should destroy first their children and then their men of war.

When we come to examine the plagues in detail, we discover that it is no arbitrary fancy which divides them into three triplets, leading up to the appalling tenth. Thus the first, fourth, and seventh, each of which begins a triplet, are introduced by a command to Moses to warn Pharaoh "in the morning" (vii. 15), or "early in the morning" (viii. 20, ix. 13). The third, sixth and ninth, on the contrary, are inflicted without any warning whatever. The story of the third plague closes with the defeat of the magicians, the sixth with their inability to stand before the king, and the ninth with the final rupture, when Moses declares, "Thou shalt see my face no more" (viii. 19, ix. 11, x. 29).

The first three are plagues of loathsomeness—bloodstained waters, frogs and lice; the next three bring actual pain and loss with them—stinging flies, murrain which afflicts the beasts, and boils upon all the Egyptians; and the third triplet are "nature-plagues" —hail, locusts and darkness. It is only after the first three plagues that the immunity of Israel is mentioned; and after the next three, when the hail is threatened, instructions are first given by which those Egyptians who fear Jehovah may also obtain protection. Thus, in orderly and solemn procession, marched the avengers of God upon the guilty land.

It has been observed, concerning the miracles of

Jesus, that not one of them was creative, and that, whenever it was possible, He wrought by the use of material naturally provided. The waterpots should be filled; the five barley-loaves should be sought out; the nets should be let down for a draught; and the blind man should have his eyes anointed, and go wash in the Pool of Siloam.

And it is easily seen that such miracles were a more natural expression of His errand, which was to repair and purify the existing system of things, and to remove our moral disease and dearth, than any exercise of creative power would have been, however it might have dazzled the spectators.

Now, the same remark applies to the miracles of Moses, to the coming of God in judgment, as to His revelation of Himself in grace; and therefore we need not be surprised to hear that natural phenomena are not unknown which offer a sort of dim hint or foreshadowing of the terrible ten plagues. Either cryptogamic vegetation or the earth borne down from upper Africa is still seen to redden the river, usually dark, but not so as to destroy the fish. Frogs and vermin and stinging insects are the pest of modern travellers. Cattle plagues make ravage there, and hideous diseases of the skin are still as common as when the Lord promised to reward the obedience of Israel to sanitary law by putting upon them none of "the evil diseases of Egypt" which they knew (Deut. vii. 15).* The locust is still dreaded. But some of the other visitations were more direful because not only their

---

* To this day, amid squalid surroundings for which nominal Christians are responsible, the immunity of the Jewish race from such suffering is conspicuous, and at least a remarkable coincidence.

intensity but even their existence was almost unprecedented: hail in Egypt was only not quite unknown; and such veiling of the sun as occurs for a few minutes during the storms of sand in the desert ought scarcely to be quoted as even a suggestion of the prolonged horror of the ninth plague.

Now, this accords exactly with the moral effect which was to be produced. The rescued people were not to think of God as one who strikes down into nature from outside, with strange and unwonted powers, superseding utterly its familiar forces. They were to think of Him as the Author of all; and of the common troubles of mortality as being indeed the effects of sin, yet ever controlled and governed by Him, let loose at His will, and capable of mounting to unimagined heights if His restraints be removed from them. By the east wind He brought the locusts, and removed them by the south-west wind. By a storm He divided the sea. The common things of life are in His hands, often for tremendous results. And this is one of the chief lessons of the narrative for us. Let the mind range over the list of the nine which stop short of absolute destruction, and reflect upon the vital importance of immunities for which we are scarcely grateful.

The purity of water is now felt to be among the foremost necessities of life. It is one which asks nothing from us except to refrain from polluting what comes from heaven so limpid. And yet we are half satisfied to go on habitually inflicting on ourselves a plague more foul and noxious than any occasional turning of our rivers into blood. The two plagues which dealt with minute forms of life may well remind us of the vast part which we are now aware that the smallest organisms play in the economy of life, as the agents of the Creator. Who gives thanks aright for the cheap blessing of the unstained light of heaven?

But we are insensible to the every-day teaching of this narrative: we turn our rivers into fluid poison; we spread all around us deleterious influences, which breed by minute forms of parasitical life the germs of cruel disease; we load the atmosphere with fumes which slay our cattle with periodical distempers, and are deadlier to vegetation than the hailstorm or the locust; we charge it with carbon so dense that multitudes have forgotten that the sky is blue, and on our Metropolis comes down at frequent intervals the darkness of the ninth plague, and all the time we fail to see that God, Who enacts and enforces every law of nature, does really plague us whenever these outraged laws avenge themselves. The miraculous use of nature in special emergencies is such as to show the Hand which regularly wields its powers.

At the same time there is no more excuse for the rationalism which would reduce the calamities of Egypt to a coincidence, than for explaining away the manna which fed a nation during its wanderings by the drug which is gathered, in scanty morsels, upon the acacia tree. The awful severity of the judgments, the series which they formed, their advent and removal at the menace and the prayer of Moses, are considerations which make such a theory absurd. The older scepticism, which supposed Moses to have taken advantage of some epidemic, to have learned in the wilderness the fords of the Red Sea,* to have discovered water, when

---

* But indeed this notion is not yet dead. "A high wind left the shallow sea so low that it became possible to ford it. Moses eagerly accepted the suggestion, and made the venture with success," etc.— *Wellhausen*, "Israel," in *Encyc. Brit.*

the caravan was perishing of thirst, by his knowledge of the habits of wild beasts, and finally to have dazzled the nation at Horeb with some kind of fireworks, is itself almost a miracle in its violation of the laws of mind. The concurrence of countless favourable accidents and strange resources of leadership is like the chance arrangement of a printer's type to make a poem.

There is a common notion that the ten plagues followed each other with breathless speed, and were completed within a few weeks. But nothing in the narrative asserts or even hints this, and what we do know is in the opposite direction. The seventh plague was wrought in February, for the barley was in the ear and the flax in blossom (ix. 31); and the feast of passover was kept on the fourteenth day of the month Abib, so that the destruction of the firstborn was in the middle of April, and there was an interval of about two months between the last four plagues. Now, the same interval throughout would bring back the first plague to September or October. But the natural discoloration of the river, mentioned above, is in the middle of the year, when the river begins to rise; and this, it may possibly be inferred, is the natural period at which to fix the first plague. They would then range over a period of about nine months. During the interval between them, the promises and treacheries of the king excited alternate hope and rage in Israel; the scribes of their own race (once the vassals of their tyrants, but already estranged by their own oppression) began to take rank as officers among the Jews, and to exhibit the rudimentary promise of national order and government; and the growing fears of their enemies fostered that triumphant sense of mastery, out of which

national hope and pride are born. When the time
came for their departure, it was possible to transmit
orders throughout all their tribes, and they came out of
Egypt by their armies, which would have been utterly
impossible a few months before. It was with them, as
it is with every man that breathes: the delay of God's
grace was itself a grace; and the slowly ripening fruit
grew mellower than if it had been forced into a
speedier maturity.

THE FIRST PLAGUE.

vii. 14-25.

It was perhaps when the Nile was rising, and
Pharaoh was coming to the bank, in pomp of state, to
make official observation of its progress, on which the
welfare of the kingdom depended, and to do homage
before its divinity, that the messenger of another
Deity confronted him, with a formal declaration of
war. It was a strange contrast. The wicked was in
great prosperity, neither was he plagued like another
man. Upon his head, if this were Menephtah, was the
golden symbol of his own divinity. Around him was
an obsequious court. And yet there was moving in his
heart some unconfessed sense of awe, when confronted
once more by the aged shepherd and his brother,
who had claimed a commission from above, and had
certainly met his challenge, and made a short end of
the rival snakes of his own seers. Once he had asked
"Who is Jehovah?" and had sent His ambassadors
to their tasks again with insult. But now he needs to
harden his heart, in order not to yield to their strange
and persistent demands. He remembers how they had
spoken to him already, "Thus saith the Lord, Israel is

My son, My firstborn, and I have said unto thee, Let My son go that he may serve Me; and thou hast refused to let him go: behold, I will slay thy son, thy firstborn" (iv. 22, R.V.). Did this awful warning come back to him, when the worn, solemn and inflexible face of Moses again met him? Did he divine the connection between this ultimate penalty and what is now announced—the turning of the pride and refreshment of Egypt into blood? Or was it partly because each plague, however dire, seemed to fall short of the tremendous threat, that he hoped to find the power of Moses more limited than his warnings? "Because sentence against an evil work is not executed speedily, therefore the heart of the sons of men is fully set in them to do evil."

And might he, at the last, be hardened to pursue the people because, by their own showing, the keenest arrow in their quiver was now sped? Whatever his feelings were, it is certain that the brothers come and go, and inflict their plagues unrestrained; that no insult or violence is attempted, and we can see the truth of the words "I have made thee as a god unto Pharaoh."

It is in clear allusion to his vaunt, "I know not Jehovah," that Moses and Aaron now repeat the demand for release, and say, "Hitherto thou hast not hearkened: behold, in this thou shalt know that I am Jehovah." What follows, when attentively read, makes it plain that the blow falls upon "the waters that are in the river," and those that have been drawn from it into canals for artificial irrigation, into reservoirs like the lakes Mœris and Mareotis, and even into vessels for immediate use.

But we are expressly told that it was possible to obtain water by digging wells. Therefore there is no point whatever in the cavil that if Moses turned all the water into blood, none was left for the operations of the magicians. But no comparison whatever existed between their petty performances and the immense and direful work of vengeance which rolled down a putrid mass of corrupt waters through the land, spoiling the great stores of water by which later drought should be relieved, destroying the fish, that important part of the food of the nation, for which Israel afterwards lusted, and sowing the seeds of other plagues, by the pollution of that balmy air in which so many of our own suffering countrymen still find relief, but which was now infected and loathsome. Even Pharaoh must have felt that his gods might do better for him than this, and that it would be much more to the point just then to undo his plague than to increase it—to turn back the blood to water than contribute a few drops more. If this was their best effort, he was already helpless in the hand of his assailant, who, by the uplifting of his rod, and the bold avowal in advance of responsibility for so great a calamity, had formally defied him. But Pharaoh dared not accept the challenge: it was effort enough for him to "set his heart" against surrender to the portent, and he sullenly turned back into the palace from the spot where Moses met him.

Two details remain to be observed. The seven days which were fulfilled do not measure the interval between this plague and the next, but the period of its infliction. And this information is not given us concerning any other, until we come to the three days of darkness.* It is important here, because the natural

---

* x. 22. The accurate Kalisch is therefore wrong in speaking of "The duration of the first plague, a statement not made with regard to any of the subsequent inflictions."—Commentary *in loco*.

discoloration lasts for three weeks, and mythical tendencies would rather exaggerate than shorten the term.

Again, it is contended that only with the fourth plague did Israel begin to enjoy exemption, because then only is their immunity recorded.* But it is strange indeed to suppose that they were involved in punishments the design of which was their relief; and in fact their exemption is implied in the statement that the Egyptians (only) had to dig wells. It is to be understood that large stores of water would everywhere be laid up, because the Nile water, however delicious, carries much sediment which must be allowed to settle down. They would not be forced, therefore, to fall back upon the polluted common sources for a supply.

And now let us contrast this miracle with the first of the New Testament. One spoiled the happiness of the guilty; the other rescued the overclouded joy of the friends of Jesus, not turning water into blood but into wine; declaring at one stroke all the difference between the law which worketh wrath, and the gospel of the grace of God. The first was impressive and public, as the revelation upon Sinai; the other appealed far more to the heart than to the imagination, and befitted well the kingdom that was not with observation, the King who grew up like a tender plant, and did not strive nor cry, the redeeming influence which was at first unobtrusive as the least of all seeds, but became a tree, and the shelter of the fowls of heaven.

---

* *Speaker's Commentary*, i., p. 242; Kalisch on viii. 18; Kiel, i. 484.

CHAPTER VIII.

THE SECOND PLAGUE.

viii. 1-15.

ALTHOUGH Pharaoh had warning of the first plague, no appeal was made to him to avert it by submission. But before the plague of frogs he was distinctly commanded, "Let My people go." It is an advancing lesson. He has felt the power of Jehovah: now he is to connect, even more closely, his suffering with his disobedience; and when this is accomplished, the third plague will break upon him unannounced—a loud challenge to his conscience to become itself his judge.

The plague of frogs was far greater than our experience helps us to imagine. At least two cases are on record of a people being driven to abandon their settlements because they had become intolerable; "as even the vessels were full of them, the water infested and the food uneatable, as they could scarcely set their feet on the ground without treading on heaps of them, and as they were vexed by the smell of the great multitude that died, they fled from that region."

The Egyptian species known to science as the Rana Mosaica, and still called by the uncommon epithet here employed, is peculiarly repulsive, and peculiarly noisy too. The superstition which adored a frog as the

"Queen of the two Worlds," and placed it upon the sacred lotus-leaf, would make it impossible for an Egyptian to adopt even such forlorn measures of self-defence as might suggest themselves. It was an unclean pest against which he was entirely helpless, and it extended the power of his enemy from the river to the land. The range of the grievance is dwelt upon in the warning: "they shall come up and enter into thine house, and into thy bedchamber, and upon thy bed . . . and into thine ovens, and into thy kneading-troughs (viii. 3). The most sequestered and the dryest spots alike would swarm with them, thrust forward into the most unsuitable places by the multitude behind.

Thus Pharaoh himself had to share, far more than in the first plague, the misery of his humblest subjects; and, although again his magicians imitated Aaron upon some small prepared plot, and amid circumstances which made it easier to exhibit frogs than to exclude them, yet there was no comfort in such puerile emulation, and they offered no hope of relieving him. From the gods that were only vanities, he turned to Jehovah, and abased himself to ask the intercession of Moses: "Intreat Jehovah that He take away the frogs from me and from my people; and I will let the people go."

The assurance would have been a hopeful one, if only the sense of inconvenience were the same as the sense of sin. But when we wonder at the relapses of men who were penitent upon sick-beds or in adversity, as soon as their trouble is at an end, we are blind to this distinction. Pain is sometimes obviously due to ourselves, and it is natural to blame the conduct which led to it. But if we blame it only for being disastrous, we cannot hope that the fruits of the Spirit will result from a sensation of the flesh. It was so with Pharaoh, as doubtless Moses expected, since God had not yet exhausted His predicted works of retribution. This anticipated fraud is much the simplest explanation of the difficult phrase, " Have thou this glory over me."

It is sometimes explained as an expression of courtesy—" I obey thee as a superior "; which does not occur elsewhere, because it is not Hebrew but Egyptian. But this suavity is quite alien to the spirit of the narrative, in which Moses, however courteous, represents an offended God. It is more natural to take it as an open declaration that he was being imposed upon, yet would grant to the king whatever advantage the fraud implied. And to make the coming relief more clearly the action of the Lord, to shut out every possibility that magician or priest should claim the honour, he bade the king name an hour at which the plague should cease.

If the frogs passed away at once, the relief might chance to be a natural one; and Pharaoh doubtless conceived that elaborate and long protracted intercessions were necessary for his deliverance. Accordingly he fixed a future period, yet as near as he perhaps thought possible; and Moses, without any express authority, promised him that it should be so. Therefore he "cried unto the Lord," and the frogs did not retreat into the river, but suddenly died where they were, and filled the unhappy land with a new horror in their decay.

But "when Pharaoh saw that there was respite, he made his heart heavy and hearkened not unto them." It is a graphic sentence: it implies rather than affirms their indignant remonstrances, and the sullen, dull, spiritless obstinacy with which he held his base and unkingly purpose.

THE THIRD PLAGUE.

viii. 16-19.

There is no sufficient reason for discarding the ordinary opinion of this plague. Gnats have been suggested (with beetles instead of flies for the fourth, since gnats and flies would scarcely make two several judgments), but these, which spring from marshy ground, would unfitly be connected with the dust whence Aaron was to evoke the pest. Sir Samuel Baker, on the other hand, has said of modern Egypt that "it seemed as if the very dust were turned into lice" (quoted in Speaker's Commentary *in loco*).

Two features in this plague deserve attention. It came without any warning whatever. The faithless king who gave his word and broke it found himself involved in fresh miseries without an opportunity of humbling himself again. He was flung back into deep waters, because he refused to fulfil the terms upon which he had been extricated.

It must be understood that the act of Aaron was a public one, performed in the sight of Pharaoh, and instantly followed by the plague. There was no doubt about the origin of the pest, and the new and alarming prospect was opened up of calamities yet to come, without a chance to avert them by submission.

Again, it will be observed that the magicians are utterly baffled just when there is no warning given, and therefore no opportunity for pre-arranged sleight of hand. And this surely favours the opinion that they had not hitherto succeeded by supernatural assistance, for there is no such evident reason why infernal aid should cease at this exact point.

It is a mistake to suppose that thereupon they confessed the mission of the brothers. In their agitation they admitted that, on their part at least, no divinity had been at work before. But they rather ascribed what they saw to the action of some vaguely indicated deity, than confessed it to be the work of Jehovah. Again it has to be asked whether this resembles more the vainglorious structure of a myth, or the course of a truthful history.

Nevertheless, their grudging and insufficient avowal was meant to induce a surrender. But "Pharaoh's heart was strong, and he hearkened not unto them." To this statement it is not added, "because the Lord had hardened him," for this had not even yet taken place; but only, "as the Lord had spoken."

THE FOURTH PLAGUE.

viii. 20-32.

When the third plague had died away, when the sense of reaction and exhaustion had replaced agitation and distress, and when perhaps the fear grew strong that at any moment a new calamity might befal the land as abruptly as the last, God orders a solemn and urgent appeal to be made to the oppressor. And the same occurs three times: after each plague which arrives unexpectedly the next is introduced by a special warning. On each of these occasions, moreover, the appeal is made in the morning, at the hour when reason ought to be clearest and the passions least agitating; and this circumstance is perhaps alluded to in the favourite phrase of Jeremiah when he would speak of condescending earnestness—" I sent my prophets, rising up early and sending them"

(Jer. xxv. 4, xxvi. 5, xxix. 19, and many more; cf. also vii. 13, and 2 Chron. xxxvi. 15). So far is the Scripture from regarding Pharaoh as propelled by destiny, as by a machine, down iron grooves to ruin.

We have now come to the group of plagues which inflict actual bodily damage, and not inconvenience and humiliation only: the dogfly (or beetle); the murrain among beasts, which was a precursor of the crowning evil that struck at human life; and the boils. Of the fourth plague the precise nature is uncertain. There is a beetle which gnaws both man and beast, destroys clothes, furniture, and plants, and even now they "are often seen in millions" (Munk, *Palestine*, p. 120). "In a few minutes they filled the whole house. . . . Only after the most laborious exertions, and covering the floor of the house with hot coals, they succeeded in mastering them. If they make such attacks during the night, the inmates are compelled to give up the houses, and little children or sick persons, who are unable to rise alone, are then exposed to the greatest danger of life" (Pratte, *Abyssinia*, p. 143, in Kalisch).

Now, this explanation has one advantage over that of dogflies—that special mention is made of their afflicting "the ground whereon they are" (ver. 21), which is less suitable to a plague of flies. But it may be that no one creature is meant. The Hebrew word means "a mixture." Jewish interpreters have gone so far as to make it mean "all kinds of noxious animals and serpents and scorpions mixed together," and although it is palpably absurd to believe that Pharaoh should have survived if these had been upon him and upon his servants, yet the expression "a mixture," following after one kind of vermin had tormented the land, need not be narrowed too exactly. With deliberate particularity the king was warned that they should come "upon thee, and upon thy servants, and upon thy people, and into thine houses, and the houses of the Egyptians shall be full of [them *], and also the ground whereon they are."

It has been supposed, from the special mention of the exemption of the land of Goshen, that this was a new thing. We have seen reason, however, to think otherwise, and the emphatic assertion now made is easy to understand. The plague was especially to be expected in low fat ground: the king may not even have been aware of the previous freedom of Israel; and in any case its importance as an evidence had not been pressed upon him. The spirit of the seventy-eighth Psalm, though not perhaps any one specific phrase, contrasts the earlier as well as the later plagues with the protection of His own people, whom He led like sheep (vers. 42-52).

After the appointed interval (the same which Pharaoh had indicated for the removal of the frogs) the plague came. We are told that the land was corrupted, but it is significant that more stress is laid upon the suffering of Pharaoh and his court in the event than in the menace. It came home to himself more cruelly than any former plague, and he at once attempted to make terms: "Go ye, sacrifice to your God in the land." It is a natural speech, at first not asking to be trusted as before by getting relief before the Hebrews actually enjoy their liberty; and yet conceding as little as possible, and in hot haste to have that little done and

---

* The Revised Version has "swarms of flies," which is clearly an attempt to meet the case. But it is worth notice that in the Psalms the expression was twice rendered "divers kinds of flies" (lxxviii. 45, cv. 31, A.V.) The word occurs only of this plague.

the relief obtained. They may even serve their God on the sacred soil, so completely has He already defeated all His rivals. But this was not what was demanded; and Moses repeated the claim of a three days' journey, basing it upon the ground, still more insulting to the national religion, that "We will sacrifice to Jehovah our God the abomination of the Egyptians," that is to say, sacred animals, which it is horror in their eyes to sacrifice. Any faith in his own creed which Pharaoh ever had is surrendered when this argument, instead of making their cause hopeless, forces him to yield—adding, however, like a thoroughly weak man who wishes to refuse but dares not, "only ye shall not go very far away: intreat for me." And again Moses concedes the point, with only the courteous remonstrance, "But let not Pharaoh deal deceitfully any more."

It is necessary to repeat that we have not a shred of evidence that Moses would have violated his compact and failed to return: it would have sufficed as a first step to have asserted the nationality of his people and their right to worship their own God: all the rest would speedily have followed. But the terms which were rejected again and again did not continue for ever to bind the victorious party: the story of their actual departure makes it plain that both sides understood it to be a final exodus; and thence came the murderous pursuit of Pharaoh (cf. xv. 9), which in itself would have cancelled any compact which had existed until then.

CHAPTER IX.

THE FIFTH PLAGUE.

ix. 1-7.

OUR Lord when on earth came not to destroy men's lives. And yet it was necessary, for our highest instruction, that we should not think of Him as revealing a Divinity wholly devoid of sternness. Twice, therefore, a gleam of the fires of justice fell on the eyes which followed Him—through the destruction once of a barren tree, and once of a herd of swine, which property no Jew should have possessed. So now, when half the gloomy round of the plagues was being completed, it was necessary to prove that life itself was staked on this desperate hazard; and this was done first by the very same expedient—the destruction of life which was not human. There is something pathetic, if one thinks of it, in the extent to which domestic animals share our fortunes, and suffer through the brutality or the recklessness of their proprietors. If all men were humane, self-controlled, and (as a natural result) prosperous, what a weight would be uplifted from the lower levels also of created life, all of which groaneth and travaileth in pain together until now! The dumb animal world is partner with humanity, and shares its fate, as each animal is dependent on its individual owner.

We have already seen the whole life of Egypt stricken, but now the lower creatures are to perish, unless Pharaoh will repent. He is once more summoned in the name of "Jehovah, God of the Hebrews," and warned that the hand of Jehovah, even a very grievous murrain (for so the verse appears to say), is "upon thy cattle which is in the field, upon the horses, upon the asses, upon the camels, upon the herds and upon the flocks." Here some particulars need observation. Herds and flocks were everywhere; but horses were a comparatively late introduction into Egypt, where they were as yet chiefly employed for war. Asses, still so familiar to the traveller, were the usual beasts of burden, and were owned in great numbers by the rich, although rash controversialists have pretended that, as being unclean, they were not tolerated in the land.

Camels, it is said, are not to be found on the monuments, but yet they were certainly known and possessed by Egypt, though there were many reasons why they should be held chiefly on the frontiers, and perhaps in connection with the Arabian mines and settlements. Upon all these "in the field" the plague should come.

The murrain still works havoc in the Delta, chiefly at the period, beginning with December, when the floods are down and the cattle are turned out into the pastures, which would this year have been signally unwholesome. It was not, then, the fact of a cattle plague which was miraculous, but its severity, its coming at an appointed time, its assailing beasts of every kind, and its exempting those of Israel. We are told that "all the cattle of Egypt died," and yet that afterwards "the hail . . . smote both man and beast" (ix. 6, 25). It is an inconsistency very

serious in the eyes of people who are too stupid or too
uncandid to observe that, just before, the mischief was
limited to those cattle which were "in the field"
(ver. 3). There were great stalls in suitable places,
to give them shelter during the inundations; and all
that had not yet been driven out to graze are
expressly exempted from the plague.

Much of Pharaoh's own property perished, but he
was the last man in the country who would feel
personal inconvenience by the loss, and therefore
nothing was more natural than that his selfish "heart
was heavy, and he did not let the people go." Not
even such an effort was needed as in the previous
plague, when we read that he made his heart heavy,
by a deliberate act.

There was nothing to indicate that he had now
reached a crisis—that God Himself in His judgment
would henceforth make bold and resolute against
crushing adversities the heart which had been obdurate
against humanity, against evidence, against honour
and plighted faith. Nothing is easier than to step over
the frontier between great nations. And in the moral
world also the Rubicon is passed, the destiny of a
soul is fixed, sometimes without a struggle, unawares.

Instead of spiritual conflict, there was intellectual
curiosity. "Pharaoh sent, and behold there was not
so much as one of the cattle of the Israelites dead.
But the heart of Pharaoh was heavy, and he did not
let the people go." This inquiry into a phenomenon
which was surprising indeed, but yet quite unable to
affect his action, recalls the spiritual condition of
Herod, who was conscience-stricken when first he
heard of Christ, and said, "It is John whom I beheaded'
(Mark vi. 16), but afterwards felt merely vulgar

curiosity and desire to behold a sign of Him. In the case of Pharaoh it was the next step to judicial infatuation. When Christ confronted Herod, He, Who had explained Himself to Pilate, was absolutely silent. And this warns us not to think that an interest in religious problems is itself of necessity religious. One may understand all mysteries, and yet it may profit him nothing. And many a reprobate soul is controversial, acute, and keenly orthodox.

THE SIXTH PLAGUE.

ix. 8-12.

At the close of the second triplet, as of the first, stands a plague without a warning, but not without the clearest connection between the blow and Him who deals it.

To the Jews Egypt was a furnace in which they were being consumed—whether literally in human sacrifice, or metaphorically in the hard labour which wasted them (Deut. iv. 20). And now the brothers were commanded to fill both hands with ashes of the furnace and throw them upon the wind,* either to symbolise the suffering which was to be spread wide over the land, or because the ashes of human sacrifices were thus presented to their evil genius, Typhon. If this were its meaning, the irony was keen, when at the same action a feverish inflammation breaking out in blains spread over all the nation.

But, apart from any such reference to their cruel idolatry, it was right that they should suffer in the

---

* The passage in Deuteronomy had not this event specially in mind, or it would have used the same term for a furnace. The word for ashes implies what can be blown upon the wind.

flesh. When the higher nature is dead, there is no appeal so sharp and certain as to the physical sensibility. And moreover, there are other sins which have their root in the flesh besides sloth and bodily indulgence. Wrath and cruelty and pride are strangely stimulated and excited by self-indulgence. Not in vain does St. Paul describe a "mind of the flesh," and reckon among the fruits of the flesh not only uncleanness and drunkenness, but, just as truly, strife, jealousies, wraths, factions, divisions, heresies (Col. ii. 18; Gal. v. 19, 20). From such evil tempers, stimulated by evil appetites, the slaves of Egypt had suffered bitterly; and now the avenging rod fell upon the bodies of their tyrants.

And we may perhaps detect especial suffering, certainly an especial triumph to be commemorated, in the failure of the magicians even to stand before the king. It is implied that they had done so until now, and this confirms the belief that after the third plague they had not acknowledged Jehovah, but merely said in their defeat, "This is the finger of a god." Until now Jannes and Jambres (two, to rival the two brothers) had withstood Moses, but now the contrast between the prophet and his victims writhing in their pain was too sharp for prejudice itself to overlook: their folly was "evident unto all men" (2 Tim. iii. 8, 9). But it was not destined that Pharaoh should yield even to so tremendous a coercion what he refused to moral influences; and as Jesus after His resurrection appeared not unto all the people (hiding this crowning evidence from the eyes which had in vain beheld so much), so "the Lord made strong the heart of Pharaoh, and he hearkened not unto them, as the Lord had spoken unto Moses." In this last expression is the explicit statement that it was now that the prediction attained fulfilment, in the manner which we have discussed already.

But even this strength of heart did not reach the height of attempting any reprisals upon the torturers. The sense of the supernatural was their defence: Moses was as a god unto Pharaoh, and Aaron was his prophet.

In the narrative of this plague there is an expression which deserves attention for another reason. The ashes, it says, "shall become dust." Is there no controversy, turning upon the too rigid and prosaic straining of a New Testament construction, which might be simplified by considering the Hebrew use of language, exemplified in such an assertion as "It shall become dust," and soon after, "It is the Lord's passover"? Do these announce transubstantiations? Did two handfuls of ashes literally become the blains upon the bodies of all the Egyptians?

THE SEVENTH PLAGUE.

ix. 13-35.

The hardening of Pharaoh's heart, we have argued, was not the debauching of his spirit, but only the strengthening of his will. "Wait on the Lord and *be of good courage*"; "*Be strong*, O Zerubbabel, saith the Lord; and *be strong*, O Joshua, son of Josadak the high priest; and *be strong*, all ye people" (Ps. xxvii. 14; Hag. ii. 4), are clear proofs that what was implied in this word was not wickedness, but only that iron determination which his choice directed in a wicked channel. And therefore it was no mockery, no insincere appeal by one who had provided against the mischance of its succeeding, when God again addressed Himself to the reason, and even to the rational fears of Pharaoh. He had only provided against a terror-stricken submission, as wholly immoral and valueless, as the ceasing to resist of one who has swooned through fright. Now, to give such an one a stimulant and thus to enable him to exercise his volition, would be different from inciting him to rebel.

The seventh plague, then, is ushered in by an expostulation more earnest, resolute and minatory than attended any of the previous ones. And this is the more necessary because human life is now for the first time at stake. First the king is solemnly reminded that Jehovah, Whom he no longer can refuse to know, is the God of the Hebrews, has a claim upon their services, and demands them. In oppressing the nation, therefore, Pharaoh usurped what belonged to the Lord. Now, this is the eternal charter of the rights of all humanity. Whoever encroaches on the just sphere of the free action of his neighbour deprives him, to exactly the same extent, of the power to glorify God by a free obedience. The heart glorifies God by submission to so hard a lot, but the co-operation of the "whole body and soul and spirit" does not visibly bear testimony to the regulating power of grace. The oppressor may contend (like some slave-owners) that he guides his human property better than it would guide itself. But one assertion he cannot make: namely, that God is receiving the loyal homage of a life spontaneously devoted; that a man and not a machine is glorifying God in this body and spirit which are God's. For the body is but a chattel. This is why the Christian doctrine of the religious equality of all men in Christ carries with it the political assertion of the equal secular rights of the whole human race. I must not transfer to myself the solemn duty of my neighbour to offer up to God the sacrifice not only of his chastened spirit but also of his obedient life.

And these words were also a lifelong admonition to every Israelite. He held his liberties from God. He was not free to be violent and wanton, and to say "I am delivered to commit all these abominations." The dignities of life were bound up with its responsibilities.

Well, it is not otherwise to-day. As truly as Moses, the champions of our British liberties were earnest and God-fearing men. Not for leave to revel, to accumulate enormous fortunes, and to excite by their luxuries the envy and rage of neglected brothers, while possessing more enormous powers to bless them than ever were entrusted to a class,—not for this our heroes bled on the field and on the scaffold. Tyrants rarely deny to rich men leave to be self-indulgent. And self-indulgence rarely nerves men to heroic effort. It is for the freedom of the soul that men dare all things. And liberty is doomed wherever men forget that the true freeman is the servant of Jehovah. On these terms the first demand for a national emancipation was enforced.

And next, Pharaoh is warned that God, who at first threatened to destroy his firstborn, but had hitherto come short of such a deadly stroke, had not, as he might flatter himself, exhausted His power to avenge. Pharaoh should yet experience "*all* My plagues." And there is a dreadful significance in the phrase which threatens to put these plagues, with regard to others, "upon thy servants and upon thy people," but with regard to Pharaoh himself "upon thine heart."

There it was that the true scourge smote. Thence came ruin and defeat. His infatuation was more dreadful than hail in the cloud and locusts on the blast, than the darkness at noon and the midnight wail of a bereaved nation. For his infatuation involved all these.

The next assertion is not what the Authorised Version made it, and what never was fulfilled. It is not, "Now I will stretch out My hand to smite thee and thy people with pestilence, and thou shalt be cut off from the earth." It says, "Now I had done this, as far as any restraint for thy sake is concerned, but in very deed for this cause have I made thee to stand" (unsmitten), "for to show thee My power, and that My name may be declared throughout all the earth" (vers. 15, 16). The course actually taken was more for the glory of God, and a better warning to others, than a sudden stroke, however crushing.

And so we find, many years after all this generation has passed away, that a strangely distorted version of these events is current among the Philistines in Palestine. In the days of Eli, when the ark was brought into the camp, they said, "Woe unto us! who shall deliver us out of the hand of these mighty gods? These are the gods that smote the Egyptians with all manner of plagues in the wilderness" (1 Sam. iv. 8). And this, along with the impression which Rahab declared that the Exodus and what followed it had made, may help us to understand what a mighty influence upon the wars of Palestine the scourging of Egypt had, how terror fell upon all the inhabitants of the land, and they melted away (Josh. ii. 9, 10).

And perhaps it may save us from the unconscious egoism which always deems that I myself shall not be treated quite as severely as I deserve, to mark how the punishment of one affects the interests of all.

Added to all this is a kind of half-ironical clemency,

an opportunity of escape if he would humble himself so far as to take warning even to a small extent. The plague was to be of a kind especially rare in Egypt, and of utterly unknown severity—such hail as had not been in Egypt since the day it was founded until now. But he and his people might, if they would, hasten to bring in their cattle and all that they had in the field. Pharaoh, after his sore experience of the threats of Moses, would find it a hard trial in any case, whether to withdraw his property or to brave the stroke. To him it was a kind of challenge. To those of his subjects who had any proper feeling it was a merciful deliverance, and a profoundly skilful education of their faith, which began by an obedience probably hesitating, but had few doubts upon the morrow. We read that he who feared the Lord among the servants of Pharaoh made his servants and his cattle flee into the houses; and this is the first hint that the plagues, viewed as discipline, were not utterly vain. The existence of others who feared Jehovah beside the Jews prepares us for the "mixed multitude" who came up along with them (xii. 38), and whose ill-instructed and probably very selfish adhesion was quite consistent with such sensual discontent as led the whole congregation into sin (Num. xi. 4).

To make the connection between Jehovah and the impending storm more obvious still, Moses stretched his rod toward heaven, and there was hail, and fire mingled with the hail, such as slew man and beast, and smote the trees, and destroyed all the vegetation which had yet grown up. The heavens, the atmosphere, were now enrolled in the conspiracy against Pharaoh: they too served Jehovah.

In such a storm, the terror was even greater than

the peril. When a great writer of our own time called attention to the elaborate machinery by which God in nature impresses man with the sense of a formidable power above, he chose a thunderstorm as the most striking example of his meaning.

"Nothing appears to me more remarkable than the array of scenic magnificence by which the imagination is appalled, in myriads of instances when the actual danger is comparatively small; so that the utmost possible impression of awe shall be produced upon the minds of all, though direct suffering is inflicted upon few. Consider, for instance, the moral effect of a single thunderstorm. Perhaps two or three persons may be struck dead within a space of a hundred square miles; and their death, unaccompanied by the scenery of the storm, would produce little more than a momentary sadness in the busy hearts of living men. But the preparation for the judgment, by all that mighty gathering of the clouds; by the questioning of the forest leaves, in their terrified stillness, which way the winds shall go forth; by the murmuring to each other, deep in the distance, of the destroying angels before they draw their swords of fire; by the march of the funeral darkness in the midst of the noonday, and the rattling of the dome of heaven beneath the chariot wheels of death;—on how many minds do not these produce an impression almost as great as the actual witnessing of the fatal issue! and how strangely are the expressions of the threatening elements fitted to the apprehensions of the human soul! The lurid colour, the long, irregular, convulsive sound, the ghastly shapes of flaming and heaving cloud, are all true and faithful in their appeal to our instinct of danger."—Ruskin, *Stones of Venice*, III. 197-8.

Such a tempest, dreadful anywhere, would be most appalling of all in the serene atmosphere of Egypt, to unaccustomed spectators, and minds troubled by their guilt. Accordingly we find that Pharaoh was less terrified by the absolute mischief done than by the "voices of God," when, unnerved for the moment, he confessed at least that he had sinned "this time" (a singularly weak repentance for his long and daring resistance, even if we explain it, "this time I confess that I have sinned"), and went on in his terror to pour out orthodox phrases and professions with suspicious fluency. The main point was the bargain which he proposed: "Intreat the Lord, for there hath been enough of mighty thunderings and hail; and I will let you go, and ye shall stay no longer."

Looking attentively at all this, we discern in it a sad resemblance to some confessions of these latter days. Men are driven by affliction to acknowledge God: they confess the offence which is palpable, and even add that God is righteous and that they are not. If possible, they shelter themselves from lonely condemnation by general phrases, such as that all are wicked; just as Pharaoh, although he would have scoffed at the notion of any national volition except his own, said, "I and my people are sinners." Above all, they are much more anxious for the removal of the rod than for the cleansing of the guilt; and if this can be accomplished through the mediation of another, they have as little desire as Pharaoh had for any personal approach to God, Whom they fear, and if possible repel.

And by these signs, every experienced observer expects that if they are delivered out of trouble they will forget their vows.

Moses was exceedingly meek. And therefore, or else because the message of God implied that other plagues were to succeed this, he consented to intercede, yet adding the simple and dignified protest, "As for thee and thy people, I know that ye will not yet fear Jehovah God."* And so it came to pass. The heart of Pharaoh was made heavy, and he would not let Israel go.

Looking back upon this miracle, we are reminded of the mighty part which atmospheric changes have played in the history of the world. Snowstorms saved Europe from the Turk and from Napoleon: the wind played almost as important a part in our liberation from James, and again in the defeat of the plans of the French Revolution to invade us, as in the destruction of the Armada. And so we read, "Hast thou entered the treasuries of the snow? or hast thou seen the treasuries of the hail, which I have reserved against the time of trouble, against the day of battle and war?" (Job xxxviii. 22-3).

---

* Except in one passage (Gen. ii. 4 to iii. 23) these titles of Deity are nowhere else combined in the books of Moses.

CHAPTER X.

THE EIGHTH PLAGUE.

x. 1-20.

THE Lord would not command His servant again to enter the dangerous presence of the sullen prince, without a reason which would sustain his faith: "For I have made heavy his heart." The pronoun is emphatic: it means to say, 'His foolhardiness is My doing and cannot go beyond My will: thou art safe.' And the same encouragement belongs to all who do the sacred will: not a hair of their head shall truly perish, since life and death are the servants of their God. Thus, in the storm of human passion, as of the winds, He says, "It is I, be not afraid"; making the wrath of man to praise Him, stilling alike the tumult of the waves and the madness of the people.

It is possible that even the merciful mitigations of the last plague were used by infatuated hearts to justify their wilfulness: the most valuable crops of all had escaped; so that these judgments, however dire, were not quite beyond endurance. Just such a course of reasoning deludes all who forget that the goodness of God leadeth to repentance.

Besides the reasons already given for lengthening out the train of judgments, it is added that Israel should teach the story to posterity, and both fathers and children should "know that I am Jehovah."

Accordingly it became a favourite title—"The Lord which brought thee up out of the land of Egypt." Even the apostates under Sinai would not reject so illustrious a memory: their feast was nominally to Jehovah; and their idol was an image of "the gods which brought thee up out of the land of Egypt" (xxxii. 4, 5).

Has *our* land no deliverances for which to be thankful? Instead of boastful self-assertion, should we not say, "We have heard with our ears, O God, and our fathers have declared unto us, the noble works that Thou didst in their days and in the old time before them?" Have we forgotten that national mercies call aloud for national thanksgiving? And in the family, and in the secret life of each, are there no rescues, no emancipations, no enemies overcome by a hand not our own, which call for reverent acknowledgment? "These things were our examples, and are written for our admonition."

The reproof now spoken to Pharaoh is sterner than any previous one. There is no reasoning in it. The demand is peremptory: "How long wilt thou refuse to humble thyself?" With it is a sharp and short command: "Let My people go, that they may serve Me." And with this is a detailed and tremendous threat. It is strange, in the face of the knowledge accumulated since the objection called for it, to remember that once this narrative was challenged, because locusts, it was said, are unknown in Egypt. They are mentioned in the inscriptions. Great misery was caused by them in 1463, and just three hundred years later Niebuhr was himself at Cairo during a plague of them. Equally arbitrary is the objection that Joel predicted locusts "such as there hath not been ever the like, neither shall be any more after them, even to the years of many generations" (ii. 2), whereas we read of these that "before them there were no such locusts as they, neither after them shall be such" (x. 14). The objection is whimsical in its absurdity, when we remember that Joel spoke distinctly of Zion and the holy mountain (ii. 1), and Exodus of "the borders of Egypt" (x. 14).

But it is true that locusts are comparatively rare in Egypt; so that while the meaning of the threat would be appreciated, familiarity would not have steeled them against it. The ravages of the locust are terrible indeed, and coming just in time to ruin the crops which had escaped the hail, would complete the misery of the land.

One speaks of the sudden change of colour by the disappearance of verdure where they alight as being like the rolling up of a carpet; and here we read "they shall cover the eye of the earth,"—a phrase peculiar to the Pentateuch (ver. 15; Num. xxii. 5, 11); and they shall eat the residue of that which has escaped, . . . and they shall fill thy houses, and the . . . houses of all the Egyptians, which neither thy fathers nor thy fathers' fathers have seen."

After uttering the appointed warning, Moses abruptly left, awaiting no negotiations, plainly regarding them as vain.

But now, for the first time, the servants of Pharaoh interfered, declared the country to be ruined, and pressed him to surrender. And yet it was now first that we read (ver. 1) that their hearts were hardened as well as his. For that is a hard heart that does not remonstrate against wrong, however plainly God reveals His displeasure, until new troubles are at hand, and which even then has no regard for the wrongs of Israel, but only for the woes of Egypt. It is a hard heart, therefore, which intends to repent upon its deathbed; for its motives are identical with these.

Pharaoh's behaviour is that of a spoiled child, who is indeed the tyrant most familiar to us. He feels that he must yield, or else why should the brothers be recalled? And yet, when it comes to the point, he tries to play the master still, by dictating the terms for his own surrender; and breaks off the negociation rather than do frankly what he must feel that it is necessary to do. Moses laid his finger accurately upon the disease when he reproached him for refusing to humble himself. And if his behaviour seem unnatural, it is worth observation that Napoleon, the greatest modern example of proud, intellectual, godless infatuation, allowed himself to be crushed at Leipsic through just the same reluctance to do thoroughly and without self-deception what he found it necessary to consent to do. "Napoleon," says his apologist, Thiers, "at length determined to retreat—a resolution humbling to his pride. Unfortunately, instead of a retreat frankly admitted . . . he determined on one which from its imposing character should not be a real retreat at all, and should be accomplished in open day." And this perversity, which ruined him, is traced back to "the illusions of pride."

Well, it was quite as hard for the Pharaoh to surrender at discretion, as for the Corsican to stoop to a nocturnal retreat. Accordingly, he asks, "Who are ye that shall go?" and when Moses very explicitly and resolutely declares that they will all go, with all their property, his passion overcomes him, he feels that to consent is to lose them for ever, and he exclaims,

"So be Jehovah with you as I will let you go and your little ones : look to it, for evil is before you"—that is to say, Your intentions are bad. "Go ye that are men, and serve the Lord, for that is what ye desire,"—no more than that is implied in your demand, unless it is a mere pretence, under which more lurks than it avows.

But he and they have long been in a state of war : menaces, submissions, and treacheries have followed each other fast, and he has no reason to complain if their demands are raised. Moreover, his own nation celebrated religious festivals in company with their wives and children, so that his rejoinder is an empty outburst of rage. And of a Jewish feast it was said, a little later, "Thou shalt rejoice before the Lord thy God, thou and thy son and thy daughter, and thy manservant and thy maidservant . . . and the stranger, and the fatherless, and the widow" (Deut. xvi. 11). There was no insincerity in the demand; and although the suspicions of the king were naturally excited by the exultant and ever-rising hopes of the Hebrews, and the defiant attitude of Moses, yet even now there is as little reason to suspect bad faith as to suppose that Israel, once released, could ever have resumed the same abject attitude toward Egypt as before. They would have come back victorious, and therefore ready to formulate new demands; already half emancipated, and therefore prepared for the perfecting of the work.

And now, at a second command as explicit as that which bade him utter the warning, Moses, anxiously watched by many, stretched out his hand over the devoted realm. At the gesture, the spectators felt that a fiat had gone forth. But the result was strangely different from that which followed his invocation, both of the previous and the following plague, when we may believe that as he raised his hand, the hail-storm burst in thunder, and the curtain fell upon the sky. Now there only arose a gentle east wind (unlike the "exceeding strong west wind" that followed), but it blew steadily all that day and all the following night. The forebodings of Egypt would understand it well: the prolonged period during which the curse was being steadily wafted toward them was an awful measure of the wide regions over which the power of Jehovah reached; and when it was morning, the east wind brought the locusts, that dreadful curse which Joel has compared to a disciplined and devastating invader, "the army of the Lord," and the first woe that heralds the Day of the Lord in the Apocalypse (Joel ii. 1-11; Rev. ix. 1-11).

The completeness of the ruin brought a swift surrender, but it has been well said that folly is the wisdom which is only wise too late, and, let us add, too fitfully. If Pharaoh had only submitted before the plague instead of after it!* If he had only respected himself enough to be faithful, instead of being too vain really to yield!

It is an interesting coincidence that, since he had this time defied the remonstrances of his advisers, his confession of sin is entirely personal: it is no longer, "I and my people are sinners," but "I have sinned against the Lord your God, and against you." This last clause was bitter to his lips, but the need for their

---

* Oddly enough, the same historian already quoted, relating the story of the same day at Leipsic, says of Napoleon's dialogue with M. de Merfeld, that he "used an expression which, if uttered at the Congress of Prague, would have changed his lot and ours. Unfortunately, it was now too late."

intercession was urgent: life and death were at stake upon the removal of this dense cloud of creatures which penetrated everywhere, leaving everywhere an evil odour, and of which a later sufferer complains, "We could not eat, but we bit a locust; nor open our mouths, but locusts filled them."

Therefore he went on to entreat volubly, "Forgive, I pray thee, my sin only this once, and intreat Jehovah your God that He may take away from me this death only."

And at the prayer of Moses, the Lord caused the breeze to veer and rise into a hurricane: "The Lord turned an exceeding strong west wind." Now, the locust can float very well upon an easy breeze, and so it had been wafted over the Red Sea; but it is at once beaten down by a storm, and when it touches the water it is destroyed. Thus simply was the plague removed.

"But the Lord made strong Pharaoh's heart," and so, his fears being conquered, his own rebellious will went on upon its evil way. He would not let Israel go.

This narrative throws light upon a thousand vows made upon sick beds, but broken when the sufferer recovers; and a thousand prayers for amendment, breathed in all the sincerity of panic, and forgotten with all the levity of security. It shows also, in the hesitating and abortive half-submission of the tyrant, the greater folly of many professing Christians, who will, for Christ's sake, surrender all their sins except one or two, and make any confession except that which really brings low their pride.

Thoroughness, decision, depth, and self-surrender, needed by Pharaoh, are needed by every soul of man.

THE NINTH PLAGUE.

x. 21-29.

We have taken it as settled that the Pharaoh of the Exodus was Menephtah, the Beloved of the God Ptah. If so, his devotion to the gods throws a curious light upon his first scorn of Jehovah, and his long continued resistance ; and also upon the threat of vengeance to be executed upon the gods of Egypt, as if they were a resisting power. But there is a special significance in the ninth plague, when we connect it with Menephtah.

In the Tombs of the Kings at Thebes there is to be seen, fresh and lifelike, the admirably sculptured effigy of this king—a weak and cruel face, with the receding forehead of his race, but also their nose like a beak, and their sharp chin. Over his head is the inscription—

> "Lord of the Two Lands, Beloved of the God Amen ;
> Lord of Diadems, Beloved of the God Ptah :
> Crowned by Amen with dominion of the world :
> Cherished by the Sun in the great abode."

This formidable personage is delineated by the court sculptor with his hand stretched out in worship, and under it is written "He adores the Sun : he worships Hor of the solar horizons."

The worship, thus chosen as the most characteristic of this king, either by himself or by some consummate artist, was to be tested now.

Could the sun help him ? or was it, like so many minor forces of earth and air, at the mercy of the God of Israel ?

There is a terrible abruptness about the coming of

the ninth plague. Like the third and sixth, it is inflicted unannounced; and the parleying, the driving of a bargain and then breaking it, by which the eighth was attended, is quite enough to account for this. Moreover, the experience of every man teaches him that each method has its own impressiveness: the announcement of punishment awes, and a surprise alarms, and when they are alternated, every possible door of access to the conscience is approached. If the heart of Pharaoh was now beyond hope, it does not follow that all his people were equally hardened. What an effect was produced upon those courtiers who so earnestly supported the recent demand of Moses, when this new plague fell upon them unawares!

But not only is there no announcement: the narrative is so concentrated and brief as to give a graphic rendering of the surprise and terror of the time. Not a word is wasted:—

"The Lord said unto Moses, Stretch out thine hand toward heaven, that there may be darkness over the land of Egypt, even darkness that may be felt. And Moses stretched forth his hand toward heaven; and there was a thick darkness in all the land of Egypt three days: they saw not one another, neither rose any from his place three days; but all the children of Israel had light in their dwellings" (vers. 21-3). We are not told anything of the emotions of the king, as the prophet strides into his presence, and before the cowering court, silently raises his hand and quenches the day. We may infer his temper, if we please, from the frantic outbreak of menace and rage in which he presently warns the man whose coming is the same thing as calamity to see his face no more. Nothing is said, again, about the evil angels by which, according to later narratives, that long night was haunted.* And after all it is more impressive to think of the blank, utter paralysis of dread in which a nation held its breath, benumbed and motionless, until vitality was almost exhausted, and even Pharaoh chose rather to surrender than to die.

As the people lay cowering in their fear, there was plenty to occupy their minds. They would remember the first dreadful threat, not yet accomplished, to slay their firstborn; and the later assertion that if pestilence had not destroyed them, it was because God would plague them with all His plagues. They would reflect upon all their defeated duties, and how the sun himself was now withdrawn at the waving of the prophet's hand. And then a ghastly foreboding would complete their dread. What was it that darkness typified, in every Oriental nation—nay, in all the world? Death! Job speaks of

"The land of darkness and of the shadow of death;
A land of thick darkness, as darkness itself;
A land of the shadow of death without any order,
And where the light is as darkness" (x. 21, 22).

With us, a mortal sentence is given in a black cap; in the East, far more expressively, the head of the culprit was covered, and the darkness which thus came upon him expressed his doom. Thus "they covered Haman's face" (Esther vii. 8). Thus to destroy "the face of the covering that is cast over all peoples and the veil that is spread over all nations," is the same thing as to "swallow up death," being the visible destruction of the embodied death-sentence (Isa. xxv. 7, 8). And

---

* Such is probably not the meaning in Ps. lxxviii. 49 (see R.V.), though from it the tradition may have sprung.

now this veil was spread over all the radiant land of Egypt. Chill, and hungry, and afraid to move, the worst horror of all that prolonged midnight was the mental agony of dire anticipation.

In other respects there had been far worse calamities, but through its effect upon the imagination this dreadful plague was a fit prelude to the tenth, which it hinted and premonished.

In the Apocryphal Book of Wisdom there is a remarkable study of this plague, regarded as retribution in kind. It avenges the oppression of Israel. "For when unrighteous men thought to oppress the holy nation, they being shut up in their houses, the prisoners of darkness, and fettered with the bonds of a long night, lay exiled from the eternal Providence" (xvii. 2). It expresses in the physical realm their spiritual misery: "For while they supposed to lie hid in their secret sins, they were scattered under a thick veil of forgetfulness" (ver. 3). It retorted on them the illusions of their sorcerers: "as for the illusions of art magick, they were put down. . . . For they, that promised to drive away terrors and troubles from a sick soul, were sick themselves of fear, worthy to be laughed at" (vers. 7, 8). In another place the Egyptians are declared to be worse than the men of Sodom, because they brought into bondage friends and not strangers, and grievously afflicted those whom they had received with feasting; "therefore even with blindness were these stricken, as those were at the doors of the righteous man." (xix. 14-17). And we may well believe that the long night was haunted with special terrors, if we add this wise explanation: "For wickedness, condemned by her own witness, is very timorous, and being pressed by conscience, always forecasteth grievous things. For"

—and this is a sentence of transcendent merit—"fear is nothing else than a betrayal of the succours that reason offereth" (xvii. 11, 12). Therefore it is concluded that their own hearts were their worst tormentors, alarmed by whistling winds, or melodious song of birds, or pleasing fall of waters, "for the whole world shined with clear light, and none were hindered in their labour: over them only was spread a heavy night, an image of that darkness which should afterward receive them: yet were they unto themselves more grievous than the darkness" (vers. 20, 21).

Isaiah, too, who is full of allusions to the early history of his people, finds in this plague of darkness an image of all mental distress and spiritual gloom. "We look for light, but behold darkness; for brightness, but we walk in obscurity: we grope for the wall like the blind, yea, we grope as those that have no eyes: we stumble at noonday as in the twilight" (lix. 10). Here the sinful nation is reduced to the misery of Egypt. But if she were obedient she would enjoy all the immunities of her forefathers amid Egyptian gloom: "Then shall thy light rise in darkness and thy obscurity as the noonday" (lviii. 10); "Darkness shall cover the earth, and gross darkness the people, but the Lord shall arise upon thee, and His glory shall be seen upon thee" (lx. 2).

And, indeed, in the spiritual light which is sown for the righteous, and the obscuration of the judgment of the impure, this miracle is ever reproduced.

The history of Menephtah is that of a mean and cowardly prince. Dreams forbade him to share the perils of his army; a prophecy induced him to submit to exile, until his firstborn was of age to recover his dominions for him; and all we know of him is admirably suited to the character represented in this narrative. He will now submit once more, and this time every one shall go; yet he cannot make a frank concession: the flocks and herds (most valuable after the ravages of the murrain and the hail) must remain as a hostage for their return. But Moses is inflexible: not a hoof shall be left behind; and then the frenzy of a baffled autocrat breaks out into wild menaces; "Get thee from me; take heed to thyself; see my face no more; for in the day thou seest my face thou shalt die." The assent of Moses was grim: the rupture was complete. And when they once more met, it was the king that had changed his purpose, and on his face, not that of Moses, was the pallor of impending death.

In the conduct of the prophet, all through these stormy scenes, we see the difference between a meek spirit and a craven one. He was always ready to intercede; he never "reviles the ruler," nor transgresses the limits of courtesy toward his superior in rank; and yet he never falters, nor compromises, nor fails to represent worthily the awful Power he represents.

In the series of sharp contrasts, all the true dignity is with the servant of God, all the meanness and the shame with the proud king, who begins by insulting him, goes on to impose on him, and ends by the most ignominious of surrenders, crowned with the most abortive of treacheries and the most abject of defeats.

CHAPTER XI.

THE LAST PLAGUE ANNOUNCED.

xi. 1-10.

THE eleventh chapter is, strictly speaking, a supplement to the tenth: the first verses speak, as if in parenthesis, of a revelation made before the ninth plague, but held over to be mentioned in connection with the last, which it now announces; and the conversation with Pharaoh is a continuation of the same in which they mutually resolved to see each other's face no more. To account for the confidence of Moses, we are now told that God had revealed to him the close approach of the final blow, so long foreseen. In spite of seeming delays, the hour of the promise had arrived; in spite of his long reluctance, the king should even thrust them out; and then the order and discipline of their retreat would exhibit the advantages gained by expectation, by promises ofttimes disappointed, but always, like a false alarm which tries the readiness of a garrison, exhibiting the weak points in their organisation, and carrying their preparations farther.

The command given already to the women (iii. 22) is now extended to them all—that they should ask of the terror-stricken people such portable things as, however precious, poorly requited their generations of unpaid and cruel toil. (It has been already shown that the word absurdly rendered " borrow" means to ask ; and is the same as when Sisera *asked* water and Jael gave him milk, and when Solomon *asked* wisdom, and did not *ask* long life, neither *asked* riches, neither *asked* the life of his enemies.) They were now to claim such wages as they could carry off, and thus the pride of Egypt was presently dedicated to construct and beautify the tabernacle of Jehovah. We read that the people found favour with the Egyptians, who were doubtless overjoyed to come to any sort of terms with them ; " moreover the man Moses was very great in the land of Egypt, in the sight of Pharaoh's servants, and in the sight of the people." This is no unbecoming vaunt : it speaks only of the high place he held, as God's deputy and herald ; and this tone of keen appreciation of the rank conceded him, compared with the utter absence of any insistence upon any action of his own, is evidence much rather of the authenticity of the work than the reverse.

By these demands expectation and faith were intensified ; while the tidings of such confidence on one side, and such tame submission on the other, goes far to explain the suspicions and the rage of Pharaoh.

With this the narrative is resumed. Moses had said, "Thou shalt see my face no more." Now he adds, "Thus saith Jehovah, About midnight" (but not on that same night, since four days of preparation for the passover were yet to come) "I will go out into the midst of Egypt." This, then, was the meaning of his ready consent to be seen no more : Jehovah Himself, Who had dealt so dreadfully with them through other hands, was now Himself to come. "And all the firstborn of Egypt shall die," from the firstborn and viceroy of the king to the firstborn of the meanest of women, and even of the cattle in their stalls. (It is surely a remarkable coincidence that Menephtah's heroic son did actually sit upon his throne, that inscriptions engraven during his life exhibit his name in the royal cartouche, but that he perished early, and long before his father.) And the wail of demonstrative Oriental agony should be such as never was heard before. But the children of Israel should be distinguished and protected by their God. And all these courtiers should come and bow down before Moses (who even then has the good feeling not to include the king himself in this abasement), and instead of Pharaoh's insulting "Get thee from me—see my face no more," they should pray him saying, "Go hence, thou and thy people that follow thee." And remembering the abject entreaties, the infatuated treacheries, and now this crowning insult, he went out from Pharaoh in hot anger. He was angry and sinned not.

The ninth and tenth verses are a kind of summary: the appeals to Pharaoh are all over, and henceforth we shall find Moses preparing his own followers for their exodus. "And the Lord (had) said unto Moses, Pharaoh will not hearken unto you, that My wonders may be multiplied in the land of Egypt. And Moses and Aaron did all these wonders before Pharaoh; and the Lord made strong Pharaoh's heart, and he did not let the children of Israel go out of his land."

In the Gospel of St. John there comes just such a period. The record of miracle and controversy is at an end, and Jesus withdraws into the bosom of His intimate circle. It is scarcely possible that the evangelist was unconscious of the influence of this passage when he wrote: "But though He had done so many signs before them, yet they believed not on Him, that the word of Isaiah the prophet might be fulfilled which he spoke, Lord, who hath believed our report? . . . For this cause they could not believe, because that Isaiah said again, He hath blinded their eyes and hardened their heart, lest they should see with their eyes and perceive with their heart, and should turn, and I should heal them" (John xii. 37-40).

This is the tragedy of Egypt repeated in Israel; and the fact that the chosen seed is now the reprobate suffices, if any doubt remain, to prove that reprobation itself was not caprice, but retribution.

CHAPTER XII.

THE PASSOVER.

xii. 1-28.

WE have now reached the birthday of the great Hebrew nation, and with it the first national institution, the feast of passover, which is also the first sacrifice of directly Divine institution, the earliest precept of the Hebrew legislation, and the only one given in Egypt.

The Jews had by this time learned to feel that they were a nation, if it were only through the struggle between their champion and the head of the greatest nation in the world. And the first aspect in which the feast of passover presents itself is that of a national commemoration.

This day was to be unto them the beginning of months; and in the change of their calendar to celebrate their emancipation, the device was anticipated by which France endeavoured to glorify the Revolution. All their reckoning was to look back to this signal event. "And this day shall be unto you for a memorial, and ye shall keep it for a feast unto the Lord; throughout your generations ye shall keep it a feast by an ordinance for ever" (xii. 14). "It shall be for a sign unto thee upon thine hand, and for a memorial between thine eyes, that the law of the Lord may be in thy mouth, for with a strong hand hath the Lord brought thee out of Egypt. Thou shalt therefore keep this ordinance in its season from year to year" (xiii. 9, 10).

Now for the first time we read of "the congregation of Israel" (xii. 3, 6), which was an assembly of the people represented by their elders (as may be seen by comparing the third verse with the twenty-first); and thus we discover that the "heads of houses" have been drawn into a larger unity. The clans are knit together into a nation.

Accordingly, the feast might not be celebrated by any solitary man. Companionship was vital to it. At every table one animal, complete and undissevered, should give to the feast a unity of sentiment; and as many should gather around as were likely to leave none of it uneaten. Neither might any of it be reserved to supply a hasty ration amid the confusion of the predicted march. The feast was to be one complete event, whole and perfect as the unity which it expressed. The very notion of a people is that of "community" in responsibilities, joys, and labours; and the solemn law by virtue of which, at this same hour, one blow will fall upon all Egypt, must now be accepted by Israel. Therefore loneliness at the feast of Passover is by the law, as well as in idea, impossible to any Jew. Every one can see the connection between this festival of unity and another, of which it is written, "We, being many, are one body, one loaf, for we are all partakers of that one loaf."

Now, the sentiment of nationality may so assert itself, like all exaggerated sentiments, as to assail others equally precious. In this century we have seen a revival of the Spartan theories which sacrificed the family to the state. Socialism and the *phalanstère* have proposed to do by public organisation, with the force of law, what natural instinct teaches us to leave to domestic influences. It is therefore worthy of notice that, as the chosen nation is carefully traced by revelation back to a holy family, so the national festival did not ignore the family tie, but consecrated it. The feast was to be eaten "according to their fathers' houses"; if a family were too small, it was to the "neighbour next unto his house" that each should turn for co-operation; and the patriotic celebration was to live on from age to age by the instruction which parents should carefully give their children (xii. 3, 26, xiii. 8).

The first ordinance of the Jewish religion was a domestic service. And this arrangement is divinely wise. Never was a nation truly prosperous or permanently strong which did not cherish the sanctities of home. Ancient Rome failed to resist the barbarians, not because her discipline had degenerated, but because evil habits in the home had ruined her population. The same is notoriously true of at least one great nation to-day. History is the sieve of God, in which He continually severs the chaff from the grain of nations, preserving what is temperate and pure and calm, and therefore valorous and wise.

In studying the institution of the Passover, with its profound typical analogies, we must not overlook the simple and obvious fact that God built His nation upon families, and bade their great national institution draw the members of each home together.

The national character of the feast is shown further because no Egyptian family escaped the blow. Opportunities had been given to them to evade some of the previous plagues. When the hail was announced, "he that feared the word of the Lord among the servants of Pharaoh made his servants and his cattle flee into the house"; and this renders the national solidarity, the partnership even of the innocent in the penalties of a people's guilt, the 'community' of a nation, more apparent now. There was not a house where there was not one dead. The mixed multitude which came up with Israel came not because they had shared his exemptions, but because they dared not stay. It was an object-lesson given to Israel, which might have warned all his generations.

And if there is hideous vice in our own land to-day, or if the contrasts of poverty and wealth are so extreme that humanity is shocked by so much luxury insulting so much squalor,—if in any respect we feel that our own land, considering its supreme advantages, merits the wrath of God for its unworthiness,—then we have to fear and strive, not through public spirit alone, but as knowing that the chastisement of nations falls upon the corporate whole, upon us and upon our children.

But if the feast of the Passover was a commemoration, it also claims to be a sacrifice, and the first sacrifice which was Divinely founded and directed.

This brings us face to face with the great question, What is the doctrine which lies at the heart of the great institution of sacrifice?

We are not free to confine its meaning altogether to that which was visible at the time. This would contradict the whole doctrine of development, the intention of God that Christianity should blossom from the bud of Judaism, and the explicit assertion that the prophets were made aware that the full meaning and the date of what they uttered was reserved for the instruction of a later period (1 Peter i. 12).

But neither may we overlook the first palpable significance of any institution. Sacrifices never could have been devised to be a blind and empty pantomime to whole generations, for the benefit of their successors. Still less can one who believes in a genuine revelation to Moses suppose that their primary meaning was a false one, given in order that some truth might afterwards develop out of it.

What, then, might a pious and well-instructed Israelite discern beneath the surface of this institution?

To this question there have been many discordant answers, and the variance is by no means confined to unbelieving critics. Thus, a distinguished living expositor says in connection with the Paschal institution, "We speak not of blood as it is commonly understood, but of blood as the life, the love, the heart,—the whole quality of Deity." But it must be answered that Deity is the last suggestion which blood would convey to a Jewish mind: distinctly it is creature-life that it expresses; and the New Testament commentators make it plain that no other notion had even then evolved itself: they think of the offering of the Body of Jesus Christ, not of His Deity.* Neither of this feast, nor of that which the gospel of Jesus has evolved from it, can we find the solution by forgetting that the elements of the problem are, not deity, but a Body and Blood.

But when we approach the theories of rationalistic thinkers, we find a perfect chaos of rival speculations.

We are told that the Hebrew feasts were really agricultural—"Harvest festivals," and that the epithet Passover had its origin in the passage of the sun into Aries. But this great festival had a very secondary

---

* Though of course the Person Whose Body was thus offered is Divine (Acts xx. 28), and this gives inestimable value to the offering.

and subordinate connection with harvest (only the waving of a sheaf upon the second day) while the older calendar which was displaced to do it honour was truly agricultural, as may still be seen by the phrase, "The feast of ingathering *at the end of the year*, when thou gatherest in thy labours out of the field" (Exod. xxiii. 16).

In dealing with unbelief we must look at things from the unbelieving angle of vision. No sceptical theory has any right to invoke for its help a special and differentiating quality in Hebrew thought. Reject the supernatural, and the Jewish religion is only one among a number of similar creations of the mind of man "moving about in worlds unrecognised." And therefore we must ask, What notions of sacrifice were entertained, all around, when the Hebrew creed was forming itself?

Now, we read that "in the early days . . . a sacrifice was a meal. . . . Year after year, the return of vintage, corn-harvest, and sheep-shearing brought together the members of the household to eat and drink in the presence of Jehovah. . . . When an honoured guest arrives there is slaughtered for him a calf, not without an offering of the blood and fat to the Deity" (Wellhausen, *Israel*, p. 76). Of the sense of sin and propitiation "the ancient sacrifices present few traces. . . . An underlying reference of sacrifice to sin, speaking generally, was entirely absent. The ancient sacrifices were wholly of a joyous nature—a merrymaking before Jehovah with music" (*ibid.*, p. 81).

We are at once confronted by the question, Where did the Jewish nation come by such a friendly conception of their deity? They had come out of Egypt, where human sacrifices were not rare. They had settled in Palestine, where such idyllic notions must have been as strange as in modern Ashantee. And we are told that human sacrifices (such as that of Isaac and of Jephthah's daughter) belong to this older period (p. 69). Are *they* joyous and festive? are they not an endeavour, by the offering up of something precious, to reconcile a Being Who is estranged? With our knowledge of what existed in Israel in the period confessed to be historical, and of the meaning of sacrifices all around in the period supposed to be mythical, and with the admission that human sacrifices must be taken into account, it is startling to be asked to believe that Hebrew sacrifices, with all their solemn import and all their freight of Christian symbolism, were originally no more than a gift to the Deity of a part of some happy banquet.

It is quite plain that no such theory can be reconciled with the story of the first passover. And accordingly this is declared to be non-historical, and to have originated in the time of the later kings. The offering of the firstborn is only "the expression of thankfulness to the Deity for fruitful flocks and herds. If claim is also laid to the human firstborn, this is merely a later generalisation" (Wellhausen, p. 88).*

But this claim is by no means the only stumbling-block in the way of the theory, serious a stumbling-

---

* Here the sceptical theorists are widely divided among themselves. Kuenen has discussed this whole theory, and rejected it as "irreconcilable with what the Old Testament itself asserts in justification of this sacrifice." And he is driven to connect it with the notion of atonement. "Jahveh appears as a severe being who must be propitiated with sacrifices." He has therefore to introduce the notion of human sacrifice, in order to get rid of the connection with the penal death of the Egyptians, and of the miraculous, which this example would establish. (*Religion of Israel*, Eng. Trans., i., 239, 240.)

block though it be. How came the bright festival to be spoiled by bitter herbs and "bread of affliction"? Is it natural that a merry feast should grow more austere as time elapses? Do we not find it hard enough to prevent the most sacred festivals from reversing the supposed process, and degenerating into revels? And is not this the universal experience, from San Francisco to Bombay? Why was' the mandate given to sprinkle the door of every house with blood, if the story originated after the feast had been centralised in Jerusalem, when, in fact, this precept had to be set aside as impracticable, their homes being at a distance? Why, again, were they bidden to slaughter the lamb "between the two evenings" (Exod. xii. 6)—that is to say, between sunset and the fading out of the light—unless the story was written long before such numbers had to be dealt with that the priests began to slaughter early in the afternoon, and continued until night? Why did the narrative set forth that every man might slaughter for his own house (a custom which still existed in the time of Hezekiah, when the Levites only slaughtered "the passovers" for those who were not ceremonially clean. 2 Chron. xxx. 17), if there were no stout and strong historical foundation for the older method?

Stranger still, why was the original command invented, that the lamb should be chosen and separated four days before the feast? There is no trace of any intention that this precept should apply to the first passover alone. It is somewhat unexpected there, interrupting the hurry and movement of the narrative with an interval of quiet expectation, not otherwise hinted at, which we comprehend and value when discovered, rather than anticipate in advance. It is the very last circumstance which the Priestly Code would have invented, when the time which could be conveniently spent upon a pilgrimage was too brief to suffer the custom to be perpetuated. The selection of the lamb upon the tenth day, the slaying of it at home, the striking of the blood upon the door, and the use of hyssop, as in other sacrifices, with which to sprinkle it, whether upon door or altar; the eating of the feast standing, with staff in hand and girded loins; the application only to one day of the precept to eat no leavened bread, and the sharing in the feast by all, without regard to ceremonial defilement,—all these are cardinal differences between the first passover and later ones. Can we be blind to their significance? Even a drastic revision of the story, such as some have fancied, would certainly have expunged every divergence upon points so capital as these. Nor could any evidence of the antiquity of the institution be clearer than its existence in a form, the details of which have had to be so boldly modified under the pressure of the exigencies of the later time.

Taking, then, the narrative as it stands, we place ourselves by an effort of the historical imagination among those to whom Moses gave his instructions, and ask what emotions are excited as we listen.

Certainly no light and joyous feeling that we are going to celebrate a feast, and share our good things with our deity. Nay, but an alarmed surprise. Hitherto, among the admonitory and preliminary plagues of Egypt, Israel had enjoyed a painless and unbought exemption. The murrain had not slain their cattle, nor the locusts devoured their land, nor the darkness obscured their dwellings. Such admonitions they needed not. But now the judgment itself is impending, and they learn that they, like the Egyptians whom they have begun to despise, are in danger from the destroying angel. The first paschal feast was eaten by no man with a light heart. Each listened for the rustling of awful wings, and grew cold, as under the eyes of the death which was, even then, scrutinising his lintels and his doorposts.

And this would set him thinking that even a gracious God, Who had "come down" to save him from his tyrants, discerned in him grave reasons for displeasure, since his acceptance, while others died, was not of course. His own conscience would then quickly tell him what some at least of those reasons were.

But he would also learn that the exemption which he did not possess by right (although a son of Abraham) he might obtain through grace. The goodness of God did not pronounce him safe, but it pointed out to him a way of salvation. He would scarcely observe, so entirely was it a matter of course, that this way must be of God's appointment and not of his own invention —that if he devised much more costly, elaborate and imposing ceremonies to replace those which Moses taught him, he would perish like any Egyptian who devised nothing, but simply cowered under the shadow of the impending doom.

Nor was the salvation without price. It was not a prayer nor a fast which bought it, but a life. The conviction that a redemption was necessary if God should be at once just and a justifier of the ungodly sprang neither from a later hairsplitting logic, nor from a methodising theological science; it really lay upon the very surface of this and every offering for sin, as distinguished from those offerings which expressed the gratitude of the accepted.

We have not far to search for evidence that the lamb was really regarded as a substitute and ransom. The assertion is part and parcel of the narrative itself. For, in commemoration of this deliverance, every firstborn of Israel, whether of man or beast, was set apart unto the Lord. The words are, "Thou shall cause to PASS OVER unto the Lord all that openeth the womb, and every firstling which thou hast that cometh of a beast; the males shall be the Lord's" (xiii. 12). What, then, should be done with the firstborn of a creature unfit for sacrifice? It should be replaced by a clean offering, and then it was said to be redeemed. Substitution or death was the inexorable rule. "Every firstborn of an ass thou shalt redeem with a lamb, and if thou wilt not redeem it, then thou shalt break its neck." The meaning of this injunction is unmistakable. But it applies also to man: "All thy firstborn of man among thy sons thou shalt redeem." And when their sons should ask "What meaneth this?" they were to explain that when Pharaoh hardened himself against letting them go from Egypt, "the Lord slew all the firstborn in the land; . . . therefore I sacrifice to the Lord all that openeth the womb being males; but all the firstborn of my sons I redeem" (xiii. 12-15).

Words could not more plainly assert that the lives of the firstborn of Israel were forfeited, that they were bought back by the substitution of another creature, which died instead, and that the transaction answered to the Passover ("thou shalt cause to pass over unto the Lord"). Presently the tribe of Levi was taken "instead of all the firstborn of the children of Israel." But since there were two hundred and seventy-three of such firstborn children over and above the number of the Levites, it became necessary to "redeem" these; and this was actually done by a cash payment of five shekels apiece. Of this payment the same phrase is used: it is "redemption-money"—the money wherewith the odd number of them is redeemed (Num. iii. 44-51).

The question at present is not whether modern taste approves of all this, or resents it: we are simply inquiring whether an ancient Jew was taught to think of the lamb as offered in his stead.

And now let it be observed that this idea has sunk deep into all the literature of Palestine. The Jews are not so much the beloved of Jehovah as His redeemed —"Thy people whom Thou hast redeemed" (1 Chron. xvii. 21). In fresh troubles the prayer is, "Redeem Israel, O Lord" (Ps. xxv. 22), and the same word is often used where we have ignored the allusion and rendered it "*Deliver* me because of mine enemies . . . *deliver* me from the oppression of men" (Ps. lxix. 18, cxix. 134). And the future troubles are to end in a deliverance of the same kind: "The *ransomed* of the Lord shall return and come with singing unto Zion" (Isa. xxxv. 10, li. 11); and at the last "I will *ransom* them from the power of the grave" (Hos. xiii. 14). In all these places, the word is the same as in this narrative.

It is not too much to say that if modern theology were not affected by this ancient problem, if we regarded the creed of the Hebrews simply as we look at the mythologies of other peoples, there would be no more doubt that the early Jews believed in propitiatory sacrifice than that Phœnicians did. We should simply admire the purity, the absence of cruel and degrading accessories, with which this most perilous and yet humbling and admonitory doctrine was held in Israel.

The Christian applications of this doctrine must be considered along with the whole question of the typical character of the history. But it is not now premature to add, that even in the Old Testament there is abundant evidence that the types were semi-transparent, and behind them something greater was discerned, so that after it was written "Bring no more vain oblations," Isaiah could exclaim, "The Lord hath laid on Him the iniquity of us all. He was led as a lamb to the slaughter. When Thou shalt make His soul a trespass-offering He shall see His seed" (Isa. i. 13, liii. 6, 7, 10). And the full power of this last verse will only be felt when we remember the statement made elsewhere of the principle which underlay the sacrifices: "the life (*or* soul) of the flesh is in the blood, and I have given it to you upon the altar to make atonement for your souls; for it is the blood that maketh atonement by reason of the life" (*or* "soul"— Lev. xvii. 11, R.V.) It is even startling to read the two verses together: "Thou shalt make His soul a trespass-offering;" "The blood maketh atonement by reason of the soul . . . the soul of the flesh is in the blood."*

It is still more impressive to remember that a Servant of Jehovah has actually arisen in Whom this doctrine has assumed a form acceptable to the best and holiest intellects and consciences of ages and civilisations widely remote from that in which it was conceived.

---

* The astonishing significance of this declaration would only be deepened if we accepted the theories now so fashionable, and believed that the later passage in Isaiah was the fruit of a period when the full-blown Priestly Code was in process of development out of "the small body of legislation contained in Lev. xvii.—xxvi." What a strange time for such a spiritual application of sacrificial language!

Another doctrine preached by the passover to every Jew was that he must be a worker together with God, must himself use what the Lord pointed out, and his own lintels and doorposts must openly exhibit the fact that he laid claim to the benefit of the institution of the Lord Jehovah's passover. With what strange feelings, upon the morrow, did the orphaned people of Egypt discover the stain of blood on the forsaken houses of all their emancipated slaves!

The lamb having been offered up to God, a new stage in the symbolism is entered upon. The body of the sacrifice, as well as the blood, is His: "Ye shall eat it in haste, it is the Lord's passover" (ver. 11). Instead of being a feast of theirs, which they share with Him, it is an offering of which, when the blood has been sprinkled on the doors, He permits His people, now accepted and favoured, to partake. They are His guests; and therefore He prescribes all the manner of their eating, the attitude so expressive of haste, and the unleavened "bread of affliction" and bitter herbs, which told that the object of this feast was not the indulgence of the flesh but the edification of the spirit, "a feast unto the Lord."

And in the strength of this meat they are launched upon their new career, freemen, pilgrims of God, from Egyptian bondage to a Promised Land.

It is now time to examine the chapter in more detail, and gather up such points as the preceding discussion has not reached.

(Ver. 1.) The opening words, "Jehovah spake unto Moses and Aaron in the land of Egypt," have all the appearance of opening a separate document, and suggest, with certain other evidence, the notion of a fragment written very shortly after the event, and afterwards incorporated into the present narrative. And they are, in the same degree, favourable to the authenticity of the book.

(Ver. 2.) The commandment to link their emancipation with a festival, and with the calendar, is the earliest example and the sufficient vindication of sacred festivals, which, even yet, some persons consider to be superstitious and judaical. But it is a strange doctrine that the Passover deserved honour better than Easter does, or that there is anything more servile and unchristian in celebrating the birth of all the hopes of all mankind than in commemorating one's own birth.

(Ver. 5.) The selection of a lamb for a sacrifice so quickly became universal, that there is no trace anywhere of the use of a kid in place of it. The alternative is therefore an indication of antiquity, while the qualities required—innocent youth and the absence of blemish, were sure to suggest a typical significance. For, if they were merely to enhance its value, why not choose a costlier animal?

Various meanings have been discovered in the four days during which it was reserved; but perhaps the true object was to give time for deliberation, for the solemnity and import of the institution to fill the minds of the people; time also for preparation, since the night itself was one of extreme haste, and prompt action can only be obtained by leisurely anticipation. We have Scriptural authority for applying it to the Antitype, Who also was foredoomed, "the Lamb slain from the foundation of the world" (Rev. xiii. 8).

But now it has to be observed that throughout the poetic literature the people is taught to think of itself as a flock of sheep. "Thou leddest Thy people like a flock by the hand of Moses and Aaron" (Ps. lxxvii. 20); "We are Thy people and the sheep of Thy pasture" (Ps. lxxix. 13); "All we like sheep have gone astray" (Isa. liii. 6); "Ye, O My sheep, the sheep of My pasture, are men" (Ezek. xxxiv. 31); "The Lord of hosts hath visited His flock" (Zech. x. 3). All such language would make more easy the conception that what replaced the forfeited life was in some sense, figuratively, in the religious idea, a kindred victim. One who offered a lamb as his substitute sang "The Lord is my shepherd." "I have gone astray like a lost sheep" (Ps. xxiii. 1, cxix. 176).

(Ver. 3, 6.) Very instructive it is that this first sacrifice of Judaism could be offered by all the heads of houses. We have seen that the Levites were presently put into the place of the eldest son, but also that this function was exercised down to the time of Hezekiah by all who were ceremonially clean, whereas the opposite holds good, immediately afterwards, in the great passover of Josiah (2 Chron. xxx. 17, xxxv. 11).

It is impossible that this incongruity could be devised, for the sake of plausibility, in a narrative which rested on no solid basis. It goes far to establish what has been so anxiously denied—the reality of the centralised worship in the time of Hezekiah. And it also establishes the great doctrine that priesthood was held not by a superior caste, but on behalf of the whole nation, in whom it was theoretically vested, and for whom the priest acted, so that they were "a nation of priests."

(Ver. 8.) The use of unleavened bread is distinctly said to be in commemoration of their haste—"for thou camest out of Egypt in haste" (Deut. xvi. 3)—but it does not follow that they were forced by haste to eat their bread unleavened at the first. It was quite as easy to prepare leavened bread as to provide the paschal lamb four days previously.

We may therefore seek for some further explanation, and this we find in the same verse in Deuteronomy, in the expression " bread of affliction." They were to receive the meat of passover with a reproachful sense of their unworthiness: humbly, with bread of affliction and with bitter herbs.

Moreover, we learn from St. Paul that unleavened bread represents simplicity and truth; and our Lord spoke of the leaven of the Pharisees and of Herod (Mark viii. 15). And this is not only because leaven was supposed to be of the same nature as corruption. We ourselves always mean something unworthy when we speak of *mixed* motives, possible though it be to act from two motives, both of them high-minded. Now, leaven represents mixture in its most subtle and penetrating form.

The paschal feast did not express any such luxurious and sentimental religionism as finds in the story of the cross an easy joy, or even a delicate and pleasing stimulus for the softer emotions, "a very lovely song of one that hath a pleasant voice, and playeth well on an instrument." No, it has vigour and nourishment for those who truly hunger, but its bread is unfermented, and it must be eaten with bitter herbs.

(Ver. 9.) Many Jewish sacrifices were "sodden," but this had to be roast with fire. It may have been to represent suffering that this was enjoined. But it comes to us along with a command to consume all the flesh, reserving none and rejecting none. Now, though boiling does not mutilate, it dissipates; a certain amount of tissue is lost, more is relaxed, and its cohesion rendered feeble; and so the duty of its complete reception is accentuated by the words "not sodden at all with water." Nor should it be a barbarous feast, such as many idolatries encouraged: true religion civilises; "eat not of it at all raw."

(Ver. 10.) Nor should any of it be left until the morning. At the first celebration, with a hasty exodus impending, this would have involved exposure to profanation. In later times it might have involved superstitious abuses. And therefore the same rule is laid down which the Church of England has carried on for the same reasons into the Communion feast—that all must be consumed. Nor can we fail to see an ideal fitness in the precept. Of the gift of God we may not select what gratifies our taste or commends itself to our desires; all is good; all must be accepted; a partial reception of His grace is no valid reception at all.

(Ver. 12.) In describing the coming wrath, we understand the inclusion equally of innocent and guilty men, because it is thus that all national vengeance operates; and we receive the benefits of corporate life at the cost, often heavy, of its penalties. The animal world also has to suffer with us; the whole creation groaneth together now, and all expects together the benefit of our adoption hereafter. But what were the judgments against the idols of Egypt, which this verse predicts, and another (Num. xxxiii. 4) declares to be accomplished? They doubtless consisted chiefly in the destruction of sacred animals, from the beetle and the frog to the holy ox of Apis—from the cat, the monkey, and the dog, to the lion, the hippopotamus, and the crocodile. In their overthrow a blow was dealt which shook the whole system to its foundation; for how could the same confidence be felt in sacred images when all the sacred beasts had once been slain by a rival invisible Spiritual Being! And more is implied than that they should share the common desolation: the text says plainly, of men and beasts the firstborn must die, but all of these. The difference in the phrase is obvious and indisputable; and in its fulfilment all Egypt saw the act of a hostile and victorious deity.

(Ver. 13.) "And the blood shall be to you for a token upon the houses where ye are." That it was a token to the destroying angel we see plainly; but why *to them?* Is it enough to explain the assertion, with some, as meaning, upon their behalf? Rather let us say that the publicity, the exhibition upon their doorposts of the sacrifice offered within, was not to inform and guide the angel, but to edify the people. They should perform an open act of faith. Their houses should be visibly set apart. "With the mouth confession" (of faith) "is made unto salvation," unto that deliverance from a hundred evasions and equivocations, and as many inward doubts and hesitations, which comes when any decisive act is done, when the die is cast and the Rubicon crossed. A similar effect upon the mind, calming and steadying it, was produced when the Israelite carried out the blood of the lamb, and by sprinkling it upon the doorpost formally claimed his exemption, and returned with the consciousness that between him and the imminent death a visible barrier interposed itself.

Will any one deny that a similar help is offered to

us of the later Church in our many opportunities of avowing a fixed and personal belief? Whoever refuses to comply with an unholy custom because he belongs to Christ, whoever joins heartily in worship at the cost of making himself remarkable, whoever nerves himself to kneel at the Holy Table although he feels himself unworthy, that man has broken through many snares; he has gained assurance that his choice of God is a reality: he has shown his flag; and this public avowal is not only a sign to others, but also a token to himself.

But this is only half the doctrine of this action. What he should thus openly avow was his trust (as we have shown) in atoning blood.

And in the day of our peril what shall be our reliance? That our doors are trodden by orthodox visitors only? that the lintels are clean, and the inhabitants temperate and pure? or that the Blood of Christ has cleansed our conscience?

Therefore (ver. 22) the blood was sprinkled with hyssop, of which the light and elastic sprays were admirably suited for such use, but which was reserved in the Law for those sacrifices which expiated sin (Lev. xiv. 49; Num. xix. 18, 19). And therefore also none should go forth out of his house until the morning, for we are not to content ourselves with having once invoked the shelter of God: we are to abide under its protection while danger lasts.

And (ver. 23) upon the condition of this marking of their doorposts the Lord should *pass over* their houses. The phrase is noteworthy, because it recurs throughout the narrative, being employed nine times in this chapter; and because the same word is found in Isaiah, again in contrast with the ruin of others, and with an interesting and beautiful expansion of the hovering poised notion which belongs to the word.*

Repeated commandments are given to parents to teach the meaning of this institution to their children, (xii. 26, xiii. 8). And there is something almost cynical in the notion of a later mythologist devising this appeal to a tradition which had no existence at all; enrolling, in support of his new institutions, the testimony (which had never been borne) of fathers who had never taught any story of the kind.

On the other hand, there is something idyllic and beautiful in the minute instruction given to the heads of families to teach their children, and in the simple words put into their mouths, "It is because of that which the Lord did for me when I came forth out of Egypt." It carries us forward to these weary days when children scarcely see the face of one who goes out to labour before they are awake, and returns exhausted when their day is over, and who himself too often needs the most elementary instruction, these heartless days when the teaching of religion devolves, in thousands of families, upon the stranger who instructs, for one hour in the week, a class in Sunday-school. The contrast is not reassuring.

When all these instructions were given to Israel, the people bowed their heads and worshipped. The bones of most of them were doomed to whiten in the wilderness. They perished by serpents and by "the

---

* So that it is used equally of the slow action of the lame, and of the lingering movements of the false prophets when there was none to answer (2 Sam. iv. 4; 1 Kings xviii. 26). " The Lord of Hosts shall come down to fight upon Mount Zion. . . . As birds flying, so will the Lord of Hosts protect Jerusalem; He will PASS OVER and preserve it" (Isa. xxxi. 4, 5).

destroyer"; they fell in one day three-and-twenty thousand, because they were discontented and rebellious and unholy. And yet they could adore the gracious Giver of promises and Slayer of foes. They would not obey, but they were quite ready to accept benefits, to experience deliverance, to become the favourites of heaven, to march to Palestine. So are too many fain to be made happy, to find peace, to taste the good word of God and the powers of the age to come, to go to heaven. But they will not take up a cross. They will murmur if the well is bitter, if they have no flesh but only angels' food, if the goodly land is defended by powerful enemies.

On these terms, they cannot be Christ's disciples.

It is apparently the mention of a mixed multitude, who came with Israel out of Egypt, which suggests the insertion, in a separate and dislocated paragraph, of the law of the passover concerning strangers (vers. 38, 43-49).

An alien was not to eat thereof: it belonged especially to the covenant people. But who was a stranger? A slave should be circumcised and eat thereof; for it was one of the benignant provisions of the law that there should not be added, to the many severities of his condition, any religious disabilities. The time would come when all nations should be blessed in the seed of Abraham. In that day the poor would receive a special beatitude; and in the meantime, as the first indication of catholicity beneath the surface of an exclusive ritual, it was announced, foremost among those who should be welcomed within the fold, that a slave should be circumcised and eat the passover.

And if a sojourner desired to eat thereof, he should

be mindful of his domestic obligations: all his males should be circumcised along with him, and then his disabilities were at an end. Surely we can see in these provisions the germ of the broader and more generous welcome which Christ offers to the world. Let it be added that this admission of strangers had been already implied at verse 19; while every form of coercion was prohibited by the words "a sojourner and a hired servant shall not eat of it," in verse 45.

THE TENTH PLAGUE.

xii. 29-36.

And now the blow fell. Infants grew cold in their mothers' arms; ripe statesmen and crafty priests lost breath as they reposed: the wisest, the strongest and the most hopeful of the nation were blotted out at once, for the firstborn of a population is its flower.

Pharaoh Menephtah had only reached the throne by the death of two elder brethren, and therefore history confirms the assertion that he "rose up," when the firstborn were dead; but it also justifies the statement that his firstborn died, for the gallant and promising youth who had reconquered for him his lost territories, and who actually shared his rule and "sat upon the throne," Menephtah Seti, is now shown to have died early, and never to have held an independent sceptre.

We can imagine the scene. Suspense and terror must have been wide spread; for the former plagues had given authority to the more dreadful threat, the fulfilment of which was now to be expected, since all negotiations between Moses and Pharaoh had been formally broken off.

Strange and confident movements and doubtless

menacing expressions among the Hebrews would also make this night a fearful one, and there was little rest for "those who feared the Lord among the servants of Pharaoh." These, knowing where the danger lay, would watch their firstborn well, and when the ashy change came suddenly upon a blooming face, and they raised the wild cry of Eastern bereavement, then others awoke to the same misery. From remote villages and lonely hamlets the clamour of great populations was echoed back; and when, under midnight skies in which the strong wind of the morrow was already moaning, the awestruck people rushed into their temples, there the corpses of their animal deities glared at them with glassy eyes.

Thus the cup which they had made their slaves to drink was put in larger measure to their own lips at last, and not infants only were snatched away, but sons around whom years of tenderness had woven stronger ties; and the loss of their bondsmen, from which they feared so much national weakness, had to be endured along with a far deadlier drain of their own life-blood. The universal wail was bitter, and hopeless, and full of terror even more than woe; for they said, "We be all dead men." Without the consolation of ministering by sick beds, or the romance and gallant excitement of war, "there was not a house where there was not one dead," and this is said to give sharpness to the statement that there was a great cry in Egypt.

Then came such a moment as the Hebrew temperament keenly enjoyed, when "the sons of them that oppressed them came bending unto them, and all they that despised them bowed themselves down at the soles of their feet." Pharaoh sent at midnight to surrender everything that could possibly be demanded, and in his abject fear added, "and bless me also"; and the Egyptians were urgent on them to begone, and when they demanded the portable wealth of the land,—a poor ransom from a vanquished enemy, and a still poorer payment for generations of forced labour,— "the Lord gave them favour" (is there not a saturnine irony in the phrase?) "in the sight of the Egyptians, so that they let them have what they asked. And they spoiled the Egyptians."

By this analogy St. Augustine defended the use of heathen learning in defence of Christian truth. Clogged by superstitions, he said, it contained also liberal instruction, and truths even concerning God—"gold and silver which they did not themselves create, but dug out of the mines of God's providence, and misapplied. These we should reclaim, and apply to Christian use" (*De Doct. Chr.*, 60, 61).

And the main lesson of the story lies so plainly upon the surface that one scarcely needs to state it. What God requires *must* ultimately be done; and human resistance, however stubborn and protracted, will only make the result more painful and more signal at the last.

Now, every concern of our obscure daily lives comes under this law as surely as the actions of a Pharaoh.

THE EXODUS.

xii. 37-42.

The children of Israel journeyed from Rameses to Succoth. Already, at the outset of their journey, controversy has had much to say about their route. Much ingenuity has been expended upon the theory which brought their early journey along the Mediterranean coast, and made the overthrow of the Egyptians take place in "that Serbonian bog where armies whole have sunk." But it may fairly be assumed that this view was refuted even before the recent identification of the sites of Rameses and Pihahiroth rendered it untenable.

How came these trampled slaves, who could not call their lives their own, to possess the cattle which we read of as having escaped the murrain, and the number of which is here said to have been very great?

Just before Moses returned, and when the Pharaoh of the Exodus appears upon the scene, we are told that "their cry came up unto God, . . . and God heard their groaning, and God remembered His covenant . . . and God saw the children of Israel, and God took knowledge of them" (ii. 23).

May not this verse point to something unrecorded, some event before their final deliverance? The conjecture is a happy one that it refers to their share in the revolt of subject races which drove Menephtah for twelve years out of his northern territories. If so, there was time for a considerable return of prosperity; and the retention or forfeiture of their chattels when they were reconquered would depend very greatly upon circumstances unknown to us. At all events, this revolt is evidence, which is amply corroborated by history and the inscriptions, of the existence of just such a discontented and servile element in the population as the "mixed multitude" which came out with them repeatedly proved itself to be.

But here we come upon a problem of another kind. How long was Israel in the house of bondage? Can we rely upon the present Hebrew text, which says that "their sojourning which they sojourned in Egypt, was four hundred and thirty years. And it came to pass at the end of the four hundred and thirty years, even the selfsame day it came to pass, that all the hosts of the Lord came out of the land of Egypt" (xii. 40, 41).

Certain ancient versions have departed from this text. The Septuagint reads, "The sojourning of the children of Israel which they sojourned in Egypt and *in the land of Canaan*, was four hundred and thirty years"; and the Samaritan agrees with this, except that it has "the sojourning of the children of Israel and *of their fathers*." The question is, which reading is correct? Must we date the four hundred and thirty years from Abraham's arrival in Canaan, or from Jacob's descent into Egypt?

For the shorter period there are two strong arguments. The genealogies in the Pentateuch range from four persons to six beween Jacob and the Exodus, which number is quite unable to reach over four centuries. And St. Paul says of the covenant with Abraham that the law which came four hundred and thirty years after" (*i.e.* after the time of Abraham) "could not disannul it" (Gal. iii. 17).

This reference by St. Paul is not so decisive as it may appear, because he habitually quotes the Septuagint, even where he must have known that it deviates from the Hebrew, provided that the deviation does not compromise the matter in hand. Here, he was in nowise concerned with the chronology, and had no reason to perplex a Gentile church by correcting it. But it was a different matter with St. Stephen, arguing his case before the Hebrew council. And he quotes plainly and confidently the prediction that the seed of Abraham should be four hundred years in bondage, and that one nation should entreat them evil four hundred years (Acts vii. 6). Again, this is the clear intention of the words in Genesis (xv. 13). And as to the genealogies, we know them to have been cut down, so that seven names are omitted from that of Ezra, and three at least from that of our Lord Himself. Certainly when we consider the great population implied in an army of six hundred thousand adult men, we must admit that the longer period is inherently the more probable of the two. But we can only assert with confidence that just when their deliverance was due it was accomplished, and they who had come down a handful, and whom cruel oppression had striven to decimate, came forth, no undisciplined mob, but armies moving in organised and regulated detachments: "the Lord did bring the children of Israel forth by their hosts" (ver. 51). "And the children of Israel went up armed out of the land of Egypt" (xiii. 18).

CHAPTER XIII.

THE LAW OF THE FIRSTBORN.

xiii. 1.

MUCH that was said in the twelfth chapter is repeated in the thirteenth. And this repetition is clearly due to a formal rehearsal, made when all "their hosts" had mustered in Succoth after their first march; for Moses says, "Remember this day, in which ye came out" (ver. 3). Already it had been spoken of as a day much to be remembered, and for its perpetuation the ordinance of the Passover had been founded.

But now this charge is given as a fit prologue for the remarkable institution which follows—the consecration to God of all unblemished males who are the firstborn of their mothers—for such is the full statement of what is claimed.

In speaking to Moses the Lord says, "Sanctify unto Me all the firstborn . . . it is Mine." But Moses addressing the people advances gradually, and almost diplomatically. First he reminds them of their deliverance, and in so doing he employs a phrase which could only have been used at the exact stage when they were emancipated and yet upon Egyptian soil: "By strength of hand the Lord brought you out *from this place*" (ver. 3). Then he charges them not to forget their rescue, in the dangerous time of their prosperity, when the Lord shall have brought them into the land which He swore to give them; and he repeats the ordinance of unleavened bread. And it is only then that he proceeds to announce the permanent consecration of all their firstborn—the abiding doctrine that these, who naturally represent the nation, are for its unworthiness forfeited, and yet by the grace of God redeemed.

God, Who gave all and pardons all, demands a return, not as a tax which is levied for its own sake, but as a confession of dependence, and like the silk flag presented to the sovereign, on the anniversaries of the two greatest of English victories, by the descendants of the conquerors, who hold their estates upon that tenure. The firstborn, thus dedicated, should have formed a sacred class, a powerful element in Hebrew life enlisted on the side of God.

For these, as we have already seen, the Levites were afterwards substituted (Num. iii. 44), and there is perhaps some allusion to this change in the direction that "all the firstborn of man thou shalt redeem" (ver. 13). But yet the demand is stated too broadly and imperatively to belong to that later modification: it suits exactly the time to which it is attributed, before the tribe of Levi was substituted for the firstborn of all.

"They are Mine," said Jehovah, Who needed not, that night, to remind them what He had wrought the night before. It is for precisely the same reason, that St. Paul claims all souls for God: "Ye are not your own, ye are bought with a price; therefore glorify God with your bodies and with your spirits, which are God's."

And besides the general claim upon us all, each of us should feel, like the firstborn, that every special mercy is a call to special gratitude, to more earnest dedication. " I beseech you, by the mercies of God, that ye present your bodies a living sacrifice " (Rom. xii. 1).

There is a tone of exultant confidence in the words of Moses, very interesting and curious. He and his nation are breathing the free air at last. The deliverance that has been given makes all the promise that remains secure. As one who feels his pardon will surely not despair of heaven, so Moses twice over instructs the people what to do when God shall have kept the oath which He swore, and brought them into Canaan, into the land flowing with milk and honey. Then they must observe His passover. Then they must consecrate their firstborn.

And twice over this emancipator and law-giver, in the first flush of his success, impresses upon them the homely duty of teaching their households what God had done for them (vers. 8, 14; cf. xii. 26).

This, accordingly, the Psalmist learned, and in his turn transmitted. He heard with his ears and his fathers told him what God did in their days, in the days of old. And he told the generation to come the praises of Jehovah, and His strength, and His wondrous works (Ps. xliv. 1, lxxviii. 4).

But it is absurd to treat these verses, as Kuenen does, as evidence that the story is mere legend: " transmitted from mouth to mouth, it gradually lost its accuracy and precision, and adopted all sorts of foreign elements." To prove which, we are gravely referred to passages like this. (*Religion of Israel*, i. 22, Eng. Vers.) The duty of oral instruction is still acknowledged, but this does not prove that the narrative is still unwritten.

From the emphatic language in which Moses urged this double duty, too much forgotten still, of remembering and showing forth the goodness of God, sprang the curious custom of the wearing of phylacteries. But the Jews were not bidden to wear signs and frontlets: they were bidden to let hallowed memories be unto them in the place of such charms as they had seen the Egyptians wear, "for a sign unto thee, upon thine hand, and for a frontlet between thine eyes, that the law of the Lord may be in thy mouth" (ver. 9). Such language is frequent in the Old Testament, where mercy and truth should be bound around their necks; their fathers' commandments should be tied around their necks, bound on their fingers, written on their hearts; and Sion should clothe herself with her converts as an ornament, and gird them upon her as a bride doth (Prov. iii. 3, vi. 21, vii. 3; Isa. xlix. 18).

But human nature still finds the letter of many a commandment easier than the spirit, a ceremony than an obedient heart, penance than penitence, ashes on the forehead than a contrite spirit, and a phylactery than the gratitude and acknowledgment which ought to be unto us for a sign on the hand and a frontlet between the eyes.

We have already observed the connection between the thirteenth verse and the events of the previous night. But there is an interesting touch of nature in the words "the firstling of an ass thou shalt redeem with a lamb." It was afterwards rightly perceived that all unclean animals should follow the same rule; but why was only the ass mentioned? Plainly because those humble journeyers had no other beast of burden. Horses pursued them presently, but even the Egyptians of that period used them only in war. The trampled

Hebrews would not possess camels. And thus again, in the tenth commandment, when the stateliest of their cattle is specified, no beast of burden is named with it but the ass: "Thou shalt not covet . . . his ox nor his ass." It is an undesigned coincidence of real value; a phrase which would never have been devised by legislators of a later date; a frank and unconscious evidence of the genuineness of the story.

Some time before this, a new and fierce race, whose name declared them to be "emigrants," had thrust itself in among the tribes of Canaan—a race which was long to wage equal war with Israel, and not seldom to see his back turned in battle. They now held all the south of Palestine, from the brook of Egypt to Ekron (Josh. xv. 4, 47). And if Moses in the flush of his success had pushed on by the straight and easy route into the promised land, the first shock of combat with them would have been felt in a few weeks. But "God led them not by the way of the Philistines, though that was near, for God said, Lest peradventure the people repent them when they see war, and they return to Egypt" (ver. 17).

From this we learn two lessons. Why did not He, Who presently made strong the hearts of the Egyptians to plunge into the bed of the sea, make the hearts of His own people strong to defy the Philistines? The answer is a striking and solemn one. Neither God in the Old Testament, nor God manifested in the flesh, is ever recorded to have wrought any miracle of spiritual advancement or overthrow. Thus the Egyptians were but confirmed in their own choice: their decision was carried further. And even Saul of Tarsus was illuminated, not coerced: he might have disobeyed the heavenly vision. He was not an insincere man suddenly coerced into earnestness, nor a coward suddenly made brave. In the moral world, adequate means are always employed for the securing of desired effects. Love, gratitude, the sense of danger and of grace, are the powers which elevate characters. And persons who live in sensuality, fraud, or falsehood, hoping to be saved some day by a sort of miracle of grace, ought to ponder this truth, which may not be the gospel now fashionable, but is unquestionably the statement of a Scriptural fact: *in the moral sphere, God works by means and not by miracle.*

A free life, the desert air, the rejection of the unfit by many visitations, and the growth of a new generation amid thrilling events, in a soul-stirring region, and under the pure influences of the law,—these were necessary before Israel could cross steel with the warlike children of the Philistines; and even then, it was not with them that he should begin.

The other lesson we learn is the tender fidelity of God, Who will not suffer us to be tempted above that we are able to bear. He led them aside into the desert, whither He still in mercy leads very many who think it a heavy judgment to be there.

THE BONES OF JOSEPH.

xiii. 19.

It is certain that Moses, in the days of his greatness, must often have mused by the sepulchre of the one Israelite before himself who held high rank in Egypt. The knowledge that Joseph's elevation was providential must have helped him at that time, now many years ago, to think rightly of his own. And now we read that Moses took the bones of Joseph with him. In the Epistle to the Hebrews (xi. 22) it is recorded as the most characteristic example of the faith of the patriarch, that instead of desiring to be carried, like his father, at once to Canaan, he made mention of the departure of the children of Israel, and gave commandment concerning his bones. To him Egypt was no longer an alien land. There only he had known honour without envy, and happiness without betrayal. There his bones could rest in quiet; but not for ever. Personal elevation, which had not rent the cord between him and his unworthy family, could still less sever the bands between him and the sacred race. Let him sleep in Egypt while his grave there was honoured: let the remembrance of him be kept fresh, to protect awhile his kindred; and when the predicted days of evil came, let his ashes share the neglect and dishonour of his people, if only they would remember his remains when the Lord would lead them forth. This confidence in their emancipation was his faith—which meant, here as always, not a clear view of truth, but an assuring grasp of it. He had straitly sworn the children of Israel saying, "God will surely visit you; and ye shall carry up my bones away hence with you."

Many a Christian might well envy a confidence so practical, so thoroughly realised, entering so naturally into the tissue of his thoughts and calculations. And their actual remembrance of him goes to show that the tradition of his faith had never completely died out, but was among the influences which kept alive the nation's hope.

And as the people bore his honoured ashes through the desert, these being dead spoke of bygone times, they linked the present and the past together, they deepened the national consciousness that Israel was a favoured people, called to no common destiny, sustained by no common promises, pressing toward no common goal.

If Israel had been wise, they would have thought of him, the Israelite in heart, though glittering in the splendours of Egypt; and would have considered well that as little as men detected his secret life from his appearance, so little could theirs be judged. To the eye, they were free from the foreign trammels in which he was seemingly entangled, yet many of them in heart turned back to all which strove in vain to bind his affections down. The lesson holds good to-day. Many a modern religionist looks askance at the "worldliness" of high office and rank and state; little dreaming that the "world" he censures is strong in his own ambitious and self-asserting spirit, and is overcome by the gentle and tranquil spirit of hundreds of those whom he condemns.

Bearing this hallowed burden, which might easily have become an object of superstitious regard, the nation moved from Succoth to Etham on the edge of the wilderness. And with them a Presence moved which rebuked all others, however venerable. The Lord went before them. It has already been pointed out that throughout the early history of this nation, just come out of an idolatrous land, and too ready to lapse back into superstition, God never reveals Himself except in fire. To Abraham and to Jacob He appeared in human form, and again to Joshua; but in the interval, never. So now they see Him by day in a pillar of cloud to guide them on the way, and by night in a pillar of fire to give them light. The glory of the nation was that manifested Presence, lacking which, Moses besought Him to carry them up no farther.

Nothing in the Exodus is more impressive, and it sank deep into the national heart. Many centuries afterwards, the ideal of a golden age was that the Lord should "create over the whole habitation of Mount Zion, and over her assemblies, a cloud of smoke by day, and the shining of a flaming fire by night" (Isa. iv. 5).

But it has been well observed that, amid the various allusions to it in Hebrew poetry, not one treats it as modern literature has done, with an eye to its marvellous sublimity and picturesque effects:

> "By day, along the astonished lands
> The cloudy pillar glided slow:
> By night, Arabia's crimsoned sands
> Returned the fiery column's glow."

The Hebrew poetry is vivid and passionate, but all its concerns are human or divine—God, and the life of man. It is not artistic, but inspired. "The modern poet is delighting in the scenic effect; the ancient chronicler was wholly occupied with the overshadowing power of God."*

---

* Hutton's *Essays*, Vol. ii., *Literary*: *The Poetry of the Old Test.*

CHAPTER XIV.

THE RED SEA.

xiv. 1-31.

IT would seem that the Israelites recoiled before a frontier fortress of Egypt at Khetam (Etham). This is probable, whatever theory of the route of the Exodus one may adopt; and it is still open to every reader to adopt almost any theory he pleases, provided that two facts are borne in mind: viz., first, that the narrative certainly means to describe a miraculous interference, not superseding the forces of nature, but wielding them in a fashion impossible to man; and second, that the phrase translated "Red Sea"* (xiii. 18, xv. 4) is the same which is confessed by all persons to have that meaning in chap. xxiii. 31, and in Numbers xxi. 4 and xxxiii. 10.

Checked, without loss or with it, they were bidden to "turn back," and encamp at Pi-hahiroth, between Migdol and the sea. And since Migdol is simply a watch-tower (there were several in the Holy Land, including that which gave her name to Mary Magdal-ene), we are to infer that from thence their inexplicable

---

* The Sea of Zuph, or reeds, the word being used of the reeds in which Moses was laid by his mother and found by Pharaoh's daughter (ii. 3, 5), rendered "flags" in the Revised Version.

movements were signalled back to Pharaoh. It was the natural signal for all the wild passions of a baffled and half-ruined tyrant to leap into flame. We are scarcely able to imagine the mental condition of men who conceived that a God Who had dealt out death and destruction might be far from invincible from another side. But ages after this, a campaign was planned upon the ingenious theory that "Jehovah is a god of the hills but He is not a god of the valleys" (1 Kings xx. 28); and plenty of people who would scorn this simple notion are still of opinion that He is a God of eternity and can save them from hell, but a little falsehood and knavery are much better able to save them from want in the meanwhile. Nay, there are many excellent persons who are not at all of opinion that the prince of this world has been dethroned.

Therefore, when his enemies recoiled from his fortresses and wandered away into the wilderness of Egypt, entangling themselves hopelessly between the sea, the mountains, and his own strongholds, it might well appear to Pharaoh that Jehovah was not a warlike deity, that he himself had now found out the weak point of his enemies, and could pursue and overtake and satisfy his lust upon them. There is a significant emphasis in the song of Miriam's triumph—"Jehovah is a man of war." At all events, it was through an imperfect sense of the universal and practical importance of Jehovah as a factor not to be neglected in his calculations, through exactly the same error which misleads every man who postpones religion, or limits the range of its influence in his daily life,—it was thus, and not through any rarer infatuation, that Pharaoh made ready six hundred chosen chariots and all the chariots of Egypt, and captains over all of them. And his court was of the same mind, saying, "What is this that we have done, that we have let Israel go from serving us?"

These words are hard to reconcile with the strange notion that until now a return after three days was expected, despite the torrent of blood which rolled between them, and the demands by which the Israelitish women had spoiled the Egyptians. Upon this theory it is not their own error, but the bad faith of their servants, which they should have cried out against.

At the sight of the army, a panic seized the servile hearts of the fugitives. First they cried out unto the Lord. But how possible it is, without any real faith, to address to Heaven the mere clamours of our alarm, and to mistake natural agitation for earnestness in prayer, we learn by the reproaches with which, after thus crying to the Lord, they assailed His servant. Were there no graves in that land of superb sepulchres —that land, now, of universal mourning? Would God that they had perished with the firstborn! Why had they been treated thus? Had they not urged Moses to let them alone, that they might serve the Egyptians?

And yet these men had lately, for the very promise of so much emancipation as they now enjoyed, bowed their heads in adoring thankfulness. As it was their fear which now took the form of supplication, so then it was their hope which took the form of praise. And we, how shall we know whether that in us which seems to be religious gladness and religious grief, is mere emotion, or is truly sacred? By watching whether worship and love continue, when emotion has spent its force, or has gone round, like the wind, to another quarter.

How did Moses feel when this outcry told him of the unworthiness and cowardice of the nation of his heart? Much as we feel, perhaps, when we see the frailties and failures of converts in the mission-field, and the lapse of the intemperate who have seemed to be reclaimed for ever. We thought that perfection was to be reached at a bound. Now we think that the whole work was unreal. Both extremes are wrong: we have much to learn from the failures of that ancient church, in which was the germ of hero, psalmist, and prophet, which was indeed the church in the wilderness, and whose many relapses were so tenderly borne with by God and His messenger.

The settled faith of Moses, and the assurances which he could give the agitated people,* contrast nobly with their alarm. But his confidence also had its secret springs in prayer, for the Lord said to him, "Wherefore criest thou unto Me? speak unto the children of Israel that they go forward."

The words are remarkable on two accounts. Can prayer ever be out of place? Not if we mean a prayerful dependent mental attitude toward God. But certainly, yes, if God has already revealed that for which we still importune Him, and we are secretly

---

* But his assurance is, "The Lord shall fight for you, and ye shall hold your peace." When Wellhausen would summarise the work of Moses, he tells us that "he taught them to regard self-assertion against the Egyptians as an article of religion" (*History*, p. 430). It would be impossible, within the compass of so many words, more completely to miss the remarkable characteristic which differentiates this whole narrative from all other revolutionary movements. Expectancy and dependence here take the place of "self-assertion."

disquieted lest His promise should fail. It is misplaced if our own duty has to be done, and we pass the golden moments in inactivity, however pious. Christ spoke of men who should leave their gift before the altar, unpresented, because of a neglected duty which should be discharged. And perhaps there are men who pray for the conversion of the heathen, or of friends at home, to whom God says, Wherefore criest thou unto Me? because their money and their faithful efforts must be given, as Moses must arouse himself to lead the people forward, and to stretch his wand over the sea.

And again the forces of nature are on the side of God: the strong wind makes the depths of the sea a way for the ransomed to pass over. History has no scene more picturesque than this wild night march, in the roar of tempest, amid the flying foam which "baptized" them unto Moses,* while the glimmering waters stood up like a rampart to protect their flanks; the full moon of passover above them, shown and hidden as the swift clouds raced before the storm, while high and steadfast overhead, unshaken by the fiercest blast, illumined by a mysterious splendour, "stood" the vast cloud which veiled like a curtain their whole host from the pursuer. This it was, and the experience of such protection that the Egyptians, overawed, came not near them, which gave them courage to enter the bed of the sea; and as they trod the strange road they found that not only were the waters driven off the surface, but the sands were left firm to traverse.

But when the blind fury of Pharaoh, "hardened"

---

* Not the adults only; nor yet by immersion, whether in the rain-cloud or the surf.

against everything but the sense that his prey was escaping, sent his army along the same track, and this after long delay, at a crisis when every moment was priceless, then a new element of terrible sublimity was added. Through the pillar of cloud and fire Jehovah looked forth on the Egyptian host, as they pressed on behind, unable to penetrate the supernatural gloom, cold fear creeping into every heart, while the chariot wheels laboured heavily in the wet sand. In that direful vision at last the question was answered, "Who is Jehovah, that I should let His people go?" Now it was the turn of those who said "Israel is entangled in the land, the wilderness hath shut them in," themselves to be taken in a worse net. For at that awful gaze the iron curb of military discipline gave way; their labouring chariots, the pride and defence of the nation, were forsaken; and a wild cry broke out, "Let us fly from the face of Israel, for Jehovah"—He who plagued us—"fighteth for them against the Egyptians." But their humiliation came too late,—for in the morning watch, at a natural time for atmospheric changes, but in obedience to the rod of Moses, the furious wind veered or fell, and the sea returned to its accustomed limits; and first, as the sands beneath became saturated, the chariots were overturned and the mail-clad charioteers went down "like lead," and then the hissing line of foam raced forward and closed around and over the shrieking mob which was the pride and strength of Egypt only an hour before.

But, as the story repeats twice over, with a very natural and glad reiteration, "the children of Israel walked on dry land in the midst of the sea, and the waters were a wall unto them on their right hand, and on their left" (ver. 29, cf. 22).

ON THE SHORE.

xiv. 30, 31.

After the haste and agitation of their marvellous deliverance the children of Israel seem to have halted for awhile at the only spot in the neighbourhood where there is water, known as the Ayoun Musa or springs of Moses to this day. There they doubtless brought into some permanent shape their rudimentary organisation. There, too, their impressions were given time to deepen. They "saw the Egyptians dead on the sea-shore," and realised that their oppression was indeed at an end, their chains broken, themselves introduced into a new life,—"baptized unto Moses." They reflected upon the difference between all other deities and the God of their fathers, Who, in that deadly crisis, had looked upon them and their tyrants out of the fiery pillar. "They feared Jehovah, and they believed in Jehovah and in His servant Moses."

"They believed in Jehovah." This expression is noteworthy, because they had all believed in Him already. "By faith 'they' forsook Egypt. By faith 'they' kept the passover and the sprinkling of blood. By faith 'they' passed through the Red Sea." But their former trust was poor and wavering compared with that which filled their bosoms now. So the disciples followed Jesus because they believed on Him; yet when His first miracle manifested forth His glory, "His disciples believed on Him there." And again they said, "By this we believe that Thou camest forth from God." And after the resurrection He said, "Because thou hast seen Me thou hast believed" (John ii. 11, xvi. 30, xx. 29). Faith needs to be edified by successive experiences, as the enthusiasm of a recruit is converted into the disciplined valour of the veteran. From each new crisis of the spiritual life the soul should obtain new powers. And that is a shallow and unstable religion which is content with the level of its initial act of faith (however genuine and however important), and seeks not to go from strength to strength.

CHAPTER XV.

THE SONG OF MOSES.

xv. 1-22.

DURING this halt they prepared that great song of triumph which St. John heard sung by them who had been victorious over the beast, standing by the sea of glass, having the harps of God. For by that calmer sea, triumphant over a deadlier persecution, they still found their adoration and joy expressed in this earliest chant of sacred victory. Because all holy hearts give like thanks to Him Who sitteth upon the throne, therefore "deep answers unto deep," and every great crisis in the history of the Church has legacies for all time and for eternity; and therefore the triumphant song of Moses the servant of God enriches the worship of heaven, as the penitence and hope and joy of David enrich the worship of the Church on earth (Rev. xv. 3).

Like all great poetry, this song is best enjoyed when it is neither commented upon nor paraphrased, but carefully read and warmly felt. There are circumstances and lines of thought which it is desirable to point out, but only as a preparation, not a substitute, for the submission of a docile mind to the influence of the inspired poem itself. It is unquestionably archaic. The parallelism of Hebrew verse is already here, but the structure is more free and unartificial than that of later poetry; and many ancient words, and words of

Egyptian derivation, authenticate its origin. So does the description of Miriam, in the fifteenth verse, as "the prophetess, the sister of Aaron." In what later time would she not rather have been called the sister of Moses? But from the lonely youth who found Aaron and Miriam together as often as he stole from the palace to his real home—the lonely man who regained both together when he returned from forty years of exile, and who sometimes found them united in opposition to his authority (Num. xii. 1, 2)—from Moses alone the epithet is entirely natural.

It is also noteworthy that Philistia is mentioned first among the foes who shall be terrified (ver. 14, R.V.), because Moses still expected the invasion to break first on them. But the unbelieving fears of Israel changed the route, so that no later poet would have set them in the forefront of his song. Thus also the terror of the Edomites is anticipated, although in fact they sturdily refused a passage to Israel through their land (Num. xx. 20). All this authenticates the song, which thereupon establishes the miraculous deliverance that inspired it.

The song is divided into two parts. Up to the end of the twelfth verse it is historical: the remainder expresses the high hopes inspired by this great experience. Nothing now seems impossible: the fiercest tribes of Palestine and the desert may be despised, for their own terror will suffice to "melt" them; and Israel may already reckon itself to be guided into the holy habitation (ver. 13).

The former part is again subdivided, by a noble and instinctive art, into two very unequal sections. With amplitude of triumphant adoration, the first ten verses tell the same story which the eleventh and twelfth compress into epigrammatical vigour and terseness. To appreciate the power of the composition, one should read the fourth, fifth, and sixth verses, and turn immediately to the twelfth.

Each of these three divisions closes in praise, and as in the "Israel in Egypt," it was probably at these points that the voices of Miriam and the women broke in, repeating the first verse of the ode as a refrain (vers. 1 and 21). It is the earliest recognition of the place of women in public worship. And it leads us to remark that the whole service was responsive. Moses and the men are answered by Miriam and the women, bearing timbrels in their hands; for although instrumental music had been sorely misused in Egypt, that was no reason why it should be excluded now. Those who condemn the use of instruments in Christian worship virtually contend that Jesus has, in this respect, narrowed the liberty of the Church, and that a potent method of expression, known to man, must not be consecrated to the honour of God. And they make the present time unlike the past, and also unlike what is revealed of the future state.

Moreover there was movement, as in very many ancient religious services, within and without the pale of revelation.* Such dances were generally slow and graceful; yet the motion and the clang of metal, and the vast multitudes congregated, must be taken into account, if we would realise the strange enthusiasm of the emancipated host, looking over the blue sea to Egypt, defeated and twice bereaved, and forward to the desert wilds of freedom.

---

* There is no warrant in the use of Scripture for Stanley's assertion that the word translated "dances" should be rendered "guitars." (Smith's *Dict. of Bible*, Article *Miriam*.)

The poem is steeped in a sense of gratitude. In the great deliverance man has borne no part. It is Jehovah Who has triumphed gloriously, and cast the horse and charioteer—there was no "rider"—into the sea. And this is repeated again and again by the women as their response, in the deepening passion of the ode. "With the breath of His nostrils the waters were piled up... He blew with His wind and the sea covered them." And such is indeed the only possible explanation of the Exodus, so that whoever rejects the miracle is beset with countless difficulties. One of these is the fact that Moses, their immortal leader, has no martial renown whatever. Hebrew poetry is well able to combine gratitude to God with honour to the men of Zebulun who jeopardised their lives unto the death, to Jael who put her hand to the nail, to Saul and Jonathan who were swifter than eagles and stronger than lions. Joshua and David can win fame without dishonour to God. Why is it that here alone no mention is made of human agency, except that, in fact, at the outset of their national existence, they were shown, once for all, the direct interposition of their God?

From gratitude springs trust: the great lesson is learned that man has an interest in the Divine power. "My strength and song is Jah," says the second verse, using that abbreviated form of the covenant name Jehovah, which David also frequently associated with his victories. "And He is become my salvation." It is the same word as when, a little while ago, the trembling people were bidden to stand still and see the salvation of God. They have seen it now. Now they give the word Salvation for the first time to the Lord as an appellation, and as such it is destined to endure. The Psalmist learns to call Him so, not only when he reproduces this verse word for word (Ps. cxviii. 14), but also when he says, "He only is my rock and my salvation" (lxii. 2), and prays, "Before Ephraim, Benjamin, and Manasseh, come for salvation to us" (lxxx. 2).

And the same title is known also to Isaiah, who says, "Behold God is my salvation," and "Be Thou their arm every morning, our salvation also in the time of trouble" (Isa. xii. 2, xxxiii. 2).

The progress is natural from experience of goodness to appropriation: He has helped me: He gives Himself to me; and from that again to love and trust, for He has always been the same: "my father," not my ancestors in general, but he whom I knew best and remember most tenderly, found Him the same Helper. And then love prompts to some return. My goodness extendeth not to Him, yet my voice can honour Him; I will praise Him, I will exalt His name. Now, this is the very spirit of evangelical obedience, the life-blood of the new dispensation racing in the veins of the old.

Where praise and exaltation are a spontaneous instinct, there is loyal service and every good work, not rendered by a hireling but a child. Had He not said, "Israel is My son"?

From exultant gratitude and trust, what is next to spring? That which is reproachfully called anthropomorphism, something which indeed easily degenerates into unworthy notions of a God limited by such restraints or warped by such passions as our own, yet which is after all a great advance towards true and holy thoughts of Him Who made man after His image and in His likeness.

Human affection cannot go forth to God without

believing that like affection meets and responds to it.
If He is indeed the best and purest, we must think
of Him as sharing all that is best and purest in our
souls, all that we owe to His inspiring Spirit.

> "So through the thunder comes a human voice,
> Saying 'O heart I made, a heart beats here.'"

If ever any religion was sternly jealous of the Divine
prerogatives, profoundly conscious of the incommunicable dignity of the Lord our God Who is one Lord,
it was the Jewish religion. Yet when Jesus was
charged with making Himself God, He could appeal to
the doctrine of their own Scripture—that the judges of
the people exercised so divine a function, and could
claim such divine support, that God Himself spoke
through them, and found representatives in them. "Is
it not written in your law, I said Ye are gods?"
(John x. 34). Not in vain did He appeal to such
scriptures—and there are many such—to vindicate
His doctrine. For man is never lifted above himself,
but God in the same degree stoops towards us, and
identifies Himself with us and our concerns. Who
then shall limit His condescension? What ground in
reason or revelation can be taken up for denying that
it may be perfect, that it may develop into a permanent
union of God with the creature whom He inspired with
His own breath? It is by such steps that the Old
Testament prepared Israel for the Incarnation. Since
the Incarnation we have actually needed help from
the other side, to prevent us from humanising our
conceptions over-much. And this has been provided in
the ever-expanding views of His creation given to us
by science, which tell us that if He draws nigh to us
it is from heights formerly undreamed of. Now, such

a step as we have been considering is taken unawares in the bold phrase "Jehovah is a man of war." For in the original, as in the English, this includes the assertion "Jehovah is a man." Of course it is only a bold figure. But such a figure prepares the mind for new light, suggesting more than it logically asserts.

The phrase is more striking when we remember that remarkable peculiarity of the Exodus and its revelations which has been already pointed out. Elsewhere God appears in human likeness. To Abraham it was so, just before, and to Manoah soon afterwards. Ezekiel saw upon the likeness of the throne the likeness of the appearance of a man (Ezek. i. 26). But Israel saw no similitude, only he heard a voice. This was obviously a safeguard against idolatry. And it makes the words more noteworthy, "Jehovah is a man of war," marching with us, our champion, into the battle. And we know Him as our fathers knew Him not,—"Jehovah is His name."

The poem next describes the overthrow of the enemy: the heavy plunge of men in armour into the deeps, the arm of the Lord dashing them in pieces, His "fire" consuming them, while the blast of His nostrils is the storm which "piles up" the waters, solid as a wall of ice, "congealed in the heart of the sea." Then the singers exultantly rehearse the short panting eager phrases, full of greedy expectation, of the enemy breathless in pursuit—a passage well remembered by Deborah, when her triumphant song closed by an insulting repetition of the vain calculations of the mother of Sisera and "her wise ladies."

The eleventh verse is remarkable as being the first announcement of the holiness of God. "Who is like unto Thee, glorious in holiness?" And what does holiness mean? The Hebrew word is apparently suggestive of "brightness," and the two ideas are coupled by Isaiah (x. 17): "The Light of Israel shall be for a fire, and his Holy One for a flame." There is indeed something in the purity of light, in its absolute immunity from stain—no passive cleanness, as of the sand upon the shore, but intense and vital—and in its remoteness from the conditions of common material substances, that well expresses and typifies the lofty and awful quality which separates holiness from mere virtue. "God is called the Holy One because He is altogether pure, the clear and spotless Light; so that in the idea of the holiness of God there are embodied the absolute moral purity and perfection of the Divine nature, and His unclouded glory (Keil, *Pent.*, ii. 99). In this thought there is already involved separation, a lofty remoteness.

And when holiness is attributed to man, it never means innocence, nor even virtue, merely as such. It is always a derived attribute: it is reflected upon us, like light upon our planet; and like consecration, it speaks not of man in himself, but in his relation to God. It expresses a kind of separation to God, and thus it can reach to lifeless things which bear a true relation to the Divine. The seventh day is thus "hallowed." It is the very name of the "Holy Place," the "Sanctuary." And the ground where Moses was to stand unshod beside the burning bush was pronounced "holy," not by any concession to human weakness, but by the direct teaching of God. Very inseparable from all true holiness is separation from what is common and unclean. Holy men may be involved in the duties of active life; but only on condition that in their bosom shall be some inner shrine, whither the din of wordliness never penetrates, and where the lamp of God does not go out.

It is a solemn truth that a kind of inverted holiness is known to Scripture. Men "sanctify themselves" (it is this very word), "and purify themselves to go into the gardens, . . . eating swine's flesh and the abomination and the mouse" (Isa. lxvi. 17). The same word is also used to declare that the whole fruit of a vineyard sown with two kinds of fruit shall be *forfeited* (Deut. xxii. 9), although the notion there is of something unnatural and therefore interdicted, which notion is carried to the utmost extreme in another derivative from the same root, expressing the most depraved of human beings.

Just so, the Greek word "anathema" means both "consecrated" and "marked out for wrath" (Luke xxi. 5 ; 1 Cor. xvi. 22: the difference in form is insignificant.) And so again our own tongue calls the saints "devoted," and speaks of the "devoted" head of the doomed sinner, being aware that there is a "separation" in sin as really as in purity. The gods of the heathen, like Jehovah, claimed an appropriate "holiness," sometimes unspeakably degraded. They too were separated, and it was through long lines of sphinxes, and many successive chambers, that the Egyptian worshipper attained the shrine of some contemptible or hateful deity. The religion which does not elevate depresses. But the holiness of Jehovah is noble as that of light, incapable of defilement. "Who among the gods is like Thee . . . glorious in holiness?" And Israel soon learned that the worshipper must become assimilated to his Ideal: "Ye shall be holy men unto Me" (xxii. 31). It is so with us. Jesus is separated from sinners. And we are to go forth unto Him out of the camp, bearing His reproach (Heb. vii. 26, xiii. 13).

The remainder of the song is remarkable chiefly for the confidence with which the future is inferred from the past. And the same argument runs through all Scripture. As Moses sang, "Thou shalt bring them in and plant them in the mountain of Thine inheritance," because "Thou stretchedst out Thy right hand, the earth * swallowed" their enemies, so David was sure that goodness and mercy should follow him all the days of his life, because God was already leading him in green pastures and beside still waters. And so St. Paul, knowing in Whom he had believed, was persuaded that He was able to keep his deposit until that day (2 Tim. i. 12).

So should pardon and Scripture and the means of grace reassure every doubting heart; for "if the Lord were pleased to kill us, He would not have . . . showed us all these things" (Judg. xiii. 23). And in theory, and in good hours, we confess that this is so. But after our song of triumph, if we come upon bitter waters we murmur; and if our bread fail, we expect only to die in the wilderness.

SHUR.

xv. 22-7.

From the Red Sea the Israelites marched into the wilderness of Shur—a general name, of Egyptian origin, for the district between Egypt and Palestine, of which Etham, given as their route in Numbers (xxxiii. 8), is

---

* This is to be taken literally; it does not mean the waves, but the quicksands in which they "drave heavily," and which, when steeped in the returning waters, engulfed them.

a subdivision. The rugged way led over stone and sand, with little vegetation and no water. And the "three days' journey" to Marah, a distance of thirty-three miles, was their first experience of absolute hardship, for not even the curtain of miraculous cloud could prevent them from suffering keenly by heat and thirst.

It was a period of disillusion. Fond dreams of ease and triumphant progress, with every trouble miraculously smoothed away, had naturally been excited by their late adventure. Their song had exulted in the prospect that their enemies should melt away, and be as still as a stone. But their difficulties did not melt away. The road was weary. They found no water. They were still too much impressed by the miracle at the Red Sea, and by the mysterious Presence overhead, for open complaining to be heard along the route; but we may be sure that reaction had set in, and there was many a sinking heart, as the dreary route stretched on and on, and they realised that, however romantic the main plan of their journey, the details might still be prosaic and exacting. They sang praises unto Him. They soon forgat His works. Aching with such disappointments, at last they reached the waters of Marah, and they could not drink, for they were bitter.

And if Marah be indeed Huwara, as seems to be agreed, the waters are still the worst in all the district. It was when the relief, so confidently expected, failed, and the term of their sufferings appeared to be indefinitely prolonged, that their self-control gave way, and they "murmured against Moses, saying, What shall we drink?" And we may be sure that wherever discontent and unbelief are working secret mischief to the soul, some event, some disappointment or temptation, will find the weak point, and the favourable moment of attack, just as the seeds of disease find out the morbid constitution, and assail it.

Now, all this is profoundly instructive, because it is true to the universal facts of human nature. When a man is promoted to unexpected rank, or suddenly becomes rich, or reaches any other unlooked-for elevation, he is apt to forget that life cannot, in any position, be a romance throughout, a long thrill, a whole song at the top note of the voice. Affection itself has a dangerous moment, when two united lives begin to realise that even their union cannot banish aches and anxieties, weariness and business cares. Well for them if they are content with the power of love to sweeten what it cannot remove, as loyal soldiers gladly sacrifice all things for the cause, and as Israel should have been proud to endure forced marches under the cloudy banner of its emancipating God.

As neither rank nor affection exempts men from the dust and tedium of life, or from its disappointments, so neither does religion. When one is "made happy" he expects life to be only a triumphal procession towards Paradise, and he is startled when "now for a season, if need be, he is in heaviness through manifold temptations." Yet Christ prayed not that we should be taken out of the world. We are bidden to endure hardness as good soldiers, and to run with patience the race which is set before us; and these phrases indicate our need of the very qualities wherein Israel failed. As yet the people murmured not ostensibly against God, but only against Moses. But the estrangement of their hearts is plain, since they made no appeal to God for relief, but assailed His agent and representative. Yet they had not because they asked not, and relief was found when Moses cried unto the Lord. Their leader was "faithful in all his house"; and instead of upbraiding his followers with their ingratitude, or bewailing the hard lot of all leaders of the multitude, whose popularity neither merit nor service can long preserve unclouded, he was content to look for sympathy and help where we too may find it.

We read that the Lord showed him a tree, which when he had cast into the waters, the waters were made sweet. In this we discern the same union of Divine grace with human energy and use of means, as in all medicine, and indeed all uses of the divinely enlightened intellect of man. It would have been easy to argue that the waters could only be healed by miracle, and if God wrought a miracle what need was there of human labour? There was need of obedience, and of the co-operation of the human will with the divine. We shall see, in the case of the artificers of the tabernacle, that God inspires even handicraftsmen as well as theologians—being indeed the universal Light, the Giver of all good, not only of Bibles, but of rain and fruitful seasons. But the artisan must labour, and the farmer improve the soil.

Shall we say with the fathers that the tree cast into the waters represents the cross of Christ? At least it is a type of the sweetening and assuaging influences of religion—a new element, entering life, and as well fitted to combine with it as medicinal bark with water, making all wholesome and refreshing to the disappointed wayfarer, who found it so bitter hitherto.

The Lord was not content with removing the grievance of the hour; He drew closer the bonds between His people and Himself, to guard them against another transgression of the kind: "there He made for them a statute and an ordinance, and there He proved them." It is pure assumption to pretend that this refers to another account of the giving of the Jewish law, inconsistent with that in the twentieth chapter, and placed at Marah instead of Sinai.* It is a transaction which resembles much rather the promises given (and at various times, although confusion and repetition cannot be inferred) to Abraham and Jacob (Gen. xii. 1-3, xv. 1, 18-21, xvii. 1-14, xxii. 15-18, xxviii. 13-15, xxxv. 10-12). He said, "If thou wilt diligently hearken to the voice of the Lord thy God, and wilt do that which is right in His eyes, and wilt give ear to His commandments, and wilt keep all His statutes, I will put none of the diseases upon thee which I have put upon the Egyptians, for I am the Lord which healeth thee." It is a compact of obedient trust on one side, and protection on the other. If they felt their own sinfulness, it asserted that He who had just healed the waters could also heal their hearts. From the connection between these is perhaps derived the comparison between human hearts and a fountain of sweet water or bitter (Jas. iii. 11).

But certainly the promised protection takes an unexpected shape. What in their circumstances leads to this specific offer of exemption from certain foul diseases—" the boil of Egypt, and the emerods, and the scurvy, and the itch, whereof thou canst not be healed" (Deut. xxviii. 27)? How does this meet the case? Doubtless by reminding them that there are better exemptions than from hardship, and worse evils than privations. If they do not realise this at the spiritual level, at least they can appreciate the threat that " He will bring upon thee again all the diseases of Egypt

---

* Wellhausen, *Israel*, p. 439.

which thou wast afraid of" (Deut. xxviii. 60). To be even a luxurious and imperial race, but infected by repulsive and hopeless ailments, is not a desirable alternative. Now, such evils, though certainly not in each individual, yet in a race, are the punishments of non-natural conditions of life, such as make the blood run slowly and unhealthily, and charge it with impure deposits. It was God who put them upon the Egyptians.

If Israel would follow His guidance, and accept a somewhat austere destiny, then the desert air and exercise, and even its privations, would become the efficacious means for their exemption from the scourges of indulgence. A time arrived when they looked back with remorse upon crimes which forfeited their immunity, when the Lord said, "I have sent among you the pestilence after the manner of Egypt; your young men have I slain with the sword" (Amos iv. 10).

But it is a significant fact that at this day, after eighteen hundred years of oppression, hardship, and persecution, of the ghetto and the old-clothes trade, the Hebrew race is proverbially exempt from repulsive and contagious disease. They also "certainly do enjoy immunity from the ravages of cholera, fever and small-pox in a remarkable degree. Their blood seems to be in a different condition from that of other people. . . . They seem less receptive of disease caused by blood poisoning than ·others" (*Journal of Victoria Institute*, xxi. 307). Imperfect as was their obedience, this covenant at least has been literally fulfilled to them.

It is by such means that God is wont to reward His children. Most commonly the seal of blessing from the skies is not rich fare, but bread and fish by the lake side with the blessing of Christ upon them; not removal from the desert, but a closer sense of the protection and acceptance of Heaven, the nearness of a loving God, and with this, an elevation and purification of the life, and of the body as well as of the soul. Not in vain has St. Paul written "The Lord for the body." Nor was there ever yet a race of men who accepted the covenant of God, and lived in soberness, temperance and chastity, without a signal improvement of the national physique, no longer unduly stimulated by passion, jaded by indulgence, or relaxed by the satiety which resembles but is not repose.

From Marah and its agitations there was a journey of but a few hours to Elim, with its twelve fountains and seventy palm trees—a fair oasis, by which they encamped and rested, while their flocks spread far and wide over a grassy and luxuriant valley.

The picture is still true to the Christian life, with the Palace Beautiful just beyond the lions, and the Delectable Mountains next after Doubting Castle.

CHAPTER XVI.

MURMURING FOR FOOD.

xvi. 1-14.

THE Israelites were now led farther away from all the associations of their accustomed life. From the waters and the palms of Elim they marched deeper into the savage recesses of the desert, haunted by fierce and hostile tribes, such as presently hung upon their rear-guard and cut off their stragglers (Deut. xxv. 18). Nor had they quite emerged from the shadow of their old oppressions, since Egyptian garrisons were scattered, though sparsely, through this district, in which gems and copper were obtained. Here, cut off from all natural modes of sustenance, the hearts of the people failed them. Such is the frequent experience of renewed souls, when privilege and joy are followed by trouble from without or from within, and the peace of God is broken by the strife of tongues, by mental perplexities, by temptations, by physical pain. It is quite as wonderful that paltry disturbances should mar for us the life divine, when once that life has become a realised experience, as that men who moved under the shadow of the marvellous cloud could be agitated by fear for their supplies. And of this our experience, what befel Israel is not a mere type or symbol, it is a case in point, a parallel example. For it also meant the breaking-in of the flesh upon the spirit, the refusal of fallen nature to rise above earthly wants and cravings even in the light of trust and acceptance, the self-assertion of the baser instincts, and the sacrifice to them of the higher life. We recognise the herd of slaves, from whence it must perplex the unbeliever to remember that the seed of immortal heroism and prophetic insight and apostolic service was yet to ripen, in their poor desire, if they must perish, to perish well fed rather than emancipated (ver. 3). Most people, we may fear, would choose to live enslaved rather than to die free men. But there is a special meanness in their regret, since die they must, that they had not died satiated, like the firstborn whom God had slain: "Would that we had died by the hand of Jehovah in the land of Egypt, when we sat by the fleshpots and when we ate bread to the full, for ye have brought us forth into this wilderness to kill this whole assembly with hunger." And to-day, among those who scorn them, how many are far less ambitious of dying holy and pure than rich, famous or powerful, having glutted their vanity if not their appetite. In the sight of angels this is not a much loftier aim; and the apostle reckoned among the works of the flesh, emulation as well as drunkenness (Gal. v. 19-21).

Tertullian draws a striking contrast between Israel, just now baptized into Moses, but caring more for appetite than for God, and Christ, after His baptism, also in the desert, fasting forty days. "The Lord figuratively retorted upon Israel His reproach" (*Baptism*, xx.)

We are not to suppose that but for their complaining God would have suffered them to hunger, although Moses declared that the reason why flesh should be given to them in the evening, and in the morning bread to the full, is "for that the Lord heareth your murmurings." But there would have been some difference in the time of the grant, to ripen their faith, some more direct manifestation of His grace, to reward their patience, if unbelief had not precipitated His design. Thus the disciples, when they awakened Jesus in the storm, received the rescue for which they clamoured, but forfeited some higher experience which would have crowned a serener confidence: "Wherefore did ye doubt?" Israel receives what is best in the circumstances, rather than the ideal best, now made unsuitable by their impatience and infidelity. But while the Lord discontinued the test of need and penury, which had proved to be too severe a discipline, He substituted the test of fulness. For we read that the removal of their suspense and anxiety by the gift of manna from heaven was "to prove them whether they will walk in My laws or no" (ver. 4). And in so doing it was seen that worldly and unthankful natures are not to be satisfied; that the disloyal at heart will complain, however favoured. For "the children of Israel wept again and said, Who will give us flesh to eat? We remember the fish which we did eat in Egypt for nought, the cucumbers and the melons and the leeks and the onions and the garlick: but now our soul is dried away; there is nothing at all: we have nought save this manna to look to" (Num. xi. 4-6). Onions and garlick were more satisfactory to gross appetites than angels' food.

At this point we learn that what is called prosperity may indeed be a result of spiritual failure; that God may sometimes abstain from strong measures with a soul because what ought to mould would only crush; and may grant them their hearts' lust, yet send lean-ness withal into their souls. Perhaps we are allowed to be comfortable because we are unfit to be heroic.

And we also learn, when prosperous, to remember that plenty, equally with want, has its moral aspect. The Lord tries fortunate men, whether they will be grateful and obedient, trusting in Him and not in uncertain riches, or whether they will forget Him who has done so great things for them, and so perish in calm weather—

> "Like ships that have gone down at sea
> When heaven was all tranquillity."

There is an experiment being tried upon the soul, curious, slow, little-suspected, but incessant, in the giving of daily bread.

In promising relief, God required of them obedience and self-control. They were to respect the Sabbath, and make provision in advance for its requirements. And this direction, given before the Mount of the Lord was reached, has an important bearing upon the question whether the Fourth Commandment was the first institution of a holy day—whether, except as a Church ordinance, the duty of sabbath-keeping has no support beyond the ceremonial law. "For that the Lord hath (already) given you the Sabbath, therefore He giveth you on the sixth day the bread of two days" (ver. 29).

While conveying the promise of relief, Moses and Aaron rebuked the people, whose murmurs against them were in reality murmurs against God, since they were but His agents, and He had been visibly their Leader. And the same rebuke applies, for exactly the same reason, to many a modern complaint against the weather, against what people call their "luck," against a thousand provoking things in which the only possible provocation must come directly from heaven. It is because our religion is so shallow, and our consciousness of God in His world so dim and rudimentary, that we utter such complaints idly, to relieve our feelings, and hear them spoken without a shock.

Such dulness is not to be removed by sounder views of doctrine, but by a more vivid realisation of God. The Israelites knew by what hand they should have fallen if they had died in Egypt; yet in fact they forgot their true Captain, and upbraided their mortal leaders. So do we confess that afflictions arise not out of the ground, yet lose the impress of divinity upon our daily lives, while we ought, like Moses, to "endure as seeing Him who is invisible."

As our Lord was in the habit of asking for some confession, or demanding some small co-operation from those He was about to bless, so the smoking flax of Hebrew faith is tended: it is a promise, and not the actual relief, which calms them. There is a curious difference in the manner of the communications now made to the people. First of all the two brothers unite their energies to hush their outcries: "At evening ye shall know that Jehovah is your leader from Egypt, and in the morning ye shall behold His glory; and what are we, that ye murmur against us?" Then Moses affirms, with all the energy of his chieftainship, that in the evening they shall eat flesh, and in the morning bread to the full. Again he asks them "What are we?" and more sternly and directly charges them with murmuring against Jehovah. And this is a good example of the true meaning of his "meekness." He is fiery enough, but not for his own greatness; rather because he feels his littleness, and that the offence is entirely against God, does he resent their conduct; absence of self-assertion is his "meekness," and thus we read of it when Miriam and Aaron spake against him, declaring that they were commissioned as well as he (Num. xii. 3). Finally, when order was restored, and some mysterious manifestation was at hand, he resumed the solemn and formal usage of conveying his orders through his brother, and in cold, compact, impressive words, said unto Aaron, "Say unto all the congregation of the children of Israel, Come near before the Lord, for He hath heard your murmurings." All this is very dignified and natural. And so is—what after ages could scarcely have invented—the impressive reticence of what follows. "They looked toward the wilderness, and behold, the glory of the Lord appeared in the cloud."

Were they not then intended to "come near"? and was it as they turned their faces to draw nigh that the Vision revealed itself and stopped them? And what was the untold sight which they beheld? The narrative belongs to a primitive age; it is quite unlike the elaborate symbolisms of Ezekiel and Daniel, or even of Isaiah, but yet this undescribed, mystic and solitary glory is not less sublime than the train which covered the Temple-floor, while, hovering above it, reverent seraphim veiled their faces and their feet, or the terrible crystal and the wheels of dreadful height, or the throne of flame whence issued a fiery stream, and before which thousands of thousands and myriads of myriads stood (Isa. vi. 2; Ezek. i. 22, 18; Dan. vii. 9, 10). But the point to observe is that it is different, more primitive, an undefined and lonely vision of awe well fitted for the desert wilds and for the gaze of men whose hearts must not be misled by the likeness of anything in heaven or earth; the glory of the Lord appearing in the cloud (most probably, but not of necessity, the cloud which guided them), and in the direction whence they were so fain to turn away.

No later inventor would have known how to say so little, much less to make that little harmonise so exactly with the lessons meant to be suggested by the wild and solemn solitudes into which they were now plunged.

And now the Lord Himself repeats the promise of relief, but first solemnly announces that He is not heedless of their ill-behaviour while He tolerates it. The question is suggested, although not asked, How long will His forbearance last?

Well for them if they learn the lesson, and "know that I am Jehovah your God," mindful of their needs, entitled to their fealty. In the evening, therefore, came a flight of quails; and in the morning they found a small round thing, small as the hoar-frost, upon the ground.

MANNA.

xvi. 15-36.

The manna which miraculously supplied the wants of Israel was to them an utterly strange food, the use of which they had to learn. Thus it was another means of severing their habitual course of life and association of ideas from their degraded past. And while we may not press too far the assertion that it was the "corn of heaven" and "angels' food" (*i.e.* "the bread of the mighty"—Psalm lxxviii. 24-5, R.V.), yet the narrative shows, even without help from later scriptures, that it was calculated to sustain their energies and yet to leave their appetites unstimulated and unpampered. For they were now called to purer joys than those of the senses—to liberty, a divine vocation, the presence of God, the revelation of His law and the unfolding of His purposes. Failing to rise to these heights, they fell far, murmured again, and perished by the destroyer, not merely to avenge the petulance of an hour, but for all that it betrayed, for treason to their vocation and radical inability to even comprehend its meaning. In the language of modern science, it answered to Nature's rejection of the unfit.

Their calling was thus, though under very different forms, that which the apostles found so hard, yet did not quite refuse: it was to mind the things of God and not the things of men.

It is well known that the manna of the Israelites bore some resemblance to a natural product of the wilderness, still exuded by certain plants during the coolness of the night, and formerly more plentiful than now, when all vegetation has been ruthlessly swept away by the Bedouin. But the differences are much greater than the resemblance. The natural product is a drug, and not a food; it is gathered only during some weeks of summer; it is not liable to speedy corruption, nor could there be any reason for preserving a specimen of this common product in the ark; it could not have sufficed, however aided by their herds and flocks, to feed one in a hundred of the Hebrew multitudes, even during the season of its production; nor could it have ceased on the same day when they ate the first ripe corn of Canaan.

And yet the resemblance is suggestive. Unbelievers find, in the links which connect most of our Scripture miracles with nature, in the undefined and gradual transition from one to the other, as from a temperate day to night, an excuse for denying that they are miraculous at all. But the instructed believer finds a confirmation of his faith. He reflects that when Fancy begins to toy with the supernatural, she spurns nature from her: the trammels under which she has long chafed are hateful to her, and she flies from them to the utmost extreme.

It could not be thus with Him by whom the system of the world was framed. He will not wantonly interfere with His own plan. He will regard nature as an elastic band to stretch, rather than as a chain to break. If He will multiply food, in the New Testament, that is no reason why His disciples should fare more delicately than Providence intended for them: they shall still eat barley loaves and fish. And so the winds help to overthrow Pharaoh and to bring the quails; and when a new thing has to be created, it approaches in its general idea to one of the few natural products of that inhospitable region.

Now let it be supposed for a moment that the supply of manna had never ceased, so that until this day men could every morning gather a day's ration off the ground. Such continuance of the provision would not make it any the less a gift; but only a more lavish boon. And yet it would clearly cease to be regarded as miraculous, an exception to the course of nature, miscalled her "laws," since men do strive to subvert the miracle by representing that such manna, however scantily, may still be found. And this may expose the folly of a wish, probably sometimes felt by all men, that some miracle had actually been perpetuated, so that we could strengthen our faith at pleasure by looking upon an exhibition of divine power. In truth, no marvel could excel that which annually multiplies the corn beneath the clod, and by the process of decay in springtime feeds the world in autumn. Only its steady recurrence throws a veil over our eyes; and it is a vain conceit that the same web would not be woven by use between man and the Worker of any other marvel that was perpetuated. Already the earth is full of the goodness of the Lord, for all who have eyes to see.

It is also to be observed that the manna was not given to teach the people sloth. They were obliged to gather it early, before the sun was hot. They had still to endure weary marches, and the care of their flocks and herds.

And, in curious harmony with the manner of all the gifts of nature, the manna sent from heaven had yet to be prepared by man: "bake that which ye will bake, and seethe that which ye will seethe." Thus God, by natural means and by the sweat of our brow, gives us our daily bread; and all knowledge, art and culture are His gifts, although elaborated by the brain and heart of generations whom He taught.

Moreover, there was a protest against the grasping, unbelieving temper which cannot trust God with to-morrow, but longs to have much goods laid up. That is the temper which forfeits the smile of God, and grinds the faces of the poor, to make an ignoble "provision" for the future. How often, since the time of Moses, has the unblessed accumulation become hateful! How often, since the time of St. James, the rust of such possession has eaten the flesh like fire! Men would be far more generous, the difference between wealth and poverty would be less portentous, and the resources of religion and charity less crippled, if we lived in the spirit of the Lord's prayer, desirous of the advance of the kingdom, but not asking to be given to-morrow's bread until to-morrow. That lesson was taught by the manner of the dispensation of the manna, but the covetousness of Israel would not learn it. The people actually strove to be dishonest in their enjoyment of a miracle. It is no wonder that Moses was wroth with them.

Among the strange properties of their supernatural food not the least curious was this: that when they came to measure what they had collected, and compare it with what Moses had bidden,* the most eager and able-bodied had nothing over, and the feeblest had no lack. Every real worker was supplied, and none was glutted. This result is apparently miraculous. St. Paul's use of it does not, as some have supposed, represent it as a result of Hebrew benevolence, sharing with the weak the more abundant supplies of the strong: the miracle is not cited as an example of charity, but of that practical equality, divinely approved, which Christian charity should reproduce; the Christian Church is bidden to do voluntarily what was done by miracle in the wilderness: " your abundance being a supply at this present time for their want, that their abundance also may become a supply for your want, that there may be equality; as it is written, He that gathered much had nothing over, and he that gathered little had no lack" (2 Cor. viii. 15).

It is quite in vain to appeal to this passage in favour of socialistic theories. In the first place it applies only to the necessities of existence; and even granting that

---

* The "omer" of this passage is not mentioned elsewhere in Scripture: it is known to have been the one-hundredth part of the homer with which careless readers sometimes confuse it, and its capacity is variously estimated, from somewhat under half a gallon to somewhat above three-quarters.

the state should enforce the principle to which it points, the duty would not extend beyond a liberal poor rate. When contributions were afterwards demanded for the sanctuary, there is no trace of a dead level in their resources: the rulers gave the gems and spices and oil, some brought gold, with some were found blue and linen and skins, and others had acacia-wood to offer (xxxv. 22-4).

In the second place, this arrangement was only temporary; and while the soil of Canaan was distinctly claimed for the Lord, the enjoyment of it by individuals was secured, and perpetuated in their families, by stringent legislation. Now, land is the kind of property which socialists most vehemently assail; but persons who appeal to Exodus must submit to the authority of Judges.

Socialism, therefore, and its coercive measures, find no more real sanction here than in the Church of Jerusalem, where the property of Ananias was his own, and the price of it in his own power. But yet it is highly significant that in both Testaments, as the Church of God starts upon its career, an example should be given of the effacing of inequalities, in the one case by miracle, in the other by such a voluntary movement as best becomes the gospel. Is not such a movement, large and free, the true remedy for our modern social distractions and calamities? Would it not be wise and Christ-like for the rich to give, as St. Paul taught the Corinthians to give, what the law could never wisely exact from them? Would not self-denial, on a scale to imply real sacrifice, and fulfilling in spirit rather than letter the apostle's aspiration for "equality," secure in return the enthusiastic adhesion to the rights of property of all that is best and noblest among the poor?

When will the world, or even the Church, awaken to the great truth that our politics also need to be steeped in Christian feeling—that humanity requires not a revolution but a pentecost—that a millennium cannot be enacted, but will dawn whenever human bosoms are emptied of selfishness and lust, and filled with brotherly kindness and compassion? Such, and no more, was the socialism which St. Paul deduced from the equality in the supply of manna.

SPIRITUAL MEAT.

xvi. 15-36.

Since the journey of Israel is throughout full of sacred meaning, no one can fail to discern a mystery in the silent ceaseless daily miracle of bread-giving. But we are not left to our conjectures. St. Paul calls manna "spiritual meat," not because it nourished the higher life (for the eaters of it murmured for flesh, and were not estranged from their lust), but because it answered to realities of the spiritual world (1 Cor. x. 3). And Christ Himself said, "It was not Moses that gave you the bread out of heaven, but My Father giveth you the true Bread from heaven," making manna the type of sustenance which the soul needs in the wilderness, and which only God can give (John vi. 32).

We note the time of its bestowal. The soul has come forth out of its bondage. Perhaps it imagines that emancipation is enough: all is won when its chains are broken: there is to be no interval between the Egypt of sin and the Promised Land of milk and honey and repose. Instead of this serene attainment, it finds that the soul requires to be fed, and no food is to be seen, but only a wilderness of scorching heat, dry sand, vacancy, and hunger. Old things have passed away, but it is not yet realised that all things have become new. Religion threatens to become a vast system for the removal of accustomed indulgences and enjoyments, but where is the recompense for all that it forbids? The soul cries out for food: well for it if the cry be not faithless, nor spoken to earthly chiefs alone!

There is a noteworthy distinction between the gift of manna and every other recorded miracle of sustenance. In Eden the fruit of immortality was ripening upon an earthly tree. The widow of Zarephath was fed from her own stores. The ravens bore to Elijah ordinary bread and flesh; and if an angel fed him, it was with a cake baken upon coals. Christ Himself was content to multiply common bread and fish, and even after His resurrection gave His apostles the fare to which they were accustomed. Thus they learned that the divine life must be led amid the ordinary conditions of mortality. Even the incarnation of Deity was wrought in the likeness of sinful flesh. But yet the incarnation was the bringing of a new life, a strange and unknown energy, to man.

And here, almost at the beginning of revelation, is typified, not the homely conditions of the inner life, but its unearthly nature and essence. Here is no multiplication of their own stores, no gift, like the quails, of such meat as they were wont to gather. They asked "What is it?" And this teaches the Christian that his sustenance is not of this world. They were fed " with manna which they knew not . . . to make them know that man doth not live by bread only, but by every word that proceedeth out of the mouth of God doth man live" (Deut. viii. 3). The root of worldliness is not in this indulgence or that, in gay clothing or an active career; but in the soul's endeavour to draw its nourishment from things below. And spirituality belongs not to an uncouth vocabulary, nor to the robes of any confraternity, to rigid rules or austere deportment; it is the blessedness of a life nourished upon the bread of heaven, and doomed to starve if that bread be not bestowed. Let not the wealthy find an insuperable bar to spirituality in his condition, nor the poor suppose that indigence cannot have its treasure upon earth; but let each man ask whence come his most real and practical impulses and energies upon life's journey. If these flow from even the purest earthly source—love of wife or child, anything else than communion with the Father of spirits, this is not the bread of life, and can no more nourish a pilgrim towards eternity than the husks which swine eat.

There is no mistaking the doctrine of the New Testament as to what this bread may be. By prayer and faith, by ordinances and sacraments rightly used, the manna may be gathered; but Jesus Himself is the Bread of life, His Flesh is meat indeed and His Blood is drink indeed, and He gives His Flesh for the life of the world. Christ is the Vine, and we are the branches, fruitful only by the sap which flows from Him. As there are diseases which cannot be overcome by powerful drugs, but by a generous and wholesome dietary, so is it with the diseases of the soul—pride, anger, selfishness, falsehood, lust. As the curse of sin is removed by the faith which appropriates pardon, so its power is broken by the steady personal acceptance of Christ; and our Bread and Wine are His new humanity, given to us, until He becomes the second Father of the race, which is begotten again in Him. An easy temper is not Christian meekness; dislike to witness pain is not Christian love. All our goodness must strike root deeper than in the sensibilities, must be nourished by the communication to us of the mind which was in Christ Jesus.

And this food is universally given, and universally suitable. The strong and the weak, the aged chieftain and little children, ate and were nourished. No stern decree excluded any member of the visible Church in the wilderness from sharing the bread from heaven: they did eat the same spiritual meat, provided only that they gathered it. Their part was to be in earnest in accepting, and so is ours; but if we fail, whom shall we blame except ourselves? In the mystery of its origin, in the silent and secret mode of its descent from above, in the constancy of its bestowal, and in its suitability for all the camp, for Moses and the youngest child, the manna prefigured Christ.

Every day a fresh supply had to be laid up, and nothing could be held over from the largest hoard. So it is with us: we must give ourselves to Christ for ever, but we must ask Him daily to give Himself to us. The richest experience, the purest aspiration, the humblest self-abandonment that was ever felt, could not reach forward to supply the morrow. Past graces will become loathsome if used instead of present supplies from heaven. And the secret of many a scandalous fall is that the unhappy soul grew self-confident: unlike St. Paul, he reckoned that he had already attained; and thereupon the graces in which he trusted became corrupt and vile.

The constant supply was not more needful than it was abundant. The manna lay all around the camp: the Bread of Life is He who stands at our door and knocks. Alas for those who murmur for grosser indulgences! Israel demanded and obtained them; but while the flesh was in their nostrils the angel of the Lord went forth and smote them. Is there no plague any longer for the perverse? What are the discords that convulse families, the uncurbed passions to which nothing is sacred, the jaded appetite and weary discontent which hates the world even as it hates itself? what but the judgment of God upon those who despise His provision, and must needs gratify themselves? Be it our happiness, as it is our duty, to trust Him to prepare our table before us, while He leads us to His Holy Land.

The Lord of the Sabbath already taught His people to respect His day. Upon it no manna fell; and we shall hereafter see the bearing of this incident upon the question whether the Sabbath is only an ordinance of Judaism. Meanwhile they who went out to gather had a sharp lesson in the difference between faith, which expects what God has promised, and presumption, which hopes not to lose much by disobeying Him.

Lastly, an omer of manna was to be kept throughout all generations, before the Testimony. Grateful remembrance of past mercies, temporal as well as spiritual, was to connect itself with the deepest and most awful mysteries of religion. So let it be with us. The bitter proverb that eaten bread is soon forgotten must never be true of the Christian. He is to remember all the way that the Lord his God hath led him. He is bidden to "forget not all His benefits, Who forgiveth all thine iniquities, Who healeth all thy diseases . . . Who satisfieth thy mouth with good things." So foolish is the slander that religion is too transcendental for the common life of man.

CHAPTER XVII.

MERIBAH.

xvii. 1-7.

THE people, miraculously fed, are therefore called to exhibit more confidence in God than hitherto, because much is required of him to whom much is given. They have now to plunge deeper into the wilderness; and after two stages which Exodus omits (Num. xxxiii. 12, 13), and just as they approach the mount of God, they find themselves without water. Even the Son of Man Himself was led into the wilderness next after the descent of the Spirit, and the avowal by the voice of God; nor is any true Christian to marvel if his seasons of special privilege are succeeded by special demands upon his firmness.

One finds himself conjecturing, very often, what nobler history, what grander analogies between type and antitype, what more gracious and lavish interpositions might have instructed us, if only the type had been less woefully imperfect—if Israel had been trustful as Moses was, and the crude material had not marred the design.

It would be more practical and edifying to reflect how often we ourselves, like Israel, might have learned and exemplified deep things of the grace of God, when all we really exhibited was the well-worn lesson of human frailty and divine forbearance.

In the story of our Lord, it has been observed that before the Pharisees directly assailed Himself, they found fault with His disciples who fasted not, or accosted them concerning Him Who ate with sinners. And so here the people really tempted God, but openly "strove with Moses," and with Aaron too, for the verb is a plural one: "Give *ye* water" (ver. 2).

But as Aaron is merely an agent and spokesman, the chief value of this tacit allusion to him, besides proving his fidelity, is to refute the notion that he sinks into comparative obscurity only after the sin of the golden calf. Already his position is one to be indicated rather than expressed; and Moses said, "Why do ye quarrel with me? wherefore do ye try the Lord?"

But the frenzy rose higher: it was he, and not a higher One, who had brought them out of Egypt; the upshot of it would only be "to kill us, and our children, and our cattle, with thirst."

Look closely at this expression, and a curious significance discloses itself. Was it mere covetousness, the spirit of the Jew Shylock lamenting in one breath his daughter and his ducats, which introduced the cattle along with the children into this complaint of dying men? Shylock himself, when death actually looked him in the face, readily sacrificed his fortune. Nor is it credible that a large number of people, really believing that a horrible death was imminent, would have spent any complaints upon their property. The language is exactly that of angry exaggeration. They have come through straits quite as desperate, and they know it well. It is not the fear of death, but the painful delay of rescue, the discomfort and misery of their condition in the meanwhile, the contrast between their sufferings and their own conception of the rights of the favourites of heaven, which is audible in this complaint. And thus their "Trial" and "Quarrel" are admirably epitomised in the phrase "Is Jehovah among us or not?" a phrase which has often since been in the heart, if not upon the lips, of men who had supposed the life divine to be one long holiday, the pilgrimage an excursion, when without are fightings and within fears, when they have great sorrow and heaviness in their hearts.

Because God is not a Judge, but a Father, the murmurs of Israel do not prevent Him from showing mercy. Accordingly, when Moses prays, he is bidden to go on before the people, bringing certain of their elders along with him for witnesses of the marvel that was to follow. Such is the Divine method. As soon as unbelief and discontent estranged the Jews of the New Testament from Christ, He would not vulgarise His miracles, nor do many mighty works among the unbelieving. After His resurrection He appeared not unto all the people, but unto witnesses chosen before. And as the Jews were chosen to bear witness to Him among the nations, so were these elders now to bear witness among the Jews, who might without their testimony have fallen into some such rationalising theory as that of Tacitus, who says that Moses discovered a fountain by examining a spot where wild asses lay.

With these witnesses, he is bidden to go to a rock in Horeb (so nearly had these murmurers approached the scene of the most awful of all manifestations of Him whose presence they debated), and there God was to stand before them upon the rock, making His universal presence a localised consciousness in their experience.

A true religion is progressive: every stage of it leans

on the past and sustains the future; and so Moses must bring with him "the rod, wherewith thou smotest the river." The dullest can see the fitness of this allusion. Among all the wonders which the shepherd's wand had wrought, the mastery over the Nile, the plague which inflicted an unwonted thirst upon the inhabitants of that well-watered field of Zoan, was most to the purpose now. To kill and to make alive are the functions of the same Being, and He Who spoiled the Egyptian river will now refresh His heritage that is weary. At the touch of the prophetic wand the waters poured forth which thenceforth supplied them through all their desert wanderings.

Reserving the symbolic meaning of this event for a future study, we have to remember meanwhile the warning which the apostle here discovered. All the people drank of the rock, yet with many of them God was not pleased. Privilege is one thing—acceptance is quite another; and it shall be more tolerable at last for Sodom and Gomorrah than for nations, churches and men, who were content to resemble soil that drinketh in the rain that cometh upon it oft, and yet to remain unfruitful. Already the conduct of Israel was such that the place was named from human worthlessness rather than Divine beneficence. Too often, it is the more conspicuous part of the story of the relations of God and man.

AMALEK.

xvii. 8-16.

Nothing can be more natural, to those who remember the value of a fountain in the East, than that Amalek should swoop down from his own territories upon

Israel, as soon as this abundant river tempted his cupidity. This unprovoked attack of a kindred nation leads to another advance in the education of the people.

They had hitherto been the sheep of God: now they must become His warriors. At the Red Sea it was said to them, "Stand still, and see the salvation of the Lord ... the Lord shall fight for you, and ye shall hold your peace" (xiv. 13). But it is not so now. Just as the function of every true miracle is to lead to a state of faith in which miracles are not required; just as a mother reaches her hand to a tottering infant, that presently the boy may go alone, so the Lord fought for Israel, that Israel might learn to fight for the Lord. The herd of slaves who came out of Egypt could not be trusted to stand fast in battle; and what a defeat would have done with them we may judge by their outcries at the very sight of Pharaoh. But now they had experience of Divine succour, and had drawn the inspiring breath of freedom. And so it was reasonable to expect that some chosen men of them at least will be able to endure the shock of battle. And if so, it was a matter of the last importance to develop and render conscious the national spirit, a spirit so noble in its unselfish readiness to die, and in its scorn of such material ills as anguish and mutilation compared with baseness and dishonour, that the re-kindling of it in seasons of peril and conflict is more than half a compensation for the horrors of a battle-field.

We do not now inquire what causes avail to justify the infliction and endurance of those horrors. Probably they will vary from age to age; and as the ties grow strong which bind mankind together, the rupture of them will be regarded with an ever-deepening shudder,

—just as England to-day would certainly refuse to make war upon our American kinsmen for a provocation which (rightly or wrongly) she would not endure from Russians. But the point to be observed is that war cannot be inherently immoral, since God instructed in war the first nation that He ever trained, not using its experience of His immediate interpositions to supersede all need of human strife, but to make valiant soldiers, and adding some of the most precious lessons of all their later experience on the battle-field and by the sword. Now, it assuredly cannot be shown that anything in itself immoral is fostered and encouraged by the Old Testament. Slavery and divorce, which it was not yet possible to extirpate, were hampered, restricted, and reduced to a minimum, being " suffered " " because of the hardness of ' their ' hearts " (Matt. xix. 8). The wildest assailant of the Pentateuch will scarcely pretend that it fosters and incites either divorce or slavery, as, beyond all question, it encourages the martial ardour of the Jews.

And yet war, though permissible, and in certain circumstances necessary, is only necessary as the lesser of two evils; it is not in itself good. Solomon, not David, could build the temple of the Lord; and Isaiah sharply contrasts the Messiah with even that providentially appointed conqueror, the only pagan who is called by God "My anointed," in that the one comes upon rulers as upon mortar, and as the potter treadeth clay, but the Other breaks not a bruised reed, nor quenches the smoking flax (Isa. xli. 25, xlii. 3, xlv. 1). The ideal of humanity is peace, and also it is happiness, but war may not yet have ceased to be a necessity of life, sometimes as ruinous to evade as any other form of suffering.

Another necessity of national development is the advancement of capable men. The empire of Napoleon would assuredly have withered, if only because its chief was as jealous of commanding genius as he was ready to advance and patronise capacity of the second order. It is a maxim that true greatness finds worthy colleagues and successors, and rejoices in them. And while the guidance of Jehovah is to be assumed throughout, it is significant that the first mention of the splendid commander and godly judge, during all whose days and the days of his contemporaries Israel served Jehovah, comes not in any express revelation or commandment of God; but the narrative relates that Moses said unto Joshua, "Choose out men for us and go out, fight with Amalek: to-morrow I will stand on the top of the hill with the rod of God in my hand." They are the words of one who had noted him already as "a man in whom is the Spirit" (Num. xxvii. 18), of one also who had unlearned, in the experience now of eighty years, the desire of glittering achievement and martial fame, who knew that the deepest fountains of real power are hidden, and was content that another should lead the headlong and victorious charge, if only it were his to hold, upon the top of the hill, the rod of God.

Once it was his own rod: with it the exiled shepherd controlled the sheep of his master; that it should be the medium of the miraculous had appeared to be an additional miracle, but now it was the very rod of God, nor was any cry to heaven more eloquent and better grounded than simply the reaching toward the skies, in long, steady, mute appeal, of that symbol of all His dealings with them—the plaguing of Egypt, the recession of the tide and its wild return, the bringing of water from the rock. Was all to be in vain? Should the wild boar waste the vine just brought out of Egypt before ever it reached the appointed vineyard? And we also should be able to plead with God the noble works that He hath done in our time. For us also there ought to be such experience as worketh hope. As long as the exertion was possible even to the heroic force which age had not abated, Moses thus prayed for his people; for the gesture was a prayer, and a grand one, and must not be criticised otherwise than as the act of a poetic and primitive genius, whose institutions throughout are full of spiritual import. While he did this, Israel prevailed; but the slow progress of the victory reminds us of these dreary centuries during which we are just able to discern some gradual advance of the kingdom of Christ on earth, but no rout, no collapse of evil. And why was this? Because the sustaining and permanent energy was not to flow from the prayers of one, however holy and however eminent; three men were together in the mountain, and the co-operation of them all was demanded; so that only when Aaron and Hur supported the sinking hand of their chief was the decisive victory given.

Now, the lesson from all this does not concern the High-priestly intercession of our Lord, for the office of Moses is consistently distinguished from the priesthood. Nor can the notion be tolerated that if our Lord requires mortal co-operation before asking and being given the heathen for His heritage, which is obviously the case, the reason can be at all expressed by that weakness which needed support.

No, the Lord our Priest is also Himself the dispenser of victory. To Him all power is given on earth, and to Him it is our duty to appeal for the triumph of His own cause. And here and there, doubtless, a Christian heart is fervent and faithful in its intercessions. To these, unknown, unsuspected by the combatants in the heat of battle,—to humble saints, some of them bed-ridden, ignorant, poverty-stricken, despised, holy souls who have no controversial skill, no missionary calling, but who possess the grace habitually to convert their wishes into prayers,—to such, perhaps, it is due that the idols of India and China are now bowing down. And when they cease to be a minority in so doing, when those who now criticise learn to sustain their flagging energies, we shall see a day of the Lord.

Observe, however, that as the active exertion of the host does not displace the silence of intercession, neither is it displaced itself: Joshua really bore his part in the discomfiture of Amalek and his host. And so it is always. The development of human energy to the uttermost is a part of the design of Him Who gave a task even to unfallen man. Let none suppose that to labour is (sufficiently and by itself) to pray; but also let none idly persuade himself that while energies and responsibilities are his, to pray is sufficiently to labour.

Thus it came to pass that Israel won its first victory in battle. Another step was taken toward the fulfilment of the promise to Abraham to make of him a great nation; and also toward the gradual transference of the national faith from a passive reliance in Divine interposition to an abiding confidence in Divine help. Let it be clearly understood that this latter is the nobler and the more mature faith.

With martial ardour, God took care to inculcate the sense of national responsibility, without which warriors become no more than brigands. So it was with

Amalek: he had not been attacked or even menaced; he had marched out from his own territories to assail an innocent and kindred race ("then *came* Amalek" ver. 8), and his attack had been cruel and cowardly, he smote the hindmost, all that were feeble and in the rear, when they were faint and weary, and he feared not God (Deut. xxv. 18). Against all such tactics the wrath of God was denounced when, because of them, Amalek was doomed to total extirpation.

Moses now built an altar, to imprint on the mind of the people this new lesson. And he called it, "The Lord is my Banner," a title which called the nation at once to valour and to obedience, which asserted that they were an army, but a consecrated one.

Now let us ask whether this simple story is at all the kind of thing which legend or myth would have created, for the first martial exploit of Israel. The obscure part played by Moses is not what we would expect; nor, even as a mediator, is the position of one whose arms must be held up a very romantic conception. If the object is to inspire the Jews for later struggles with more formidable foes, the story is ill-contrived, for we read of no surprising force of Amalek, and no inspiriting exploit of Joshua. Everything is as prosaic as the real course of events in this poor world is wont to be. And on that account it is all the more useful to us who live prosaic lives, and need the help of God among prosaic circumstances.

CHAPTER XVIII.

JETHRO.

xviii. 1-27.

THE defeat of Amalek is followed by the visit of Jethro; the opposite pole of the relation between Israel and the nations, the coming of the Gentiles to his brightness. And already that is true which repeats itself all through the history of the Church, that much secular wisdom, the art of organisation, the structure and discipline of societies, may be drawn from the experience and wisdom of the world.

Moses was under the special guidance of God, as really as any modern enthusiast can claim to be. When he turned for aid or direction to heaven, he was always answered. And yet he did not think scorn of the counsel of his kinsman. And although eighty years had not dimmed the fire of his eyes, nor wasted his strength, he neglected not the warning which taught him to economise his force; not to waste on every paltry dispute the attention and wisdom which could govern the new-born state.

Jethro is the kinsman, and probably the brother-in-law of Moses; for if he were the father-in-law, and the same as Reuel in the second chapter, why should a new name be introduced without any mark of identification? When he hears of the emancipation of Israel from Egypt, he brings back to Moses his two sons and Zipporah, who had been sent away, after the angry scene at the circumcision of the younger, and before he entered Egypt with his life in his hand. Now he was a great personage, the leader of a new nation, and the conqueror of the proudest monarch in the world. With what feelings would the wife and husband meet? We are told nothing of their interview, nor have we any reason to qualify the unfavourable impression produced by the circumstances of their parting, by the schismatic worship founded by their grandchildren, and by the loneliness implied in the very names of Gershom and Eliezer—" A-stranger-there," and "God-a-Help."

But the relations between Moses and Jethro are charming, whether we look at the obeisance rendered to the official minister of God by him whom God had honoured so specially, by the prosperous man to the friend of his adversity, or at the interest felt by the priest of Midian in all the details of the great deliverance of which he had heard already, or his joy in a Divine manifestation, probably not in all respects according to the prejudices of his race, or his praise of Jehovah as "greater than all gods, yea, in the thing wherein they dealt proudly against them" (ver. 11, R.V.). The meaning of this phrase is either that the gods were plagued in their own domains, or that Jehovah had finally vanquished the Egyptians by the very element in which they were most oppressive, as when Moses himself had been exposed to drown.

There is another expression, in the first verse, which deserves to be remarked. How do the friends of a successful man think of the scenes in which he has borne a memorable part? They chiefly think of them in connection with their own hero. And amid all the story of the Exodus, in which so little honour is given to the human actor, the one trace of personal exultation is where it is most natural and becoming; it is in the heart of his relative: "When Jethro . . . heard of all that the Lord had done *for Moses* and for Israel."

We are told, with marked emphasis, that this Midianite, a priest, and accustomed to act as such with Moses in his family, "took a burnt-offering and sacrifices for God; and Aaron came, and all the elders of Israel, to eat bread with Moses' father-in-law before God." Nor can we doubt that the writer of the Epistle to the Hebrews, who laid such stress upon the subordination of Abraham to Melchizedek, would have discerned in the relative position of Jethro and Aaron another evidence that the ascendency of the Aaronic priesthood was only temporary. We shall hereafter see that priesthood is a function of redeemed humanity, and that all limitations upon it were for a season, and due to human shortcoming. But for this very reason (if there were no other) the chief priest could only be He Who represents and embodies all humanity, in Whom is neither Jew nor Greek, barbarian, Scythian, bond nor free, because He is all and in all.

In the meantime, here is recognised, in the history of Israel, a Gentile priesthood.

And, as at the passover, so now, the sacrifice to God is partaken of by His people, who are conscious of acceptance by Him. Happy was the union of innocent festivity with a sacramental recognition of God. It is the same sentiment which was aimed at by the primitive Christian Church in her feasts of love, genuine meals in the house of God, until licence and appetite spoiled them, and the apostle asked " Have ye not houses to eat and drink in?" (1 Cor. xi. 22). Shall there never come a time when the victorious and pure Church of the latter days shall regain what we have forfeited, when the doctrine of the consecration of what is called "secular life" shall be embodied again in forms like these? It speaks to us meanwhile in a form which is easily ridiculed (as in Lamb's well-known essay), and yet singularly touching and edifying if rightly considered, in the asking for a blessing upon our meals.

On the morrow, Jethro saw Moses, all day long, deciding the small matters and great which needed already to be adjudicated for the nation. He who had striven, without a commission, himself to smite the Egyptian and lead out Israel, is the same self-reliant, heroic, not too discreet person still.

But the true statesman and administrator is he who employs to the utmost all the capabilities and energies of his subordinates. And Jethro made a deep mark in history when he taught Moses the distinction between the lawgiver and the judge, between him who sought from God and proclaimed to the people the principles of justice and their form, and him who applied the law to each problem as it arose.

"It is supposed, and with probability," writes Kalisch (*in loco*), "that Alfred the Great, who was well versed in the Bible, based his own Saxon constitution of sheriffs in counties, etc., on the example of the Mosaic division (comp. *Bacon on English Government*, i. 70)." And thus it may be that our own nation owes its free institutions almost directly to the generous interest in the well-being of his relative, felt by an Arabian priest, who cherished, amid the growth of idolatries all around him, the primitive belief in God, and who rightly held that the first qualifications of a capable judge were ability, and the fear of God, truthfulness and hatred of unjust gain.

We learn from Deuteronomy (i. 9-15), that Moses allowed the people themselves to elect these officials, who became not only their judges but their captains.

From the whole of this narrative we see clearly that the intervention of God for Israel is no more to be regarded as superseding the exercise of human prudence and common-sense, than as dispensing with valour in the repulse of Amalek, and with patience in journeying through the wilderness.

THE TYPICAL BEARINGS OF THE HISTORY.

WE are now about to pass from history to legislation. And this is a convenient stage at which to pause, and ask how it comes to pass that all this narrative is also, in some sense, an allegory. It is a discussion full of pitfalls. Countless volumes of arbitrary and fanciful interpretation have done their worst to discredit every attempt, however cautious and sober, at finding more than the primary signification in any narrative.* And whoever considers the reckless, violent and inconsistent methods of the mystical commentators may be forgiven if he recoils from occupying the ground which they have wasted, and contents himself with simply drawing the lessons which the story directly suggests.

But the New Testament does not warrant such a surrender. It tells us that leaven answers to malice, and unleavened bread to sincerity; that at the Red Sea the people were baptized; that the tabernacle and the altar, the sacrifice and the priest, the mercy-seat and the manna, were all types and shadows of abiding Christian realities.

It is more surprising to find the return of the infant Jesus connected with the words "When Israel was a

---

* Take as an example the assertion of Bunyan that the sea in the Revelation is a sea of glass, because the laver in the tabernacle was made of the brazen looking-g'asses of the women. (*Solomon's Temple*, xxxvi. 1.)

child then I loved him, and I called My son out of Egypt,"—for it is impossible to doubt that the prophet was here speaking of the Exodus, and had in mind the phrase "Israel is My son, My first-born: let My son go, that he may serve Me" (Matt. i. 15; Hos. xi. 1; Exod. iv. 22).

How are such passages to be explained? Surely not by finding a superficial resemblance between two things, and thereupon transferring to one of them whatever is true of the other. No thought can attain accuracy except by taking care not to confuse in this way things which superficially resemble each other.

But no thought can be fertilising and suggestive which neglects real and deep resemblances, resemblances of principle as well as incident, resemblances which are due to the mind of God or the character of man.

In the structure and furniture of the tabernacle, and the order of its services, there are analogies deliberately planned, and such as every one would expect, between religious truth shadowed forth in Judaism, and the same truth spoken in these latter days unto us in the Son.

But in the emancipation, the progress, and alas! the sins and chastisements of Israel, there are analogies of another kind, since here it is history which resembles theology, and chiefly secular things which are compared with spiritual. But the analogies are not capricious; they are based upon the obvious fact that the same God Who pitied Israel in bondage sees, with the same tender heart, a worse tyranny. For it is not a figure of speech to say that sin is slavery. Sin does outrage the will, and degrade and spoil the life. The sinner does obey a hard and merciless master. If his true home is in the kingdom of God, he is, like Israel, not only a slave but an exile. Is God the God of the Jew only? for otherwise He must, being immutable, deal with us and our tyrant as He dealt with Israel and Pharaoh. If He did not, by an exertion of omnipotence, transplant them from Egypt to their inheritance at one stroke, but required of them obedience, co-operation, patient discipline, and a gradual advance, why should we expect the whole work and process of grace to be summed up in the one experience which we call conversion? Yet if He did, promptly and completely, break their chains and consummate their emancipation, then the fact that grace is a progressive and gradual experience does not forbid us to reckon ourselves dead unto sin. If the region through which they were led, during their time of discipline, was very unlike the land of milk and honey which awaited the close of their pilgrimage, it is not unlikely that the same God will educate his later Church by the same means, leading us also by a way that we know not, to humble and prove us, that He may do us good at the latter end.

And if He marks, by a solemn institution, the period when we enter into covenant relations with Himself, and renounce the kingdom and tyranny of His foe, is it marvellous that the apostle found an analogy for this in the great event by which God punctuated the emancipation of Israel, leading them out of Egypt through the sea depths and beneath the protecting cloud?

If privilege, and adoption, and the Divine good-will, did not shelter them from the consequences of ingratitude and rebellion, if He spared not the natural branches, we should take heed lest He spare not us.

Such analogies are really arguments, as solid as those of Bishop Butler.

But the same cannot be maintained so easily of some others. When that is quoted of our Lord upon the cross which was written of the paschal lamb, "a bone shall not be broken" (Exod. xii. 46, John xix. 36), we feel that the citation needs to be justified upon different grounds. But such grounds are available. He was the true Lamb of God. For His sake the avenger passes over all His followers. His flesh is meat indeed. And therefore, although no analogy can be absolutely perfect, and the type has nothing to declare that His blood is drink indeed, yet there is an admirable fitness, worthy of inspired record, in the consummating and fulfilment in Him, and in Him alone of three sufferers, of the precept "A bone of Him shall not be broken." It may not be an express prophecy which is brought to pass, but it is a beautiful and appropriate correspondence, wrought out by Providence, not available for the coercion of sceptics, but good for the edifying of believers.

And so it is with the calling of the Son out of Egypt. Unquestionably Hosea spoke of Israel. But unquestionably too the phrase "My Son, My Firstborn" is a startling one. Here is already a suggestive difference between the monotheism of the Old Testament and the austere jealous logical orthodoxy of the Koran, which protests "It is not meet for God to have any Son, God forbid" (Sura xix. 36). Jesus argued that such a rigid and lifeless orthodoxy as that of later Judaism, ought to have been scandalised, long before it came to consider His claims, by the ancient and recognised inspiration which gave the name of gods to men who sat in judgment as the representatives of Heaven. He claimed the right to carry still further the same principle—namely, that deity is not selfish and incommunicable, but practically gives itself away, in transferring the exercise of its functions. From such condescension everything may be expected, for God does not halt in the middle of a path He has begun to tread.

But if this argument of Jesus were a valid one (and the more it is examined the more profound it will be seen to be), how significant will then appear the term " My Son," as applied to Israel!

In condescending so far, God almost pledged Himself to the Incarnation, being no dealer in half measures, nor likely to assume rhetorically a relation to mankind to which in fact He would not stoop.

Every Christian feels, moreover, that it is by virtue of the grand and final condescension that all the preliminary steps are possible. Because Abraham's seed was one, that is Christ, therefore ye (all) if ye are Christ's, are Abraham's seed, heirs according to promise (Gal. iii. 16, 29).

But when this great harmony comes to be devoutly recognised, a hundred minor and incidental points of contact are invested with a sacred interest.

No doctrinal injury would have resulted, if the Child Jesus had never left the Holy Land. No infidel could have served his cause by quoting the words of Hosea. Nor can we now cite them against infidels as a prophecy fulfilled. But when He does return from Egypt our devotions, not our polemics, hail and rejoice in the coincidence. It reminds us, although it does not demonstrate, that He who is thus called out of Egypt is indeed the Son.

The sober historian cannot prove anything, logically and to demonstration, by the reiterated interventions in history of atmospheric phenomena. And yet no devout thinker can fail to recognise that God has reserved the hail against the time of trouble and war.

In short, it is absurd and hopeless to bid us limit our contemplation, in a divine narrative, to what can be demonstrated like the propositions of Euclid. We laugh at the French for trying to make colonies and constitutions according to abstract principles, and proposing, as they once did, to reform Europe "after the Chinese manner." Well, religion also is not a theory: it is the true history of the past of humanity, and it is the formative principle in the history of the present and the future.

And hence it follows that we may dwell with interest and edification upon analogies, as every great thinker confesses the existence of truths, "which never can be proved."

In the meantime it is easy to recognise the much simpler fact, that these things happened unto them by way of example, and they were written for our admonition.

CHAPTER XIX.

AT SINAI.

xix. 1-25.

IN the third month from the Exodus, and on the self-same day (which addition fixes the date precisely), the people reached the wilderness of Sinai. This answers fairly to the date of Pentecost, which was afterwards connected by tradition with the giving of the law. And therefore Pentecost was the right time for the gift of the Holy Ghost, bringing with Him the law of the spirit of life in Christ Jesus, and that freedom from servile Jewish obedience which is not attained by violating law, but by being imbued in its spirit, by the love which is the fulfilling of the law.

There is among the solemn solitudes of Sinai a wide amphitheatre, reached by two converging valleys, and confronted by an enormous perpendicular cliff, the Ras Sufsâfeh—a "natural altar," before which the nation had room to congregate, awed by the stern magnificence of the approach, and by the intense loneliness and desolation of the surrounding scene, and thus prepared for the unparalleled revelation which awaited them.

It is the manner of God to speak through nature and the senses to the soul. We cannot imagine the youth of the Baptist spent in Nazareth, nor of Jesus in the desert. Elijah, too, was led into the wilderness to receive the vision of God, and the agony of Jesus was endured at night, and secluded by the olives from the paschal moon. It is by another application of the same principle that the settled Jewish worship was bright with music and splendid with gold and purple; and the notion that the sublime and beautiful in nature and art cannot awaken the feelings to which religion appeals, is as shallow as the notion that when these feelings are awakened all is won.

What happens next is a protest against this latter extreme. Awe is one thing: the submission of the will is another. And therefore Moses was stopped when about to ascend the mountain, there to keep the solemn appointment that was made when God said, "This shall be the token unto thee that I have sent thee: When thou hast brought forth the people out of Egypt, ye shall serve God upon this mountain" (iii. 12). His own sense of the greatness of the crisis perhaps needed to be deepened. Certainly the nation had to be pledged, induced to make a deliberate choice, now first, as often again, under Joshua and Samuel, and when Elijah invoked Jehovah upon Carmel. (Josh. xxiv. 24; 1 Sam. xii. 14; 1 Kings xviii. 21, 39.)

It is easy to speak of pledges and formal declarations lightly, but they have their warrant in many such Scriptural analogies, nor should we easily find a church, careful to deal with souls, which has not employed them in some form, whether after the Anglican and Lutheran fashion, by confirmation, or in the less formal methods of other Protestant communions, or even by delaying baptism itself until it becomes, for the adult in Christian lands, what it is to the convert from false creeds.

Therefore the Lord called to Moses as he climbed

the steep, and offered through him a formal covenant to the people.

"Thus shalt thou say to the house of Jacob,* and tell the children of Israel: Ye have seen what I did unto the Egyptians, and how I bare you on eagles' wings, and brought you unto Myself."

The appeal is to their personal experience and their gratitude: will this be enough? will they accept His yoke, as every convert must, not knowing what it may involve, not yet having His demands specified and His commandments before their eyes, content to believe that whatever is required of them will be good, because the requirement is from God? Thus did Abraham, who went forth, not knowing whither, but knowing that he was divinely guided. "Now, therefore, if ye will obey My voice indeed and keep My covenant, then ye shall be a peculiar treasure unto Me from among all peoples; for all the earth is Mine, and ye shall be unto Me a kingdom of priests and a holy nation."

Thus God conveys to them, more explicitly than hitherto, the fact that He is the universal Lord, not ruling one land or nation only, nor, as the Pentateuch is charged with teaching, their tutelary deity among many others. Thus also the seeds are sown in them of a wholesome and rational self-respect, such as the Psalmist felt, who asked "What is man, that Thou art mindful of him?" yet realised that such mindful-

---

* This phrase is not found elsewhere in the Pentateuch. Is it fancy which detects in it a desire to remind them of their connection with the least worthy rather than the noblest of the Patriarchs? One would not expect, for instance, to read, Fear not, thou worm Abraham, or even Israel; but the name of Jacob at once calls up humble associations.

ness gave to man a real dignity, made him but little lower than the angels, and crowned him with glory and honour.

Abolish religion, and mankind will divide into two classes,—one in which vanity, unchecked by any spiritual superior, will obey no restraints of law, and another of which the conscious pettiness will aspire to no dignity of holiness, and shrink from no dishonour of sin. It is only the presence of a loving God which can unite in us the sense of humility and greatness, as having nothing and yet possessing all things, and valued by God as His "peculiar treasure."*

And with a reasonable self-respect should come a noble and yet sober dignity—"Ye shall be a kingdom of priests," a dynasty (for such is the meaning) of persons invested with royal and also with priestly rank. This was spoken just before the law gave the priesthood into the hands of one tribe; and thus we learn that Levi and Aaron were not to supplant the nation, but to represent it.

Now, this double rank is the property of redeemed humanity: we are "a kingdom and priests unto God." Yet the laity of the Corinthian Church were rebuked for a self-asserting and mutinous enjoyment of their rank: "Ye have reigned as kings without us"; and others there were in this Christian dispensation who "perished in the gainsaying of Korah" (1 Cor. iv. 8; Jude 11).

If the words "He hath made us a kingdom and

---

* This word is the same which occurs in the verse so beautifully but erroneously rendered "They shall be Mine, saith the Lord of hosts, in the day when I make up My jewels" (Mal. iii. 17, A.V.). "They shall be Mine . . . in the day that I do make, even a peculiar treasure" (R.V.).

priests" furnish any argument against the existence of an ordained ministry now, then there should have been no Jewish priesthood, for the same words are here. And is it supposed that this assertion only began to be true when the apostles died? Certainly there is a kind of self-assertion in the ministry which they condemn. But if they are opposed to its existence, alas for the Pastoral Epistles! It was because the function belonged to all, that no man might arrogate it who was not commissioned to act on behalf of all.

But while the individual may not assert himself to the unsettling of church order, the privilege is still common property. All believers have boldness to enter into the holiest place of all. All are called upon to rule for God "over a few things," to establish a kingdom of God within, and thus to receive a crown of life, and to sit with Jesus upon His throne. The very honours by which Israel was drawn to God are offered to us all, as it is written, "We are the circumcision," "We are Abraham's seed and heirs according to the promise" (Phil. iii. 3 ; Gal. iii. 29).

To this appeal the nation responded gladly. They could feel that indeed they had been sustained by God as the eagle bears her young—not grasping them in her claws, like other birds, but as if enthroned between her wings, and sheltered by her body, which interposed between the young and any arrow of the hunter. Thus, say the Rabbinical interpreters, did the pillar of cloud intervene between Israel and the Egyptians. If the image were to be pressed so far, we could now find a much closer analogy for the eagle " preferring itself to be pierced rather than to witness the death of its young" (Kalisch). But far more tender, and very touching in its domestic homeliness, is the metaphor of Him Whose discourses teem with allusions to the Old Testament, yet Who preferred to compare Himself to a hen gathering her chickens under her wing.

With the adhesion of Israel to the covenant, Moses returned to God. And the Lord said, "Lo, I come unto thee in a thick cloud, that the people may hear when I speak with thee, and may also believe thee for ever."

The design was to deepen their reverence for the Lawgiver Whose law they should now receive; to express by lessons, not more dreadful than the plagues of Egypt, but more vivid and sublime, the tremendous grandeur of Him Who was making a covenant with them, Who had borne them on His wings and called them His firstborn Son, Whom therefore they might be tempted to approach with undue familiarity, were it not for the mountain that burned up to heaven, the voice of the trumpet waxing louder and louder, and the Appearance so fearful that Moses said, "I exceedingly fear and quake" (τὸ φαντάζομενον—Heb. xii. 21).

When thus the Deity became terrible, the envoy would be honoured also.

But it is important to observe that these terrible manifestations were to cease. Like the impressions produced by sickness, by sudden deaths, by our own imminent danger, the emotion would subside, but the conviction should remain: they should believe Moses for ever. Emotions are like the swellings of the Nile: they subside again; but they ought to leave a fertilising deposit behind.

That the impression might not be altogether passive, and therefore ephemeral, the people were bidden to "sanctify themselves"; all that is common and secular must be suspended for awhile; and it is worth notice that, as when the family of Jacob put away their strange gods, so now the Israelites must wash their clothes (cf. Gen. xxxv. 2). For one's vestment is a kind of outer self, and has been with the man in the old occupations from which he desires to purify himself. It was therefore that when Jehu was made king, and when Jesus entered Jerusalem in triumph, men put their garments under their chief to express their own subjection (2 Kings ix. 13; Matt. xxi. 7). Much of the philosophy of Carlyle is latent in these ancient laws and usages.

Moreover, the mountain was to be fenced from the risk of profanation by any sudden impulsive movement of the crowd, and even a beast that touched it should be slain by such weapons as men could hurl without themselves pursuing it. Only when the trumpet blew a long summons might the appointed ones come up to the mount (ver. 13).

On the third day, after a soul-searching interval, there were thunders and lightnings, and a cloud, and the trumpet blast; and while all the people trembled, Moses led them forth to meet with God. Again the narrative reverts to the terrible phenomena—the fire like the smoke of a furnace (called by an Egyptian name which only occurs in the Pentateuch), and the whole mountain quaking. Then, since his commission was now to be established, Moses spake, and the Lord answered him with a voice. And when he again climbed the mountain, it became necessary to send him back with yet another warning, whether his example was in danger of emboldening others to exercise their newly given priesthood, or the very excess of terror exercised its well-known fascinating power, as men in a burning ship have been seen to leap into the flames.

And the priests also, who come near to God, should sanctify themselves. It has been asked who these were, since the Levitical institutions were still non-existent (ver. 22, cf. 24). But it is certain that the heads of houses exercised priestly functions; and it is not impossible that the elders of Israel who came to eat before God with Jethro (xviii. 12) had begun to perform religious functions for the people. Is it supposed that the nation had gone without religious services for three months?

It has been remarked by many that the law of Moses appealed for acceptance to popular and even democratic sanctions. The covenant was ratified by a plébiscite. The tremendous evidence was offered equally to all. For, said St. Augustine, "as it was fit that the law which was given, not to one man or a few enlightened people, but to the whole of a populous nation, should be accompanied by awe-inspiring signs, great marvels were wrought . . . before the people" (*De Civ. Dei*, x. 13).

We have also to observe the contrast between the appearance of God on Sinai and His manifestation in Jesus. And this also was strongly wrought out by an ancient father, who represented the Virgin Mary, in the act of giving Jesus into the hands of Simeon, as saying, "The blast of the trumpet does not now terrify those who approach, nor a second time does the mountain, all on fire, cause terror to those who come nigh, nor does the law punish relentlessly those who would boldly touch. What is present here speaks of love to man; what is apparent, of the Divine compassion." (Methodius *De Sym. et Anna*, vii.)

But we must remember that the Epistle to the Hebrews regards the second manifestation as the more solemn of the two, for this very reason: that we have not come to a burning mountain, or to mortal penalties for carnal irreverence, but to the spiritual mountain Zion, to countless angels, to God the Judge, to the spirits of just men made perfect, and to Jesus Christ. If they escaped not, when they refused Him Who warned on earth, much more we, who turn away from Him Who warneth from heaven (Heb. xii. 18-25).

There is a question, lying far behind all these, which demands attention.

It is said that legends of wonderful appearances of the gods are common to all religions; that there is no reason for giving credit to this one and rejecting all the rest; and, more than this, that God absolutely could not reveal Himself by sensuous appearances, being Himself a Spirit. In what sense and to what extent God can be said to have really revealed Himself, we shall examine hereafter. At present it is enough to ask whether human love and hatred, joy and sorrow, homage and scorn can manifest themselves by looks and tones, by the open palm and the clenched fist, by laughter and tears, by a bent neck and by a curled lip. For if what is most immaterial in our own soul can find sensuous expression, it is somewhat bold to deny that a majesty and power beyond anything human may at least be conceived as finding utterance, through a mountain burning to the summit and reeling to the base, and the blast of a trumpet which the people could not hear and live.

But when it is argued that wondrous theophanies are common to all faiths, two replies present themselves. If all the races of mankind agree in believing that there is a God, and that He manifests Himself wonderfully, does that really prove that there is no

God, or even that He never manifested Himself wondrously? We should certainly be derided if we insisted that such a universal belief proved the truth of the story of Mount Sinai, and perhaps we should deserve our fate. But it is more absurd by far to pretend that this instinct, this intuition, this universal expectation that God would some day, somewhere, rend the veil which hides Him, does actually refute the narrative.

We have also to ask for the production of those other narratives, sublime in their conception and in the vast audience which they challenged, sublimely pure alike from taint of idolatrous superstition and of moral evil, profound and far-reaching in their practical effect upon humanity, which deserve to be so closely associated with the giving of the Mosaic law that in their collapse it also must be destroyed, as the fall of one tree sometimes breaks the next. But this narrative stands out so far in the open, and lifts its head so high, that no other even touches a bough of it when overturned.

Is it seriously meant to compare the alleged disappearance of Romulus, or the secret interviews of Numa with his Egeria, to a history like this? Surely one similar story should be produced, before it is asserted that such stories are everywhere.

CHAPTER XX.

THE LAW.

xx. 1-17.

WE have now reached that great event, one of the most momentous in all history, the giving of the Ten Commandments. And it is necessary to consider what was the meaning of this event, what part were they designed to play in the religious development of mankind.

1. St. Paul tells us plainly what they did *not* effect. By the works of the law could no flesh be justified: to the father of the Hebrew race faith was reckoned instead of righteousness; the first of their royal line coveted the blessedness not of the obedient but of the pardoned; and Habakkuk declared that the just should live by his faith, while the law is not of faith, and offers life only to the man that doeth these things (Rom. iv. 3, 6; Gal. iii. 12). In the doctrinal scheme of St. Paul there was no room for a compromise between salvation by faith and reliance upon our own performance of any works, even those simple and obvious duties which are of world-wide obligation.

2. But he never meant to teach that a Christian is free from the obligation of the moral law. If it is not true that we can keep it and so earn heaven, it is equally false that we may break it without penalty or

remorse. What he insisted upon was this : that obligation is one thing, and energy is another ; the law is good, but it has not the gift of pardon or of inspiration ; by itself it will only reveal the feebleness of him who endeavours to perform it, only force into direst contrast the spiritual beauty of the pure ideal and the wretchedness of the sinner, carnal, sold under sin. In this respect, indeed, the law was its own witness. For if, among all the millions of its children, one had lived by obedience, how could he have shared in its elaborate sacrificial apparatus, in the hallowing of the altar from pollution by the national uncleanness, in the sprinkling of the blood of the offering for sin ? Take the case of the highest official. A sinless high priest under the law would have been paralysed by his virtue, for his duty on the greatest day of all the year was to make atonement first for his own sins.

3. The law being an authorised statement of what innocence means, and therefore of the only terms upon which a man might hope to live by works, is an organic whole, and we either keep it as a whole or break it. Such is the meaning of the words, he that offendeth in one point is guilty of all ; because He who gave the seventh commandment gave also the sixth—so that if one commit no adultery, yet kill, he has become a transgressor of the law in its integrity (James ii. 11). The challenge of God to human self-righteousness is not one which can be half met. If we have not thoroughly kept it, we have thoroughly failed.

4. But this failure of man does not involve any failure, in the law, to accomplish its intended work. It is, as has been said, a challenge. The sense of our inability to meet it is the best introduction to Him Who came not to call the righteous but sinners to

repentance, and thus the law became a tutor to bring men to Christ. It awoke the conscience, brought home the sense of guilt, and entered, that sin might abound in us, whose ignorance had not known sin without it. It was strictly that which Moses most frequently calls it—the Testimony.

5. Finally, however, the teaching of Scripture is not that Christians are condemned to live always in a condition of baffled striving, hopeless longing, conscious transgression of a code which testifies against them. The old and carnal nature gravitates downward, to selfishness and sin, as surely as by a law of the physical universe. But the law of the spirit of life in Christ Jesus emancipates us from that law of sin and death—the higher nature doing, by the very quality of its life, what the lower nature cannot be driven to do, by dread of hell or by desire of heaven. The creature of earth becomes a creature of air, and is at home in a new sphere, poised on its wings upon the breeze. Love is the fulfilling of the law. And the Christian is free from its dictation, as affectionate men are free from any control of the laws which command the maintenance of wife and child, not because they may defy the statutes, but because their volition and the statutes concide. Liberty is not lawlessness—it is the reciprocal harmony of law and the will.

And thus the grand paradox of Luther is entirely true: "Unless faith be without any, even the smallest works, it does not justify, nay, it is not faith. And yet it is impossible for faith to be without works—earnest, many and great." We are justified by faith without the works of the law, and yet we do not make void the law by faith—nay, we establish the law.

All this agrees exactly with the contrast, so often urged, between the giving of the Law and the utterance of the Sermon on the Mount. The former echoes across wild heights, and through savage ravines; the latter is heard on the grassy slopes of the hillside which overlooks the smiling Lake of Galilee. The one is spoken in thunder and graven upon stone: the other comes from the lips, into which grace is poured, of Him Who was fairer than the children of men. The former repeats again and again the stern warning, "'Thou shalt not!" The latter crowns a sevenfold description of a blessedness, which is deeper than joy, though pensive and even weeping, by adding to these abstract descriptions an eighth, which applies them, and assumes them to be realised in His hearers— "Blessed are *ye*." If so much as a beast touched the mountain it should be stoned. But Simeon took the Divine Infant in his arms.

And this is not because God has become gentler, or man worthier: it is because God the Law-giver upon His throne has come down to be God the Helper. But the beatitudes could never have been spoken, if the law had not been imposed: the blessedness of a hunger and thirst for righteousness was created by the majestic and spiritual beauty of the unattained commandment.

Yes, it had a spiritual beauty. For, however formal, external, and even shallow, the commandments may appear to flippant modern babblers, St. Paul bewailed the contrast between the law, which was spiritual, and his own carnal heart. And he, who had kept all the letter from his youth, was only the more vexed and haunted by the fleeting consciousness of a higher "good thing" unattained. Did not one table say

"Thou shalt not covet," and the other promise mercy to thousands of those that love?

This leads us to consider the structure and arrangement of the Decalogue. Scripture itself tells us that there were "ten words" or precepts, written upon both sides of two tables. But various answers have been given at different times, to the question, How shall we divide the ten?

The Jews of a later period made a first commandment of the words, "I am the Lord thy God," which is not a commandment at all. And they restored the proper number, thus exceeded, by uniting in one the prohibition of other gods and of idolatry; although the worship of the golden calf, almost immediately after the law was given, suffices to establish the distinction. For then, as well as under Gideon, Micah and Jeroboam, the sin of idolatry fell short of apostasy to a wholly different god (Judg. viii. 23, 27, xvii. 3, 5; 1 Kings xii. 28). The worship of images dishonours God, even if it be His semblance that they claim. In this arrangement, the tables were allotted five commandments each.

Another curious arrangement was devised, apparently by St. Augustine; and the weight of his authority imposed it upon Western Christianity until the Reformation, and upon the Latin and Lutheran churches unto this day. Like the former, it adds the second commandment to the first, but it divides the tenth. And it gives to the first table three commandments, "since the number of commandments which concern God seem to hint at the Trinity to careful students," while the seven commandments of the second table suggest the Sabbath. Such mystical references are no longer weighty arguments. And the proposed division of the tenth commandment seems quite precluded by the fact that in Exodus we read, "Thou shalt not covet thy neighbour's house nor his wife," while in Deuteronomy the order is reversed; so that its advocates are divided among themselves as to whether the coveting of a house or a wife is to attain the dignity of separate mention.

The ordinary English arrangement assigns to the tables four commandments and six respectively. And the noble catechism of the Church of England appears to sanction this arrangement by including among "my duties to my neighbour" that of loving, honouring and succouring my father and mother. There are several objections to this arrangement. It is unsymmetrical. There seems to be something more sacred and divine about my relationship with my father and mother than those which connect me with my neighbour. The first table begins with the gravest offence, and steadily declines to the lowest; sin against the unique personality of God being followed by sin against His spirituality of nature, His name, and His holy day. If now the sin against His earthly representative, the very fountain and sanction of all law to childhood, be added to the first table, the same order will pervade those of the second—namely, sin against my neighbour's life, his family, his property, his reputation, and lastly, his interest in my inner self, in the wishes that are unspoken, the thoughts and feelings which

> "I wad nae tell to nae man."

We thus obtain both the simplest division and the clearest arrangement. In Romans xiii. 9 the fifth commandment is not enumerated when rehearsing the actions which transgress the second table. In the

Hebrew text of Deuteronomy all the later commandments are joined with the sixth by the copulative (represented along with the negative fairly enough in our English by "Neither"), which seems to indicate that these five were united together in the author's mind. But the fifth stands alone, like all those of the first table. Now, it is clear that such an arrangement gives great sanction and weight to the sacred institution of the family.

Finally, the comprehensiveness and spirituality of the law may be observed in this; that the first table forbids sin against God in thought, word and deed; and the second table forbids sin against man in deed, word and thought.

THE PROLOGUE.

xx. 2.

The Decalogue is introduced by the words "I am the Lord thy God, which brought thee out of the land of Egypt, out of the house of bondage."

Here, and in the previous chapter, is already a great advance upon the time when it was said to them "The God of thy fathers, the God of Abraham, of Isaac, and of Jacob, hath appeared." Now they are expected to remember what He has done for themselves. For, although religion must begin with testimony, it ought always to grow up into an experience. Thus it was that many of the Samaritans believed on Jesus because of the word of the woman; but presently they said, "Now we believe, not because of thy speaking, for we have heard Him ourselves, and know." And thus the disciples who heard John the Baptist speak, and so followed Jesus, having come and seen where He abode, could say, "We have found the Messiah."

This prologue is vitally connected with both tables of the law. In relation to the first, it recognises the instinct of worship in the human heart. In vain shall we say Do not worship idols, until the true object of adoration is supplied, for the heart must and will prostrate itself at some shrine. A leader of modern science confesses "the immovable basis of the religious sentiment in the nature of man," adding that "to yield this sentiment reasonable satisfaction is the problem of problems at the present hour."* It is indeed a problem for the unbelief which, because it professes to be scientific, cannot shut its eyes to the fact that men whose faith in Christ has suffered shipwreck are everywhere seen to be clinging to strange planks—spiritualism, esoteric Buddhism, and other superstitions,—which prove that man must and will reverence something more than streams of tendencies, or beneficial results to the greatest numbers. The Law of Moses abolishes superstition by no mere negation, but by the proclamation of a true God.

Moreover, it declares that this God is knowable, which flatly contradicts the brave assertion of modern agnostics that the notion of a God is not even "thinkable." That assertion is a bald and barren platitude in the only sense in which it is not contrary to the experience of all mankind. As we cannot form a complete and perfect, nor even an adequate notion of God, so no man ever yet conceived a complete and adequate notion of his neighbour, nor indeed of himself. But as we can form a notion of one another, dim and

* Prof. Tyndall, *Belfast Address*, p. 60. What progress has scientific unbelief made since 1874 in solving this "question of questions for the present hour"? It has perfected the phonograph, but it has not devised a creed.

fragmentary indeed, yet more or less accurate and fit to guide our actions, so has every nation and every man formed some notion of deity. Nor could even the agnostic declare that God is unthinkable, unless the word God, of which he makes this assertion, conveyed to him *some* idea, some thought, more or less worthy of the thinking. The ancient Jew never dreamed that he could search out the Almighty to perfection, yet God was known to him by His actions (the only means by which we know our fellow-men); and the combined terror and loving-kindness of these at once warned him against revolt, and appealed to his loyalty for obedience.

In relation to the second table, the prologue was both an argument and an appeal. Why should a man hope to prosper by estranging his best Friend, his Emancipator and Guide? And even if disobedience could obtain some paltry advantage, how base would he be who snatched at it, when forbidden by the God Who broke his chains, and brought him out of the house of bondage—a Benefactor not ungenial and remote, but One Who enters into closest relations with him, calling Himself "Thy God"!

Now, a greater emancipation and a closer personal relationship belong to the Church of Christ. When a Christian hears that God is unthinkable, he ought to be able to answer, 'God is my God, and He has brought my soul out of its house of bondage.'

Moreover, his emancipation by Christ from many sins and inner slaveries ought to be a fact plain enough to constitute the sorest of problems to the observing world.

It must be observed, besides, that the Law, which was the centre of Judaism, does not appeal chiefly to the meaner side of human nature. Hell is not yet known, for the depths of eternity could not be uncovered before the clouds had rolled away from its heights of love and condescension; or else the sanity and balance of human nature would have been overthrown. But even temporal judgments are not set in the foremost place. As St. Paul, who knew the terrors of the Lord, more commonly and urgently besought men by the mercies of God, so were the ancient Jews, under the burning mountain, reminded rather of what God had bestowed upon them, than of what He might inflict if they provoked Him. And our gratitude, like theirs, should be excited by His temporal as well as His spiritual gifts to us.

THE FIRST COMMANDMENT.

"Thou shalt have none other gods before Me." – xx. 3.

When these words fell upon the ears of Israel, they conveyed, as their primary thought, a prohibition of the formal worship of rival deities, Egyptian or Sidonian gods. Following immediately upon the proclamation of Jehovah, their own God, they declared His intolerance of rivalry, and enjoined a strict and jealous monotheism. For God was a reality. Races who worshipped idealisations or personifications might easily make room for other poetic embodiments of human thought and feeling; but Jehovah would vindicate His rights. He had proved himself very real in Egypt. Other gods would not displace Him: He would observe them: they would be "before Me."* God does not quit the scene when man forgets Him.

---

* "Or *beside Me*" (R.V.) The preposition is so vague that either of our English words may suggest quite too definite a meaning, as

Now, it is hard for us to realise the charm which the worship of false gods possessed for ancient Israel. To comprehend it we must reflect upon the universal ignorance which made every phenomenon of nature a portentous manifestation of mysterious and varied power, which they could by no means trace back to a common origin, while the crash and discord of the results appeared to indicate opposing wills behind. We must reflect how closely akin is awe to worship, and how blind and unintelligent was the awe which storm and earthquake and pestilence then excited. We must remember the pressure upon them of surrounding superstitions armed with all the civilisation and art of their world. Above all, we must consider that the gods which seduced them were not of necessity supreme: homage to them was very fairly consistent with a reservation of the highest place for another; so that false worship in its early stages need not have been much more startling than belief in witchcraft, or in the paltry and unimaginative "spirits" which, in our own day, are reputed to play the banjo in a dark room, and to untie knots in a cabinet. Is it for us to deride them?

To oppose all such tendencies, the Lord appealed not to philosophy and sound reason. These are not the parents of monotheism: they are the fruit of it. And so is our modern science. Its fundamental principle is faith in the unity of nature, and in the extent to which the same laws which govern our little world reach through the vast universe. And that faith is directly traceable to the conviction that all the universe is the work of the same Hand.

---

when "before Me" is made to mean "in My angry eyes," or "beside Me" is taken to hint at resentment for intrusion upon the same throne.

"One God, one law, one element;"—the preaching of the first was sure to suggest the other two. Nor could any race which believed in a multitude of gods labour earnestly to reduce various phenomena to one cause. Monotheism is therefore the parent of correct thinking, and could not draw its sanctions thence. No: the law appeals to the historical experience of Israel; it is content to stand and fall by that; if they acknowledged the claim of God upon their loyalty, all the rest followed. Their own story made good this claim. And so does the whole story of the Church, and the whole inner life of every man who knows anything of himself, bear witness to the religion of Jesus.

Never let us weary of repeating that while we have ample controversial resource, while no missile can pierce the chain-armour of the Christian evidences, connected and interwoven into a great whole, and while the infidelity which is called scientific is really infidel only so far as it begs its case (which is an unscientific thing to do), nevertheless the strength of our position is experimental. If the experience which testifies to Jesus were historical alone, I might refuse to give it credit: if it were only personal, I might ascribe it to enthusiasm. But as long as a great cloud of living witnesses, and all the history of the Church, declare the reality of His salvation, while I myself feel the sufficiency of what He offers (or else the bitter need of it), so long the question is not between conflicting theories, but between theories and facts. To have another god is to place him beside One Whom we already have, and Who has wrought for us the great emancipation. It is not an error in theological science: it is ingratitude and treason.

But it very soon became evident that men could apostatise from God otherwise than in formal worship, chant and sacrifice and prostration: "This people honoureth me with their mouths, but their hearts are far from Me." God asks for love and trust, and our litanies should express and cultivate these. Whatever steals away these from the Lord is really His rival, and another god. "What is it to have a God? or what is God?" Luther asks. And he answers, "He is God, and is so called, from Whose goodness and power thou dost confidently promise all good things to thyself, and to Whom thou dost fly from all adverse affairs and pressing perils. So that to have a God is nothing else than to trust Him and believe in Him with all the heart, even as I have often alleged that the reliance of the heart constitutes alike one's God and one's idol.... In what thing soever thou hast thy mind's reliance and thine heart fixed, that is beyond doubt thy God" (*Larger Catechism*).

And again: "What sort of religion is this, to bow not the knees to riches and honour, but to offer them the noblest part of you, the heart and mind? It is to worship the true God outwardly and in the flesh, but the creature inwardly and in spirit" (*X. Præcepta Witt. Prædicata*).

It was on this ground that he included charms and spells among the sins against this commandment, because, though "they seem foolish rather than wicked, yet do they lead to this too grave result, that men learn to rely upon the creature in trifles, and so fail in great things to rely upon God" (*Ibid.*)

This view of false worship is frequent in Scripture itself. The Chaldeans were idolaters of an elaborate and imposing ritual, but their true deities were not to be found in temples. They adored what they really trusted upon, and that was their military prowess—the god of the modern commander, who said that Providence sided with the big battalions. The Chaldean is "he whose might is his god," whereas the sacred warrior has the Lord for his strength and shield and very present help in battle. Nay, regarding men "as the fishes of the sea," and his own vast armaments as the fisher's apparatus to sweep them away, the Chaldean, it is said, "sacrificeth unto his net, and burneth incense unto his drag; because by them his portion is fat and his meat plenteous" (Hab. i. 11, 14-16). Multitudes of humbler people practise a similar idolatry. They say to God "Give us this day our daily bread"; but they really ascribe their maintenance to their profession or their trade; and so this is the true object of their homage. They, too, burn incense to their drag.

Others had no thought of a higher blessedness than animal enjoyment. Their god was their belly. They set the excitement of wine in the place of the fulness of the Spirit, or preferred some depraved union upon earth to the honour of being one spirit with the Lord (Phil. iii. 19; Eph. v. 18; 1 Cor. vi. 16, 17). And some tried to combine the world and righteousness; not to lose heaven while grasping wealth, and receiving here not only good things, but the only good things they acknowledged—*their* good things (Luke xvi. 25). As the Samaritans feared the Lord and served graven images, so these were fain to serve God and mammon (2 Kings xvii. 41; Matt. vi. 24).

Now, these departures from the true Centre of all love and Source of all light were really a homage to His great rival, "the god of this world." Whenever men seek to obtain any prize by departing from God, they do reverence to him who falsely said of all the kingdoms of the earth, and their glory, "These things are delivered unto me, and to whomsoever I will I give them." They deny Him to Whom indeed all power is committed in heaven and earth.

What is the remedy, then, for all such formal or virtual apostasies? It is to "have" the true God—which means, not only to know and confess, but to be in real relationship with Him.

Despite His so-called self-sufficiency, man is not very self-sufficing, after all. The vast endowments of Julius Cæsar did not prevent him from chafing because, at the age when he was still obscure, Alexander had conquered the world. To be Julius Cæsar was not enough for him. Nor is any man able to stand alone. In the Old Testament Joshua said, "If it seem evil unto you to serve the Lord, choose you this day whom ye will serve,"—implying that they must obey some one and will do better to choose a service than to drift into one (Josh. xxiv. 15). And in the New Testament Jesus declared that no man can serve two masters; but added that he would not break with both and go free, he was sure to love and cleave to one of them. Now, he only is proof against apostasy, who has realised the wants of the soul within him, and the powerlessness of all creatures to satisfy or save, and then, turning to the cross of Christ, has found his sufficiency in Him. "Lord, to whom shall we go? Thou hast the words of everlasting life." Marvellous it is to think that underneath the stern words "Thou shalt have none other," lies all the condescension of the privilege "Thou shalt have . . . Me."

THE SECOND COMMANDMENT.

"Thou shalt not make unto thee a graven image, . . . thou shalt not bow down thyself unto them, nor serve them."—xx. 4-6.

How far does the second of these clauses modify the first? Men there are who maintain the severe independence of the former, so that it forbids the presence of any image or likeness in the house of God, even for innocent purposes of adornment. But the Decalogue is not a liturgical directory: what it forbids in church it forbids anywhere; and on this theory the statues in Parliament Square would be idolatrous, as well as those in Westminster Abbey. And such Christians are more Judaical than the Jews, who were taught to place in the very Holy of Holies golden cherubim overshadowing the mercy-seat, and to represent them again upon its curtains.

It is therefore plain that the precept never forbade imagery, but idolatry, which is the making of images to satisfy the craving of men's hearts for a sensuous worship—the making of them "unto thee." The second clause qualifies and elucidates the first. And what the commandment prohibits is any attempt to help our worship by representing the object of adoration to the senses.

The higher and more subtle idolatries do not conceive that wood or gold is actually transformed into their deities; but only that the deities are locally present in the images, which express their attributes—power in a hundred hands, beneficence in a hundred breasts. But in thus expressing, they degrade and cramp the conception.

They may perhaps evade the reproach of Isaiah that they warm themselves with a portion of timber, and roast meat with another portion, and make the remainder a god (Isa. xliv. 15-17), by urging that the timber is not the god, but an abode which he chooses because it expresses his specific qualities. But they cannot evade the reproach of St. Paul, that being ourselves the offspring of God, we ought not to compare Him to the workmanship of our hands, graven with art and man's device (Acts xvii. 29).

A truly spiritual worship is intellectually as well as morally the most elevating exercise of the soul, which it leads onward and upward, making of all that it knows and thinks a vestibule, beyond which lie higher knowledge and deeper feeling as yet unattained.

Why is Gothic architecture better adapted for religious buildings than any Grecian or Oriental style? Because its long aisles, vaulted roofs and pointed arches, leading the vision up to the unseen, tell of mystery, and draw the mind away beyond the visible and concrete to something greater which it hints; while rounded arches and definite proportions shut in at once the vision and the mind. The difference is the same as between poetry and logic.

And so it is with worship. We fetter and cramp our thoughts of deity when we bind them to even the loftiest conceptions which have ever been shut up in marble or upon canvas. The best image that ever took shape is inferior to the poorest spiritual conception of God, in this respect if in no other—that it has no expansiveness, it cannot grow. And in connecting our prayers with it, we virtually say, 'This satisfies my conception of God.'

It is not to be condemned merely as inadequate, for so are all our highest thoughts of deity; nor only because average humanity (which is supposed to stand most in need of the help and suggestion of art) will never learn the fine distinctions by which subtle intellects withhold from the image itself the worship which it evokes, and which goes out in its direction. It is still more mischievous because, even for the trained theologian, it is the petrifaction of what is meant to develop and expand, the solidification of the inadequate, the accepting of what is human as our idea of the divine.

Nor will it long continue to be merely inadequate. Experience proves that ideas, like air and water, cannot be confined without stagnating. Idolatries not only fail to develop, they degenerate; and systems, however orthodox they may appear at starting, which connect worship with palpable imagery, are doomed to sink into superstition.

To this precept there is added a startling and painful caution—" For I the Lord thy God am a jealous God." That a man should be jealous is no passport to our friendship: we think of unreasonable estrangements, exaggerated demands, implacable and cruel resentments. It would not enter the average mind to doubt that one is highly praised when another says of him, 'I never traced in his words or actions the slightest stain of jealousy.' And yet we are to think of God Himself as the jealous God.

Upon reflection, however, we must admit that a man is not condemned as jealous-minded because he is capable of jealousy, but because he has an unjust and unreasonable tendency towards it. It is a narrowing and suspicious quality when it operates without due cause, a vindictive and cruel one when it operates in excessive measure. But what should we think of a parent who felt no jealousy if the heart of his child were stolen from him by intriguing servants or by frivolous comrades? Now, God has called Israel His son, even His firstborn. The truth is that with us jealousy is dangerous and frequently perverted, because we are bad judges of the measure of our own rights, especially when our affections are involved. But some measure of jealousy is the necessary pain of love neglected, love wronged or slighted by those upon whom it has a claim. Jealousy is the shadow thrown where the sunshine of love is intercepted, and it is strong in proportion to the strength of the light. It operates in the heart exactly like the sense of justice in the reason. Justice expects a recompense where it has given service, and jealousy asks for love where it has given affection.

And therefore, when God tells us that He is jealous, He implies that He condescends to love us, to look for a return, to desire more from us than outward service. We cannot be jealous concerning things which are indifferent to us. Even the jealousy of rival competitors for business or for place may be measured by the desire of each for that which the other would engross. The politician is not jealous of the millionaire, nor the capitalist of the prime minister.

Now, if God is jealous when the enemies of our soul would steal away our loyalty, it surely follows that we shall not be left to contend with those enemies alone: He values us; He is upon our side; He will help us to overcome them.

And now we begin to see why this attribute is connected with the second commandment and not the first. The apostate who betakes himself to another god is almost beyond the reach of this tender and intimate emotion: he is still loved, for God loves all men; but yet perhaps the chord is unstrung which trembles responsive to this plaintive note.

When a man who confesses God begins to weary of spiritual intercourse with the Lord of spirits, when he can no longer worship One whose actual presence is realised because His voice is heard within, when the likeness of man or brute, or brightness of morning, or marvel of life or its reproductiveness, contents him as a representation of God the invisible, then his heart is beginning to go after the creature, to content itself with artistic loveliness or majesty, to let go the grasp as upon a living hand, by which alone the soul may be sustained when it stumbles, or guided when it would err.

To those who are within His covenant—to us, therefore, as to His ancient Israel—He says, "I the Lord thy God am a jealous God." Because I am "thy God."

The assertion of a Divine jealousy is but one difficulty of this remarkable verse. The Lord goes on to describe Himself as "visiting the iniquity of the fathers upon the children unto the third and fourth generation of them that hate Me, and showing mercy unto thousands of them that love Me and keep My commandments." And is this reasonable? To punish the child, to be avenged upon the children's children, for sins which are not their own? We know how often the sceptic has made gain out of this representation—which is but his own unauthorised gloss, since in reality God has said nothing about punishing the righteous with the wicked. It is not true that all sad and disastrous consequences are penal; many are disciplinary, and even to the people of God some are surgical, cutting away what would lead to disease and death. Are no evil consequences probable, if men brought up amid scenes dishonouring to God were treated exactly like those who have since childhood felt as it were the hand of a Father upon their head? For themselves it is best and kindest that so deep a loss could come home to their consciousness in pain.

At all events, the assertion so early made in Scripture is confirmed in all the experience of the race. Insanity, idiocy, scrofula, consumption, are too often, though not always, the hereditary results of guilt. Sins of the flesh are visited upon the bodily system. Sins of the temper, such as pride, cynicism and frivolity, are felt in the mental structure of the race. And the sins which offend directly against God, do they bring no results with them? Ask of the investigators of the new science of heredity and transmitted peculiarities, whether it stops short of the highest and holiest parts of human nature. Or consider the ravages which victory and consequent wealth have made, again and again, in the character of whole nations.

There is no doctrine impugned in Scripture, which men have less prospect of shaking off, even if they close their Bibles for ever, than this. If it were not there, we should be perplexed at a want of conformity between the ways of God in nature and what is asserted of Him in His Book.

But it is either slander or blindness to represent this law, viewed in its entirety, as other than benevolent. The transmission of the result of evil is only a part of the vast law which has bound men together in nations and families, as partners and members with each other. It is clear that distinctive advantages cannot be bestowed upon the children of the good, as such, unless the same advantages be withheld from the evil race beside them. If the prizes of a university are won by knowledge, the result is that ignorance is "visited," in the withholding of them. And if, in the vaster university of life, health, affluence, good repute and a clear intellect are the transmitted results of virtue, then disease, poverty, neglect and incompetence become the dire bequest of the unrighteous.

There is no choice, therefore, except either to carry out this law, or else to bid every man in the world begin life, not as "the heir of all the ages," but absolutely destitute of all that has been acquired by his fellow-men.

Sometimes a hint is given us of what this would be. There is brought occasionally into civilised communities, from the depths of forests, a creature without language or decency or intellect, with low forehead and brutal appetites, who in his early childhood had wandered away and been lost,—brought up, men say, by the strange compassion of some lower creature, and now sunken well-nigh to its level. To this degradation we should all come, if it were not for the transmitted inheritance of our fathers. And so vast is the upward force of this grand law, that it is steadily though slowly upheaving the whole mass; and the lowest of to-day, visited for ancestral failings by sinking to the bottom, is higher than if he had been left absolutely alone.

This over-weight of good is clearly seen by comparing the clauses, for the sins of the fathers are visited upon the children to the third and fourth generation, but mercy is shown in them that love God upon a wholly different scale. Even "unto thousands" would enormously counterbalance three generations. But the Revised Version rightly suggests "a thousand generations" in the margin, and supports it by one of its very rare references. It is plainly stated in Deuteronomy vii. 9, that He "keepeth covenant and mercy with them that love Him and keep His commandments unto a thousand generations."

Lastly, it is to be observed that in all this passage the gospel is shining through the law. It is not a question of just dealing, but of emotion. God is not a master exacting taskwork, but a Father, jealous if we refuse our hearts. He visits sin upon the posterity "of them that hate," not only of them that disobey Him. And when our hearts sink, we who are responsible for generations yet to be, as we reflect upon our frailty, our ignorance and our sins, upon the awful consequences which may result from one heedless act—nay, from a gesture or a look—He reminds us that He does not requite those who serve Him only with a measured wage, but shows "mercy" upon those who love Him unto a thousand generations.

THE THIRD COMMANDMENT.

"Thou shalt not take the name of the Lord thy God in vain."—xx. 7.

What is the precise force of this prohibition? The word used is ambiguous: sometimes it must be rendered as here, as in the verses "*Vain* is the help of man," and "Except the Lord build the house, their labour is but *vain* that build it" (Psalm cviii. 12, cxxvii. 1). But sometimes it clearly means false, as in the texts "Thou shalt not raise a *false* report," and "swearing *falsely* in making a covenant" (Exod. xxiii. 1; Hos. x. 4). Yet again, it hangs midway between the two ideas, as when we read of "*lying* vanities," and again, "trusting in vanity and speaking *lies*" (Psalm xxxi. 6; Isa. lix. 4).

In favour of the rendering "falsely" it is urged that our Lord quotes it as "said to them of old time 'Thou shalt not forswear thyself'" (Matt. v. 33). But it is by no means clear that He quotes this text: the citation is closer to the phraseology of Lev. xix. 12, and it is found in a section of the Sermon which does not confine its citations to the Decalogue (cf. ver. 38).

The Authorised rendering seems the more natural when we remember that civic duty had not yet come upon the stage. When we have learned to honour only one God, and not to degrade nor materialise our conception of Him, the next step is to inculcate, not yet veracity toward men when God has been invoked, but reverence, in treating the sacred name.

We have already seen the miserable superstitions by which the Jews endeavoured to satisfy the letter while outraging the spirit of this precept. In modern times some have conceived that all invocation of the Divine Name is unlawful, although St. Paul called God for a witness upon his soul, and the strong angel shall yet swear "by Him Who liveth for ever and ever" (2 Cor. i. 23; Rev. x. 6).

As it is not a temple but a desert which no foot ever treads, so the sacred name is not honoured by being unspoken, but by being spoken aright.

Swearing is indeed forbidden, where it has actually disappeared, namely, in the mutual intercourse of Christian people, whose affirmation should suffice their brethren, while the need of stronger sanctions "cometh of evil," even of the consciousness of a tendency to untruthfulness, which requires the stronger barrier of an oath. But our Lord Himself, when adjured by the living God, responded to the solemn authority of that adjuration, although His death was the result.

The name of God is not taken in vain when men who are conscious of His nearness, and act with habitual reference to His will, mention Him more frequently and familiarly than formalists approve. It is abused when the insincere and hollow professor joins in the most solemn act of worship, honours Him with the lips while the heart is far from Him —nay, when one strives to curb Satan, and reclaim his fellow-sinner, by the use of good and holy phrases, in which his own belief is merely theoretical; and fares like the sons of Sceva, who repeated an orthodox adjuration, but fled away overpowered and wounded. Or if the truth unworthily spoken assert its inherent power, that will not justify the hollowness of his profession, and in vain will he plead at last, "Lord, Lord, have we not in Thy name cast out devils, and in Thy name done many marvellous acts?"

The only safe rule is to be sure that our conception of God is high and real and intimate; to be habitually humble and trustful in our attitude toward Him; and then to speak sincerely and frankly, as then we shall not fail to do. The words which rise naturally to the lips of men who think thus cannot fail to do Him honour, for out of the fulness of the heart the mouth speaketh.

And the prevalent notion that God should be mentioned seldom and with bated breath is rather an evidence of men's failure habitually to think of Him aright, than of filial and loving reverence. There is a large and powerful school of religion in our own day, whose disciples talk much more of their own emotions and their own souls than St. Paul did, and much less about God and Christ. Some day the proportions will be restored. In the great Church of the future men will not morbidly shrink from confessing their inner life, but neither will it be the centre of their contemplation and their discourse: they will be filled with the fulness of God; out of the abundance of their hearts their mouths will speak; His name shall be continually in their mouth, and yet they shall not take the name of the Lord their God in vain.

THE FOURTH COMMANDMENT.

xx. 8-11.

It cannot be denied that the commandment to honour the Sabbath day occupies a unique place among the ten. It is, at least apparently, a formal precept embedded in the heart of a moral code, and good men have thought very differently indeed about its obligation upon the Christian Church.

The great Continental reformers, Lutheran and Calvinistic alike, who subscribed the Confession of Augsburg, there affirmed that "Scripture hath abolished the Sabbath by teaching that all Mosaic ceremonies may be omitted since the gospel has been revealed" (II. vii. 28). The Scotch reformers, on the other hand, declared that God "in His Word, by a positive moral and perpetual commandment, binding all men in all ages, hath particularly appointed one day in seven for a Sabbath, to be kept holy unto Him" (*Westminster Confess.*, XXI. vii.). They are even so bold as to declare that this day "from the beginning of the world to the resurrection of Christ was the last day of the week, and from the resurrection of Christ was changed into the first day of the week"; but this proposition would be as hard to prove as the contrary assertion, still maintained by some obscure religionists, that the change of day, for however sufficient and sublime a reason, was beyond the capacity of the Church of Christ to enact.

Amid these conflicting opinions the doctrinal formularies of the Church of England are characteristically guarded and prudent; but her worshippers are bidden to seek mercy from the Lord for past violations of this law, and an inclination of heart to keep it in the future; and when the Ten have been recited, they pray that "all these Thy laws" may be written upon their hearts. There is no doubt, therefore, about the opinion of our own Reformers concerning the divine obligation of the commandment.

In examining the problem thus presented to us, our chief light must be that of Scripture itself. Is the Sabbath what the Lutheran confession called it, a mere "Mosaic ceremony," or does it rest upon sanctions which began earlier and lasted longer than the precept to abstain from shell-fish, or to sanctify the firstborn of cattle?

Does its presence in the Decalogue disfigure that great code, as the intrusion of these other precepts would do? When we find a Gentile church reminded that the next precept to this "is the first commandment with promise" (Eph. vi. 2), can we suppose that the tables to which St. Paul appealed, and the promise which he cited at full length, were both cancelled; that in so far as a moral element existed in them, that portion of course survived their repeal, but the code itself was gone? If so, the temporal promise went with it, and its quotation by St. Paul is strange. Strange also, upon this supposition, was the stress which he habitually laid upon the law as a convicting power, and as being only repealed in the letter so far as it was fulfilled by the spontaneous instinct of love, which was the fulfilling of the law.

The position of the commandment among a number of moral and universal duties cannot but weigh heavily in its favour. It prompts us to ask whether our duty to God is purely negative, to be fulfilled by a policy of non-intervention, not worshipping idols, nor blaspheming. Something more was already intimated in the promise of mercy to them "that love Me." For love is chiefly the source of active obedience: while fear is satisfied by the absence of provocation, love wants not only to abstain from evil but to do good. And how may it satisfy this instinct when its object is the eternal God, Who, if He were hungry, would not tell us? It finds the necessary outlet in worship, in adoring communion, in the exclusion for awhile of worldly cares, in the devotion of time and thought to Him. Now, the foundation upon which all the institutions of religion may be securely built, is the day of rest. Call it external, formal, unspiritual if you will; say that it is a carnal ordinance, and that he who keeps it in spirit is free from the obligation of the letter. But then, what about the eighth commandment? Are we absolved also from the precept "Thou shalt not steal," because it too is concerned with external actions, because "this . . . thou shalt not steal . . . and if there be any other commandment, it is briefly comprehended in this one saying, Thou shalt love thy neighbour as thyself"? Do we say, the spirit has abolished the letter: love is the rescinding of the law? St. Paul said the very opposite: love is the fulfilling of the law, not its destruction; and thus he re-echoed the words of Jesus, "I am not come to destroy the law, but to fulfil."

All men know that the formal regulations which defend property are relaxed as the ties of love and mutual understanding are made strong; that to enter unannounced is not a trespass, that the same action which will be prosecuted as a theft by a stranger, and resented as a liberty by an acquaintance, is welcomed as a graceful freedom, almost as an endearment, by a friend. And yet the commandment and the rights of property hold good: they are not compromised, but glorified, by being spiritualised. As it is between man and his brother, so should it be between us and our Divine Father. We have learned to know Him very differently from those who shuddered under Sinai: the whole law is not now written upon tables of stone, but upon fleshly tables of the heart. But among the precepts which are thus etherialised and yet established, why should not the fourth commandment retain its place? Why should it be supposed that it must vanish from the Decalogue, unless the gathering of sticks deserves stoning? The institution, and the ceremonial application of it to Jewish life, are entirely different things; just as respect for property is a fixed obligation, while the laws of succession vary.

Bearing this distinction in mind, we come to the question, Was the Sabbath an ordinance born of Mosaism, or not? Grant that the word "Remember," if it stood alone, might conceivably express the emphasis of a new precept, and not the recapitulation of an existing one. Grant also that the mention in Genesis of the Divine rest might be made by anticipation, to be read with an eye to the institution which would be mentioned later. But what is to be made of the fact that on the seventh day manna was withheld from the camp, before they had arrived at Horeb, and therefore before the commandment had been written by the finger of God upon the stone? Was this also done by anticipation? Upon any supposition, it aimed at teaching the nation that the obligation of the day was not based upon the positive precept, but the precept embodied an older and more fundamental obligation.

How is the Sabbath spoken of in those prophecies which set least value upon the merely ceremonial law?

Isaiah speaks of mere ritual as slightly as St. Paul. To fast and afflict one's soul is nothing, if in the day of fasting one smites with the fist and oppresses his labourers. To loose the bonds of wickedness, to free the oppressed, to share one's bread with the hungry, this is the fast which God has chosen, and for him who fasts after this fashion the light shall break forth like sunrise, and his bones shall be strong, and he himself like an unfailing water-spring. Now, it is the same chapter which thus waives aside mere ceremonial in contempt, which lavishes the most ample promises on him who turns away his foot from the Sabbath, and calls the Sabbath a delight, and the holy of the Lord, honourable, and honours it (Isa. lviii. 5-11, 13-14).

There is no such promise in Jeremiah, for the observance of any merely ceremonial law, as that which bids the people to honour the Sabbath day, that there may enter into their gates kings and princes riding in chariots and upon horses, and that the city may remain for ever (Jer. xvii. 24, 25).

And Ezekiel declares that in the day when God made Himself known to His people in the land of Egypt, He gave them statutes and judgments and His sabbaths (Ezek. xx. 11, 12). Now, this phrase is a clear allusion to the word of God in Jeremiah, that "I spake not unto their fathers in the day when I brought them out of Egypt, concerning burnt-offerings or sacrifices, but this thing I commanded them, saying, Hearken unto My voice," etc. (Jer. vii. 23). And it sharply contrasts the sacredness of God's abiding ordinances with the temporary institutions of the sanctuary. But it reckons the Sabbath among the former.

It is objected that our Lord Himself treated the Sabbath lightly, as a worn-out ordinance. But He was "a minister of the circumcision," and always discussed the lawfulness of His Sabbath miracles as a Jew with Jews. Thus He argued that men, admittedly under the law, baked the shewbread, circumcised children, and even rescued cattle from jeopardy upon the seventh day. He appealed to the example of David, who met a sufficiently urgent necessity by eating the consecrated bread, "which was not lawful for him to eat" (Matt. xii. 4).

He did not hint that the law of the sabbath had disappeared, but insisted that it was meant to serve man and not to oppress him: that "the sabbath was made for man, and not man for the sabbath" (Mark ii. 27).

Now, there is not in the life of Christ an assertion, so broad and strong as that the Sabbath was made for the human race, which can be narrowed down to a discussion of any merely local and temporary institution. He Who stood highest, and saw the widest horizons, declared that the Sabbath was intended for humanity, and not for a section or a sect of it. Not because He was the King of the Jews, but because He was the Son of Man, the ripe fruit and the leader of the world-wide race which it was given to bless, therefore He was also its Lord.

And in Him, so are we. Like all things present and things to come, it is our help, we are not its slaves.

There is something abject in the notion of a Christian freeman, who has been for a long week imprisoned in some gloomy and ill-ventilated workshop, whose lungs would be purified, and therefore his spirits uplifted, and therefore his reason and his affections invigorated, and therefore his worship rendered more fresh, warm and reasonable, by the breathing of a purer air, yet whose conception of a day of rest is so slavish that he dares not "rest" from the pollution of an infected atmosphere, and from the closeness of a London court, because he conceives it imperative to "rest" only from that bodily exercise, to enjoy which would be to him the most real and the most delightful repose of all.

But there are other things more abject still; and one of them is the miserable insincerity of the affluent and luxurious, using the exceptional case of him whose week-days are thus oppressed, to excuse their own wanton neglect of religious ordinances, accepting at the hands of Christianity the sacred holiday, but ignoring utterly the fact that the Lord sanctified and hallowed it, that it is to be called the holy of the Lord, and to be honoured, and that we are free from the letter of the precept only in so far as we rise to the spirit of it, in loving and true communion with the Father of spirits.

Another utterance of Jesus throws a strong light upon the nature and the limits of our obligation. "My Father worketh even until now, and I work" (John v. 17) is an appeal to the fact that in the long sabbath of God His world is not deserted; creation may be suspended, but the bounties of Providence go on;

and therefore Christ also felt that His day of rest was not one of torpor, that in healing the impotent man upon the Sabbath He was but following the example of Him by whose rest the day was sanctified. All works of beneficent love, all that ministers to human recovery from anguish, and carries out the Divine purposes of grace for body or soul, rescue from danger, healing of disease, reformation of guilt, are sanctioned by this defence of Christ.

They need not plead that the commandment is abrogated, but that Jesus of Nazareth, of the seed of David, found nothing in such liberties inconsistent with the duties of a devout Hebrew.

THE FIFTH COMMANDMENT.

"Honour thy father and thy mother: that thy days may be long upon the land which the Lord thy God giveth thee."—xx. 12.

This commandment forms a kind of bridge between the first table and the second. Obedience to parents is not merely a neighbourly virtue; we do not honour them simply as our fellow-men: they are the vice-gerents of God to our childhood; through them He supplies our necessities, defends our feebleness, and pours in light and wisdom upon our ignorance; by them our earliest knowledge of right and wrong is imparted, and upon the sanction of their voice it long depends.

It is clear that parental authority cannot be undermined, nor filial disobedience and irreverence gain ground, without shaking the foundations of our religious life, even more perhaps than of our social conduct.

Accordingly this commandment stands before the

sixth, not because murder is a less offence against society, but because it is more emphatically against our neighbour, and less directly against God.

The human infant is dependent and helpless for a longer period, and more utterly, than the young of any other animal. Its growth, which is to reach so much higher, is slower, and it is feebler during the process. And the reason of this is plain to every thoughtful observer. God has willed that the race of man should be bound together in the closest relationships, both spiritual and secular; and family affection prepares the heart for membership alike of the nation and the Church. With this inner circle the wider ones are concentric. The pathetic dependence of the child nourishes equally the strong love which protects, and the grateful love which clings. And from our early knowledge of human generosity, human care and goodness, there is born the capacity for belief in the heart of the great Father, from Whom every family in heaven and earth derived its Greek name of Fatherhood (Eph. iii. 15).

Woe to the father whose cruelty, selfishness, or evil passions make it hard for his child to understand the Archetype, because the type is spoiled! or whose tyranny and self-will suggest rather the stern God of reprobation, or of servile, slavish subjection, than the tender Father of freeborn sons, who are no more under tutors and governors, but are called unto freedom.

But how much sorer woe to the son who dishonours his earthly parent, and in so doing slays within himself the very principle of obedience to the Father of spirits!

No earthly tie is perfect, and therefore no earthly obedience can be absolute. Some crisis comes in every life when the most innocent and praiseworthy affection becomes a snare—when the counsel we most relied upon would fain mislead our conscience—when a man, to be Christ's disciple, must "hate father and mother," as Christ Himself heard the temptation of the evil one speaking through chosen and beloved lips, and said "Get thee behind Me, Satan." Even then we shall respect them, and pray as Christ prayed for His failing apostle, and when the storm has spent itself they shall resume their due place in the loving heart of their Christian offspring.

So Jesus, when Mary would interrupt His teaching, said "Who is My mother?" But imminent death could not prevent Him from pitying her sorrow, and committing her to His beloved disciple as to a son.

From the letter of this commandment streams out a loving influence to sanctify all the rest of our relationships. As the love of God implies that of our brother also, so does the honour of parents involve the recognition of all our domestic ties.

And even unassisted nature will tend to make long the days of the loving and obedient child; for life and health depend far less upon affluence and luxury than upon a well-regulated disposition, a loving heart, a temper which can obey without chafing, and a conscience which respects law. All these are being learned in disciplined and dutiful households, which are therefore the nurseries of happy and righteous children, and so of long-lived families in the next generation also. Exceptions there must be. But the rule is clear, that violent and curbless lives will spend themselves faster than the lives of the gentle, the loving, the law-abiding and the innocent.

THE SIXTH COMMANDMENT.

"Thou shalt do no murder."—xx. 13.

We have now clearly passed to the consideration of man's duty to his fellow-man, as a part of his duty to his Maker. It is no longer as holding a divinely appointed relation to us, but simply as he is a man, that we are bidden to respect his person, his family, his property, and his fair fame.

And the influence of the teaching of our Lord is felt in the very name which we all give to the second table of the law. We call it "our duty to our neighbour." But we do not mean to imply that there lives on the surface of the globe one whom we are free to assault or to pillage. The obligation is universal, and the name we give it echoes the teaching of Him who said that no man can enter the sphere of our possible influence, even as a wounded creature in a swoon whom we may help, but he should thereupon become our neighbour. Or rather, we should become his; for while the question asked of Him was "Who is my neighbour?" (whom should I love?) Jesus reversed the problem when He asked in turn not To whom was the wounded man a neighbour? but Who was a neighbour unto him? (who loved him?)

Social ethics, then, have a religious sanction. It is the constant duty and effort of the Church of God to saturate the whole life of man, all his conduct and his thought, with a sense of sacredness; and as the world is for ever desecrating what is holy, so is religion for ever consecrating what is secular.

In these latter days men have thought it a proof of grace to separate religion from daily life. The Antinomian, who maintains that his orthodox beliefs or feelings absolve him from the obligations of morality, joins hands with the Italian brigand who hopes to be forgiven for cutting throats because he subsidises a priest. The enthusiast who insists that all sins, past and future, were forgiven him when he believed, approaches far nearer than he supposes to the fanatic of another creed, who thinks a formal confession and an external absolution sufficient to wash away sin. All of them hold the grand heresy that one may escape the penalties without being freed from the power of evil; that a life may be saved by grace without being penetrated by religion, and that it is not exactly accurate to say that Jesus saves His people from their sins.

It is scarcely wonderful, when some men thus refuse to morality the sanctions of religion, that others propose to teach morality how she may go without them. In spite of the experience of ages, which proves that human passions are only too ready to defy at once the penalties of both worlds, it is imagined that the microscope and the scalpel may supersede the Gospel as teachers of virtue; that the self-interest of a creature doomed to perish in a few years may prove more effectual to restrain than eternal hopes and fears; and that a scientific prudence may supply the place of holiness. It has never been so in the past. Not only Judæa, but Egypt, Greece, and Rome, were strong as long as they were righteous, and righteous as long as their morality was bound up in their religion. When they ceased to worship they ceased to be self-controlled, nor could the most urgent and manifest self-interest, nor all the resources of lofty philosophy, withhold them from the ruin which always accompanies or follows vice.

Is it certain that modern science will fare any better? So far from deepening our respect for human nature and for law, she is discovering vile origins for our most sacred institutions and our deepest instincts, and whispering strange means by which crime may work without detection and vice without penalty. Never was there a time when educated thought was more suggestive of contempt for one's self and for one's fellow-man, and of a prudent, sturdy, remorseless pursuit of self-interest, which may be very far indeed from virtuous. The next generation will eat the fruit of this teaching, as we reap what our fathers sowed. The theorist may be as pure as Epicurus. But the disciples will be as the Epicureans.

Is there anything in the modern conception of a man which bids me spare him, if his existence dooms me to poverty and I can quietly push him over a precipice? It is quite conceivable that I can prove, and very likely indeed that I can persuade myself, that the shortening of the life of one hard and grasping man may brighten the lives of hundreds. And my passions will simply laugh at the attempt to restrain me by arguing that great advantages result from the respect for human life upon the whole. Appetites, greeds, resentments do not regard their objects in this broad and colourless way; they grant the general proposition, but add that every rule has its exceptions. Something more is needed: something which can never be obtained except from a universal law, from the sanctity of all human lives as bearing eternal issues in their bosom, and from the certainty that He who gave the mandate will enforce it.

It is when we see in our fellow-man a divine creature

of the Divine, made by God in His own image, marred and defaced by sin, but not beyond recovery, when his actions are regarded as wrought in the sight of a Judge Whose presence supersedes utterly the slightness, heat and inadequacy of our judgment and our vengeance, when his pure affections tell us of the love of God which passeth knowledge, when his errors affright us as dire and melancholy apostacies from a mighty calling, and when his death is solemn as the unveiling of unknown and unending destinies, then it is that we discern the sacredness of life, and the awful presumption of the deed which quenches it. It is when we realise that he is our brother, holding his place in the universe by the same tenure by which we hold our own, and dear to the same Father, that we understand how stern is the duty of repressing the first resentful movements within our breast which would even wish to crush him, because they are a rebellion against the Divine ordinance and against the Divine benevolence.

Is it asked, how can all this be reconciled with the lawfulness of capital punishment? The death penalty is frequent in the Mosaic code. But Scripture regards the judge as the minister and agent of God. The stern monotheism of the Old Testament " said, Ye are Gods," to those who thus pronounced the behest of Heaven; and private vengeance becomes only more culpable when we reflect upon the high sanction and authority by which alone public justice presumes to act.

Now, all these considerations vanish together, when religion ceases to consecrate morality. The judgment of law differs from my own merely as I like it better, and as I am a party (perhaps unwillingly) to the general consent which creates it; he whom I would assail is doomed in any case to speedy and complete extinction; his longer life is possibly burdensome to himself and to society; and there exists no higher Being to resent my interference, or to measure out the existence which I think too protracted. It is clear that such a view of human life must prove fatal to its sacredness; and that its results would make themselves increasingly felt, as the awe wore away which old associations now inspire.

THE SEVENTH COMMANDMENT.

"Thou shalt not commit adultery."—xx. 14.

This commandment follows very obviously from even the rudest principle of justice to our neighbour. It is among those that St. Paul enumerates as "briefly comprehended in this saying, Thou shalt love thy neighbour as thyself."

And therefore nothing need here be said about the open sin by which one man wrongs another. Wild and evil theories may be abroad, new schemes of social order may be recklessly invented and discussed; yet, when the institution of the permanent family is assailed, every thoughtful man knows full well that all our interests are at stake in its defence, and the nation could no more survive its overthrow than the Church.

But when our Lord declared that to excite desire through the eyes is actually this sin, already ripe, He appealed to some deeper and more spiritual consideration than that of social order. What He pointed to is the sacredness of the human body—so holy a thing that impurity, and even the silent excitement of passion, is a wrong done to our nature, and a dishonour to the temple of the Holy Ghost.

Now, this is a subject upon which it is all the more necessary to write, because it is hard to speak about.

What is the human body, in the view of the Christian? It is the one bond, as far as we know in all the universe, between the material and the spiritual worlds, one of which slopes thence down to inert molecules, and the other upward to the throne of God.

Our brain is the engine-room and laboratory whereby thought, aspiration, worship express themselves and become potent, and even communicate themselves to others.

But it is a solemn truth that the body not only interprets passively, but also influences and modifies the higher nature. The mind is helped by proper diet and exercise, and hindered by impure air and by excess or lack of food. The influence of music upon the soul has been observed at least since the time of Saul. And hereafter the Christian body, redeemed from the contagion of the fall, and promoted to a spiritual impressibility and receptiveness which it has never yet known, is meant to share in the heavenly joys of the immortal spirit before God. This is the meaning of the assertion that it is sown a natural ($=$ *soulish*) body, but shall be raised a spiritual body. In the meantime it must learn its true function. Whatever stimulates and excites the animal at the cost of the immortal within, will in the same degree cloud and obscure the perception that a man's life consisteth not in his pleasures, and will keep up the illusion that the senses are the true ministers of bliss. The soul is attacked through the appetites at a point far short of their physical indulgence. And when lawless wishes are deliberately toyed with, it is clear that lawless acts are not hated, but only avoided through fear of consequences. The reins which govern the life are no longer in the hands of the spirit, nor is it the will which now refuses to sin. How, then, can the soul be alert and pure? It is drugged and stupified: the offices of religion are a dull form, and its truths are hollow unrealities, assented to but unfelt, because unholy impulses have set on fire the course of nature, in what should have been the temple of the Holy Ghost.

Moreover, the Christian life is not one of mere submission to authority; its true law is that of ceaseless upward aspiration. And since the union of husband and wife is consecrated to be the truest and deepest and most far-reaching of all types of the mystical union between Christ and His Church, it demands an ever closer approach to that perfect ideal of mutual love and service.

And whatever impairs the sacred, mysterious, all-pervading unity of a perfect wedlock is either the greatest of misfortunes or of crimes.

If it be frailty of temper, failure of common sympathies, an irretrievable error recognised too late, it is a calamity which may yet strengthen the character by evoking such pity and helpfulness as Christ the Bridegroom showed for the Church when lost. But if estrangement, even of heart, come through the secret indulgence of lawless reverie and desire, it is treason, and criminal although the traitor has not struck a blow, but only whispered sedition under his breath in a darkened room.

THE EIGHTH COMMANDMENT.

"Thou shalt not steal."—xx. 15.

There is no commandment against which human ingenuity has brought more evasions to bear than this.

Property itself is theft, says the communist. "It is no grave sin," says the Roman text-book, "to steal in moderation"; and this is defined to be, "from a pauper less than a franc, from a daily labourer less than two or three, from a person in comfortable circumstances anything under four or five francs, or from a very rich man ten or twelve francs. And a servant whom force or necessity compels to accept an unjust payment, may secretly compensate himself, because the workman is worthy of his hire."* A moment's reflection discovers this to be the most naked rationalism, choosing some of the commandments of God for honour, and some for contempt as "not very grave," and wholly ignoring the principle that whoever attacks the code at any one point "is guilty of all," because he has despised it as a code, as an organic system.

Nothing is easier than to confuse one's conscience about the ethics of property. For the arrangements of various nations differ: it is a geographical line which defines the right of the elder son against his brothers, of sons against daughters, and of children against a wife; and the demand is still more capricious which the state asserts against them all, under the name of succession duty, and which it makes upon other property in the form of a multitude of imposts and taxes. Can all these different arrangements be alike binding? Add to this variability the immense national revenues, which are apparently so little affected by individual contributions, and it is no wonder if men fail to see that honesty to the public is a duty as immutable and stern as any other duty to their neighbour. Unfortunately the evil spreads. The

---

* Gury, Compend., i., secs. 607, 623.

same considerations which make it seem pardonable to rob the nation apply also to the millionaire ; and they tempt many a poor man to ask whether he need respect the wealth of a usurer, or may not adjust the scales of Mine and Thine, which law causes to hang unfairly.

It is forgotten that a nation has at least the same authority as a club to regulate its own affairs, to fix the relative position and the subscription of its members. Common honesty teaches me that I must conform to these rules or leave the club ; and this duty is not at all affected by the fact that other associations have different rules. In three such societies God Himself has placed us all—the family, the Church, and the nation ; and therefore I am directly responsible to God for due respect to their laws. It is not true that the statute-book is inspired, any more than that the regulations of a household are divinely given. Yet a Divine sanction, such as rests upon the parental rule of fallible human creatures, hallows also national law. I may advocate a change in laws of which I disapprove, but I am bound in the meantime to obey the conditions upon which I receive protection from foreign foes and domestic fraud, and which cannot be subjected to the judgment of every individual, except at the cost of a dissolution of society, and a state of anarchy compared with which the worst of laws would be desirable.

This revolt of the individual is especially tempting when selfishness deems itself wronged, as by the laws of property. And the eighth commandment is necessary to protect society not merely against the violence of the burglar and the craft of the impostor, but also against the deceitfulness of our own hearts, asking What harm is in the evasion of an impost ? What right has a successful speculator to his millions? Why should I not do justice to myself when law refuses it?

There is always the simple answer, Who made me a judge in my own case?

But when we regard the matter thus, it becomes clear that honesty is not mere abstinence from pillage. The community has larger claims than this upon us, and is wronged if we fail to discharge them.

The rich man robs the poor if he does not play his part in the great organisation by which he is served so so well: every one robs the community who takes its benefits and returns none; and in this sense the bold saying is true, that every man lives by one of two methods—by labour or by theft.

St. Paul does not exhort men to refrain from theft merely in order to be harmless, but to do good. That is the alternative contemplated when he says, "Let the thief steal no more, but rather let him labour, working with his hands the thing that is good, that he may have whereof to give to him that hath need" (Eph. iv. 28).

THE NINTH COMMANDMENT.

"Thou shalt not bear false witness against thy neighbour."— xx. 16.

St. James called the tongue a world of iniquity. And against its lawlessness, which inflames the whole course of nature, each table of the law contains a warning. For it is equally ready to profane the name of God, and to rob our neighbour of his fair fame.

Jesus Christ regarded verbal professions as a very poor thing, and asked, "Why call ye Me Lord, Lord, and do not the things which I command you? He aimed a parable at the hollowness of merely saying, "I go, sir." But, worthless though such phrases be, the act which substitutes professions for actual service is no trifle; and our Lord felt the importance of words, empty or sincere, so profoundly as to stake upon this one test the eternal destinies of His people: "By thy words thou shalt be justified, and by thy words thou shalt be condemned." Now, the tongue is thus important because it is so prompt and willing a servant of the mind within. We scarcely think of it as a servant at all: our words do not seem to be more than "expressions," manifestations of what is within us.

But a thought, once expressed, is transformed and energetic as a bullet when the charge is fired; it modifies other minds, and the word which we took to be far less potent than a deed becomes the mover of the fateful deeds of many men. And thus, being at once powerful and unsuspected, it is the most treacherous and subtle of all the forces which we wield.

And the ninth commandment does not undertake to bridle it by merely forbidding us in a court of justice to wrong our fellow-man by perjury.

We transgress it whenever we conceive a strong suspicion and repeat it as a thing we know; when we allow the temptation of a biting epigram to betray us into an unkind expression not quite warranted by the facts; when we vindicate ourselves against a charge by throwing blame where it probably but not certainly ought to lie; or when we are not content to vindicate ourselves without bringing a countercharge which it would perplex us to be asked to prove; when we give way to that most shallow and meanest of all attempts at cleverness which claims credit for penetration because it can discover base motives for innocent actions, so that high-mindedness becomes pride, and charity withers up into love of patronising, and forbearance shrivels into lack of spirit. The pattern and ideal of such cleverness is the east wind, which makes all that is fair and sensitive to shut itself up, forbids the bud to expand into a blossom, and puts back the coming of the springtime and of the singing bird.

There are very gifted persons who have never found out that a kindly and winning phrase may have as much literary merit as a stinging one, and it is quite as fine a thing to be like the dew on Hermon as to shoot out arrows, even bitter words.

It is a pity that our harsh judgments always speak more loudly and confidently than our kindly ones, but the reason is plain: angry passion prompts the former, and its voice is loud; while the calm reflection which tones down and sweetens the judgment softens also the expression of it.

It has to be remembered, also, that false witness can reach to nations, organisations, political movements as well as individuals. The habit of putting the worst construction upon the intentions of foreign powers is what feeds the mutual jealousies that ultimately blaze out in war. The habit of thinking of rival politicians as deliberately false and treasonable is what lowers the standard of the noblest of secular pursuits, until each party, not to be undone, protests too much, raises its voice to a falsetto to scream its rival down, and relaxes its standard of righteousness lest it should be outdone by the unscrupulousness of its rival.

And there is yet another neighbour, against whom

false witness is woefully rife, both in the Church and in society. That neighbour is mankind at large. There is a prevalent theory of human sinfulness which unconsciously scoffs at the appeals of the gospel, striving indeed to influence me by love, gratitude, admiration for the Perfect One, and desire to be like Him, by the hope of holiness and the shame of vileness, but telling me at the same time that I have no sympathies whatever except with evil. The observation of every day shows that man's nature is corrupt, but it also shows that he is not a fiend—that he has fallen indeed, but remembers yet in what image he was made. But the world cannot upbraid the Church for these exaggerations, since they are but the echo of its own.

> "I do believe,
> Though I have found them not, that there may be
> Words which are things, hopes which will not deceive,
> And virtues which are merciful, nor weave
> Snares for the failing; I would also deem
> O'er others' griefs that some sincerely grieve;
> That two, or one, are almost what they seem,
> That goodness is no name, and happiness no dream.
> *Childe Harold*, III., cxiv.

Cynicism is false witness; and if it does not greatly wrong any one of our fellow-men, it injures both society and the cynic. If he is of a coarse fibre, it excuses him to himself in becoming the hard and unloving creature which he fancies that all men are. If he is too proud or too self-respecting to yield to this temptation, it isolates him, it chills and withers his sympathies for people quite as good as himself, whom he thinks of as the herd.

As for the more flagrant sins, so for this, the remedy

is love. Love sympathises, makes allowance for frailty, discovers the germs of good, hopeth all things, taketh not account of evil.

THE TENTH COMMANDMENT.

"Thou shalt not covet . . . anything that is his."—xx. 17.

It will be remembered that the order of the catalogue of objects of desire is different in Exodus and in Deuteronomy. In the latter "thy neighbour's wife" is first, as of supreme importance; and therefore it has been thought possible to convert it into a separate commandment.

But this the order in Exodus forbids, by placing the house first, and then the various living possessions which the householder gathers around him. What is thought of is the gradual process of acquisition, and the right of him who wins first a house, then a wife, servants, and cattle, to be secure in the possession of them all. Now, between foes, we saw that the evil temper is what leads to the evil deed, and the man who nurses hatred is a murderer at heart. Just so the householder is not rendered safe, and certainly not happy in the enjoyment of his rights, by the seventh commandment and the eighth, unless care be taken to prevent the accumulation of those forces which will some day break through them both. To secure cities against explosion, we forbid the storage of gunpowder and dynamite, and not only the firing of magazines.

But the moral law is not given to any man for his neighbour's sake chiefly. It is for me: statutes whereby I myself may live. And as the Psalmist pondered on them, they expanded strangely for his perception. "I have kept Thy testimonies," he says; but presently asks to be quickened,—"So shall I *observe* the testimony of Thy mouth,"—and prays, "Give me understanding, that I may *know* Thy testimonies." And at the last, he confesses that he has "gone astray like a lost sheep" (Ps. cxix. 22, 88, 125, 176). Starting with a literal innocence, he comes to feel a deep inward need, need of vitality to obey, and even of power to understand aright. If the sacrifices of God are a broken spirit, it follows that they are a spirit, and inward loyalty is the necessary condition upon which external obedience can be accepted. The cheers of a traitor, the flattery of one who scorns, the ritual of a hypocrite, these are quite as valuable, as indications of what is within, as a reluctant relinquishment to my neighbour of what is his. I must not covet. Plainly this is the sharpest and most searching precept of all; and accordingly St. Paul asserts that without this he would not have suffered the deep internal discontent, the consciousness of something wrong, which tortured him, even although no mortal could reproach him, even though, touching the righteousness of the law, he was blameless. He had not known coveting, except the law had said "Thou shalt not covet."

Here, then, we perceive with the utmost clearness what St. Paul so clearly discerned—the true meaning of the Law, its convicting power, its design to work not righteousness, but self-despair as the prelude of self-surrender. For who can, by resolving, govern his desires? Who can abstain not only from the usurping deed, but from the aggressive emotion? Who will not despair when he learns that God desireth truth in the inward parts? But this despair is the way to that better hope which adds, "In the hidden part Thou shalt make me to know wisdom. Purge me with hyssop, and I shall be clean."

And as a strong interest or affection has power to destroy in the soul many weaker ones, so the love of God and our neighbour is the appointed way to overcome the desire of taking from our neighbour what God has given to him, refusing it to us.

THE LESSER LAW.

xx. 18—xxiii. 33.

With the close of the Decalogue and its universal obligations, we approach a brief code of laws, purely Hebrew, but of the deepest moral interest, confessed by hostile criticism to bear every mark of a remote antiquity, and distinctly severed from what precedes and follows by a marked difference in the circumstances.

This is evidently the book of the Covenant to which the nation gave its formal assent (xxiv. 7), and is therefore the germ and the centre of the system afterwards so much expanded.

And since the adhesion of the people was required, and the final covenant was ratified as soon as it was given, before any of the more formal details were elaborated, and before the tabernacle and the priesthood were established, it may fairly claim the highest and most unique position among the component parts of the Pentateuch, excepting only the Ten Commandments.

Before examining it in detail, the impressive circumstances of its utterance have to be observed.

It is written that when the law was given, the voice of the trumpet waxed louder and louder still. And as the multitude became aware that in this tempestuous and growing crash there was a living centre, and a voice of intelligible words, their awe became insufferable: and instead of needing the barriers which excluded them from the mountain, they recoiled from their appointed place, trembling and standing afar off. "And they said unto Moses, Speak thou with us and we will hear, but let not God speak with us lest we die." It is the same instinct that we have already so often recognised, the dread of holiness in the hearts of the impure, the sense of unworthiness, which makes a prophet cry, "Woe is me, for I am undone!" and an apostle, "Depart from me, for I am a sinful man."

Now, the New Testament quotes a confession of Moses himself, well-nigh overwhelmed, "I do exceedingly fear and quake" (Heb. xii. 21). And yet we read that he "said unto the people, Fear not, for God is come to prove you, and that His fear may be before your faces, that ye sin not" (xx. 20). Thus we have the double paradox,—that he exceedingly feared, yet bade them fear not, and yet again declared that the very object of God was that they might fear Him.

Like every paradox, which is not a mere contradiction, this is instructive.

There is an abject fear, the dread of cowards and of the guilty, which masters and destroys the will—the fear which shrank away from the mount and cried out to Moses for relief. Such fear has torment, and none ought to admit it who understands that God wishes him well and is merciful.

There is also a natural agitation, at times inevitable though not unconquerable, and often strongest in the highest natures because they are the most finely strung. We are sometimes taught that there is sin in that instinctive recoil from death, and from whatever brings it close, which indeed is implanted by God to prevent foolhardiness, and to preserve the race. Our duty, however, does not require the absence of sensitive nerves, but only their subjugation and control. Marshal Saxe was truly brave when he looked at his own trembling frame, as the cannon opened fire, and said, "Aha! tremblest thou? thou wouldest tremble much more if thou knewest whither I mean to carry thee to-day." Despite his fever-shaken nerves, he was perfectly entitled to say to any waverer, "Fear not."

And so Moses, while he himself quaked, was entitled to encourage his people, because he could encourage them, because he saw and announced the kindly meaning of that tremendous scene, because he dared presently to draw near unto the thick darkness where God was.

And therefore the day would come when, with his noble heart aflame for a yet more splendid vision, he would cry, "O Lord, I beseech Thee show me Thy glory"—some purer and clearer irradiation, which would neither baffle the moral sense, nor conceal itself in cloud.

Meanwhile, there was a fear which should endure, and which God desires: not panic, but awe; not the terror which stood afar off, but the reverence which dares not to transgress. "Fear not, for God is come to prove you" (to see whether the nobler emotion or the baser will survive), "and that His fear may be before your faces" (so as to guide you, instead of pressing upon you to crush), "that ye sin not."

How needful was the lesson, may be seen by what followed when they were taken at their word, and the pressure of physical dread was lifted off them. "They soon forgat God their Saviour . . . they made a calf in Horeb, and worshipped the work of their own hands." Perhaps other pressures which we feel and lament to-day, the uncertainties and fears of modern life, are equally required to prevent us from forgetting God.

Of the nobler fear, which is a safeguard of the soul and not a danger, it is a serious question whether enough is alive among us.

Much sensational teaching, many popular books and hymns, suggest rather an irreverent use of the Holy Name, which is profanation, than a filial approach to a Father equally revered and loved. It is true that we are bidden to come with boldness to the throne of Grace. Yet the same Epistle teaches us again that our approach is even more solemn and awful than to the Mount which might be touched, and the profaning of which was death; and it exhorts us to have grace whereby we may offer service well-pleasing to God with reverence and awe, "for our God is a consuming fire" (Heb. iv. 16, xii. 28). That is the very last grace which some Christians ever seem to seek.

When the people recoiled, and Moses, trusting in God, was brave and entered the cloud, they ceased to have direct communion, and he was brought nearer to Jehovah than before.

What is now conveyed to Israel through him is an expansion and application of the Decalogue, and in turn it becomes the nucleus of the developed law. Its great antiquity is admitted by the severest critics; and it is a wonderful example of spirituality and searching depth, and also of such germinal and fruitful principles as cannot rest in themselves, literally applied, but must lead the obedient student on to still better things.

It is not the function of law to inspire men to obey

it; this is precisely what the law could not do, being weak through the flesh. But it could arrest the attention and educate the conscience. Simple though it was in the letter, David could meditate upon it day and night. In the New Testament we know of two persons who had scrupulously respected its precepts, but they both, far from being satisfied, were filled with a divine discontent. One had kept all these things from his youth, yet felt the need of doing some good thing, and anxiously demanded what it was that he lacked yet. The other, as touching the righteousness of the law, was blameless, yet when the law entered, sin revived and slew him. For the law was spiritual, and reached beyond itself, while he was carnal, and thwarted by the flesh, sold under sin, even while externally beyond reproach.

This subtle characteristic of all noble law will be very apparent in studying the kernel of the law, the code within the code, which now lies before us.

Men sometimes judge the Hebrew legislation harshly, thinking that they are testing it, as a Divine institution, by the light of this century. They are really doing nothing of the sort. If there are two principles of legislation dearer than all others to modern Englishmen, they are the two which these flippant judgments most ignore, and by which they are most perfectly refuted.

One is that institutions educate communities. It is not too much to say that we have staked the future of our nation, and therefore the hopes of humanity, upon our conviction that men can be elevated by ennobling institutions,—that the franchise, for example, is an education as well as a trust.

The other, which seems to contradict the first, and does actually modify it, is that legislation must not move too far in advance of public opinion. Laws may be highly desirable in the abstract, for which communities are not yet ripe. A constitution like our own would be simply ruinous in Hindostan. Many good friends of temperance are the reluctant opponents of legislation which they desire in theory but which would only be trampled upon in practice, because public opinion would rebel against the law. Legislation is indeed educational, but the danger is that the practical outcome of such legislation would be disobedience and anarchy.

Now, these principles are the ample justification of all that startles us in the Pentateuch.

Slavery and polygamy, for instance, are not abolished. To forbid them utterly would have substituted far worse evils, as the Jews then were. But laws were introduced which vastly ameliorated the condition of the slave, and elevated the status of woman—laws which were far in advance of the best Gentile culture, and which so educated and softened the Jewish character, that men soon came to feel the letter of these very laws too harsh.

That is a nobler vindication of the Mosaic legislation than if this century agreed with every letter of it. To be vital and progressive is a better thing than to be correct. The law waged a far more effectual war upon certain evils than by formal prohibition, sound in theory but premature by centuries. Other good things besides liberty are not for the nursery or the school. And "we also, when we were children, were held in bondage" (Gal. iv. 3).

It is pretty well agreed that this code may be divided into five parts. To the end of the twentieth chapter it deals directly with the worship of God. Then follow thirty-two verses treating of the personal rights of man as distinguished from his rights of property. From the thirty-third verse of the twenty-first chapter to the fifteenth verse of the twenty-second, the rights of property are protected. Thence to the nineteenth verse of the twenty-third chapter is a miscellaneous group of laws, chiefly moral, but deeply connected with the civil organisation of the state. And thence to the end of the chapter is an earnest exhortation from God, introduced by a clearer statement than before of the manner in which He means to lead them, even by that mysterious Angel in Whom "is My Name."

Part I.—The Law of Worship.

xx. 22-26.

It is no vain repetition that this code begins by reasserting the supremacy of the one God. That principle underlies all the law, and must be carried into every part of it. And it is now enforced by a new sanction,—"Ye yourselves have seen that I have talked with you from heaven: ye shall not make *other gods* with Me; gods of silver or gods of gold ye shall not make unto you (vers. 22, 23). The costliest material of this low world should be utterly contemned in rivalry with that spiritual Presence revealing Himself out of a wholly different sphere; and in so far as they remembered Him, and the Voice which had thrilled their nature to its core, in so far would they be free from the desire for any carnal and materialised divinity to go before them.

Impressed with such views of God, their service of Him would be moulded accordingly (24, 25). It is true that nothing could be too splendid for His sanctuary, and Bezaleel was presently to be inspired, that the work of the tabernacle might be worthy of its destination. Spirituality is not meanness, nor is art without a consecration of its own. But it must not intrude too closely upon the solemn act wherein the soul seeks the pardon of the Creator. The altar should not be a proud structure, richly sculptured and adorned, and offering in itself, if not an object of adoration, yet a satisfying centre of attention for the worshipper. It should be simply a heap of sods. And if they must needs go further, and erect a more durable pile, it must still be of materials crude, inartistic, such as the earth itself affords, of unhewn stone. A golden casket is fit to convey the freedom of some historic city to a prince, but the noblest offering of man to God is too humble to deserve an ostentatious altar.

"If thou lift up a tool upon it thou hast polluted it:" it has lost its virginal simplicity; it no longer suits a spontaneous offering of the heart, it has become artificial, sophisticated, self-conscious, polluted.

It is vehemently urged that these verses sanction a plurality of altars (so that one might be of earth and another of stone), and recognise the lawfulness of worship in other places than at a central appointed shrine. And it is concluded that early Judaism knew nothing of the exclusive sanctity of the tabernacle and the temple.

This argument forgets the circumstances. The Jews had been led to Horeb, the mount of God. They were soon to wander away thence through the wilderness. Altars had to be set up in many places, and might be of different materials. It was an important announcement that in every place where God would record His name He would come unto them and bless them. But certainly the inference leans rather toward than against the belief that it was for Him to select every place which should be sacred.

The last direction given with regard to worship is a homely one. It commands that the altar must not be approached with steps, lest the clothes of the priest should be disturbed and his limbs uncovered. Already we feel that we have to reckon with the temper as well as the letter of the precept. It is divinely unlike the frantic indecencies of many pagan rituals. It protests against all infractions of propriety, even the slightest, such as even now discredit many a zealous movement, and bear fruit in many a scandal. It rebukes all misdemeanour, all forgetfulness in look and gesture of the Sacred Presence, in every worshipper, at every shrine.

CHAPTER XXI.

THE LESSER LAW (continued).

PART II.—RIGHTS OF THE PERSON.

xxi. 1-32.

The first words of God from Sinai had declared that He was Jehovah Who brought them out of slavery. And in this remarkable code, the first person whose rights are dealt with is the slave. We saw that a denunciation of all slavery would have been premature, and therefore unwise; but assuredly the germs of emancipation were already planted by this giving of the foremost place to the rights of the least of all and the servant of all.

As regards the Hebrew slave, the effect was to reduce his utmost bondage to a comparatively mild apprenticeship. At the worst he should go free in the seventh year; and if the year of jubilee intervened, it brought a still speedier emancipation. If his debt or misconduct had involved a family in his disgrace, they should also share his emancipation, but if while in bondage his master had provided for his marriage with a slave, then his family must await their own appointed period of release. It followed that if he had contracted a degrading alliance with a foreign slave, his freedom would inflict upon him the pang of final severance from his dear ones. He might, indeed, escape this pain, but only by a deliberate and humiliating act, by formally renouncing before the judges his liberty, the birthright of his nation ("they are My servants, whom I brought forth out of Egypt, they shall not be sold as bondservants"—Lev. xxv. 42), and submitting to have his ear pierced, at the doorpost of his master's house, as if, like that, his body were become his master's property. It is uncertain, after this decisive step, whether even the year of jubilee brought him release; and the contrary seems to be implied in his always bearing about in his body an indelible and degrading mark. It will be remembered that St. Paul rejoiced to think that his choice of Christ was practically beyond recall, for the scars on his body marked the tenacity of his decision (Gal. vi. 17). He wrote this to Gentiles, and used the Gentile phrase for the branding of a slave. But beyond question this Hebrew of Hebrews remembered, as he wrote, that one of his race could incur lifelong subjection only by a voluntary wound, endured because he loved his master, such as he had received for love of Jesus.

When the law came to deal with assaults it was impossible to place the slave upon quite the same level as the freeman. But Moses excelled the legislators of Greece and Rome, by making an assault or chastisement which killed him upon the spot as worthy of death as if a freeman had been slain. It was only the victim who lingered that died comparatively unavenged (20, 21). After all, chastisement was a natural right of the master, because he owned him ("he is his money"); and it would be hard to treat an excess of what was permissible, inflicted perhaps under provocation which made some punishment necessary, on the same lines with an assault that was entirely lawless. But there was this grave restraint upon bad temper,—that the loss of any member, and even of the tooth of a slave, involved his instant manumission. And this carried with it the principle of moral responsibility for every hurt (26, 27).

It was not quite plain that these enactments extended to the Gentile slave. But in accordance with the assertion that the whole spirit of the statutes was elevating, the conclusion arrived at by the later authorities was the generous one.

When it is added that man-stealing (upon which all our modern systems of slavery were founded) was a capital offence, without power of commutation for a fine (xxi. 16), it becomes clear that the advocates of slavery appeal to Moses against the outraged conscience of humanity without any shadow of warrant either from the letter or the spirit of the code.

There remains to be considered a remarkable and melancholy sub-section of the law of slavery.

In every age degraded beings have made gain of the attractions of their daughters. With them, the law attempted nothing of moral influence. But it protected their children, and brought pressure to bear upon the tempter, by a series of firm provisions, as bold as the age could bear, and much in advance of the conscience of too many among ourselves to-day.

The seduction of any unbetrothed maiden involved marriage, or the payment of a dowry. And thus one door to evil was firmly closed (xxii. 16).

But when a man purchased a female slave, with the intention of making her an inferior wife, whether for himself or for his son (such only are the purchases here dealt with, and an ordinary female slave was treated upon the same principles as a man), she was far from being the sport of his caprice. If indeed he repented at once, he might send her back, or transfer her to another of her countrymen upon the same terms, but when once they were united she was protected against his fickleness. He might not treat her as a servant or domestic, but must, even if he married another and probably a chief wife, continue to her all the rights and privileges of a wife. Nor was her position a temporary one, to her damage, as that of an ordinary slave was, to his benefit.

And if there was any failure to observe these honourable terms, she could return with unblemished reputation to her father's home, without forfeiture of the money which had been paid for her (xxi. 7-11).

Does any one seriously believe that a system like the African slave trade could have existed in such a humane and genial atmosphere as these enactments breathed? Does any one who knows the plague spot and disgrace of our modern civilisation suppose for a moment that more could have been attempted, in that age, for the great cause of purity? Would to God that the spirit of these enactments were even now respected! They would make of us, as they have made of the Hebrew nation unto this day, models of domestic tenderness, and of the blessings in health and physical vigour which an untainted life bestows upon communities.

By such checks upon the degradation of slavery, the Jew began to learn the great lesson of the sanctity of manhood. The next step was to teach him the value of life, not only in the avenging of murder, but also in the mitigation of such revenge. The blood-feud was too old, too natural a practice to be suppressed at once; but it was so controlled and regulated as to become little more than a part of the machinery of justice.

A premeditated murder was inexpiable, not to be ransomed; the murderer must surely die. Even if he fled to the altar of God, intending to escape thence to a city of refuge when the avenger ceased to watch, he should be torn from that holy place: to shelter him would not be an honour, but a desecration to the shrine (xxi. 12, 14). According to this provision Joab and Adonijah suffered. For the slayer by accident or in hasty quarrel, "a place whither he shall flee" would be provided, and the vague phrase indicates the antiquity of the edict (ver. 13). This arrangement at once respected his life, which did not merit forfeiture, and provided a penalty for his rashness or his passion.

It is because the question in hand is the sanctity of man, that the capital punishment of a son who strikes or curses a parent, the vicegerent of God, and of a kidnapper, is interposed between these provisions and minor offences against the person (15-17).

Of these latter, the first is when lingering illness results from a blow received in a quarrel. This was not a case for the stern rule, eye for eye and tooth for tooth,—for how could that rule be applied to it?—but the violent man should pay for his victim's loss of time, and for medical treatment until he was thoroughly recovered (18, 19).

But what is to be said to the general law of retribution in kind? Our Lord has forbidden a Christian, in his own case, to exact it. But it does not follow that it was unjust, since Christ plainly means to instruct private persons not to exact their rights, whereas the magistrate continues to be "a revenger to execute justice." And, as St. Augustine argued shrewdly, "this command was not given for exciting the fires of hatred, but to restrain them. For who would easily be satisfied with repaying as much injury as he received? Do we not see men slightly hurt athirst for slaughter and blood? . . . Upon this immoderate and unjust vengeance, the law imposed a just limit, not that what was quenched might be kindled, but that what was burning might not spread." (Cont. Faust, xix. 25.)

It is also to be observed that by no other precept were the Jews more clearly led to a morality still higher than it prescribed. Their attention was first drawn to the fact that a compensation in money was nowhere forbidden, as in the case of murder (Num. xxxv. 31). Then they went on to argue that such compensation must have been intended, because its literal observance teemed with difficulties. If an eye were injured but not destroyed, who would undertake to inflict an equivalent hurt? What if a blind man destroyed an eye? Would it be reasonable to quench utterly the sight of a one-eyed man who had only destroyed one-half of the vision of his neighbour? Should the right hand of a painter, by which he maintains his family, be forfeited for that of a singer who lives by his voice? Would not the cold and premeditated operation inflict far greater mental and even physical suffering than a sudden wound received in a moment of excitement? By all these considerations, drawn from the very principle which underlay the precept, they learned to relax its pressure in actual life. The law was already their schoolmaster, to lead them beyond itself (*vide* Kalisch *in loco*).

Lastly, there is the question of injury to the person, wrought by cattle.

It is clearly to deepen the sense of reverence for human life, that not only must the ox which kills a man be slain, but his flesh may not be eaten; thus carrying further the early aphorism "at the hand of every beast will I require ... your blood" (Gen. ix. 5). This motive, however, does not betray the lawgiver into injustice: "the owner of the ox shall be quit"; the loss of his beast is his sufficient penalty.

But if its evil temper has been previously observed, and he has been warned, then his recklessness amounts to blood-guiltiness, and he must die, or else pay whatever ransom is laid upon him. This last clause recognises the distinction between his guilt and that of a deliberate manslayer, for whose crime the law distinctly prohibited a composition (Num. xxxv. 31).

And it is expressly provided, according to the honourable position of woman in the Hebrew state, that the penalty for a daughter's life shall be the same as for that of a son.

As a slave was exposed to especial risk, and his position was an ignoble one, a fixed composition was appointed, and the amount was memorable. The ransom of a common slave, killed by the horns of the wild oxen, was thirty pieces of silver, the goodly price that Messiah was prized at of them (Zech. xi. 13).

Part III.—Rights of Property.

xxi. 33—xxii. 15.

The vital and quickening principle in this section is the stress it lays upon man's responsibility for negligence, and the indirect consequences of his deed. All sin is selfish, and all selfishness ignores the right of others. Am I my brother's keeper? Let him guard his own property or pay the forfeit. But this sentiment would quickly prove a disintegrating force in the community, able to overthrow a state. It is the ignoble negative of public spirit, patriotism, all by which nations prosper. And this early legislation is well devised to check it in detail. If an ox fall into a pit or cistern, from which I have removed the cover, I must pay the value of the beast, and take the carcase for what it may be worth. I ought to have considered the public interest (xxi. 33). If I let my cattle stray into my neighbour's field or vineyard, there must be no wrangling about the quality of what he has consumed: I must forfeit an equal quantity of the best of my own field or vineyard (xxii. 5). If a fire of my kindling burn his grain, standing or piled, I must make restitution: I had no right to kindle it where he was brought into hazard (xxii. 6). This is the same principle which had already pronounced it murder to let a vicious ox go loose. And it has to do with graver things than oxen and fires,—with the teachers of principles rightly called incendiary, the ingenious theorists who let loose abstract speculations pernicious when put into practice, the well-behaved questioners of morality, and the law-abiding assailants of the foundations which uphold law.

It is quite in the same spirit that I am accountable for what I borrow or hire, and even for its accidental death (since for the time being it was mine, and so should the loss be); but if I hired the owner with his beast, it clearly continued to be in his charge (14, 15). But again, my responsibility may not be pressed too far. If I have not borrowed property, but consented to keep it for the owner, the risk is fairly his, and if it be stolen, the presumption is not against my integrity, although I may be required to clear myself on oath before the judges (7, 8). But I am accountable in such a case for cattle, because it was certainly understood that I should watch them; and if a wild beast have torn any, I must prove my courage and vigilance by rescuing the carcase and producing it (10—13).

But I must not be plunged into litigation without a compensating hazard on the other side: he whom God shall condemn shall pay double unto his neighbour (9).

It only remains to be observed, with regard to theft, that when cattle was recovered yet alive, the thief restored double, but when his act was consummated by slaughtering what he had taken, then he restored a sheep fourfold, and for an ox five oxen, because his villainy was more high-handed. And we still retain the law which allows the blood of a robber at night to be shed, but forbids it in the day, when help can more easily be had.

All this is reasonable and enlightened law; founded, like all good legislation, upon clear and satisfactory principles, and well calculated to elevate the tone of the public feeling, to be not only so many specific enactments, but also the germinant seeds of good.

CHAPTER XXII.

THE LESSER LAW (continued).

PART IV.

xxii. 16—xxiii. 19.

THE Fourth section of this law within the law consists of enactments, curiously disconnected, many of them without a penalty, varying greatly in importance, but all of a moral nature, and connected with the well-being of the state. It is hard to conceive how the systematic revision of which we hear so much could have left them in the condition in which they stand.

It is enacted that a seducer must marry the woman he has betrayed, and if her father refuse to give her to him, then he must pay the same dower as a bridegroom would have done (xxii. 16, 17). And presently the sentence of death is launched against a blacker sensual crime (19). But between the two is interposed the celebrated mandate which doomed the sorceress to death, remarkable as the first mention of witchcraft in Scripture, and the only passage in all the Bible where the word is in the feminine form—a witch, or sorceress; remarkable also for a far graver reason, which makes it necessary to linger over the subject at some length.

SORCERY.

"Thou shalt not suffer a sorceress to live."—xxii. 18.

The world knows only too well what sad and shameful inferences have been drawn from these words. Unspeakable terrors, estrangement of natural sympathy, tortures and cruel deaths, have been inflicted on many thousands of the most forlorn creatures upon earth (creatures who were sustained in their sufferings by no high ardour of conviction or fanaticism, not being martyrs but simply victims), because it was held that Moses, in declaring that witches should not live, affirmed the reality of witchcraft. No sooner did the argument cease to be dangerous to old women than it became formidable to religion; for now it was urged that, since Moses was in error about the reality of witchcraft, his legislation could not have been inspired.

What are we to say to this?

In the first place it must be observed that the existence of a sorcerer is one thing, and the reality of his powers is quite another. What was most sad and shameful in the mediæval frenzy was the burning to ashes of multitudes who made no pretensions to traffic with the invisible world, who frequently held fast their innocence while enduring the agonies of torture, who were only aged and ugly and alone. Upon any theory, the prohibition of sorcery by the Pentateuch was no more answerable for these iniquities than its other prohibitions for the lynch law of the backwoods.

On the other hand, there were real professors of the black art: men did pretend to hold intercourse with spirits, and extorted great sums from their dupes in return for bringing them also into communion with superhuman beings. These it is reasonable to call sorcerers, whether we accept their professions or not, just as we speak of thought-readers and of mediums without being understood to commit ourselves to the pretensions of either one or other. In point of fact, the existence, in this nineteenth century after Christ, of sorcerers calling themselves mediums, is much more surprising than the existence of other sorcerers in the time of Moses or of Saul; and it bears startling witness to the depth in human nature of that craving for traffic with invisible powers which the law prohibited so sternly, but the roots of which neither religion nor education nor scepticism has been able wholly to pluck up.

Again, from the point of view which Moses occupied, it is plain that such professors should be punished. They are virtually punished still, whenever they obtain money under pretence of granting interviews with the departed. If we now rely chiefly upon educated public opinion to stamp out such impositions, that is because we have decided that a struggle between truth and falsehood upon equal terms will be advantageous to the former. It is a subdivision of the debate between intolerance and free thought. Our theory works well, but not universally well, even under modern conditions and in Christian lands. And assuredly Moses could not proclaim freedom of opinion, among uneducated slaves, amid the pressure of splendid and of seductive idolatries, and before the Holy Ghost was given. To complain of Moses for proscribing false religions would be to denounce the use of glass for seedlings because the full-grown plant flourishes in the open air.

Now, it would have been preposterous to proscribe

false religions and yet to tolerate the sorcerer and the sorceress. For these were the active practitioners of another worship than that of God. They might not profess idolatry; but they offered help and guidance from sources which Jehovah frowned upon, rival sources of defence or knowledge.

The holy people was meant to grow up under the most elevating of all influences, reliance upon a protecting God, Who had bidden His children to subdue the world as well as to replenish it, and of Whom one of their own poets sang that He had put all things under the feet of man. Their true heritage was not bounded by the strip of land which Joshua and his followers slowly conquered; to them belonged all the resources of nature which science, ever since, has wrested from the Philistine hands of barbarism and ignorance. And this nobler conquest depended upon the depth and sincerity of man's feeling that the world is well-ordered and stable and the heritage of man, not a chaos of various and capricious powers, where Pallas inspires Diomed to hunt Venus bleeding off the field, or where the incantations of Canidia may disturb the orderly movements of the skies. Who could hope to discover by inductive science the secrets of such a world as this?

The devices of magic cut the links between cause and effect, between studious labour and the fruits which sorcery bade men to steal rather than to cultivate. What gambling was to commerce, that was witchcraft to philosophy, and the mischief no more depended on the validity of its methods than upon the soundness of the last device for breaking the bank at Monte Carlo.

If one could actually extort their secrets from the

dead, or win for luxury and sloth a longer life than is bestowed upon temperance and labour, he would succeed in his revolt against the God of nature. But the revolt was the endeavour; and the sorcerer, however falsely, professed to have succeeded; and preached the same revolt to others. In religion he was therefore an apostate, and in the theocracy a traitor against the King, one whose life was forfeited if it was prudent to exact the penalty.

And when we consider the fascination wielded by such pretensions, even in ages when the stability of nature is an axiom, the dread which false religions all around and their terrible rituals must have inspired, the superstitious tendencies of the people and their readiness to be misled, we shall see ample reasons for treading out the first sparks of so dangerous a fire.

Beyond this it is vain to pretend that the law of Moses goes. It was right in declaring the sorcerer and the sorceress to be real and dangerous phenomena. It never declared their pretensions to be valid though illegitimate. And in one noteworthy passage it proclaims that a real sign or a wonder could only proceed from God, and when it accompanied false teaching was still a sign, though an ominous one, implying that the Lord would prove them (Deut. xiii. 1-3). This does not look very like an admission of the existence of rival powers, inferior though they might be, who could interfere with the order of His world.

Sorcery in all its forms will die when men realise indeed that the world is His, that there is no short or crooked way to the prizes which He offers to wisdom and to labour, that these rewards are infinitely richer and more splendid than the wildest dreams of magic, and that it is literally true that all power, in earth as well as heaven, is committed into the Hands which were pierced for us. In such a conception of the universe, incantations give place to prayers, and prayer does not seek to disturb, but to carry forward and to consummate, the orderly rule of Love.

The denunciation of witchcraft is quite naturally followed, as we now perceive, by the reiteration of the command that no sacrifice may be offered to any god except Jehovah (20). Strange and hateful offerings were an integral part of witchcraft, long before the hags of Macbeth brewed their charm, or the child in Horace famished to yield a spell.

THE STRANGER.

xxii. 21, xxiii. 9.

Immediately after this, a ray of sunlight falls upon the sombre page.

We read an exhortation rather than a statute, which is repeated almost literally in the next chapter, and in both is supported by a beautiful and touching reason. "A stranger shalt thou not wrong, neither shall ye oppress him: for ye were strangers in the land of Egypt." "A stranger shall ye not oppress, for ye know the heart of a stranger, seeing ye were strangers in the land of Egypt" (xxii. 21, xxiii. 9).

The "stranger" of these verses is probably the settler among them, as distinguished from the traveller passing through the land. His want of friends and ignorance of their social order would place him at a disadvantage, of which they are forbidden to avail themselves, either by legal process (for the first passage is connected with jurisprudence), or in the affairs of common life. But the spirit of the commandment could not fail to influence their treatment of all foreigners; and simple and commonplace though it appear to us, it would have startled many of the wisest and greatest peoples of antiquity, and would have fallen as strangely upon the ears of the Greeks of Pericles, as of the modern Bedouin, with whom Israel had kinship. A foreigner, as such, was a foe: to wrong him was a paradox, because he had no rights: kinship, or else alliance or treaty was required to entitle the weaker to any better treatment than it suited the stronger to allow.

Yet we find a precept reiterated in this Jewish code which involves, in its inevitable though slow development, the abolition of negro slavery, the respect by powerful and civilised nations of the rights of indigenous tribes, the most boundless advance of philanthropy, through the most generous recognition of the fraternity of man.

However sternly the sword of Joshua might fall, it struck not at the foreigner, as such, but at those tribes, guilty and therefore accursed of God, the cup of whose iniquity was full. And yet there was enough of carnage to prove that so gracious a commandment as this could not have risen spontaneously in the heart of early Judaism. Does it seem to be made more natural, by any proposed shifting of the date?

The reason of the precept is beautifully human. It rests upon no abstract basis of common rights, nor prudential consideration of mutual advantage.

In our time it is sometimes proposed to build all morality upon such foundations; and strange consequences have already been deduced in cases where the proposed sanction has not seemed to apply. But, in fact, no advance in virtue has ever been traced to self-interest, although, after the advance took place, self-interest has always found its account in it. A progressive community is made of good men, and the motive to which Moses appeals is compassion fed by memory : " For ye were strangers in the land of Egypt " (xxii. 21); " For ye know the heart of a stranger, seeing ye were strangers in the land of Egypt " (xxiii. 9).

The point is not that they may again be carried into captivity : it is that they have felt its bitterness, and ought to recoil from inflicting what they writhed under.

Now, this appeal is a master-stroke of wisdom. Much cruelty, and almost all the cruelty of the young, springs from ignorance, and that slowness of the imagination which cannot realise that the pains of others are like our own. Feeling them to be so, the charities of the poor toward one another frequently rise almost to sublimity. And thus, when suffering does not ulcerate the heart and make it savage, it is the most softening of all influences. In one of the most threadbare lines in the classics, the queen of Carthage boasts that

"I, not ignorant of woe,
To pity the distressful know."

And the boldest assertion in Scripture of the natural development of our Saviour's human powers, is that which declares that "In that He Himself hath suffered, being tempted, He is able to succour them that are tempted" (Heb. ii. 18).

To this principle, then, Moses appeals, and by the appeal he educates the heart. He bids the people reflect on their own cruel hardships, on the hateful character of their tyrants, on their own greater hatefulness if they follow the vile example, after such bitter experience of its character. He does not yet rise to the grand level of the New Testament morality, Do all to thy neighbour which it is not servile and dependent to will that he should do for thee. But he attains to the level of that precept of Confucius and Zoroaster which has been so unworthily compared with it: Do not unto thy neighbour what thou wouldest not that he should do to thee—a precept which mere indifference obeys. Nay, he excels it; for the mental and spiritual attitude of one who respects his helpless neighbour because he so much resembles himself, will surely not be content without relieving the griefs that have so closely touched him. Thus again the legislation of Moses looks beyond itself.

Now, if the Jew should be merciful because he had himself known calamity, what implicit confidence may we repose upon the Man of sorrows and acquainted with grief?

In the same spirit they are warned against afflicting the widow or the orphan. And the threat which is added joins hand with the exhortation which preceded. They should not oppress the stranger, because they had been strangers and oppressed. Now the argument advances. The same God Who then heard their cry will hear the cry of the forlorn, and avenge them, according to the judicial fate which He had just announced, in kind, by bringing their own wives to widowhood and their children to orphanage (xxii. 22-4).

To their brethren they should not lend money upon usury; but loans are no more recommended than afterwards by Solomon: the words are "if thou lend" (ver. 25). And if the raiment of the borrower were taken for a pledge, it must be returned for him to use at night, or else God will hear his cry, because, it is added very significantly and briefly, "I am gracious" (ver. 27). It is the most exalting of all motives: Be merciful, for I am merciful: ye shall be the children of your Father.

Again is to be observed the influence reaching beyond the prescription—the motive which cannot be felt without many other and larger consequences than the restoration of pledges at sunset.

How comes this precept to be followed by the words, "Thou shalt not curse God nor blaspheme a ruler" (ver. 28)? and is not this again somewhat strangely followed by the order not to delay to offer the firstfruits of the soil, to consecrate the firstborn son, and to devote the firstborn of cattle at the same age when a son ought to be circumcised? (vers. 29, 30).

If any link can be discovered, it is in the sense of communion with God, suggested by the recent appeal to His character as a motive that should weigh with man. Therefore they must not blaspheme Him, either directly or through His agents, nor tardily yield Him what He claims. Therefore it is added, "Ye shall be holy men unto Me," and from the sense of dignity which religion thus inspires, a homely corollary is deduced—"Ye shall not eat any flesh that is torn of beasts in the field" (ver. 31). The bondmen of Egypt must learn a high-minded self-respect.

CHAPTER XXIII.

THE LESSER LAW (continued).

xxiii. 1-19.

THE twenty-third chapter begins with a series of commands bearing upon the course of justice; but among these there is interjected very curiously a command to bring back the stray ox or ass of an enemy, and to help under a burden the over-weighted ass of him that hateth thee, even "if thou wouldest forbear to help him." It is just possible that the lawgiver, urging justice in the bearing of testimony, interrupts himself to speak of a very different manner in which the action may be warped by prejudice, but in which (unlike the other) it is lawful to show not only impartiality but kindness. The help of the cattle of one's enemy shows that in the bearing of testimony we should not merely abstain from downright wrong. And it is a fine example of the spirit of the New Testament, in the Old.

"Thou shalt not take up a false report" (ver. 1) is a precept which reaches far. How many heedless whispers, conjectures lightly spoken because they were amusing, yet influencing the course of lives, and inferences uncharitably drawn, would have been still-born if this had been remembered!

But when the scandal is already abroad, the temptation to aid its progress is still greater. Therefore it is added, "Put not thine hand with the wicked to be an unrighteous witness." Whatever be the menace or the bribe, however the course of opinion seem to be decided, and the assent of an individual to be harmless because the result is sure, or blameless because the responsibility lies elsewhere, still each man is a unit, not an "item," and must act for himself, as hereafter he must give account. Hence it results inevitably that "Thou shalt not follow a multitude to do evil, neither shalt thou speak in a cause to turn aside after a multitude to wrest judgment" (ver. 2). The blind impulses of a multitude are often as misleading as the solicitations of the bad, and to aspiring temperaments much more seductive. There is indeed a strange magnetism in the voice of the public. Every orator knows that a great assembly acts upon the speaker as really as he acts upon it: its emotions are like a rush of waters to sweep him away, beyond his intentions or his ordinary powers. Yet he is the strongest individual there; no other has at all the same opportunity for self-assertion, and therefore its power over others must be more complete than over him.

This is one reason for the institution of public worship. Men neglect the house of God because they can pray as well at home, and encourage wanton subdivisions of the Church because they think there is no very palpable difference between competing denominations, or even because competition may be as useful in religion as in trade, as if our competition with the world and the devil for souls would not sufficiently animate us, without competing with one another. But in acting thus they weaken the effect for good of one of the mightiest influences which work evil among us, the influence of association. Men are always persuading themselves that they need not be better than their neighbours, nor ashamed of doing what every one does. And yet no voice joins in a cry without deepening it: every one who rushes with a crowd makes its impulse more difficult to stem; his individuality is not lost by its partnership with a thousand more; and he is accountable for what he contributes to the result. He has parted with his self-control, but not with the inner forces which he ought to have controlled.

Against this dangerous influence of the world, Christ has set the contagion of godliness within His Church, and every avoidable subdivision enfeebles this salutary counter-influence.

Moses warns us, therefore, of the danger of being drawn away by a multitude to do evil; but he is thinking especially of the peril of being tempted to "speak" amiss. Who does not know it? From the statesman who outruns his convictions rather than break with his party, and who cannot, amid deafening cheers, any longer hear his conscience speak, down to the humblest who fails to confess Christ before hostile men, and therefore by-and-by denies Him, there is not one whose speech and silence have never been in danger of being set to the sympathies of his own little public like a song to music.

That Moses was really thinking of this tendency to court popularity, is plain from the next clause—"Neither shalt thou favour a poor man in his cause" (ver. 3).

It is an admirable caution. Men there are who would scorn the opposite injustice, and from whom no rich man could buy a wrongful decision with gold or favour, but who are habitually unjust, because they load the other scale. The beam ought to hang straight. When justice is concerned, the poor man's friend is almost as contemptible as his foe, and he has taken a bribe, if not in the mean enjoyment of democratic popularity, yet in his own pride—the fancy that he has done a magnanimous act, the attitude in which he poses.

As in law so in literature. There once was a tendency to describe magnanimous persons of quality, and repulsive clodhoppers and villagers. Times have changed, and now we think it much more ingenious and high-toned to be quite as partial and disingenuous, reversing the cases. Neither is true, and therefore neither is artistic. No class in society is deficient in noble qualities, or in base ones. Nor is the man of letters at all more independent, who flatters the democracy in a democratic age, than he who flattered the aristocracy when they had all the prizes to bestow.

Other precepts forbid bribery, command that the soil shall rest in the seventh year, when its spontaneous produce shall be for the poor, and further recognise and consecrate relaxation, by instituting (or more probably adopting into the code) the three feasts of Passover, Pentecost, and Tabernacles. The section closes with the words "Thou shalt not seethe a kid in his mother's milk" (ver. 19). Upon this clause much ingenuity has been expended. It makes occult reference to some superstitious rite. It is the name for some unduly stimulating compound. But when we remember that, just before, the sabbatical fruit which the poor left ungleaned was expressly reserved for the beasts of the field, that men were bidden to help the overladen ass of their enemies, and that care is taken elsewhere that the ox should not be muzzled when treading out grain, that the birdnester should not take the dam with the young, and that neither cow nor ewe should be slain on the same day with its young (Deut. xxv. 4, xxii. 6; Lev. xxii. 28), the simplest meaning seems also the most probable. Men, who have been taught respect for their fellow-men, are also to learn a fine sensibility even in respect to the inferior animals. Throughout all this code there is an exquisite tendency to form a considerate, humane, delicate and high-minded nation.

It remained, to stamp upon the human conscience a deep sense of responsibility.

Part V.—Its Sanctions.

xxiii. 20-33.

This summary of Judaism being now complete, the people have to learn what mighty issues are at stake upon their obedience. And the transition is very striking from the simplest duty to the loftiest privilege: "Thou shalt not seethe a kid in his mother's milk. Behold, I send an Angel before thee. . . . Beware of him: for My Name is in him" (19-21).

We have now to ask how much this mysterious phrase involves; who was the Angel of whom it speaks?

The question is not, How much did Israel at that moment comprehend? For we are distinctly told that prophets were conscious of speaking more than they understood, and searched diligently but in vain what the spirit that was in them did signify (1 Peter i. 11).

It would, in fact, be absurd to seek the New Testament doctrine of the Logos full-blown in the Pentateuch. But it is mere prejudice, unphilosophical and presumptuous, to shut one's eyes against any evidence which may be forthcoming that the earliest books of Scripture were tending towards the last conclusions of theology; that the slender overture to the Divine oratorio indicates already the same theme which thunders from all the chorus at the close.

It is scarcely necessary to refute the position that a mere "messenger" is intended, because angels have not yet "appeared as personal agents separate from God." Kalisch himself has amply refuted his own theory. For, he says, "we are compelled . . . to refer it to Moses and his successor Joshua" (*in loco*). So then He Who will not forgive their transgressions is he who prayed that if God would not pardon them, his own name might be blotted from the book of life. He, to whom afterwards God said "I will proclaim the name of the Lord before thee" (xxxiii. 19), is the same of Whom God said "My name is in Him." This position needs no examination; but the perplexities of those who reject the deeper interpretation is a strong confirmation of its soundness. We have still to choose between the promise of a created angel, and some manifestation and interposition of God, distinguished from Jehovah and yet one with Him. This latter view is an evident preparation for clearer knowledge yet to come. It is enough to stamp the dispensation which puts it forth as but provisional, and therefore bears witness to that other dispensation which has the key to it. And it is exactly what a Christian would expect to find somewhere in this summary of the law.

What, then, do we read elsewhere about the Angel

of Jehovah? What do we find, especially, in these early books?

A difficulty has to be met at the very outset. The issue would be decided offhand, if it could be shown that the Angel of this verse is the same who is offered, as a poor substitute for their Divine protector, in the thirty-third chapter. But no contrast can be clearer than between the encouraging promise before us, and the sharp menace which then plunged Israel into mourning. Here is an Angel who must not be provoked, who will not pardon you, because "My Name is in Him." There is an angel who will be sent because God will not go up, . . . lest He consume them (vers. 2, 3). He is not the Angel of God's presence, but of His absence. When the intercession of Moses won from God a reversal of the sentence, He then said "My Presence (My Face) shall go with thee, and I will give thee rest,"* but Moses answers, not yet reassured, "If Thy Presence (Thy Face) go not up with us, carry us not up hence. For wherein shall it be known that I have found grace in Thy sight? . . . Is it not that Thou goest with us? And the Lord said, I will do this thing also that thou hast spoken" (14-17).

Moreover, Isaiah, speaking of this time, says that "In all their affliction He was afflicted, and the Angel of His Presence (His Face) saved them" (Isa. lxiii. 9).

Thus we find that some angel is to be sent because God will not go up: that thereupon the nation mourns,

---

* Even if the rendering were accepted, "Must My Presence (My Face) go with thee?" (Can I not be trusted without a direct Presence?) the argument would not be affected, because Moses presses for the favour and obtains it.

although in this twenty-third chapter they had received as a gladdening promise, the assurance of an Angel escort in Whom is the name of God; that in response to prayer God promises that His Face shall accompany them, so that it may be known that He Himself goes with them; and finally that His Face in Exodus is the Angel of His Face in Isaiah. The prophet at least had no doubt whether the gracious promise in the twenty-third chapter answered, in the thirty-third chapter, to the third verse or the fourteenth—to the menace, or to the restored favour.

This difficulty being now converted into an evidence, we turn back to examine other passages.

When the Angel of the Lord spoke to Hagar, "she called the name of Jehovah that spake unto her El Roi" (Gen. xvi. 11, 13). When God tempted Abraham, "the Angel of Jehovah called unto him out of heaven, and said, ... I know that thou fearest God, seeing thou hast not withheld thy son ... from Me" (Gen. xxii. 11, 12). When a man wrestled with Jacob, he thereupon claimed to have seen God face to face, and called the place Peniel, the Face (Presence) of God (Gen. xxxii. 4, 30). But Hosea tells us that "He had power with God: yea, he had power over the Angel, ... and there He spake with us, even Jehovah, the God of hosts" (Hos. xii. 3, 5). Even earlier, in his exile, the Angel of the Lord had appeared unto him and said, "I am the God of Bethel ... where thou vowedst a vow unto Me." But the vow was distinctly made to God Himself: "I will surely give the tenth to Thee" (xxxi. 11, 13; xxviii. 20, 22). Is it any wonder that when this patriarch blessed Joseph, he said, "The God before whom my fathers Abraham and Isaac did walk, the God which hath fed me all my life long unto this day, the Angel which hath redeemed me from all evil, (may He) bless the lads" (xlviii. 15, 16)?

In Exodus iii. 2 the Angel of the Lord appeared out of the bush. But presently He changes into Jehovah Himself, and announces Himself to be Jehovah the God of their fathers (iii. 2, 4, 15). In Exodus xiii. 21 Jehovah went before Israel, but the next chapter tells how "the Angel of the Lord which went before Israel removed and went behind" (xiv. 19); while Numbers (xx. 16) says expressly that "He sent an Angel and brought us out of Egypt."

By the comparison of these and many later passages (which is nothing but the scientific process of induction, leaning not on the weight of any single verse, but on the drift and tendency of all the phenomena) we learn that God was already revealing Himself through a Medium, a distinct personality whom He could send, yet not so distinct but that His name was in Him, and He Himself was the Author of what He did.

If Israel obeyed Him, He would bring them into the promised land (ver. 23); and if there they continued unseduced by false worships, He would bless their provisions, their bodily frame, their children; He would bring terror and a hornet against their foes; He would clear the land before them as fast as their population could enjoy it; He would extend their boundaries yet farther, from the Red Sea, where Solomon held Ezion Geber (1 Kings ix. 26), to the Mediterranean, and from the desert where they stood to the Euphrates, where Solomon actually possessed Palmyra and Thiphsah (2 Chron. viii. 4; 1 Kings iv. 24).

CHAPTER XXIV.

THE COVENANT RATIFIED. THE VISION OF GOD.

xxiv.

THE opening words of this chapter ("Come up unto the Lord") imply, without explicitly asserting, that Moses was first sent down to convey to Israel the laws which had just been enacted.

This code they unanimously accepted, and he wrote it down. It is a memorable statement, recording the origin of the first portion of Holy Scripture that ever existed as such, whatever earlier writings may now or afterwards have been incorporated in the Pentateuch. He then built an altar for God, and twelve pillars for the tribes, and sacrificed burnt-offerings and peace-offerings unto the Lord. Sin-offerings, it will be observed, were not yet instituted; and neither was the priesthood, so that young men slew the offerings. Half of the blood was poured upon the altar, because God had perfected His share in the covenant. The remainder was not used until the law had been read aloud, and the people had answered with one voice, "All that the Lord hath commanded will we do, and will be obedient." Thereupon they too were sprinkled with the blood, and the solemn words were spoken, "Behold the blood of the covenant which the Lord hath made with you concerning all these words." The people were now finally bound: no later covenant of the same kind will be found in the Old Testament.

And now the principle began to work which was afterwards embodied in the priesthood. That principle, stated broadly, was exclusion from the presence of God, relieved and made hopeful by the admission of representatives. The people were still forbidden to approach, under pain of death. But Moses and Aaron were no longer the only ones to cross the appointed boundaries. With them came the two sons of Aaron, (afterwards, despite their privilege, to meet a dreadful doom,) and also seventy representatives of all the newly covenanted people. Joshua, too, as the servant of Moses, was free to come, although unspecified in the summons (vers. 1, 13).

"They saw the God of Israel," and under His feet the blueness of the sky like intense sapphire. And they were secure: they beheld God, and ate and drank.

But in privilege itself there are degrees: Moses was called up still higher, and left Aaron and Hur to govern the people while he communed with his God. For six days the nation saw the flanks of the mountain swathed in cloud, and its summit crowned with the glory of Jehovah like devouring fire. Then Moses entered the cloud, and during forty days they knew not what had become of him. Was it time lost? Say rather that all time is wasted except what is spent in communion, direct or indirect, with the Eternal.

The narrative is at once simple and sublime. We are sometimes told that other religions besides our own rely for sanction upon their supernatural origin. "Zarathustra, Sâkya-Mooni and Mahomed pass among their followers for envoys of the Godhead; and in the estimation of the Brahmin the Vedas and the laws of Manou are holy, divine books" (Kuenen, *Religion of Israel*, i. 6). This is true. But there is a wide difference between nations which assert that God privately appeared to their teachers, and a nation which asserts that God appeared to the public. It is not upon the word of Moses that Israel is said to have believed; and even those who reject the narrative are not entitled to confound it with narratives utterly dissimilar. There is not to be found anywhere a parallel for this majestic story.

But what are we to think of the assertion that God was seen to stand upon a burning mountain?

He it is Whom no man hath seen or can see, and in His presence the seraphim veil their faces.

It will not suffice to answer that Moses "endured as seeing Him that is invisible" (Heb. xi. 27), for the paraphrase is many centuries later, and hostile critics will rule it out of court as an after-thought. At least, however, it proves that the problem was faced long ago, and tells us what solution satisfied the early Church.

With this clue before us, we ask what notion did the narrative really convey to its ancient readers? If our defence is to be thoroughly satisfactory, it must show an escape from heretical and carnal notions of deity, not only for ourselves, but also for careful readers from the very first.

Now it is certain that no such reader could for one moment think of a manifestation thorough, exhaustive, such as the eye receives of colour and of form. Because the effect produced is not satisfaction, but desire. Each new vision deepens the sense of the unseen. Thus we read first that Moses and Aaron,

Nadab and Abihu and the seventy elders, saw God, from which revelation the people felt and knew themselves to be excluded. And yet the multitude also had a vision according to its power to see; and indeed it was more satisfying to them than was the most profound insight enjoyed by Moses. To see God is to sail to the horizon: when you arrive, the horizon is as far in front as ever; but you have gained a new consciousness of infinitude. "The appearance of the glory of the Lord was seen like devouring fire in the eyes of the children of Israel" (ver. 17). But Moses was aware of a glory far greater and more spiritual than any material splendour. When theophanies had done their utmost, his longing was still unslaked, and he cried out, "Show me, I pray Thee, Thy glory" (xxxiii. 18). To his consciousness that glory was still veiled, which the multitude sufficiently beheld in the flaming mountain. And the answer which he received ought to put the question at rest for ever, since, along with the promise "All My goodness shall pass before thee," came the assertion "Thou shalt not see My face, for no man shall see Me and live."

So, then, it is not our modern theology, but this noble book of Exodus itself, which tells us that Moses did not and could not adequately see God, however great and sacred the vision which he beheld. From this book we learn that, side by side with the most intimate communion and the clearest possible unveiling of God, grew up the profound consciousness that only some attributes and not the essence of deity had been displayed.

It is very instructive also to observe the steps by which Moses is led upward. From the burning bush to the fiery cloud, and thence to the blazing mountain, there was an ever-deepening lesson of majesty and awe. But in answer to the prayer that he might really see the very glory of his Lord, his mind is led away upon entirely another pathway: it is "All My goodness" which is now to "pass before" him, and the proclamation is of "a God full of compassion and gracious," yet retaining His moral firmness, so that He "will by no means clear the guilty."

What can cloud and fire avail, toward the manifesting of a God Whose essence is His love? It is from the Old Testament narrative that the New Testament inferred that Moses endured as seeing indeed, yet as seeing Him Who is inevitably and for ever invisible to eyes of flesh: he learned most, not when he beheld some form of awe, standing on a paved work of sapphire stone and as it were the very heaven for clearness, but when hidden in a cleft of the rock and covered by the hand of God while He passed by.

On one hand the people saw the glory of God: on the other hand it was the best lesson taught by a far closer access, still to pray and yearn to see that glory. The seventy beheld the God of Israel: for their leader was reserved the more exalting knowledge, that beyond all vision is the mystic overshadowing of the Divine, and a voice which says "No man shall see Me and live." The difference in heart is well typified in this difference in their conduct, that they saw God and ate and drank, but he, for forty days, ate not. Satisfaction and assurance are a poor ideal compared with rapt aspiration and desire.

Thus we see that no conflict exists between this declaration and our belief in the spirituality of God.

We have still to ask what is the real force of the

assertion that God was in some lesser sense seen of Israel, and again, more especially, of its leaders.

What do we mean even by saying that we see each other?—that, observing keenly, we see upon one face cunning, upon another sorrow, upon a third the peace of God? Are not these emotions immaterial and invisible as the essence of God Himself? Nay, so invisible is the reality within each bosom, that some day all that eye hath seen shall fall away from us, and yet the true man shall remain intact.

Man has never seen more than a hint, an outcome, a partial self-revelation or self-betrayal of his fellow-man.

> "Yes, in the sea of life in-isled,
> With echoing straits between us thrown,
> Dotting the shoreless watery wild,
> We mortal millions live *alone*.
>
> . . . . . .
>
> God bade betwixt 'our' shores to be
> The unplumb'd, salt, estranging sea."

And yet, incredible as the paradox would seem, if it were not too common to be strange, the play of muscles and rush of blood, visible through the skin, do reveal the most spiritual and immaterial changes. Even so the heavens declare that very glory of God which baffled the undimmed eyes of Moses. So it was, also, that when rended rocks and burning skies revealed a more immanent action of Him Who moves through all nature always, when convulsions hitherto undreamed of by those dwellers in Egyptian plains overwhelmed them with a new sense of their own smallness and a supreme Presence, God was manifested there.

Not unlike this is the explanation of St. Augustine.

"We need not be surprised that God, invisible as He is, appeared visibly to the patriarchs. For, as the sound which communicates the thought conceived in the silence of the mind is not the thought itself, so the form by which God, invisible in His own nature, became visible, was not God Himself. Nevertheless it was He Himself Who was seen under that form, as the thought itself is heard in the sound of the voice; and the patriarchs recognised that, although the bodily form was not God, they saw the invisible God. For, though Moses was conversing with God, yet he said, "If I have found grace in Thy sight, show me Thyself" (*De Civ. Dei*, x. 13). And again: "He knew that he saw corporeally, but he sought the true vision of God spiritually" (*De Trin.*, ii. 27).

It has still to be added that His manifestation is exactly suited to the stage now reached in the education of Israel. Their fathers had already "seen God" in the likeness of man: Abraham had entertained Him; Jacob had wrestled with Him. And so Joshua before Ai, and Manoah by the rock at Zorah, and Ezekiel by the river Chebar, should see the likeness of a man. We who believe the doctrine of a real Incarnation can well perceive that in these passing and mysterious glimpses God was not only revealing Himself in the way which would best prepare humanity for His future coming in actual manhood, but also in the way by which, meanwhile, the truest and deepest light could be thrown upon His nature, a nature which could hereafter perfectly manifest itself in flesh. Why, then, do not the records of the Exodus hint at a human likeness? Why did they "behold no similitude"? Clearly because the masses of Israel were utterly unprepared to receive rightly such a vision. To them the likeness of man would have meant no more than the likeness of a flying eagle or a calf. Idolatry would have followed, but no sense of sympathy, no consciousness of the grandeur and responsibility of being made in the likeness of God. Anthropomorphism is a heresy, although the Incarnation is the crowning doctrine of the faith.

But it is hard to see why the human likeness of God should exist in Genesis and Joshua, but not in the history of the Exodus, if that story be a post-Exilian forgery.

This is not all. The revelations of God in the desert were connected with threats and prohibitions: the law was given by Moses; grace and truth came by Jesus Christ. And with the different tone of the message a different aspect of the speaker was to be expected. From the blazing crags of Sinai, fenced around, the voice of a trumpet waxing louder and louder, said "Thou shalt not!" On the green hill by the Galilæan lake Jesus sat down, and His disciples came unto Him, and He opened His mouth and said "Blessed."

Now, the conscience of every sinner knows that the God of the commandments is dreadful. It is of Him, not of hell, that Isaiah said "The sinners in Zion are afraid; trembling hath surprised the godless ones. Who among us shall dwell with the devouring fire? who among us shall dwell with everlasting burnings?" (Isa. xxxiii. 14).

For him who rejects the light yoke of the Lord of Love, the fires of Sinai are still the truest revelation of deity; and we must not deny Sinai because we know Bethlehem. We must choose between the two.

CHAPTER XXV.

THE SHRINE AND ITS FURNITURE.

xxv. 1-40.

THE first direction given to Moses on the mountain is to prepare for the making of a tabernacle wherein God may dwell with man. For this he must invite offerings of various kinds, metals and gems, skins and fabrics, oil and spices; and the humblest man whose heart is willing may contribute toward an abode for Him Whom the heaven of heavens cannot contain.

Strange indeed is the contrast between the mountain burning up to heaven, and the lowly structure of the wood of the desert, which was now to be erected by subscription.

And yet the change marks not a lower conception of deity, but an advance, just as the quiet and serene communion of a saint with God is loftier than the most agitating experience of the convert.

. This is the first announcement of a fixed abiding presence of God in the midst of men, and it is therefore the precursor of much. St. John certainly alluded to this earliest dwelling of God on earth when he wrote, "The Word was made flesh, and tabernacled among us" (John i. 14). A little later it was said, "Ye also are builded together for an habitation of God" (Eph. ii. 22); and again the very words used at first of the tabernacle are applied to faithful souls: "We are a temple of the living God, as God said, I will dwell in them and walk in them" (2 Cor. vi. 16; Lev. xxvi. 11). For God dwelt on earth in the Messiah hidden by the veil, that is to say His flesh (Heb. x. 20), and also in the hearts of all the faithful. And a yet fuller communion is to come, of which the tabernacle in the wilderness was a type, even the descent of the Holy City, when the true tabernacle of God shall be with men, and He shall tabernacle with them (Rev. xxi. 3).

It may seem strange that after the commandment "Let them make Me a sanctuary" the whole chapter is devoted to instructions, not for the tabernacle but for its furniture. But indeed the four articles enumerated in this chapter present a wonderfully graphic picture of the nature and terms of the intercourse of God with man. On one side is His revelation of righteousness, but righteousness propitiated and become gracious, and this is symbolised by the ark of the testimony and the mercy-seat. On the other side the consecration both of secular and sacred life is typified by the table with bread and wine, and by the golden candlestick. Except thus, no tabernacle could have been the dwelling of the Lord, nor ever shall be.

And this is the true reason why the altar of incense is not even mentioned until a later chapter (xxx.). We do homage to God because He is present: it is rather the consequence than the condition of His abode with us.

The first step towards the preparation of a shrine for God on earth is the enshrining of His will: Moses should therefore make first of all an ark, wherein to treasure up "the testimony which I shall give thee," the two tables of the law (xxv. 16). In it were also

the pot of manna and Aaron's rod which budded
(Heb. ix. 4), and beside it was laid the whole book of
the law, for a testimony, alas! against them (Deut.
xxxi. 26).

Thus the ark was to treasure up the expression of
the will of God, and the relics which told by what
mercies and deliverances He claimed obedience. It
was a precious thing, but not the most precious, as we
shall presently learn; and therefore it was not made
of pure gold, but overlaid with it. That it might be
reverently carried, four rings were cast and fastened to
it at the lower corners, and in these four staves, also
overlaid with gold, were permanently inserted.

The next article mentioned is the most important
of all.

It would be a great mistake to suppose that the
mercy-seat was a mere lid, an ordinary portion of the
ark itself. It was made of a different and more costly
material, of pure gold, with which the ark was only
overlaid. There is separate mention that Bezaleel
"made the ark, . . . and he made the mercy-seat"
(xxxvii. 1, 6), and the special presence of God in the
Most Holy Place is connected much more intimately
with the mercy-seat than with the remainder of the
structure. Thus He promises to "appear in the cloud
above the mercy-seat" (Lev. xvi. 2). And when it is
written that "Moses heard the Voice speaking unto
him from above the mercy-seat which is upon the ark
of the testimony" (Num. vii. 89), it would have been
more natural to say directly "from above the ark"
unless some stress were to be laid upon the interposing
slab of gold. In reality no distinction could be sharper
than between the ark and its cover, from whence to
hear the voice of God. And so thoroughly did all

the symbolism of the Most Holy Place gather around this supreme object, that in one place it is actually called "the house of the mercy-seat" (1 Chron. xxviii. 11).

Let us, then, put ourselves into the place of an ancient worshipper. Excluded though he is from the Holy Place, and conscious that even the priests are shut out from the inner shrine, yet the high priest who enters is his brother: he goes on his behalf: the barrier is a curtain, not a wall.

But while the Israelite mused upon what was beyond, the ark, as we have seen, suggests the depth of his obligation; for there is the rod of his deliverance and the bread from heaven which fed him; and there also are the commandments which he ought to have kept. And his conscience tells him of ingratitude and a broken covenant; by the law is the knowledge of sin.

It is therefore a sinister and menacing thought that immediately above this ark of the violated covenant burns the visible manifestation of God, his injured Benefactor.

And hence arises the golden value of that which interposes, beneath which the accusing law is buried, by means of which God "hides His face from our sins."

The worshipper knows this cover to be provided by a separate ordinance of God, after the ark and its contents had been arranged for, and finds in it a vivid concrete representation of the idea "Thou hast cast all my sins behind Thy back" (Isa. xxxviii. 17). That this was its true intention becomes more evident when we ascertain exactly the meaning of the term which we have, not too precisely, rendered "mercy-seat."

The word "seat" has no part in the original; and we are not to think of God as reposing on it, but as revealing Himself above. The erroneous notion has probably transferred itself to the type from the heavenly antitype, which is "the throne of grace," but it has no countenance either in the Greek or the Hebrew name of the Mosaic institution. Nor is the notion expressed that of gratuitous and unbought "mercy." When Jehovah showeth mercy unto thousands, the word is different. It is true that the root means "to cover," and is once employed in Scripture in that sense (Gen. vi. 14); but its ethical use is generally connected with sacrifice; and when we read of a "sin-offering for *atonement*," of the half-shekel being an "*atonement*-money," and of "the day of *atonement*," the word is a simple and very similar development from the same root with this which we render *mercy-seat* (Exod. xxx. 10, 16; Lev. xxiii. 27, etc.).

The Greek word is found twice in the New Testament: once when the cherubim of glory overshadow the *mercy-seat*, and again when God hath set forth Christ to be a *propitiation* (Heb. ix. 5; Rom. iii. 25). The mercy-seat is therefore to be thought of in connection with sin, but sin expiated and thus covered and put away.

We know mysteries which the Israelite could not guess of the means by which this was brought to pass. But as he watched the high priest disappearing into that awful solitude, with God, as he listened to the chime of bells, swung by his movements, and announcing that still he lived, two conditions stood out broadly before his mind. One was the bringing in of incense: "Thou shalt bring a censer full of burning coals of fire from before the altar, that the cloud of the incense may cover the mercy-seat" (Lev. xvi. 13). Now, the connection between prayer and incense was quite familiar to the Jew; and he could not but understand that the blessing of atonement was to be sought and won by intense and burning supplication. And the other was that invariable demand, the offering of a victim's blood. All the sacrifices of Judaism culminated in the great act when the high priest, standing in the most holy and the most occult spot in all the world, sprinkled "blood upon the mercy-seat eastwards, and before the mercy-seat sprinkled of the blood with his finger seven times" (Lev. xvi. 14).

Thus the crowning height of the Jewish ritual was attained when the blood of the great national sacrifice was offered not only before God, but, with special reference to the covering up of the broken and accusing law, before the mercy-seat.

No wonder that on either side of it, and moulded of the same mass of metal, were the cherubim in an attitude of adoration, their outspread wings covering it, their faces bent, not only as bowing in reverence before the Divine presence, but, as we expressly read, "toward the mercy-seat shall the faces of the cherubim be." For the meaning of this great symbol was among the things which "the angels desire to look into."

We now understand how much was gained when God said "There will I meet thee, and I will commune with thee from above the mercy-seat" (ver. 22). It was an assurance, not only of the love which desires obedience, but of the mercy which passes over failure.*

---

* This investigation offers a fine example of the folly of that kind of interpretation which looks about for some sort of external and arbitrary resemblance, and fastens upon that as the true meaning. Nothing is more common among these expounders than to declare that the wood and gold of the ark are types of the human and Divine natures of our Lord. If either ark or mercy-seat should be compared to Him, it is obviously the latter, which speaks of mercy. But this was of pure gold.

Thus far, there has been symbolised the mind of God, His righteousness and His grace.

The next articles have to do with man, his homage to God and his witness for Him.

There is first the table of the shewbread (vers. 23-30), overlaid with pure gold, surrounded, like the ark, with "a crown" or moulding of gold, for ornament and the greater security of the loaves, and strengthened by a border of pure gold carried around the base, which was also ornamented with a crown, or moulding. Close to this border were rings for staves, like those by which the ark was borne. The table was furnished with dishes upon which, every Sabbath day, new shewbread might be conveyed into the tabernacle, and the old might be removed for the priests to eat. There were spoons also, by which to place frankincense upon each pile of bread; and "flagons and bowls to pour out withal." What was thus to be poured we do not read, but there is no doubt that it was wine, second only to bread as a requisite of Jewish life, and forming, like the frankincense, a link between this weekly presentation and the meal-offerings. But all these were subordinate to the twelve loaves, one for each tribe, which were laid in two piles upon the table. It is clear that their presentation was the essence of the rite, and not their consumption by the priests, which was possibly little more than a safe-guard against irreverent treatment. For the word shewbread is literally bread of the face or presence, which word is used of the presence of God, in the famous prayer "If Thy presence go not with me, carry us not up hence" (xxxiii. 15). And of whom, other than God, can it here be reasonably understood? Now Jacob, long before, had vowed "Of all that Thou givest me, I will surely give the tenth to Thee" (Gen. xxviii. 22). And it was an edifying ordinance that a regular offering should be made to God of the staple necessaries of existence, as a confession that all came from Him, and an appeal, clearly expressed by covering it with frankincense, which typified prayer (Lev. xxiv. 7) that He would continue to supply their need.

Nor is it overstrained to add, that when this bread was given to their priestly representatives to eat, with all reverence and in a holy place, God responded, and gave back to His people that which represented the necessary maintenance of the tribes. Thus it was, "on the behalf of the children of Israel, an everlasting covenant" (Lev. xxiv. 8).

The form has perished. But as long as we confess in the Lord's Prayer that the wealthiest does not possess one day's bread ungiven—as long, also, as Christian families connect every meal with a due acknowledgment of dependence and of gratitude—so long will the Church of Christ continue to make the same confession and appeal which were offered in the shewbread upon the table.

The next article of furniture was the golden candlestick (vers. 31-40). And this presents the curious phenomenon that it is extremely clear in its typical import, and in its material outline; but the details of the description are most obscure, and impossible to be gathered from the Authorised Version. Strictly speaking, it was not a lamp, but only a gorgeous lampstand, with one perpendicular shaft, and six branches, three springing, one above another, from each side of the shaft, and all curving up to the same height. Upon these were laid the seven lamps, which were altogether separate in their construction (ver. 37). It was of pure gold, the base and the main shaft being of one piece of beaten metal. Each of the six branches was ornamented with three cups, made like almond blossoms; above these a "knop," variously compared by Jewish writers to an apple and a pomegranate, and still higher, a flower or bud. It is believed that there was a fruit and flower above each of the cups, making nine ornaments on each branch. The "candlestick" in ver. 34 can only mean the central shaft, and upon this there were "four cups with their knops and flowers" instead of three. With the lamp were tongs, and snuff-dishes in which to remove the charred wick from the temple.

As we are told that when the Lord called the child Samuel, "the lamp of God was not yet gone out" (1 Sam. iii. 3), it follows that the lights were kept burning only during the night.

We have now to ascertain the spiritual meaning of this stately symbol. There are two other passages in Scripture which take up the figure and carry it forward. In Zechariah (iv. 2-12) we are taught that the separation of the lamps is a mere incident; they are to be conceived of as organically one, and moreover as fed by secret ducts with oil from no limited supply, but from living olive trees, vital, rooted in the system of the universe. Whatever obscurity may veil those "two sons of oil" (and this is not the place to discuss the subject), we are distinctly told that the main lesson is that of lustre derived from supernatural, invisible sources. Zerubbabel is confronted by a great mountain of hindrance, but it shall become a plain before him, because the lesson of the vision of the candlestick is this—"Not by might, nor by power, but by My Spirit, saith the Lord." A lamp gives light not because the gold shines, but because the oil burns; and yet the oil is the one thing which the eye sees not. And so the Church is a witness for her Lord, a light shining in a dark place, not because of its learning or culture, its noble ritual, its stately buildings or its ample revenues. All these things her children, having the power, ought to dedicate. The ancient symbol put art and preciousness in an honourable place, worthily upholding the lamp itself; and in the New Testament the seven lamps of the Apocalypse were still of gold. But the true function of a lamp is to be luminous, and for this the Church depends wholly upon its supply of grace from God the Holy Ghost. It is "not by might, nor by power, but by My Spirit, saith the Lord."

Again, in the Revelation, we find the New Testament Churches described as lamps, among which their Lord habitually walks. And no sooner have the seven churches on earth been warned and cheered, than we are shown before the throne of God seven torches (burning by their own incandescence—*vide* Trench, *N. T. Synonyms*, p. 162), which are the seven spirits of God, answering to His seven light-bearers upon the earth (Rev. iv. 5).

Lastly, the perfect and mystic number, seven, declares that the light of the Church, shining in a dark place, ought to be full and clear, no imperfect presentation of the truth: "they shall light the lamps, to give light over against it."

Because this lamp shines with the light of the Church, exhibiting the graces of her Lord, therefore a special command is addressed to the people, besides the call for contributions to the work in general, that they shall bring pure olive oil, not obtained by heat and pressure, but simply beaten, and therefore of the best quality, to feed its flame.

It is to burn, as the Church ought to shine in all darkness of the conscience or the heart of man, from evening to morning for ever. And the care of the ministers of God is to be the continual tending of this blessed and sacred flame.

THE PATTERN IN THE MOUNT.

xxv. 9, 40.

Twice over (vers. 9, 40, and cf. xxvi. 30, xxvii. 8, etc.) Moses was reminded to be careful to make all things after the pattern shown him in the mount. And these words have sometimes been so strained as to convey the meaning that there really exists in heaven a tabernacle and its furniture, the grand original from which the Mosaic copy was derived.

That is plainly not what the Epistle to the Hebrews understands (Heb. viii. 5). For it urges this admonition as a proof that the old dispensation was a shadow of ours, in which Christ enters into heaven itself, and our consciences are cleansed from dead works to serve the living God. The citation is bound indissolubly with all the demonstration which follows it.

We are not, then, to think of a heavenly tabernacle, exhibited to the material senses of Moses, with which all the details of his own work must be identical.

Rather we are to conceive of an inspiration, an ideal, a vision of spiritual truths, to which all this work in gold and acacia-wood should correspond. It was thus that Socrates told Glaucon, incredulous of his republic, that in heaven there is laid up a pattern, for him that wishes to behold it. Nothing short of this would satisfy the inspired application of the words in the Epistle to the Hebrews, where the readers, who were Jewish converts, are asked to recognise in this verse evidence that the light of the new dispensation illuminated the institutions of the old.

Without this pervading sentiment, the most elaborate specifications of weight and measurement, of cup and pomegranate and flower, could never have produced the required effect. An ideal there was, a divinely designed suggestiveness, which must be always present to his superintending vigilance, as once it shone upon his soul in sacred vision or trance; a suggestiveness which might possibly be lost amid correct elaborations, like the soul of a poem or a song, evaporating through a rendering which is correct enough, yet in which the spirit, even if that alone, has been forgotten.

It is surely a striking thing to find this need of a pervading sentiment impressed upon the author of the first piece of religious art that ever was recognised by heaven.

For it is the mysterious all-pervading charm of such a dominant sentiment which marks the impassable difference between the lowliest work of art, and the highest piece of art-manufacture which is only a manufactured article.

And assuredly the recognition of this principle among a people whose ancient history shows but little interest in art, calls for some attention from those who regard the tabernacle itself as a fiction, and its details as elaborated in Babylonia, in the priestly interest. (Kuenen, *Relig. of Israel*, ii. 148).

The problem of problems for all who deny the divinity of the Old Testament is to explain the curious position which its institutions are consistent in accepting. They rest on the authority of heaven, and yet they are not definitive, but provisional. They are always looking forward to another prophet like their founder, a new covenant better than the present one, a high priest after the order of a Canaanite enthroned at the right hand of Jehovah, a consecration for every pot in the city like that of the vessels in the temple (Deut. xviii. 15; Jer. xxxi. 31; Ps. cx. 1, 4; Zech. xiv. 20). And here, "in the priestly interest," is an avowal that the Divine habitation which they boast of is but the likeness and shadow of some Divine reality concealed. And these strange expectations have proved to be the most fruitful and energetic principles in their religion.

This very presence of the ideal is what will for ever make the highest natures quite certain that the visible universe is no mere resultant of clashing forces without a soul, but the genuine work of a Creator. The universe is charged throughout with the most powerful appeals to all that is artistic and vital within us; so that a cataract is more than water falling noisily, and the silence of midnight more than the absence of disturbance, and a snow mountain more than a storehouse to feed the torrents in summer, being also poems, appeals, revelations, whispers from a spirit, heard in the depth of ours.

Does any one, listening to Beethoven's funeral march, doubt the utterance of a soul, as distinct from clanging metal and vibrating chords? And the world has in it this mysterious witness to something more than heat and cold, moisture and drought: something which makes the difference between a well-filled granary and a field of grain rippling golden in the breeze. This is not a coercive argument for the hostile logic-monger 1 it is an appeal for the open heart. "He that hath ears to hear, let him hear."

To fill the tabernacle of Moses with spiritual meaning, the ideal tabernacle was revealed to him in the Mount of God.

Let us apply the same principle to human life. There also harmony and unity, a pervading sense of beauty and of soul, are not to be won by mere obedience to a mandate here and a prohibition there. Like Moses, it is not by labour according to specification that we may erect a shrine for deity. Those parables which tell of obedient toil would be sadly defective, therefore, without those which speak of love and joy, a supper, a Shepherd bearing home His sheep, a prodigal whose dull expectation of hired service is changed for investiture with the best robe and the gold ring, and welcome of dance and music.

How shall our lives be made thus harmonious, a spiritual poem and not a task, a chord vibrating under the musician's hand? How shall thought and word, desire and deed, become like the blended voices of river and wind and wood, a witness for the divine? Not by mere elaboration of detail (though correctness is a condition of all true art), but by a vision before us of the divine life, the Ideal, the pattern shown to all, and equally to be imitated (strange though it may seem) by peasant and prince, by woman and sage and child.

CHAPTER XXVI.

THE TABERNACLE

xxvi.

WE now come to examine the structure of the tabernacle for which the most essential furniture has been prepared.

Some confusion of thought exists, even among educated laymen, with regard to the arrangements of the temple; and this has led to similar confusion (to a less extent) concerning the corresponding parts of the tabernacle. "The temple" in which the Child Jesus was found, and into which Peter and John went up to pray, ought not to be confounded with that inner shrine, "the temple," in which it was the lot of the priest Zacharias to burn incense, and into which Judas, forgetful of all its sacredness in his anguish, hurled his money to the priests (Luke ii. 46; Acts iii. 3; Luke i. 9; Matt. xxvii. 5). Now, the former of these corresponded to "the court of the tabernacle," an enclosure open to the skies, and containing two important articles, the altar of burnt sacrifices and the laver. This was accessible to the nation, so that the sinner could lay his hand upon the head of his offering, and the priests could purify themselves before entering their own sacred place, the tabernacle proper, the shrine. But when we come to the structure itself, some attention is still necessary, in order to derive any clear notion from the description; nor can this easily be done by an English reader without substituting the Revised Version for the Authorised. He will then discover that we have a description, first of the "curtains of the tabernacle" (vers. 1-6), and then of other curtains which are not considered to belong to the tabernacle proper, but to "the tent over the tabernacle" (7-13), being no part of the rich ornamental interior, but only a protection spread above it; and over this again were two further screens from the weather (14), and finally, inside all, are "the boards of the tabernacle"—of which boards the two actual apartments were constructed (15-30)—and the veil which divided the Holy from the Most Holy Place (31-3).

"The curtains of the tabernacle" were ten, made of linen, of which every thread consisted of fine strands twisted together, "and blue and purple and scarlet," with cherubim not embroidered but woven into the fabric (1).

These curtains were sewn together, five and five, so as to make two great curtains, each slightly larger than forty-two feet by thirty, being twenty-eight cubits long by five times four cubits broad (2, 3). Finally these two were linked together, each having fifty loops for that purpose at corresponding places at the edge, which loops were bound together by fifty golden clasps (4-6). Thus, when the nation was about to march, they could easily be divided in the middle and then folded in the seams.

This costly fabric was regarded as part of the true tabernacle: why, then, do we find the outer curtains mentioned before the rest of the tabernacle proper is described?

Certainly because these rich curtains lie immediately underneath the coarser ones, and are to be considered along with "the tent" which covered all (7). This consisted of curtains of goats' hair, of the same size, and arranged in all respects like the others, except that their clasps were only bronze, and that the curtains were eleven in number, instead of ten, so that half a curtain was available to hang down over the back, and half was to be doubled back upon itself at the front of "the tabernacle," that is to say, the richer curtains underneath. The object of this is obvious: it was to bring the centre of the goatskin curtains over the edge of the linen ones, as tiles overlap each other, to shut out the rain at the joints. But this implies, what has been said already, that the curtains of the tabernacle should lie close to the curtains of the tent.

Over these again was an outer covering of rams' skins dyed red, and a covering of sealskins above all (14). This last, it is generally agreed, ran only along the top, like a ridge tile, to protect the vulnerable part of the roof. And now it has to be remembered that we are speaking of a real tent with sloping sides, not a flat cover laid upon the flat inner structure of boards, and certain to admit the rain. By calling attention to this fact, Mr. Fergusson succeeded in solving all the problems connected with the measurements of the tabernacle, and bringing order into what was little more than chaos before (*Smith's Bible Dict.*, "Temple").

The inner tabernacle was of acacia wood, which was the only timber of the sanctuary. Each board stood ten cubits high, and was fitted by tenons into two silver sockets, which probably formed a continuous base. Each of these contained a talent of silver, and was therefore more than eighty pounds weight; and they were probably to some extent sunk into the ground for a foundation (xxxviii. 27). There were twenty boards on each side; and as they were a cubit and a half broad, the length of the tabernacle was about forty-five feet (16-18). At the west end there were six boards (22), which, with the breadth of the two posts or boards for the corners (23-4) just gives ten cubits, or fifteen feet, for the width of it. Thus the length of the tabernacle was three times its breadth; and we know that in the Temple (where all the proportions were the same, the figures being doubled throughout) the subdividing veil was so hung as to make the inner shrine a perfect square, leaving the holy place twice as long as it was broad.

The posts were held in their places by wooden bars, which were overlaid with gold (as the boards also were, ver. 29) and fitted into golden rings. Four such bars, or bolts, ran along a portion of each side, and there was a fifth great bar which stretched along the whole forty-five feet from end to end. Thus the edifice was firmly held together; and the wealth of the material makes it likely that they were fixed on the inside, and formed a part of the ornament of the edifice (26-9).

When the two curtains were fastened together with clasps, they gave a length of sixty feet. But we have seen that the length of the boards when jointed together was only forty-five feet. This gives a projection of seven feet and a half (five cubits) for the front and rear of the tent beyond the tabernacle of boards; and when the great curtains were drawn tight, sloping from the ridge-pole fourteen cubits on each side, it has been shown (assuming a right-angle at the top) that they reached within five cubits of the ground, and extended five cubits beyond the sides, the same distance as at the front and rear. The next instructions concern the veil which divided the two chambers of the sanctuary. This was in all respects like "the curtain of the tabernacle," and similarly woven with cherubim. It was hung upon four pillars; and the even number seems to prove that there was no higher one in the centre, reaching to the roof—which seems to imply that there was a triangular opening above the veil, between the Holy and the Most Holy Place (31, 32).

But here a difficult question arises. There is no specific measurement of the point at which this subdividing veil was to stretch across the tent. The analogy of the Temple inclines us to believe that the Most Holy Place was a perfect cube, and the Holy Place twice as long as it was broad and high. There is evident allusion to this final shape of the Most Holy Place in the description of the New Jerusalem, of which the length and breadth and height were equal. And yet there is strong reason to suspect that this arrangement was not the primitive one. For Moses was ordered to stretch the veil underneath the golden clasps which bound together the two great curtains of the tabernacle (ver. 33). But these were certainly in the middle. How, then, could the veil make an unequal division below? Possibly fifteen feet square would have been too mean a space for the dimensions of the Most Holy Place, although the perfect cube became desirable, when the size was doubled.

A screen of the same rich material, but apparently not embroidered with cherubim, was to stretch across the door of the tent; but this was supported on five pillars instead of four, clearly that the central one might support the ridge-bar of the roof. And their sockets were of brass (vers. 36, 37).

The tabernacle, like the Temple, had its entrance on the east (ver. 22); and in the case of the Temple this was the more remarkable, because the city lay at the other side, and the worshippers had to pass round the shrine before they reached the front of it. The object was apparently to catch the warmth of the sun. For a somewhat similar reason, every pagan temple in the ancient world, with a few well-defined exceptions which are easily explained, also faced the east; and the worshippers, with their backs to the dawn, saw the first beams of the sun kindling their idol's face. The orientation of Christian churches is due to the custom which made the neophyte, standing at first in his familiar position westward, renounce the devil and all his works, and then, turning his back upon his idols, recite the creed with his face eastward.

What ideas would be suggested by this edifice to the worshipper will better be examined when we have examined also the external court.

CHAPTER XXVII.

THE OUTER COURT.

xxvii.

BEFORE describing the tabernacle, its furniture was specified. And so, when giving instructions for the court of the tabernacle, the altar has to be described: "Thou shalt make the altar of acacia wood." The definite article either implies that an altar was taken for granted, a thing of course; or else it points back to chap. xx. 24, which said "An altar of earth shalt thou make." Nor is the acacia wood of this altar at all inconsistent with that precept, it being really not an altar but an altar-case, and "hollow" (ver. 8)—an arrangement for holding the earth together, and preventing the feet of the priests from desecrating it. At each corner was a horn, of one piece with the framework, typical of the power which was there invoked, and practically useful, both to bind the sacrifice with cords, and also for the grasp of the fugitive, seeking sanctuary (Ps. cxviii. 27; 1 Kings i. 50). This arrangement is said to have been peculiar to Judaism. And as the altar was outside the tabernacle, and both symbolism and art prescribed simpler materials, it was overlaid with brass (vers. 1, 2). Of the same material were the vessels necessary for the treatment of the fire and blood (ver. 3). A network of brass protected the lower part of the altar; and at half the height a ledge projected, supported by this network, and probably wide enough to allow the priests to stand upon it when they ministered (vers. 4, 5). Hence we read that Aaron " came down from offering " (Lev. ix. 22). Lastly, there was the same arrangement of rings and staves to carry it as for the ark and the table (vers. 6, 7).

It will be noticed that the laver in this court, like the altar of incense within, is reserved for mention in a later chapter (xxx. 18) as being a subordinate feature in the arrangements.

The enclosure was a quadrangle of one hundred cubits by fifty; it was five cubits high, and each cubit may be taken as a foot and a half. The linen which enclosed it was upheld by pillars with sockets of brass; and one of the few additional facts to be gleaned from the detailed statement that all these directions were accurately carried out is that the heads of all the pillars were overlaid with silver (xxxviii. 17). The pillars were connected by rods (fillets) of silver, and a hanging of fine-twined linen was stretched by means of silver hooks (9-13). The entrance was twenty cubits wide, corresponding accurately to the width, not of the tabernacle, but of "the tent" as it has been described (reaching out five cubits farther on each side than the tabernacle), and it was closed by an embroidered curtain (14-17). This fence was drawn firmly into position and held there by brazen tent-pins; and we here incidentally learn that so was the tent itself (19).

[FOR VERSES 20, 21, see page 423.]

We are now in a position to ask what sentiment all

these arrangements would inspire in the mind of the simple and somewhat superstitious worshippers.

Approaching it from outside, the linen enclosure (being seven feet and a half high) would conceal everything but the great roof of the tent, one uniform red, except for the sealskin covering along the summit. A gloomy and menacing prospect, broken possibly by some gleams, if the curtain of the gable were drawn back, from the gold with which every portion of the shrine within was plated.

So does the world outside look askance upon the Church, discerning a mysterious suggestion everywhere of sternness and awe, yet with flashes of strange splendour and affluence underneath the gloom.

In this place God is known to be: it is a tent, not really "of the congregation," but "of meeting" between Jehovah and His people: "the tent of meeting before the Lord, where I will meet with you, . . . and there I will meet with the children of Israel" (xxix. 42-3). And so the Israelite, though troubled by sin and fear, is attracted to the gate, and enters. Right in front stands the altar: this obtrudes itself before all else upon his attention: he must learn its lesson first of all. Especially will he feel that this is so if a sacrifice is now to be offered, since the official must go farther into the court to wash at the laver, and then return; so that a loss of graduated arrangement has been accepted in order to force the altar to the front. And he will soon learn that not only must every approach to the sacred things within be heralded by sacrifice upon this altar, but the blood of the victim must be carried as a passport into the shrine. Surely he remembers how the blood of the lamb saved his own life when the firstborn of Egypt died: he knows that it is written "The life (or soul) of the flesh is in the blood: and I have given it to you upon the altar to make atonement for your souls (or lives): for it is the blood that maketh atonement by reason of the life (or soul)" (Lev. xvii. 11).

No Hebrew could watch his fellow-sinner lay his hand on a victim's head, and confess his sin before the blow fell on it, without feeling that sin was being, in some mysterious sense, "borne" for him. The intricacies of our modern theology would not disturb him, but this is the sentiment by which the institutions of the tabernacle assuredly ministered comfort and hope to him. Strong would be his hope as he remembered that the service and its solace were not of human devising, that God had "given it to him upon the altar to make atonement for his soul."

Taking courage, therefore, the worshipper dares to lift up his eyes. And beyond the altar he sees a vision of dazzling magnificence. The inner roof, most unlike the sullen red of the exterior, is blazing with various colours, and embroidered with emblems of the mysterious creatures of the sky, winged, yet not utterly afar from human in their suggestiveness. Encompassed and looked down into by these is the tabernacle, all of gold. If the curtain is raised he sees a chamber which tells what the earth should be—a place of consecrated energies and resources, and of sacred illumination, the oil of God burning in the sevenfold vessel of the Church. Is this blessed place for him, and may he enter? Ah, no! and surely his heart would grow heavy with consciousness that reconciliation was not yet made perfect, when he learned that he must never approach the place where God had promised to meet with him.

Much less might he penetrate the awful chamber

within, the true home of deity. There, he knows, is the record of the mind of God, the concentrated expression of what is comparatively easy to obey in act, but difficult beyond hope to love, to accept and to be conformed to. That record is therefore at once the revelation of God and the condemnation of His creature. Yet over this, he knows well, there is poised no dead image such as were then adored in Babylonian and Egyptian fanes, but a spiritual Presence, the glory of the invisible God. Nor was He to be thought of as in solitude, loveless, or else needing human love: above Him were the woven seraphim of the curtain, and on either side a seraph of beaten gold—types, it may be, of all the created life which He inhabits, or else pictures of His sinless creatures of the upper world. And yet this pure Being, to Whom the companionship of sinful man is so little needed, is there to meet with man; and is pleased not to look upon His violated law, but to command that a slab, inestimably precious, shall interpose between it and its Avenger. By whom, then, shall this most holy floor be trodden? By the official representative of him who gazes, and longs, and is excluded. He enters not without blood, which he is careful to sprinkle upon all the furniture, but chiefly and seven times upon the mercy-seat.

Thus every worshipper carries away a profound consciousness that he is utterly unworthy, and yet that his unworthiness has been expiated; that he is excluded, and yet that his priest, his representative, has been admitted, and therefore that he may hope. The Holy Ghost did not declare by sign that no way into the Holiest existed, but only that it was not yet made manifest. Not yet.

This leads us to think of the priest,

CHAPTER XXVIII

"THE HOLY GARMENTS."

xxviii.

THE tabernacle being complete, the priesthood has to be provided for. Its dignity is intimated by the command to Moses to bring his brother Aaron and his sons near to himself (clearly in rank, because the object is defined, "that he may minister unto Me"), and also by the direction to make "holy garments for glory and for beauty." But just as the furniture is treated before the shrine, and again before the courtyard, so the vestments are provided before the priesthood is itself discussed.

The holiness of the raiment implies that separation to office can be expressed by official robes in the Church as well as in the state; and their glory and beauty show that God, Who has clothed His creation with splendour and with loveliness, does not dissever religious feeling from artistic expression.

All that are wise-hearted in such work, being inspired by God as really, though not as profoundly, as if their task were to foretell the advent of Messiah, are to unite their labours upon these garments.

The order in the twenty-eighth chapter is perhaps that of their visible importance. But it will be clearer to describe them in the order in which they were put on.

Next the flesh all the priests were clad from the loins to the thighs in close-fitting linen: the indecency of many pagan rituals must be far from them, and this was a perpetual ordinance, "that they bear not iniquity and die" (xxviii. 42-3).

Over this was a tight-fitting "coat" (a shirt rather) of fine linen, white, but woven in a chequered pattern, without seam, like the robe of Jesus, and bound together with a girdle (39-43).

These garments were common to all the priests; but their "head-tires" differed from the impressive mitre of the high priest. The rest of the vestments in this chapter belong to him alone.

Over the "coat" he wore the flowing "robe of the ephod," all blue, little seen from the waist up, but uncovered thence to the feet, and surrounded at the hem with golden pomegranates, the emblem of fruitfulness, and with bells to enable the worshippers outside to follow the movements of their representative. He should die if this expression of his vicarious function were neglected (31-35).

Above this robe was the ephod itself—a kind of gorgeous jacket, made in two pieces which were joined at the shoulders, and bound together at the waist by a cunningly woven band, which was of the same piece. This ephod, like the curtains of the tabernacle, was of blue and purple and scarlet and fine-twined linen; but added to these were threads of gold, and we read, as if this were a novelty which needed to be explained, that they beat the gold into thin plates and then cut it into threads (xxxix. 3, xxviii. 6-8).

Upon the shoulders were two stones, rightly perhaps called onyx, and set in "ouches"—of filagree work, as the word seems to say. Upon them were engraven the names of the twelve tribes, the burden of whose sins and sorrows he should bear into the presence of his God, " for a memorial " (9-12).

Upon the ephod was the breastplate, fastened to it by rings and chains of twisted gold, made to fold over into a square, a span in measurement, and blazing with twelve gems, upon which were engraved, as upon the onyxes on the shoulders, the names of the twelve tribes. All attempts to derive edification from the nature of these jewels must be governed by the commonplace reflection that we cannot identify them; and many of the present names are incorrect. It is almost certain that neither topaz, sapphire nor diamond could have been engraved, as these stones were, with the name of one of the twelve tribes (13-30).

"In the breastplate" (that is, evidently, between the folds as it was doubled), were placed those mysterious means of ascertaining the will of God, the Urim and the Thummim, the Lights and the Perfections; but of their nature, or of the manner in which they became significant, nothing can be said that is not pure conjecture (30).

Lastly, there was a mitre of white linen, and upon it was laced with blue cords a gold plate bearing the inscription " HOLY TO JEHOVAH " (36, 37).

No mention is made of shoes or sandals; and both from the commandment to Moses at the burning bush, and from history, it is certain that the priests officiated with their feet bare.

The picture thus completed has the clearest ethical significance. There is modesty, reverence, purity, innocence typified by whiteness, the grandeur of the office of intercession displayed in the rich colours and precious jewels by which that whiteness was relieved, sympathy expressed by the names of the people in the breastplate that heaved with every throb, of his heart, responsibility confessed by the same names upon the shoulder, where the government was said to press like a load (Isa. ix. 6); and over all, at once the condition and the explanation of the rest, upon the seat of intelligence itself, the golden inscription on the forehead, "Holy to Jehovah."

Such was the import of the raiment of the high priest: let us see how it agrees with the nature of his office.

THE PRIESTHOOD.

What, then, are the central ideas connected with the institution of a priesthood?

Regarding it in the broadest way, and as a purely human institution, we may trace it back to the eternal conflict in the breast of man between two mighty tendencies—the thirst for God and the dread of Him, a strong instinct of approach and a repelling sense of unworthiness.

In every age and climate, man prays. If any curious inquirer into savage habits can point to the doubtful exception of a tribe seemingly without a ritual, he will not really show that religion is one with superstition; for they who are said to have escaped its grasp are never the most advanced and civilised among their fellows upon that account,—they are the most savage and debased, they are to humanity what the only people which has formally renounced God is fast becoming among the European races.

Certainly history cannot exhibit one community, progressive, energetic and civilised, which did not feel that more was needful and might be had than its own resources could supply, and stretch aloft to a Supreme Being the hands which were so deft to handle the weapon and the tool. Certainly all experience proves that the foundations of national greatness are laid in national piety, so that the practical result of worship, and of the belief that God responds, has not been to dull the energies of man, but to inspire him with the self-respect befitting a confidant of deity, and to brace him for labours worthy of one who draws, from the sense of Divine favour, the hope of an infinite advance.

And yet, side by side with this spiritual gravitation, there has always been recoil and dread, such as was expressed when Moses hid his face because he was afraid to look upon God.

Now, it is not this apprehension, taken alone, which proves man to be a fallen creature: it is the combination of the dread of God with the desire of Him. Why should we shrink from our supreme Good, except as a sick man turns away from his natural food? He is in an unnatural and morbid state of body, and we of soul.

Thus divided between fear and attraction, man has fallen upon the device of commissioning some one to represent him before God. The priest on earth has come by the same road with so many other mediators— angel and demigod, saint and virgin.

At first it has been the secular chief of the family, tribe or nation, who has seemed least unworthy to negotiate as well with heaven as with centres of interest upon earth. But by degrees the duty has everywhere been transferred into professional hands, patriarch and king recoiling, feeling the inconsistency of his earthly duties with these sacred ones, finding his hands to be too soiled and his heart too heavily weighted with sin for the tremendous Presence into which the family or the tribe would press him. And yet the union of the two functions might be the ideal; and the sigh of all truly enlightened hearts might be for a priest sitting upon his throne, a priest after the order of Melchizedek. But thus it came to pass that an official, a clique, perhaps a family, was chosen from among men in things pertaining to God, and the institution of the priesthood was perfected.

Now, this is the very process which is recognised in Scripture; for these two conflicting forces were altogether sound and right. Man ought to desire God, for Whom he was created, and Whose voice in tne garden was once so welcome: but also he ought to shrink back from Him, afraid now, because he is conscious of his own nakedness, because he has eaten of the forbidden fruit.

Accordingly, as the nation is led out from Egypt, we find that its intercourse with heaven is at once real and indirect. The leader is virtually the priest as well, at whose intercession Amalek is vanquished and the sin of the golden calf is pardoned, who entered the presence of God and received the law upon their behalf, when they feared to hear His voice lest they should die, and by whose hand the blood of the covenant was sprinkled upon the people, when they had sworn to obey all that the Lord had said (xvii. 11, xxxii. 30, xx. 19, xxiv. 8).

Soon, however, the express command of God provided for an orthodox and edifying transfer of the priestly function from Moses to his brother Aaron. Some such division of duties between the secular chief and the religious priest would no doubt have come, in Israel as elsewhere, as soon as Moses disappeared; but it might have come after a very different fashion, associated with heresy and schism.

Especially would it have been demanded why the family of Moses, if the chieftainship must pass away from it, could not retain the religious leadership. We know how cogent such a plea would have appeared; for, although the transfer was made publicly and by his own act, yet no sooner did the nation begin to split into tribal subdivisions, amid the confused efforts of each to conquer its own share of the inheritance, than we find the grandson of Moses securely establishing himself and his posterity in the apostate and semi-idolatrous worship of Shechem (Judg. xviii. 30, R.V.).

And why should not this illustrious family have been chosen?

Perhaps because it was so illustrious. A priesthood of that great line might seem to have earned its office, and to claim special access to God, like the heathen priests, by virtue of some special desert. Therefore the honour was transferred to the far less eminent line of Aaron, and that in the very hour when he was lending his help to the first great apostacy, the type of the many idolatries into which Israel was yet to fall. So, too, the whole tribe of Levi was in some sense consecrated, not for its merit, but because, through the sin of its founder, it lacked a place and share among its brethren, being divided in Jacob and scattered in Israel by reason of the massacre of Shechem (Gen. xlix. 7).

Thus the nation, conscious of its failure to enjoy intercourse with heaven, found an authorised expression for its various and conflicting emotions. It was not worthy to commune with God, and yet it could not rest without Him. Therefore a spokesman, a representative, an ambassador, was given to it. But he was chosen after such a fashion as to shut out any suspicion that the merit of Levi had prevailed where that of Israel at large had failed. It was not because Levi executed vengeance on the idolaters that he was chosen, for the choice was already made, and made in the person of Aaron, who was so far from blameless in that offence.

And perhaps this is the distinguishing peculiarity of the Jewish priest among others : that he was chosen from among his brethren, and simply as one of them ; so that while his office was a proof of their exclusion, it was also a kind of sacrament of their future admission, because he was their brother and their envoy, and entered not as outshining but as representing them, their forerunner for them entering. The almond rod of Aaron was dry and barren as the rest, until the miraculous power of God invested it with blossoms and fruit.

Throughout the ritual, the utmost care was taken to inculcate this double lesson of the ministry. Into the Holy Place, whence the people were excluded, a whole family could enter. But there was an inner shrine, whither only the high priest might penetrate, thus reducing the family to a level with the nation ; " the Holy Ghost this signifying, that the way into the Holy Place hath not yet been made manifest, while as the first tabernacle (the outer shrine—ver. 6) was yet standing" (Heb. ix. 8).

Thus the people felt a deeper awe, a broader separation. And yet, when the sole and only representative who was left to them entered that "shrine, remote, occult, untrod," they saw that the way was not wholly barred against human footsteps : the lesson suggested was far from being that of absolute despair, —it was, as the Epistle to the Hebrews said, " Not yet." The prophet Zechariah foresaw a time when the bells of the horses should bear the same consecrating legend that shone upon the forehead of the priest: HOLY UNTO THE LORD (Zech. xiv. 20).

It is important to observe that the only book of the New Testament in which the priesthood is discussed dwells quite as largely upon the difference as upon the likeness between the Aaronic and the Messianic priest. The latter offered but one Sacrifice for sins, the former offered for himself before doing so for the people (Heb. x. 12). The latter was a royal Priest, and of the order of a Canaanite (Heb. vii. 1-4), thus breaking down all the old system at one long-predicted blow—for if He were on earth He could not so much as be a priest at all (Heb. viii. 4)—and with it all the old racial monopolies, all class distinctions, being Himself of a tribe as to which Moses spake nothing concerning priests (Heb. vii. 14). Every priest standeth, but this priest hath for ever sat down, and even at the right hand of God (Heb. x. 11, 12).

In one sense this priesthood belongs to Christ alone. In another sense it belongs to all who are made one with Him, and therefore a kingly priesthood unto God. But nowhere in the New Testament is the name by which He is designated bestowed upon any earthly minister by virtue of his office. The presbyter is never called *sacerdos*. And perhaps the heaviest blow ever dealt to popular theology was the misapplying of the New Testament epithet (elder, presbyter or priest) to designate the sacerdotal functions of the Old Testament, and those of Christ which they foreshadowed. It is not the word "priest" that is at fault, but some other word for the Old Testament official which is lacking, and cannot now be supplied.

CHAPTER XXIX.

THE CONSECRATION SERVICES.

xxix.

THE priest being now selected, and his raiment so provided as that it shall speak of his office and its glory, there remains his consecration.

In our day there is a disposition to make light of the formal setting apart of men and things for sacred uses. If God, we are asked, has called one to special service, is not that enough? What more can earth do to commission the chosen of the sky? But the plain answer which we ought to have the courage to return is that this is not at all enough. For God Himself had already called Paul and Barnabas when He said to such folk as Simeon Niger and Lucius of Cyrene and Manaen, "Separate Me Barnabas and Saul for the work whereunto I have called them" (Acts xiii. 1-4). And these obscure people not only laid their hands upon the great apostle, but actually sent him forth. Now, if he was not exempted from the need of an orderly commission by the marvellous circumstances of his call, by his apostleship not of man, by the explicit announcement that he was a chosen vessel to bear the sacred name before kings and peoples, it is startling to be told of some shallow modern evangelist, who works for no Church and submits to no discipline, that he can dispense with the sanction of human ordination because he is so clearly sent of heaven.

The example of the Old Testament will no doubt be brushed aside as if the religion which Jesus learned and honoured were a mere human superstition. Or else it would be natural to ask, Is it because the offices and functions of Judaism were more formal, more perfunctory than ours, that a greater spiritual grace went with their appointments than with the laying on of hands in the Christian Church, a rite so clearly sanctioned in the New Testament?

It is written of Joshua that Moses was to lay his hands upon him, because already the Spirit was in him; and of Timothy that he had unfeigned faith, and that prophecies went before concerning him (Num. xxvii. 18; 1 Tim. i. 18; 2 Tim. i. 5). But in neither dispensation did special grace fail to accompany the official separation to sacred office: Joshua was full of the Spirit of Wisdom, for Moses had laid his hands upon him; and Timothy was bidden to stir into flame that gift of God which was in him through the laying on of the Apostle's hands (Deut. xxxiv. 9; 2 Tim. i. 6).

Accordingly there is great stress laid upon the orderly institution of the priest. And yet, to make it plain that his authority is only "for his brethren," Moses, the chief of the nation, is to officiate throughout the ceremony of consecration. He it is who shall offer the sacrifices upon the altar, and sprinkle the blood, not upon the first day only, but throughout the ceremonies of the week.

In the first place certain victims must be held in readiness—a bullock and two rams; and with these must be brought in one basket unleavened bread, and unleavened cakes made with oil, and unleavened wafers on which oil is poured. Then, at the door of the tent of the meeting of man with God, a ceremonial washing must follow, in a laver yet to be provided. Here the assertion that purity is needed, and that it is not inherent, is too plain to be dwelt upon.

But such details as the assuming of the existence of a laver, for which no directions have yet been given (and presently also of the anointing oil, the composition of which is still untold), deserve notice. They are much more in the manner of one who is working out a plan, seen already by his mental vision, but of which only the salient and essential parts have been as yet stated, than of any priest of the latter days, who would first have completed his catalogue of the furniture, and only then have described the ceremonies in which he was accustomed to see all this apparatus take its appointed place.

What we actually find is quite natural to a creative imagination, striking out the broad design of the work and its uses first, and then filling in the outlines. It is not natural at a time when freshness and inspiration have departed, and squared timber, as we are told, has taken the place of the living tree.

The priest, when cleansed, was next to be clad in his robes of office, with the mitre on his head, and upon the mitre the golden plate, with its inscription, which is here called, as the culminating object in all his rich array, "the holy crown" (ver. 6).

And then he was to be anointed. Now, the use of oil, in the ceremony of investiture to office, is peculiar to revealed religion. And whether we suppose it to refer to the oil in a lamp, invisible, yet the secret source of all its illuminating power, or to that refreshment and renovated strength bestowed upon a weary traveller when his head is anointed with oil, in either case it expresses the grand doctrine of revealed religion—that no office may be filled in one's own strength, but that the inspiring help of God is offered, as surely as responsibilities are imposed. "The Spirit of the Lord God is upon Me, because He hath anointed Me."

With these three ceremonies—ablution, robing and anointing—the first and most personal section of the ritual ended. And now began a course of sacrifices to God, advancing from the humblest expression of sin, and appeal to heaven to overlook the unworthiness of its servant, to that which best exhibited conscious acceptance, enjoyment of privilege, admission to a feast with God. The bullock was a sin-offering: the word is literally *sin*, and occurs more than once in the double sense: "let him offer for his *sin* which he hath *sinned* a young bullock ... for a *sin*(-*offering*)" (Lev. iv. 3, v. 6, etc.). And this is the explanation of the verse which has perplexed so many: "He made Him to be sin for us, Who knew no sin" (2 Cor. v. 21). The doctrine that pardon comes not by a cheap and painless overlooking of transgression, as a thing indifferent, but by the transfer of its consequences to a victim divinely chosen, could not easily find clearer expression than in this word. And it was surely a sobering experience, and a wholesome one, when Aaron, in his glorious robes, sparkling with gems, and bearing on his forehead the legend of his holy calling, laid his hand, beside those of his children and successors, upon the doomed creature which was made sin for him. The gesture meant confession, acceptance of the appointed expiation, submission to be freed from guilt by a method so humiliating and admonitory. There was no undue exaltation in the mind of any priest whose heart went with this "remembrance of sins."

The bullock was immediately slain at the door of "the tent of meeting"; and to show that the shedding of his blood was an essential part of the rite, part of it was put with the finger on the horns of the altar, and the remainder was poured out at the base. Only then might the fat and the kidney be burned upon the altar; but it is never said of any sin-offering, as presently of the burnt-offering and the peace-offerings, that it is "a sweet savour before Jehovah" (vers. 18, 25)—a phrase which is only once extended to a trespass-offering for a purely unconscious lapse (Lev. iv. 31). The sin-offering is, at the best, a deplorable necessity. And therefore the notion of a gift, welcome to Jehovah, is carefully shut out: no portion of such an offering may go to maintain the priests: all must be burned "with fire without the camp; it is a sin-offering" (ver. 14). Rightly does the Epistle to the Hebrews emphasize this fact: "The bodies of those beasts whose blood is brought into the Holy Place . . . as an offering for sin" are burned without the camp. The bodies of other sacrifices were not reckoned unfit for food.* And so there is a striking example of humility, as well as an instructive coincidence, in the fact that Jesus suffered without the gate, being the true Sin-offering, "that He might sanctify the people through His own blood" (Heb. xiii. 11, 12).

Thus, by sacrifice for sin, the priest is rendered fit to

---

* Neither, it must be added, were the bodies of certain sin-offerings of the lower grade, and in which the priest was not personally concerned (Lev. x. 17, etc.).

offer up to God the symbol of a devoted life. Again, therefore, the hands of Aaron and his sons are laid upon the head of the ram, because they come to offer what represents themselves in another sense than that of expiation—a sweet savour now, an offering made by fire unto Jehovah (ver. 18). And to show that it is perfectly acceptable to Him, the whole ram shall be burnt upon the altar, and not now without the camp: "it is a burnt-offering unto the Lord." Such is the appointed way of God with man—first expiation, then devotion.

The third animal was a "peace-offering" (ver. 28). This is wrongly explained to mean an offering by which peace is made, for then there could be no meaning in what went before. It is the offering of one who is now in a state of peace with God, and who is therefore himself, in many cases, allowed to partake of what he brings. But on this occasion some quite peculiar ceremonies were introduced, and the ram is called by a strange name—"the ram of consecration." When Aaron and his sons have again declared their connection with the animal by laying their hands upon it, it is slain. And then the blood is applied to the tip of their right ear, the thumb of their right hand, and the great toe of their right foot, that the ear may hearken, and the best energies obey, and their life become as that of the consecrated animal, their bodies being presented, a living sacrifice, holy, acceptable to God. Then the same blood, with the oil which spoke of heavenly anointing, was sprinkled upon them and upon their official robes, and all were hallowed. Then the fattest and richest parts of the animal were taken, with a loaf, a cake, and a wafer from the basket, and placed in the hands of Aaron and his sons. This was their formal investiture with official rights; although not yet performing service, it was as priests that they received these; and their hands, swayed by those of Moses, solemnly waved them before the Lord in formal presentation, after which the pieces were consumed by fire. The breast was likewise waved, and became the perpetual property of Aaron and his sons—although on this occasion it passed from their hands to be the portion of Moses, who officiated. The remainder of the flesh, seethed in a holy place, belonged to Aaron and his sons. No stranger (of another family) might eat it, and what was left until morning should be consumed by fire, that is to say, destroyed in a manner absolutely clean, seeing no corruption.

For seven days this rite of consecration was repeated; and every day the altar also was cleansed, rendering it most holy, so that whatever touched it was holy.

Thus the people saw their representative and chief purified, accepted and devoted. Thenceforward, when they too brought their offerings, and beheld them presented (in person or through his subordinates) by the high priest with holiness emblazoned upon his brow, they gained hope, and even assurance, since one so consecrated was bidden to present their intercession; and sometimes they saw him pass into secret places of mysterious sanctity, bearing their tribal name on his shoulder and his bosom, while the chime of golden bells announced his movements, ministering there for them.

But the nation as a whole, with which this historical book is chiefly interested, saw in the high priest the means of continually rendering to God the service of its loyalty. Every day began and closed with the burnt-offering of a lamb of the first year, along with a meal-offering of fine flour and oil, and a drink-offering of wine. This would be a sweet savour unto God, not after the carnal fashion in which sceptics have interpreted the words, but in the same sense in which the wicked are a smoke in His nostrils from a continually burning fire.

And where this offering was made, the Omnipresent would meet with them. There He would convey His mind to His priest. There also He would meet with all the people—not occasionally, as amid the more impressive but less tolerable splendours of Sinai, but to dwell among them and be their God. And they should know that all this was true, and also that for this He led them out of Egypt: "I am Jehovah their God."

CHAPTER XXX.

INCENSE.

xxx. 1-10.

THE altar of incense was not mentioned when the tent of meeting was being prepared and furnished. But when, in the Divine idea, this is done, when all is ready for the intercourse of God and man, and the priest and the daily victims are provided for, something more than this formal routine of offerings might yet be sought for. This material worship of the senses, this round of splendour and of tragedy, this blaze of gold and gold-encrusted timber, these curtains embroidered in bright colours, and ministers glowing with gems, this blood and fire upon the altar, this worldly sanctuary,—was it all? Or should it not do as nature ever does, which seems to stretch its hands out into the impalpable, and to grow all but spiritual while we gaze; so that the mountain folds itself in vapour, and the ocean in mist and foam, and the rugged stem of the tree is arrayed in fineness of quivering frondage, and it may be of tinted blossom, and around it breathes a subtle fragrance, the most impalpable existence known to sense? Fragrance indeed is matter passing into the immaterial, it is the sigh of the sensuous for the spiritual state of being, it is an aspiration.

And therefore an altar, smaller than that of burnt-offering, but much more precious, being plated all around and on the top with gold (a "golden altar") (xxxix. 38), is now to be prepared, on which incense of sweet spices should be burned whenever a burnt-offering spoke of human devotion, and especially when the daily lamb was offered, every morning and every night.

This altar occupied a significant position. Of necessity, it was without the Most Holy Place, or else it would have been practically inaccessible; and yet it was spiritually in the closest connection with the presence of God within. The Epistle to the Hebrews reckons it among the furniture of the inner shrine* (Heb. ix. 4), close to the veil of which it stood, and within which its burning odours made their sweetness palpable. In the temple of Solomon it was "the altar that belonged to the oracle" (1 Kings vi. 22). In Leviticus (xvi. 12) incense was connected especially with that spot in the Most Holy Place which best expressed the grace that it appealed to, and "the cloud of incense" was to "cover the mercy-seat." Therefore Moses was bidden to put this altar "before the veil that is by the ark of the testimony, before the mercy-seat" (ver. 6).

It can never have been difficult to see the meaning of the rite for which this altar was provided. When Zacharias burned incense the multitude stood without,

---

* For it is incredible that, in a catalogue of furniture which included Aaron's rod and the pot of manna, this altar should be omitted, and "a golden censer," elsewhere unheard of, substituted. The gloss is too evidently an endeavour to get rid of a difficulty. But in idea and suggestion this altar belonged to the Most Holy. That shrine "had" it, though it actually stood outside.

praying. The incense in the vial of the angel of the Apocalypse was the prayers of the saints (Luke i. 10; Rev. viii. 3). And, long before, when the Psalmist thought of the priest approaching the veil which concealed the Supreme Presence, and there kindling precious spices until their aromatic breath became a silent plea within, it seemed to him that his own heart was even such an altar, whence the perfumed flame of holy longings might be wafted into the presence of his God, and he whispered, "Let my prayer be set forth before Thee as incense" (Ps. cxli. 2).

Such being the import of the type, we need not wonder that it was a perpetual ordinance in their generations, nor yet that no strange perfume might be offered, but only what was prescribed by God. The admixture with prayer of any human, self-asserting, intrusive element, is this unlawful fragrance. It is rhetoric in the leader of extempore prayer; studied inflexions in the conductor of liturgical service; animal excitement, or sentimental pensiveness, or assent which is merely vocal, among the worshippers. It is whatever professes to be prayer, and is not that but a substitute. And formalism is an empty censer.

But, however earnest and pure may seem to be the breathing of the soul to God, something unworthy mingles with what is best in man. The very altar of incense needs to have an atonement made for it once in the year throughout their generations with the blood of the sin-offering of atonement. The prayer of every heart which knows its own secret will be this:

> "Forgive what seemed my sin in me,
> What seemed my worth since I began;
> For merit lives from man to man
> And not from man, O Lord, to Thee."

THE CENSUS.

xxx. 11-16.

Moses by Divine command was soon to number Israel, and thus to lay the foundation for its organisation upon the march. A census was not, therefore, supposed to be presumptuous or sinful in itself; it was the vain-glory of David's census which was culpable.

But the honour of being numbered among the people of God should awaken a sense of unworthiness. Men had reason to fear lest the enrolment of such as they were in the host of God should produce a pestilence to sweep out the unclean from among the righteous. At least they must make some practical admission of their demerit. And therefore every man of twenty years who passed over unto them that were numbered (it is a picturesque glimpse that is here given into the method of enrolment) should offer for his soul a ransom of half a shekel after the shekel of the sanctuary. And because it was a ransom, the tribute was the same for all; the poor might not bring less, nor the rich more. Here was a grand assertion of the equality of all souls in the eyes of God—a seed which long ages might overlook, but which was sure to fructify in its appointed time.

For indeed the madness of modern levelling systems is only their attempt to level down instead of up, their dream that absolute equality can be obtained, or being obtained can be made a blessing, by the envious demolition of all that is lofty, and not by all together claiming the supreme elevation, the measure of the stature of manhood in Jesus Christ.

It is not in any *phalanstère* of Fourier or Harmony

Hall of Owen, that mankind will ever learn to break a common bread and drink of a common cup; it is at the table of a common Lord.

And so this first assertion of the equality of man was given to those who all ate the same spiritual meat and drank the same spiritual drink.

This half-shekel gradually became an annual impost, levied for the great expenses of the Temple. Thus Joash made a proclamation throughout Judah and Jerusalem, to bring in for the Lord the tax that Moses, the servant of God, laid upon Israel in the wilderness" (2 Chron. xxiv. 9).

And it was the claim for this impost, too rashly conceded by Peter with regard to his Master, which led Jesus to distinguish clearly between His own relation to God and that of others, even of the chosen race.

He paid no ransom for His soul. He was a Son, in a sense in which no other, even of the Jews, could claim to be so. Now, the kings of the earth did not levy tribute from their sons; so that, if Christ paid, it was not to fulfil a duty, but to avoid being an offence. And God Himself would provide, directly and miraculously, what He did not demand from Jesus. Therefore it was that, on this one occasion and no other, Christ Who sought figs when hungry, and when athirst asked water at alien hands, met His own personal requirement by a miracle, as if to protest in deed, as in word, against any burden from such an obligation as Peter's rashness had conceded.

And yet, with that marvellous condescension which shone most brightly when He most asserted His prerogative, He admitted Peter also to a share in this miraculous redemption-money, as He admits us all to a share in His glory in the skies. Is it not He only

Who can redeem His brother, and give to God a ransom for him?

It is the silver thus levied which was used in the construction of the sanctuary. All the other materials were free-will offerings; but even as the entire tabernacle was based upon the ponderous sockets into which the boards were fitted, made of the silver of this tax, so do all our glad and willing services depend upon this fundamental truth, that we are unworthy even to be reckoned His, that we owe before we can bestow, that we are only allowed to offer any gift because He is so merciful in His demand. Israel gladly brought much more than was needed of all things precious. But first, as an absolutely imperative ransom, God demanded from each soul the half of three shillings and sevenpence.

THE LAVER.

xxx. 17-21.

For the cleansing of various sacrifices, but especially for the ceremonial washing of the priests, a laver of brass was to be made, and placed upon a separate base, the more easily to be emptied and replenished.

We have seen already that although its actual use preceded that of the altar, yet the other stood in front of it, as if to assert, to the very eyes of all men, that sacrifice precedes purification. But the use of the laver was not by the man as man, but by the priest as mediator. In his office he represented the absolute purity of Christ. And therefore it was a capital offence to enter the tabernacle or to burn a sacrifice without first having washed the hands and feet. At his inauguration, the whole person of the priest was bathed, and thenceforth he needed not save to remove the stains of contact with the world.

When the laver was actually made, an interesting fact was recorded about its materials: "He made the laver of brass, and the base of it of brass, of the mirrors of the serving-women which served at the door of the tent of meeting" (xxxviii. 8). Thus their instruments of personal adornment were applied to further a personal preparation of a more solemn kind, like the ointment with which a penitent woman anointed the feet of Jesus. There is a fitness which ought to be considered in the direction of our gifts, not as a matter of duty, but of good taste and charm. And thus also they continually saw the monument of their self-sacrifice. There is an innocent satisfaction, far indeed from vanity, when one looks at his own work for God.

THE ANOINTING OIL AND THE INCENSE.

xxx. 22-38.

We have already seen the meaning of the anointing oil and of the incense.

But we have further to remark that their ingredients were accurately prescribed, that they were to be the best and rarest of their kind, and that special skill was demanded in their preparation.

Such was the natural dictate of reverence in preparing the symbols of God's grace to man, and of man's appeal to God.

With the type of grace should be anointed the tent and the ark, and the table of shewbread and the candlestick, with all their implements, and the altar of incense, and the altar of burnt sacrifice and the laver. All the import of every portion of the Temple worship could be realized only by the outpouring of the Spirit of grace.

It was added that this should be a holy anointing oil, not to be made, much less used, for common purposes, on pain of death. The same was enacted of the incense which should burn before Jehovah: "according to the composition thereof ye shall not make for yourselves; it shall be unto thee holy for the Lord: whosoever shall make like unto that, to smell thereto, he shall be cut off from his people."

And this was meant to teach reverence. One might urge that the spices and frankincense and salt were not in themselves sacred: there was no consecrating efficacy in their combination, no charm or spell in the union of these, more than of any other drugs. Why, then, should they be denied to culture? Why should her resources be thus restricted? Does any one suppose that such arguments belong peculiarly to the New Testament spirit, or that the saints of the older dispensation had any superstitious views about these ingredients? If it was through such notions that they abstained from vulgarising its use, then they were on the way to paganism, through a materialised worship.

But in truth they knew as well as we that gums were only gums, just as they knew that the Most High dwelleth not in temples made with hands. And yet they were bidden to reverence both the shrine and the apparatus of His worship, for their own sakes, for the solemnity and sobriety of their feelings, not because God would be a loser if they did otherwise. And we may well ask ourselves, in these latter days, whether the constant proposal to secularise religious buildings, revenues, endowments and seasons does really indicate greater religious freedom, or only greater freedom from religious control.

And we may be sure that a light treatment of sacred subjects and sacred words is a very dangerous symptom: it is not the words and subjects alone that are being secularised, but also our own souls.

There is in our time a curious tendency among men of letters to use holy things for a mere perfume, that literature may "smell thereto."

A novelist has chosen for the title of a story "Just as I am." An innocent and graceful poet has seen a smile,—

> "'Twas such a smile,
> Aaron's twelve jewels seemed to mix
> With the lamps of the golden candlesticks."

Another is bolder, and sings of the war of love,—

> "In the great battle when the hosts are met
> On Armageddon's plain, with spears beset."

Another thinks of Mazzini as the

> "Dear lord and leader, at whose hand
> The first days and the last days stand,"

and again as he who

> "Said, when all Time's sea was foam,
> 'Let there be Rome,' and there was Rome."

And Victor Hugo did not shrink from describing, and that with a strange and scandalous ignorance of the original incidents, the crucifixion by Louis Napoleon of the Christ of nations.

Now, Scripture is literature, besides being a great deal more; and, as such, it is absurd to object to all allusions to it in other literature. Yet the tendency of which these extracts are examples is not merely toward allusion, but desecration of solemn and sacred thoughts: it is the conversion of incense into perfumery.

There is another development of the same tendency, by no means modern, noted by the prophet when he complains that the message of God has become as the "very lovely song of one who hath a pleasant voice and playeth well on an instrument." Wherever divine service is only appreciated in so far as it is "well rendered," as rich music or stately enunciation charm the ear, and the surroundings are æsthetic,—wherever the gospel is heard with enjoyment only of the eloquence or controversial skill of its rendering, wherever religion is reduced by the cultivated to a thrill or to a solace, or by the Salvationist to a riot or a romp, wherever Isaiah and the Psalms are only admired as poetry, and heaven is only thought of as a languid and sentimental solace amid wearying cares,—there again is a making of the sacred balms to smell thereto.

And as often as a minister of God finds in his holy office a mere outlet for his natural gifts of rhetoric or of administration, he also is tempted to commit this crime.

CHAPTER XXXI.

BEZALEEL AND AHOLIAB.

xxxi. 1-18.

NEXT after this marking off so sharply of the holy from the profane, this consecration of men to special service, this protection of sacred unguents and sacred gums from secular use, we come upon a passage curiously contrasted, yet not really antagonistic to the last, of marvellous practical wisdom, and well calculated to make a nation wise and great.

The Lord announces that He has called by name Bezaleel, the son of Uri, and has filled him with the Spirit of God. To what sacred office, then, is he called? Simply to be a supreme craftsman, the rarest of artisans. This also is a divine gift. "I have filled him with the Spirit of God in wisdom and in understanding and in knowledge and in all manner of workmanship, to devise cunning works, to work in gold and in silver and in brass and in cutting of stones for setting, and in carving of wood, to work in all manner of workmanship,"—that is to say, of manual dexterity. With him God had appointed Aholiab; "and in the hearts of all the wise-hearted I have put wisdom." Thus should be fitly made the tabernacle and its furniture, and the finely wrought garments, and the anointing oil and the incense.

So then it appears that the Holy Spirit of God is to be recognised in the work of the carpenter and the jeweller, the apothecary and the tailor. Probably we object to such a statement, so baldly put. But inspiration does not object. Moses told the children of Israel that Jehovah had filled Bezaleel with the Spirit of God, and also Aholiab, for the work "of the engraver . . . and of the embroiderer . . . and of the weaver" (xxxv. 31, 35).

It is quite clear that we must cease to think of the Divine Spirit as inspiring only prayers and hymns and sermons. All that is good and beautiful and wise in human art is the gift of God. We feel that the supreme Artist is audible in the wind among the pines; but is man left to himself when he marshals into more sublime significance the voices of the wind among the organ tubes? At sunrise and sunset we feel that

"On the beautiful mountains the pictures of God are hung";

but is there no revelation of glory and of freshness in other pictures? Once the assertion that a great masterpiece was "inspired" was a clear recognition of the central fire at which all genius lights its lamp: now, alas! it has become little more than a sceptical assumption that Isaiah and Milton are much upon a level. But the doctrine of this passage is the divinity of all endowment; it is quite another thing to claim Divine authority for a given product sprung from the free human being who is so richly crowned and gifted.

Thus far we have smoothed our way by speaking only of poetry, painting, music—things which really compete with nature in their spiritual suggestiveness. But Moses spoke of the robe-maker, the embroiderer, the weaver, and the perfumer.

Nevertheless, the one is carried with the other. Where shall we draw the line, for example, in architecture or in ironwork? And there is another consideration which must not be overlooked. God is assuredly in the growth of humanity, in the progress of true civilisation—in all, the recognition of which makes history philosophical. It is not only the saints who feel themselves to be the instruments of a Greater than they. Cromwell and Bismarck, Columbus, Raleigh and Drake, William the Silent and William the Third, felt it. Mr. Stanley has told us how the consciousness that he was being used grew up in him, not through fanaticism but by slow experience, groping his way through the gloom of Central Africa.

But none will deny that one of the greatest factors in modern history is its industrial development. Is there, then, no sacredness here?

The doctrine of Scripture is not that man is a tool, but that he is responsible for vast gifts, which come directly from heaven—that every good gift is from above, that it was God Himself Who planted in Paradise the tree of knowledge.

Nor would anything do more to restrain the passions, to calm the impulses and to elevate the self-respect of modern life, to call back its energies from the base competition for gold, and make our industries what dreamers persuade themselves that the mediæval industries were, than a quick and general perception of what is meant when faculty goes by such names as talent, endowment, gift—of the glory of its use, the tragedy of its defilement. Many persons, indeed, reject this doctrine because they cannot believe that man has power to abase so high a thing so sadly. But what, then, do they think of the human body?

What connection is there between all this and the reiteration of the law of the Sabbath? Not merely that the moral law is now made a civic statute as well, for this had been done already (xxiii. 12). But, as our Lord has taught us that a Jew on the Sabbath was free to perform works of mercy, it might easily be supposed lawful, and even meritorious, to hasten forward the construction of the place where God would meet His people. But He who said "I will have mercy and not sacrifice" said also that to obey was better than sacrifice. Accordingly this caution closes the long story of plans and preparations. And when Moses called the people to the work, his first words were to repeat it (xxxv. 2).

Finally, there was given to Moses the deposit for which so noble a shrine was planned—the two tables of the law, miraculously produced.

If any one, without supposing that they were literally written with a literal finger, conceives that this was the meaning conveyed to a Hebrew by the expression "written with the finger of God," he entirely misses the Hebrew mode of thought, which habitually connects the Lord with an arm, with a chariot, with a bow made naked, with a tent and curtains, without the slightest taint of materialism in its conception. Did not the magicians, failing to imitate the third plague, say "This is the finger of a God"? Did not Jesus Himself "cast out devils by the finger of God"? (Ex. viii. 19; Luke xi. 20).

CHAPTER XXXII.

THE GOLDEN CALF.

xxxii.

WHILE God was thus providing for Israel, what had Israel done with God? They had grown weary of waiting: had despaired of and slighted their heroic leader, ("this Moses, the man that brought us up,") had demanded gods, or a god, at the hand of Aaron, and had so far carried him with them or coerced him that he thought it a stroke of policy to save them from breaking the first commandment by joining them in a breach of the second, and by infecting "a feast to Jehovah" with the licentious "play" of paganism. At the beginning, the only fitness attributed to Aaron was that "he can speak well." But the plastic and impressible temperament of a gifted speaker does not favour tenacity of will in danger. Demosthenes and Cicero, and Savonarola, the most eloquent of the reformers, illustrate the tendency of such genius to be daunted by visible perils.

God now rejects them because the covenant is violated. As Jesus spoke no longer of "My Father's house," but "your house, left unto you desolate," so the Lord said to Moses, "thy people which thou broughtest up."

But what are we to think of the proposal to destroy them, and to make of Moses a great nation?

We are to learn from it the solemn reality of intercession, the power of man with God, Who says not that He will destroy them, but that He will destroy them if left alone. Who can tell, at any moment, what calamities the intercession of the Church is averting from the world or from the nation?

The first prayer of Moses is brief and intense; there is passionate appeal, care for the Divine honour, remembrance of the saintly dead for whose sake the living might yet be spared, and absolute forgetfulness of self. Already the family of Aaron had been preferred to his, but the prospect of monopolising the Divine predestination has no charm for this faithful and patriotic heart. No sooner has the immediate destruction been arrested than he hastens to check the apostates, makes them exhibit the madness of their idolatry by drinking the water in which the dust of their pulverised god was strewn; receives the abject apology of Aaron, thoroughly spirit-broken and demoralised; and finding the sons of Levi faithful, sends them to the slaughter of three thousand men. Yet this is he who said "O Lord, why is Thy wrath hot against Thy people?" He himself felt it needful to cut deep, in mercy, and doubtless in wrath as well, for true affection is not limp and nerveless: it is like the ocean in its depth, and also in its tempests. And the stern action of the Levites appeared to him almost an omen; it was their "consecration," the beginning of their priestly service.

Again he returns to intercede; and if his prayer must fail, then his own part in life is over: let him too perish among the rest. For this is evidently what he means and says: he has not quite anticipated the spirit of Christ in Paul willing to be anathema for his brethren (Rom. ix. 3), nor has the idea of a vicarious human sacrifice been suggested to him by the institutions of the sanctuary. Yet how gladly would he have died for his people, who made request that he might die among them!

How nobly he foreshadows, not indeed the Christian doctrine, but the love of Christ Who died for man, Who from the Mount of Transfiguration, as Moses from Sinai, came down (while Peter would have lingered) to bear the sins of His brethren! How superior He is to the Christian hymn which pronounces nothing worth a thought, except how to make my own election sure.

CHAPTER XXXIII.

PREVAILING INTERCESSION.

xxxiii.

AT this stage the first concession is announced: Moses shall lead the people to their rest, and God will send an angel with him.

We have seen that the original promise of a great Angel in whom was the Divine Presence was full of encouragement and privilege (xxiii. 20). No unbiassed reader can suppose that it is the sending of this same Angel of the Presence which now expresses the absence of God, or that He Who then would not pardon their transgression " because My Name is in Him" is now sent because God, if He were in the midst of them for a moment, would consume them. Nor, when Moses passionately pleads against this degradation, and is heard in this thing also, can the answer " My Presence shall go with thee" be merely the repetition of those evil tidings. Yet it was the Angel of His Presence Who saved them. All this has been already treated, and what we are now to learn is that the faithful and sublime urgency of Moses did really save Israel from degradation and a lower covenant.

It was during the progress of this mediation that Moses distracted by a double anxiety—afraid to absent himself from his wayward followers, equally afraid to be so long withdrawn from the presence of God as the descending of Sinai and returning thither would involve—made a noble adventure of faith. Inspired by the conception of the tabernacle, he took a tent, "his tent," and pitched it outside the camp, to express the estrangement of the people, and this he called the Tent of the Meeting (with God), but in the Hebrew it is never called the Tabernacle. And God did condescend to meet him there. The mystic cloud guarded the door against presumptuous intrusion, and all the people, who previously wist not what had become of him, had now to confess the majesty of his communion, and they worshipped every man at his tent door.

It would seem that the anxious vigilance of Moses caused him to pass to and fro between the tent and the camp, "but his minister, Joshua the son of Nun, departed not out of the tent."

The dread crisis in the history of the nation was now almost over. God had said, "My Presence shall go with thee, and I will give thee rest,"—a phrase which the lowly Jesus thought it no presumption to appropriate, saying, "*I* will give you rest," as He also appropriated the office of the Shepherd, the benevolence of the Physician, the tenderness of the Bridegroom, and the glory of the King and the Judge, all of which belonged to God.

But Moses is not content merely to be secure, for it is natural that he who best loves man should also best love God. Therefore he pleads against the least withdrawal of the Presence: he cannot rest until repeatedly assured that God will indeed go with him; he speaks as if there were no "grace" but that. There are many people now who think it a better proof of being religious to feel either anxious or comforted about their own salvation, their election, and their going to heaven. And these would do wisely to consider how it comes to pass that the Bible first taught men to love and to follow God, and afterwards revealed to them the mysteries of the inner life and of eternity.

CHAPTER XXXIV.

THE VISION OF GOD.

xxxiv.

IT was when God had most graciously assured Moses of His affection, that he ventured, in so brief a cry that it is almost a gasp of longing, to ask, "Show me, I pray Thee, Thy glory" (xxxiii. 18).

We have seen how nobly this petition and the answer condemn all anthropomorphic misunderstandings of what had already been revealed; and also how it exemplifies the great law, that they who see most of God, know best how much is still unrevealed. The elders saw the God of Israel and did eat and drink: Moses was led from the bush to the flaming top of Sinai, and thence to the tent where the pillar of cloud was as a sentinel; but the secret remained unseen, the longing unsatisfied, and the nearest approach to the Beatific Vision reached by him with whom God spake face to face as with a friend, was to be hidden in a cleft of the rock, to be aware of an awful Shadow, and to hear the Voice of the Unseen.

It was a fit time for the proclamation which was then made. When the people had been righteously punished and yet graciously forgiven, the name of the Self-Existent expanded and grew clearer,—" Jehovah, Jehovah, a God full of compassion and gracious, slow to anger and plenteous in mercy and truth, keeping mercy for thousands, forgiving iniquity and transgression and sin, and that will by no means clear the guilty, visiting the iniquity of the fathers upon the children and upon the children's children, upon the third and upon the fourth generation." And as Moses made haste and bowed himself, it is affecting to hear him again pleading for that beloved Presence which even yet he can scarce believe to be restored, and instead of claiming any separation through his fidelity and his honours, praying "Pardon our iniquity and our sin, and take us for Thine inheritance" (xxxiv. 10).

Thereupon the covenant is given, as if newly, but without requiring its actual re-enactment; and certain of the former precepts are rehearsed, chiefly such as would guard against a relapse into idolatry when they entered the good land where God would bestow on them prosperity and conquest.

As Moses had broken the former tablets, the task was imposed on him of hewing out the slabs on which God renewed His awful sanction of the Decalogue, the fundamental statutes of the nation. And they who had failed to endure his former absence, were required to be patient while he tarried again upon the mountain, forty days and nights.

With his return a strange incident is connected. Unknown by himself, the "skin of his face shone by reason of His speaking with him," and Aaron and the people recoiled until he called to them. And thenceforth he lived a strange and isolated life. At each new interview the glory of his countenance was renewed, and when he conveyed his revelation to the people, they beheld the lofty sanction, the light of God upon his face. Then he veiled his face until next he approached his God, so that none might see what changes came there, and whether—as St. Paul seems to teach us—the lustre gradually waned.

His revelation, the apostle argues, was like this occasional and fading gleam, while the moral glory of the Christian system has no concealments: it uses great frankness; there is nothing withdrawn, no veil upon the face. Nor is it given to one alone to behold as in a mirror the glory of the Lord, and to share its lustre. We all, with face unveiled, share this experience of the deliverer (2 Cor. iii. 12, 18).

But the incident itself is most instructive. Since he had already spent an equal time with God, yet no such results had followed, it seems that we receive what we are adapted to receive, not straitened in Him but in our own capabilities; and as Moses, after his vehemence of intercession, his sublimity of self-negation, and his knowledge of the greater name of God, received new lustre from the unchangeable Fountain of light, so does all true service and earnest aspiration, while it approaches God, elevate and glorify humanity.

We learn also something of the exaltation of which matter is capable. We who have seen coarse bulb and soil and rain transmuted by the sunshine into radiance of bloom and subtlety of perfume, who have seen plain faces illuminated from within until they were almost angelic,—may we not hope for something great and rare for ourselves, and the beloved who are gone, as we muse upon the profound word, "It is raised a spiritual body"?

And again we learn that the best religious attainment is the least self-conscious: Moses wist not that the skin of his face shone.

CHAPTERS XXXV—XL.

THE CONCLUSION.

THE remainder of the narrative sets forth in terms almost identical with the directions already given, the manner in which the Divine injunctions were obeyed. The people, purified in heart by danger, chastisement and shame, brought much more than was required. A quarter of a million would poorly represent the value of the shrine in which, at the last, Moses and Aaron approached their God, while the cloud covered the tent and the glory filled the tabernacle, and Moses failed to overcome his awe and enter.

Thenceforth the cloud was the guide of their halting and their march. Many a time they grieved their God in the wilderness, yet the cloud was on the tabernacle by day, and there was fire therein by night, throughout all their journeyings.

That cloud is seen no longer; but One has said, "Lo, I am with you all the days." If the presence is less material, it is because we ought to be more spiritual.

Looking back upon the story, we can discern more clearly what was asserted when we began—the forming and training of a nation.

They are called from shameful servitude by the devotion of a patriot and a hero, who has learned in failure and exile the difference between self-confidence and faith. The new name of God, and His remembrance of their fathers, inspire them at the same time with awe and hope and nationality. They see the hollowness of earthly force, and of superstitious worships, in the abasement and ruin of Egypt. They are taught by the Paschal sacrifice to confess that the Divine favour is a gift and not a right, that their lives also are justly forfeited. The overthrow of Pharaoh's army and the passage of the Sea brings them into a new and utterly strange life, in an atmosphere and amid scenes well calculated to expand and deepen their emotions, to develop their sense of freedom and self-respect, and yet to oblige them to depend wholly on their God. Privation at Marah chastens them. The attack of Amalek introduces them to war, and forbids their dependence to sink into abject softness. The awful scene of Horeb burns and brands his littleness into man. The covenant shows them that, however little in themselves, they may enter into communion with the Eternal. It also crushes out what is selfish and individualising, by making them feel the superiority of what they all share over anything that is peculiar to one of them. The Decalogue reveals a holiness at once simple and profound, and forms a type of character such as will make any nation great. The sacrificial system tells them at once of the pardon and the heinousness of sin. Religion is both exalted above the world and infused into it, so that all is consecrated. The priesthood and the shrine tell them of sin and pardon, exclusion and hope; but that hope is a common heritage, which none may appropriate without his brother.

The especial sanctity of a sacred calling is balanced

by an immediate assertion of the sacredness of toil, and the Divine Spirit is recognised even in the gift of handicraft.

A tragic and shameful failure teaches them, more painfully than any symbolic system of curtains and secret chambers, how little fitted they are for the immediate intercourse of heaven. And yet the ever-present cloud, and the shrine in the heart of their encampment, assure them that God is with them of a truth.

Could any better system be imagined by which to convert a slavish and superstitious multitude into a nation at once humble and pure and gallant—a nation of brothers and of worshippers, chastened by a genuine sense of ill desert and of responsibility, and yet braced and fired by the conviction of an exalted destiny?

To do this, and also to lead mankind to liberty, to rescue them from sensuous worship, and prepare them for a system yet more spiritual, to teach the human race that life is not repose but warfare, pilgrimage and aspiration, and to sow the seeds of beliefs and expectations which only an atoning Mediator and an Incarnate God could satisfy, this was the meaning of the Exodus.

BY THE SAME AUTHOR.

Third Edition. Crown 8vo, cloth, 7s. 6d.

THE GOSPEL ACCORDING TO ST. MARK.

Academy.—"Dr. Chadwick has performed his task admirably. He keeps close to his subject, avoiding irrelevant and lengthy comment. He is thoughtful and penetrating in his criticism, and yet concise and epigrammatic when he wishes."

Scotsman.—"It is at once scholarly, popular, and orthodox, and written in clear, vigorous English."

Record.—"Dr. Chadwick's style is characteristic, thoughtful, clear, and vigorous. He is never commonplace or trivial."

English Churchman.—"A valuable, interesting, and delightful work, almost every page of which contains something worthy of quotation."

Christian.—"If the volumes to come be like the one before us they may be sure of a warm welcome. Dr. Chadwick has caught something of the vividness of style and onward rush which characterise the writer he expounds. Sober in judgment, markedly Scriptural in tone, well acquainted with exegetical lore, and qualified by patient investigations to give an individual opinion on disputed points, he makes good his claim to help and instruct students of Mark's Gospel."

Methodist Recorder.—"We are glad to say that the beginning of a very promising series is, in our opinion, distinctly good, and that Dean Chadwick has hit the mark specially aimed at exceedingly well. We have found ourselves many sparkling and memorable sentences in his pages. We hope the 'Expositor's Bible' has many other volumes in store as instructive as the first instalment."

Expositor.—"Dean Chadwick's readers, even in the first pages, become aware that they are in the company of a thoroughly original writer, who repeats nothing, echoes nothing, imitates no one. It is with a feeling of thankfulness his readers follow him from passage to passage of the Gospel, finding new truth in familiar words and incidents, and, unable to confine themselves to the limits they had set for their day's reading, are lured on to trespass on to-morrow's portion. There is every quality here that is desirable in an expositor—reverence for his text, sufficient information about it, sympathetic insight, and keen observation of men and manners. Equally successful in opening up the significance of the text and in applying it to present conditions of life, Dean Chadwick has given us an admirable specimen of what an expositor's Bible should be."

London Quarterly Review.—"Dr. Chadwick's exposition is thoughtful and penetrating; his sentences are sharp and crisp. . . . Often bright aphoristic sayings occur which are likely to print themselves on the memory of the reader. The expositor would almost seem to resemble his subject in the practical and condensed, yet graphic, style in which he has done his expository work."

Rock.—"The style of the commentary is, like its subject, forcible and terse."

Church Bells.—"We have never yet read any commentary which we liked so well. The preacher will find it full of materials for sermons, fresh and vigorous, and yet calm and well-weighed."

LONDON : HODDER & STOUGHTON, 27, PATERNOSTER ROW, E.C.

SPECIAL ANNOUNCEMENT.

THE EXPOSITOR'S BIBLE.

Edited by W. ROBERTSON NICOLL, M.A., LL.D.,
Editor of *The Expositor.*

THIRD YEAR'S ISSUE.

Price 7s. 6d. each Volume.

Judges and Ruth.

By the Rev. R. A. WATSON, M.A., Author of "Gospels of Yesterday." [*Ready.*

The Prophecies of Jeremiah.

WITH A SKETCH OF HIS LIFE AND TIMES.

By the Rev. C. J. BALL, M.A., Chaplain of Lincoln's Inn; Contributor to Bishop Ellicott's "Commentary," "The Speaker's Commentary," etc. [*Ready.*

The Book of Exodus.

By the Very Rev. G. A. CHADWICK, D.D., Dean of Armagh, Author of "The Gospel of St. Mark," etc. [*Ready.*

The Gospel of St. Matthew.

By the Rev. J. MONRO GIBSON, D.D., London, Author of "The Ages before Moses," "The Mosaic Era," etc.

The Prophecies of Isaiah, Vol. II.

Completing the work.

By the Rev. GEORGE ADAM SMITH, M.A.

The Acts of the Apostles.

By the Rev. G. T. STOKES, D.D., Professor of Ecclesiastical History in the University of Dublin.

THE EXPOSITOR'S BIBLE.

FIRST SERIES.

Price 7s. 6d. each Volume.

Fourth Edition.

The Book of Genesis.

By Rev. Professor MARCUS DODS, D.D.

"The style of this book is so simple, the march of the thought so strong and unencumbered, and there is in the ripe result such a perfect assimilation of varied erudition, that none but fellow-craftsmen will realise the amount of study, industry, and many-sided ability that was requisite to produce it."—*Professor Elmslie, D.D.*

Third Edition.

The First Book of Samuel.

By the Rev. Professor W. G. BLAIKIE, D.D., LL.D.

"There can be no doubt of the care and thoroughness with which Dr. Blaikie has executed his task. From his own point of view he has produced a solid and able piece of work."—*Academy.*

Third Edition.

The Second Book of Samuel.

By the Rev. Professor W. G. BLAIKIE, D.D., LL.D.

"Of the utmost value to preachers and teachers, being very full of suggestive thoughts."—*English Churchman.*

Third Edition.

The Gospel according to St. Mark.

By the Very Rev. G. A. CHADWICK, D.D., Dean of Armagh.

"Dr. Chadwick has performed his task admirably. He keeps close to his subject, avoiding irrelevant and lengthy comment. He is thoughtful and penetrating in his criticism, and yet concise and epigrammatic when he wishes."—*Academy.*

"It is at once scholarly, popular, and orthodox, and written in clear, vigorous English."—*Scotsman.*

Fourth Edition.

The Epistles to the Colossians and Philemon.

By the Rev. ALEXANDER MACLAREN, D.D.

"In nothing Dr. Maclaren has written is there more of beauty, of spiritual insight, or of brilliant elucidation of Scripture. Indeed, Dr. Maclaren is here at his best."—*Expositor.*

"The book is pre-eminently one for ministers, but there is nothing in the exposition which may not prove a boon to any diligent student of the Word of God. It contains a wealth of thought for preachers."—*Rock.*

Third Edition.

The Epistle to the Hebrews.

By Rev. Principal T. C. EDWARDS, D.D., Author of "A Commentary on the First Epistle to the Corinthians."

"He has entered into the spirit and purport of what truly he calls 'one of the greatest and most difficult books of the New Testament' with a systematic thoroughness and fairness which cannot be too highly commended. Henceforth English students of this portion of the New Testament will have only themselves to blame if they cannot trace the connection of thought and final purport of this epistle."—*Academy.*

THE EXPOSITOR'S BIBLE.
SECOND SERIES.
Price 7s. 6d. each Volume.

Fifth Edition.
The Book of Isaiah. Vol. I. Chapters I.—XXXIX.
By the Rev. GEORGE ADAM SMITH, M.A., Aberdeen. With Map.

"This is a very attractive book. Mr. George Adam Smith has evidently such a mastery of the scholarship of his subject that it would be a sheer impertinence for most scholars, even though tolerable Hebraists, to criticise his translations; and certainly it is not the intention of the present reviewer to attempt anything of the kind, to do which he is absolutely incompetent. All we desire is to let English readers know how very lucid, impressive, and, indeed, how vivid a study of Isaiah is within their reach—the fault of the book, if it has a fault, being rather that it finds too many points of connection between Isaiah and our modern world, than that it finds too few. In other words, no one can say that the book is not full of life."—*Spectator.*

Second Edition.
The First Epistle to the Corinthians.
By the Rev. Professor MARCUS DODS, D.D.

"A clear, close, unaffected, unostentatious exposition, not verse by verse, but thought after thought of this most interesting, perhaps, and certainly most various, of all the Apostle's writings."—*London Quarterly Review.*

Second Edition.
The Epistle to the Galatians.
By the Rev. Professor G. G. FINDLAY, B.A., Headingley College, Leeds.

"Professor G. G. Findlay discloses a minute acquaintance with his subject, an earnest desire to penetrate its inmost meaning, and a marked capacity of illustrating and enforcing the text."—*Record.*

Second Edition.
The Pastoral Epistles.
By the Rev. ALFRED PLUMMER, D.D., Master of University College, Durham.

"It is an admirable example of what popular theology ought to be—presuming a somewhat high level of education and interest in its readers, and built throughout upon sound erudition and sensible, devout, and well-disciplined reflection."—*Saturday Review.*

The Epistles of St. John.
By WILLIAM ALEXANDER, D.D., D.C.L., Brasenose College, Oxford, Lord Bishop of Derry and Raphoe.

"Full of felicities of exegesis. . . . Brilliant and valuable."—*Literary Churchman.*
"The discourses are eloquent and impressive, and show a thorough knowledge of the subject."—*Scotsman.*

The Revelation of St. John.
By Rev. Prof. W. MILLIGAN, D.D., of the University of Aberdeen.

"The most delightful work on the Apocalypse that we have read. The practical and spiritual teaching even of the most recondite and mysterious passages is made plain."—*Methodist Recorder.*

THE THEOLOGICAL EDUCATOR.
Price 2s. 6d. each Volume. Fcap. 8vo.

The Language of the New Testament.
By Rev. WILLIAM HENRY SIMCOX, M.A., Rector of Harlaxton.

"The distinctive peculiarities of New Testament Greek are defined with exactness, the gradations by which one grammatical usage passes into another are clearly traced, the frontier between grammar and exegesis marked with unusual sense and discrimination. In a word, this is the most living grammar of the New Testament we have."—*Expositor.*

Outlines of Christian Doctrine.
By the Rev. H. C. G. MOULE, M.A., Principal of Ridley Hall, Cambridge. Fifth Thousand.

"Marked throughout by the most careful and critical knowledge of Scripture, more particularly of the New Testament, and the most patient weighing and comparison of parallel texts. . . . It forms an admirable introduction to the subject, and seems in intellectual power to even surpass any other of Mr. Moule's published writings."—*Record.*

An Introduction to the New Testament.
By Rev. Professor MARCUS DODS, D.D. Now Ready. Fourth Edition.

"The authenticity, authorship, history, object, and general character of each book are discussed with admirable condensation and lucidity, and with ample critical knowledge."—*Scotsman.*

A Manual of Christian Evidences.
By the Rev. C. A. ROW, M.A., Prebendary of St. Paul's. Fifth Thousand.

"A veritable *multum in parvo*, clear, cogent, and concise, without being sketchy or superficial."—*Saturday Review.*

An Introduction to the Textual Criticism of the New Testament.
By the Rev. Professor B. B. WARFIELD, D.D. Third Thousand.

A Hebrew Grammar.
By the Rev. W. H. LOWE, M.A., Joint Author of "A Commentary on the Psalms," etc., etc.; Hebrew Lecturer, Christ's College, Cambridge. Second Thousand.

An Exposition of the Apostles' Creed.
By the Rev. J. E. YONGE, M.A., Late Fellow of King's College, Cambridge, and Assistant-Master in Eton College.

A Manual of the Book of Common Prayer.
Showing its History and Contents.
By the Rev. CHARLES HOLE, B.A., King's College, London.

A Manual of Church History.
By the Rev. A. C. JENNINGS, M.A. In Two Vols.
Vol. I.—From the First to the Tenth Century.
Vol. II.—From the Eleventh to the Nineteenth Century.

COMPLETION OF THE OLD TESTAMENT.

THE SERMON BIBLE.

Each Volume contains upwards of Five Hundred Sermon Outlines and Several Thousand References. Strongly bound in half buckram.

Price 7s. 6d. each.

VOLUME I.
Genesis to 2 Samuel.

"A very complete guide to the sermon literature of the present day."—*Scotsman.*

"We do not hesitate to pronounce this the most practically useful work of its kind at present extant. It is not a commentary, but a *Thesaurus* of sermons on texts arranged consecutively, chapter after chapter and book after book... We are bound to say that the object announced by the compilers is on the way to be realised, and here will be given the essence of the best homiletic literature of this generation."—*Literary Churchman.*

VOLUME II.
1 Kings to Psalm LXXVI.

"Preachers anxious to discover the best books out of which they may discover golden thoughts on any particular text, for use in their sermons, will doubtless be glad of the volume before us, which aims at being a guide-book, pointing out where sermons and articles on those texts may be found. In addition to this, extracts from sermons are given in the book itself."—*English Churchman.*

"A hearty word of commendation can be said of the selected and condensed outlines of sermons in this volume, most of which are by well-known preachers. They will be of considerable service."—*Nonconformist.*

VOLUME III.
Psalm LXXVII. to The Song of Solomon.

"Like its two predecessors, the third volume is distinguished by the perfect catholicity of the selections, the admirable condensation of the sermons and expositions that are quoted, and the fulness of the references to the best sermon literature on each of the texts. It is beyond question the richest treasury of modern homiletics which has ever issued from the press."—*Christian Leader.*

VOLUME IV.
Isaiah to Malachi.

"A marvellous amount of information is here presented in compact and readable form at a very moderate price."—*Methodist Recorder.*

"A great number of the best contemporary sermons are here rendered generally available in a very convenient form, and at a very low price indeed."—*Literary Churchman.*

LONDON : HODDER & STOUGHTON, 27, PATERNOSTER ROW.

www.ingramcontent.com/pod-product-compliance
Lightning Source LLC
Chambersburg PA
CBHW022107300426
44117CB00007B/621